This incisive reinterpretation of Hume contests standard views by placing Hume's writings on religion securely within the context of his ethical concerns, and giving due attention to the *History of England* and the *Natural History of Religion*. Arguing that important aspects of Hume's writings on religion and moral philosophy can only be understood in light of his worries about the social effects of religion, Jennifer Herdt reveals the links between Hume's concept of sympathy in the *Treatise* and his preoccupation with the destructiveness of religious faction. Sympathy and the related capacity to achieve understanding by entering into foreign points of view are crucial to Hume's attempt to secularize moral philosophy and neutralize religious zeal and faction. By tracing these concepts throughout Hume's corpus and setting his discussions of topics ranging from the nature of moral approval to the role of tragedy within the full scope of eighteenth-century thought, Herdt is able not only to shed new light on the coherence of Hume's authorship, but also to revise our understanding of the period in which he lived and wrote. This book offers an example of the importance of concrete social and political concerns to the history of ethics and modern religious thought, and suggests that Hume's writings can provide the basis for a non-relativist, non-confessional approach to culture and history.

CAMBRIDGE STUDIES IN
RELIGION AND CRITICAL THOUGHT 3

RELIGION AND FACTION IN HUME'S MORAL PHILOSOPHY

CAMBRIDGE STUDIES IN
RELIGION AND CRITICAL THOUGHT

Edited by
WAYNE PROUDFOOT, *Columbia University*
JEFFREY L. STOUT, *Princeton University*
NICHOLAS WOLTERSTORFF, *Yale University*

Current events confirm the need to understand religious ideas and institutions critically, yet radical doubts have been raised about how to proceed and about the ideal of critical thought itself. Meanwhile, some prominent scholars have urged that we turn the tables, and view modern society as the object of criticism and a religious tradition as the basis for critique. Cambridge Studies in Religion and Critical Thought is a series of books intended to address the interaction of critical thinking and religious traditions in this context of uncertainty and conflicting claims. It will take up questions such as the following, either by reflecting on them philosophically or by pursuing their ramifications in studies of specific figures and movements: is a coherent critical perspective on religion desirable or even possible? What sort of relationship to religious tradition ought a critic to have? What, if anything, is worth saving from the Enlightenment legacy or from critics of religion like Hume and Feuerbach? The answers offered, while varied, will uniformly constitute distinguished, philosophically informed, and critical analyses of particular religious topics.

Titles already published in the series

RELIGION AND FACTION IN HUME'S MORAL PHILOSOPHY

JENNIFER A. HERDT

New College of the University of South Florida

CAMBRIDGE
UNIVERSITY PRESS

PUBLISHED BY THE PRESS SYNDICATE OF THE UNIVERSITY OF CAMBRIDGE
The Pitt Building, Trumpington Street, Cambridge CB2 1RP, United Kingdom

CAMBRIDGE UNIVERSITY PRESS
The Edinburgh Building, Cambridge CB2 2RU, United Kingdom
40 West 20th Street, New York, NY 10011-4211, USA
10 Stamford Road, Oakleigh, Melbourne 3166, Australia

First published 1997

Printed in the United Kingdom at the University Press, Cambridge

Typeset in Baskerville 11/12½ pt in Poltype™   [VN]

A catalogue record for this book is available from the British Library

Library of Congress cataloguing in publication data
Herdt, Jennifer A., 1967–
Religion and faction in Hume's moral philosophy / Jennifer A. Herdt.
p.   cm. – (Cambridge Studies in Religion and Critical Thought; 3)
Includes bibliographical references and index.
ISBN 0 521 55442 X
1. Hume, David, 1711–1776.   2. Sympathy.
3. Hume, David, 1711–1776 – Ethics.
4. Hume, David, 1711–1776 – Religion.
I. Title.   II. Series.
B1499.SH47   1997
192–dc21   96-48933
CIP

ISBN 0 521 55442 X hardback

To my parents

Contents

Preface

Modern religious thought and ethics are customarily seen as emerging in reaction to developments in epistemology, most notably the rise of the new science, which created new standards for justified belief and rendered traditional authorities problematic. As J. B. Schneewind comments, "when we teach a course called 'the history of modern philosophy,' we usually teach the history of epistemology and metaphysics, and we do not ordinarily offer a comparable course, held to be of equal importance, on the history of modern ethics. The history of ethics is seen, if it is seen at all, as a dependent variable." Schneewind concedes that "of course it is possible that there is no really independent life to the history of thought about morality, that modern ethics simply arose out of changes in the best views available about knowledge and the ultimate constitution of the universe. I believe, however, that this is not so."[1] In what follows, I attempt to retell an episode of this history in a way which resists allowing the tail of epistemology to wag the dog of critical reflection about ethics, religion, and society.

The sixteenth- and seventeenth-century religious wars created a situation in which it was perilous to appeal to specifically sectarian Christian doctrines in support of social and political proposals, because such appeals tended only to fan the flames of religious conflict. There was an urgent need for shared vocabularies in which to conceive of human society and common welfare beyond the boundaries of sectarian identities and loyalties. The long-term outcome has been the secularization of public discourse and the marginalization of religious ethics and modern religious thought.[2] Many of the key figures in this process of secularization were, of course, themselves religious, and held beliefs about the particular nature of the deity and the appropriate way in which to worship and serve such a deity. Nevertheless, for strategic purposes they employed non-sectarian justifications for their public social and political proposals.

This book focuses on the eighteenth-century Scottish philosopher, critic, and historian David Hume, and his role in this story of the search for shared public vocabularies which would secure social peace and engender common prosperity. I will seek to establish the following claims:

(1) That Hume's project for the secularization of moral philosophy is best understood when placed in the tradition of modern natural law, but that it is self-consciously more radical than the accounts of his predecessors, who, while scrupulously avoiding any appeal to a deity possessing identifiable sectarian features, continued to invoke or surreptitiously assume Providence at crucial points in their accounts of morality.

(2) That a major effort of the *Treatise* is to replace Providence with a wholly non-theological concept which can play a similar role in assuring the connection between morality and human flourishing without, however, reducing morality to a hidden expression of self-interest. Such a concept could, according to Hume, render religious beliefs (and hence disagreements about religious beliefs) irrelevant to human life in society and thus harmless.

(3) That the concept with which Hume replaces Providence in the *Treatise* is sympathy, and that therefore Hume's role in the process of secularization cannot be understood apart from sympathy and its progress throughout his writings.

(4) That Hume recognizes that the immediate form which sympathy takes is unreliable in that it is variable and tends to reinforce existing factions, and that Hume's notion of "extensive" sympathy and his discussions of the correction of sympathy are an attempt to respond to this problem. This, in turn, pushes Hume in the direction of providing a normative account of the formation of good moral judgment, as opposed to a causal account of the origin of moral distinctions.

(5) That this normative account, which can be traced through Hume's essays of criticism and his *History of England*, explores the possibilities of developing the capacity to enter sympathetically into the points of view of others. This sympathetic understanding can be employed in seeking to overcome factional divisions and in developing good moral judgment.

(6) That a crucial theme of Hume's essays of criticism and his *History of England* is that religious zeal and sectarian loyalties interfere with the role of sympathy and related capacities associated with moral judgment

among religious believers. Religious belief, far from providing
basis for morality, tends to distort moral judgment.

(7) That, while Hume believed that history has the potential of
the exemplary form of sympathetic activity (despite the bad example
by sectarian histories), he argues that the points of view of those who hold
irrational religious beliefs and lead artificial religious lives cannot be
sympathetically entered into. While zeal and factional allegiances create
artificial and illegitimate barriers among different groups, beliefs and
ways of life which are absurd, contradictory, and unintelligible create
insurmountable and legitimate barriers to sympathetic understanding.

(8) That the scope of Hume's capacity for sympathetic understanding
is adequate only if he is correct in his assessment of theism as utterly
contradictory and unintelligible, but that even if Hume is wrong and
therefore himself guilty of a failure of sympathetic understanding, he
nevertheless takes an important step toward illustrating the possibility of
a secular historiography. He shows that history does not and should not
pretend to forswear substantive moral judgments, but that sympathetic
understanding of historical actors is a prerequisite of good judgment. His
reflections and practice help to reveal the basic prerequisites for such
understanding as well as the pitfalls and temptations which await those
who try to define its outer limits.

In the past, Hume's thought has been studied primarily from the point
of view of epistemological concerns. This approach has tended to
fragment his work. Hume the philosopher has often been cast as a
cheerful and unconcerned skeptic, an approach which renders his
political essays and *History of England* anomalous and adventitious. But
when Hume's preoccupation with securing the conditions for social
peace and prosperity is appreciated, Hume's writings form an intelligible
whole and the significance of Hume's "non-philosophical" works can be
grasped. The standard approach to Hume's work misconstrues the
nature of the challenge he poses to modern religious thought. An
adequate response to Hume's critique of religion cannot remain at the
level of epistemology, but must address Hume's analysis of the way in
which irrationality and self-deception in religious belief create and
preserve zealous sectarian identities and violent factions which threaten
to destroy social concord.

There are many individuals to whom I wish to express my gratitude.
Had it not been for the encouragement of Jeffrey Stout, who suggested
that the Cambridge series in Religion and Critical Thought would be the

ideal context for this book, the manuscript would no doubt have languished several years longer on my hard drive. In addition, along with Victor Preller and Alan Ryan, Jeffrey Stout generously read drafts and revisions of the manuscript, offering suggestions which are reflected on nearly every page. Wayne Proudfoot and Nicholas Wolterstorff, who edit the series in Religion and Critical Thought together with Jeffrey Stout, read the manuscript and gave it a green light, while Alex Wright and later Ruth Parr, my editors at Cambridge, capably guided me through the process of preparing the manuscript. Alex Wright also located two anonymous readers who contributed immeasurably, not only by their attention to particulars, but also by challenging me to clarify the nature of my basic claims. The project was further enriched and strengthened by the critical insights of others who read one or more chapters along the way: Annette Baier, Julia Driver, Bob Gibbs, Amy Gutmann, Doug Langston, Mark Larrimore, Heather Nadelman, Jerry Schneewind, and Cornel West. Scott Davis was kind enough to read the entire manuscript and offer many detailed and perceptive comments. A draft of chapter 4 benefited from lively discussion in the faculty-graduate colloquium of the Center for Human Values at Princeton University.

I am also grateful for the financial support I received from the Whiting Foundation, from the Woodrow Wilson Foundation through its program of Mellon Fellowships in the Humanities, and from the New College Foundation in the form of summer research support. Small portions of chapter 5 have previously appeared in the *American Journal of Theology and Philosophy* 16.3 (1995). I wish to thank Tyron Inbody, editor of *AJTP*, for permission to use the material in a different context here.

Finally, I am fortunate enough to have married the man who is my best conversation partner. To my husband, Jan-Lüder Hagens, go my thanks, not only for constant encouragement, but also for intense and inspiring discussions.

1 J. B. Schneewind, "The Divine Corporation and the history of ethics," in *Philosophy in History: Essays on the Historiography of Philosophy*, ed. Richard Rorty, J. B. Schneewind, and Quentin Skinner (Cambridge University Press, 1984), 173–174.

2 On the autonomy of morals as it arises out of the crisis of authority created by the Wars of Religion, see Jeffrey Stout, *The Flight from Authority: Religion, Morality, and the Quest for Autonomy* (University of Notre Dame Press, 1981). Quentin Skinner discusses the secularization of political discourse in *The Foundations of Modern Political Thought*, vol. 2, *The Age of Reformation* (Cambridge University Press, 1978).

Abbreviations

Hume's works are cited in the text according to the following abbreviations and by page numbers, except in the case of the *History of England*, for which volume and chapter are also given. Full citations are given in the bibliography.

FD	*Four Dissertations*
D	*Dialogues Concerning Natural Religion*
E	*Enquiries Concerning Human Understanding and Morals*
H	*History of England*
LDH	*Letters of David Hume*
MPL	*Essays Moral, Political, and Literary*
NHR	*Natural History of Religion*
T	*A Treatise of Human Nature*

Introduction

Hume's account of sympathy is often dismissed as an unfortunate example of associationist psychology, which Hume introduces in the *Treatise* but thankfully has the sense to take out of the restatement of his moral theory in the *Enquiry Concerning the Principles of Morals*. A very different account of sympathy and its significance forms the starting point of this study of Hume. I begin with the *Treatise*, but continue through Hume's essays on aesthetics, his works on religion, and finally the *History of England*, finding in sympathy a key to the relationship between Hume's moral philosophy and his concern with the effects of religious belief on moral judgment. Sympathy first appears as a passive experience of connectedness, but, when the inadequacies of this notion become apparent, Hume introduces distinctions among different kinds of sympathy and talks of the "correction" of sympathy. In the *Enquiry* and thereafter, the term "sympathy" appears less frequently. Nevertheless, the notion of entering sympathetically into the "situation" or "point of view" of others continues to play a vital role in Hume's thought. The natural partiality of sympathy can only be corrected through sympathy's extension and correction, not by attempting to eradicate it. Hume's later writings therefore attend carefully to the ways in which the original form of limited sympathy threatens to reinforce and inflame factional divisions (as among religious zealots), and testify as well to the need to develop an active and intentional form of sympathetic understanding which seeks to enter into foreign situations and points of view. Sympathy thus unites Hume's theory of moral judgment with his preoccupation with social conflict and his critique of the artificiality of religious lives.

The concept of sympathy had gained currency during the seventeenth century as part of the effort to refute the Hobbesian insistence that all human action is fundamentally self-interested. The Latitudinarian divines argued that pity and general benevolence, because they arise out of instinctive sympathetic responses, are just as basic, unreflective principles of human action as is self-interest. In chapter 1, I discuss this background against which sympathy emerges as a salient feature of the moral life. This involves exploring Hume's links to the tradition of modern natural law, with its attempt to show that the study of human nature can give us information about how we ought to live in order to avoid conflict and achieve peace.

In the *Treatise*, as I discuss in the second chapter, Hume first attempts to give this passive, automatic form of sympathy a scientific analysis and then invokes it to account for a wide range of social phenomena, from love of relatives to national character to infectious laughter. While this sort of sympathy testifies to the fact that human beings cannot be understood apart from society, it is limited to those close to us. Far from supporting a theory of universal or general benevolence, as its advocates had supposed, it tends to reinforce pre-existing bonds, strengthening factional loyalties and prejudices. Although Hume refrains from reducing all principles of human action to self-interest, his initial analysis of sympathy calls into question attempts to invoke it in support of an instinctive universal benevolence.

After highlighting sympathy's moral ambiguity, Hume goes on to give sympathy a central role in his theory of moral judgment. I argue that giving sympathy this novel role was crucial to his attempt to appropriate Hutcheson's ethical theory, while at the same time undermining Hutcheson's apologetic project. In Hume's account, the principle of sympathy replaces Providence in illuminating the connection between our ethical judgments and human flourishing. Hume argues that sympathy with those affected by actions or character traits is the source of moral distinctions. The passive, automatic form of sympathy which Hume had appropriated was, however, inadequate to account for the stability and disinterestedness of moral judgments, and so Hume introduces a contrast between "weak" or "limited" sympathy and "extensive" sympathy; it is the latter, he says, which is at work in moral judgment. Something much like the former will reappear in later works, playing a troubling role in the genesis and spread of factional zeal and enthusiasm. There are points at which Hume's account of the relation between sympathy and moral distinctions is ambiguous, and, while I will strive to clarify the relationship, I will be just as interested in exploring the significance of the remaining ambiguities. One important location of ambiguity is in the second *Enquiry*, where Hume introduces a new term, the "sentiment of humanity," thereby (apparently) displacing sympathy from its central role in his moral theory.

Having considered the background to Hume's moral theory and his deployment of sympathy in the *Treatise* and the second *Enquiry*, I go on in the third chapter to discuss sympathy in relation to eighteenth-century debates on the pleasures of tragedy. At this point, it begins to be clear that the function of sympathy in Hume's thought is to show not simply Providence to be irrelevant to morality, but also that appreciating the role of sympathy in moral judgment can shed light on the nature of various malfunctions of judgment among religious believers. Hume's contributions to the debate on tragedy unveil the misplaced fears behind Scottish Evangelical opposition to theater, showing it to reflect pathologies of belief which grow out of a rejection of this-worldly existence and which lead to the distortion of sympathetic capacities. Calvinists' fear of the theater is symptomatic of their more general fear of being drawn too much into earthly pains and pleasures; they resist theater's ability to move and touch the soul. Freed from this fear, one may enjoy the artistic achievements of dramatic tragedy while retaining the ability to distinguish it from the real-world tragedy which requires an active response and perhaps even some sort of intervention.

In the fourth chapter, I turn to another of Hume's essays, "Of the standard of taste." Like Hume's writings on tragedy, this essay is misunderstood if read merely as a contribution to aesthetic theory. In "Of the standard of taste," Hume continues to refine his understanding of judgment by recognizing that the capacity for good judgment does not emerge automatically as the result of an equilibration process, but that it involves active cultivation and training. This active effort to attain a full-bodied understanding of various points of view, an effort which Hume explores here and in "A dialogue," is intimately related to the notion of extensive sympathy and its correction, but, in order to give due weight to its intentionality, it might better be termed "sympathetic understanding." The continuities between Hume's earlier discussions of sympathy and his later discussions of the development of taste are cast into bold relief when Hume's accounts are held up against his contemporaries' understandings of sympathy and his successors' explorations of the sympathetic imagination.

Hume does not provide a formula or utilitarian calculus for calculating how different points of view are to be related to one another in arriving at moral judgment, but I argue that this movement away from a mechanical model which promises correct output should be seen as a recognition of the nature of actual practical judgment, not as a theoretical failure. What Hume does attempt is to give a priori definition to the activity of sympathetic understanding by identifying the limits of its scope. "Of the standard of taste" is often read as claiming that we cannot enter into the sentiments of those whose morals differ from our own. I argue, however, that Hume sets the limit, not at moral differences *per se*, but at "artificial" manners which are dictated by speculative religious or philosophical beliefs. The irrationality and incomprehensibility of such artificial lives block attempts by outsiders to place themselves in the artificial "situations" of religious believers.

The *History of England* provides an opportunity to learn more about Hume's fully developed view of the nature and possibility of sympathetically entering into foreign points of view. This should not be surprising, for Hume regarded history as the exemplary form of sympathetic activity and as the training ground for moral judgment. In writing the *History*, he both puts his theory into practice and reflects on that practice and its theory. Moreover, it is in the *History of England* that sympathetic understanding comes up against what Hume has defined as the limits of its scope – the "artificial lives" of religious believers. The final chapter therefore relates Hume's discussions of sympathy and related concepts to his analysis of the irrationality of religious belief in the *Natural History of Religion* and the *History of England*.

In the *History*, Hume strives to understand how it is that religious zeal comes into being and why it poses such a grave threat to social peace and stability. Religious believers do not simply possess a false theoretical understanding of the relationship between morals and religion; more dangerously, religious zeal (which spreads by "contagion" or passive sympathy) warps their substantive moral judgments and beliefs, their capacity to apprehend moral distinctions. Hume's conclusion, in "Of the standard of taste," about the incapacity of an outsider to come to a sympathetic understanding of religious believers and their situations may prove, however, to have been premature. Causal explanations which wholly circumvent the intentions of the believers properly come into play only where a person's intentions are so ridden with internal contradictions as to be incoherent. Does religious belief properly belong in this category? If not, then there is room for "outsiders" of a religious group to sympathetically understand the points of view of "insiders" whose beliefs they take to be false. Hume clearly sees this as a possibility when he considers polytheism, but is less sanguine when he turns to the forms of theism with which he was familiar.

Just as extensive sympathy in the *Treatise* is the solution to the internal civil war created by conflicting and changing points of view (interests), the corresponding intentional capacity which I am terming sympathetic understanding emerges in Hume's later writings as a potential solution to the external conflict and violence of religious factionalism. In entering into the situations of others, we are able to look beyond factional prejudices to the shared goods of human existence, rooting moral judgment firmly in this-worldly human flourishing. To utterly devalue this existence, in contrast, is to lose the basis for understanding others, healing factional conflict, and living in peace. Hume's analysis of zeal and bigotry makes an important contribution to identifying the logical limits of the capacity to enter sympathetically into others' points of view. But Hume may be precipitous in his identification of religious lives as self-contradictory and "artificial" and thus too quick to see barriers precluding sympathetic understanding. Hume believes that sympathetic understanding (and not the fiction of general benevolence) can be the key not only to engaging constructively with cultural difference, but also to resolving religious violence and to securing the conditions for social peace and prosperity. But he thinks that this possibility will be fully realized only if religious believers can be lured away from their "artificial" lives. If, however, their lives are not as artificial as he thinks, if not all theists are zealots, then sympathetic understanding is a present possibility and not simply a future hope.

Insofar as interpretation is never mere repetition, it is always in some sense a constructive enterprise. In the course of exploring the role of sympathy in Hume's thought, I have not hesitated to clarify my interpretation by supplying my own distinctions and descriptive terminology. By distinguishing more clearly between the different sorts of sympathy which Hume discusses, I am able to avoid confusion while highlighting the continuity between extensive sympathy in the *Treatise* and Hume's later reflections on moral and aesthetic judgment and the theory and practice of historiography. This, in turn, helps to place Hume more precisely within the broader context of ongoing discussions of sympathy.

Hume for instance opposes "limited" and "weak" sympathy to "extensive" and "strong" sympathy, which implies that there is a continuum of degrees of sympathy rather than qualitatively different forms of sympathy. I will argue, however, that careful attention to Hume's discussion supports the conclusion that limited sympathy is qualitatively different from extensive sympathy. I should make clear, moreover, that my occasional references to "active" and "passive" sympathy are not intended to congrue precisely with either "limited" or "extensive" sympathy. Extensive sympathy seems, in Hume's initial account, to be just as passive as limited sympathy. It should become clear, however, that Hume's characterization of what he calls extensive sympathy is refined and developed even within the *Treatise*, as Hume puts extensive sympathy to work in accounting for moral evaluation. The term "active" sympathy attempts to capture the continuities between corrected, extensive sympathy in the *Treatise* and related capacities which Hume discusses – without attaching a particular name to them – in later works, while indicating the effort and intentionality which distinguishes these from the official account of sympathy in the *Treatise*.

The term "sympathetic understanding," which I also employ, has the added advantage of drawing attention to the ways in which this form of sympathy functions as a hermeneutic principle. Other scholars have discussed sympathy in Hume in similar terms, but without clarifying the relationship between this sort of sympathy and the other related notions which Hume discusses.[1] I hope in the following chapters to provide this clarification. What does "sympathetic understanding" have to do wtih sympathy as fellow-feeling? How can it be justified in light of Hume's emphasis on feelings and passions and his concomitant criticism of reason's overblown claims? Sympathy as understanding is, I take it, a *prerequisite* to sympathy as fellow-feeling (the latter being involved, for example, in the phenomenon of pity). This contrasts with limited, passive sympathy, which is a sort of emotional infection and need not be present in either sympathy as understanding or sympathy as fellow-feeling. It is not, I hold, sympathy as fellow-*feeling* which is necessary for moral judgment, but rather sympathetic understanding. Sympathetic understanding must, however, be directly concerned with others' desires and fears and hopes for the good, with how things *matter* to them, and in this sense has to do with passionate, value-laden reality, not with the stripped-down world of abstract reason.

Although Hume admits that sympathy is highly variable, while moral judgments are constant, he continues to insist that extensive sympathy accounts for moral distinctions. That is, in the end he uses the term "extensive sympathy" to indicate the corrected sentiments of the "steady and general points of view" required for moral judgment. It is this morally relevant form of "extensive sympathy" which I characterize as active and isolate with the term "sympathetic understanding." What is needed for good moral judgment is not a *moral* point of view, but rather a *sympathetic* point of view. The term "moral point of view" implies a position of detachment, a view from nowhere, rather than the impartial involvedness advocated by Hume.[2] In addition, it hides the fact that for

Hume there is no single moral point of view which is applicable to every situation, but rather that good moral judgment requires entering sympathetically into different "situations" or "points of view" depending on who in particular is involved.

One of the contributions of this study is the new perspective it gives on the reasons behind Hume's critique of religion by attending to sympathy's place in understanding and judgment. From this perspective, religious factions, and the way in which their irrational zeal disrupts the activity of sympathy, take center stage. Most writers who have explored the subject of Hume and religion have taken Hume's discussions of the justification of religious belief to be the core of his writing on religion. This focus accords with the traditional twentieth-century view of Hume as motivated primarily by epistemological concerns, and reinforces the standard epistemology-driven approach to the history of modern religious thought as a whole. The *Dialogues Concerning Natural Religion,* with its philosophical attacks on the argument from design, has understandably been the starting-point – and often the ending-point as well – of such studies of Hume's critique of religion.[3] This approach does not cope well, however, with the fact that Hume's concern with religion ranges far beyond a narrow emphasis on the epistemological status of religious belief to include the sources of religious belief in fear of unknown causes, the emergence of theism from polytheism, the psychological nature and impact of religious belief and practice, the sources of religious controversy, and the impact of religion on morality.

J. C. A. Gaskin's 1978 work on *Hume's Philosophy of Religion,* now a classic, set out to remedy the overemphasis on the *Dialogues* by drawing attention to the broad scope of Hume's writings on religion and showing that they fit together coherently. Nevertheless, Gaskin failed to question the assumption that Hume's driving concern is with the justification of religious belief. His overall conclusion is that Hume's "failure to find any convincing reasons for religious belief in the arguments of natural religion leads him first to consider its possible status as a 'natural instinct,' and finally to search for its causes in human nature ... Hume's conclusions about religion form a coherent whole and ... his critique moves steadily towards one crucial conclusion with its consequences for personal religion and morality. This conclusion is that natural order may possibly take its origin from an intelligent being, but if it does then that being has no moral claim upon or interest in mankind."[4] This leaves out any consideration of the effects of religion on society, which Gaskin claimed were "the concern of Hume the historian and moralist rather than Hume the philosopher," and therefore outside of the scope of his book, despite the fact that it claimed to be concerned with Hume's discussions of religion as a whole. In the second edition of the book, Gaskin added a new chapter on "The corruptions caused by religion," which gave greater attention to the issue of religious corruptions of morality, but the starting-point in natural religion's arguments for belief in God remained the same.[5]

To give another example, in his introduction to a collection of selections from Hume called *Hume on Religion*, which was published in 1963, Richard Wollheim sought to grasp the reasons underlying Hume's sustained and comprehensive interest in religion.[6] He first considers the possibility that Hume was working out his own personal religious conflict, but rejects this thesis as being wholly unsupported by evidence from Hume's published writings as well as his correspondence, which indicate that Hume had no trace of vital religious faith nor any anguish at its lack. Second, Wollheim denies that Hume was driven by a desire to free mankind from error and superstition. Here he points to Hume's pessimism about eradicating religious belief and to his conservatism. Wollheim finally concludes that Hume's main concern was with religion insofar as it fell afoul of his epistemology and the proper limits of human understanding. Once again, epistemology takes center stage and religion is seen as worthy of concern only insofar as it makes illegitimate claims to knowledge.

But why should Hume be so interested in the limits of human understanding and justified knowledge? In recent years this assumption has begun to seem less self-explanatory, and a few scholars of Hume, both those concerned with Hume's views of religion and those concerned with other aspects of his work, have begun to conceive of the possibility that Hume's epistemological concerns might be secondary to his moral or political concerns. Kenneth Merrill and Donald Wester, for example, claim that Hume's interest in the logical-epistemological problems surrounding religion and morality is "ancillary to Hume's overriding concern with the practical-moral affairs of what he calls the common life of man" and claim that Hume's rejection of traditional theism is based "on the irresolvable conflict between the motives that animate religion (on the one hand) and ordinary morality (on the other)."[7] Keith Yandell asserts that Hume is worried about the damage which religious belief causes to human nature, in particular that he "is concerned about the degree to which being pulled back and forth from one religious pole (acceptance of a sort of diaphanous theism) to another (acceptance of polytheism) may weaken our capacity for belief."[8] The movement beyond epistemology has been accompanied by increased interest in writings other than the *Dialogues*. Yandell, for example, claims that the *Natural History of Religion*, rather than the *Dialogues*, should be regarded as Hume's central work on religion.

While these new directions are encouraging, I believe that no understanding of Hume's preoccupation with religion and the scope of his critique of it is complete if it does not range beyond the works overtly addressed to religion to include the *History of England*, the political writings, and the essays on aesthetic topics. In the concept of sympathy, the connections between Hume's theory of moral judgment and his critique of religion become salient. Moreover, following sympathy and related notions through Hume's thought allows us to see that Hume's epistemological concerns are not just secondary to practical and moral affairs, as Merrill and Wester claim, but that they are actually driven by his concerns about the threat posed by religious belief and practice to the peace and prosperity of society, and not merely "society" and "religious belief" in the abstract, but eighteenth-century Scottish society and the factions of the Church of Scotland in particular. To understand Hume on religion, is, therefore, to take a large step in the direction of understanding the concerns and motivations behind the entire corpus of his work, and to place him in the context of the history of modern religious, ethical, and political thought.

The importance of Hume's *History of England* to his understanding of religion has been largely overlooked. Antony Flew, for example, in the introduction to his collection of Hume's writings on religion (which has the merit of including several letters and small excerpts from longer works), feels he must justify excluding the *Treatise*, which he acknowledges as having been regarded by Hume's contemporaries as making a strong statement regarding religion, but he makes no mention whatsoever of the *History of England*.[9] James Noxon takes it to be important that "in his histories [Hume] is constantly attentive to the role played by religious institutions in the course of events and to the influence of religious belief upon the conduct of men of affairs," but he regards the *History* more as evidence of Hume's continued interest in religion than as a primary source for understanding Hume's critique of religion.[10] Richard Popkin and David Fate Norton, in their *David Hume: Philosophical Historian*, took a stand on the importance of Hume's *History* and played a key role in bringing it to the attention of other scholars. They noted something which the modern reader is likely to overlook – that "Hume's was an attempt, and one of the first," as Popkin writes, "to portray human history as meaningful and comprehensive in its own secular terms, according to a complex of human and natural factors."[11] They were, however, primarily interested in Hume from the standpoint of historiography, not in the light shed on Hume's corpus by the detailed content of his *History*.

Donald Siebert's recent work, *The Moral Animus of David Hume*, is a noteworthy exception; it begins to fill an important gap in Hume scholarship in its recognition that the *History of England* is crucial to understanding Hume's preoccupation with the problems posed by religion to society and in its willingness to dive into the concrete details of the *History*.[12] Nicholas Phillipson's presentation of the *History of England* as the peak of Hume's intellectual career also breaks new ground in its analysis of "parties of principle," in particular religious factions, as the bane of a society with a mixed constitution.[13] I hope in what follows to explore further these new directions in the understanding of Hume's thought.

One of the first questions to ask about the *History* is why a Scottish philosopher would write a history of England in which Scotland played only a peripheral role. Was Hume a self-hating Anglophile? The *History* was certainly written for an English readership, not just a Scottish one, and Hume never wished to be the target of English anti-Scottish sentiment (witness his attempt to eliminate all Scotticisms from his spelling). But Hume's fascination with things English reflects an intense Scottish patriotism, not an antipathy toward Scotland. Hume shared with other leading intellectuals in eighteenth-century Scotland (including Adam Smith, Allan Ramsay, and other members of the "Select Society") a concern with understanding and promoting the conditions for social peace and prosperity in Scotland.[14]

These thinkers saw Scotland as a poor and backward nation, particularly in comparison with the prosperity of nearby trading states. They regarded economic independence and prosperity, along with the acquisition of modern institutions, manners, and values, as the route by which Scotland could take its rightful place among the civilized and cosmopolitan nations.[15] Social peace and security were seen as fostering, not only happiness, but also virtue. It should not be surprising that Smith wrote both the *Wealth of Nations* and the *Theory of Moral Sentiments*. Both were part of a single project. At the turn of the century, Scottish leaders believed that, if Scotland could create a self-sufficient economy, primarily by engaging in international trade, this would foster and reflect

Scotland's distinctive identity and sense of community. Free trade with England and the American colonies seemed absolutely necessary if Scotland was to escape its perceived poverty and economic dependence, and to this end Scotland, in 1707, sacrificed its privilege of an autonomous parliament and accepted political union with England. But union with England was followed by a period of economic depression rather than of growth, a turn of events which stimulated further reflection in following decades on the conditions for prosperity. The loss of local political culture, meanwhile, created a vacuum in Scottish society which was filled with a flowering of intellectual activity: "Edinburgh saw a proliferation of Spectatorial clubs and societies, practising the virtues of polite conversation and enlightened taste while discussing the economic, cultural and even – given an age in which manners seemed no unimportant part of morality – the moral improvement of Scottish life. The locus of virtue shifted decisively from the civic to the civil, from the political and military to that blend of the economic, cultural and moral which we call the social for short."[16]

Hume was particularly concerned with the problems of warfare and internal faction. These seemed to him to pose the greatest threats to the flourishing of society, since they invariably disrupt trade and destroy social peace and stability: "Factions subvert government, render laws impotent, and beget the fiercest animosities among men of the same nation, who ought to give mutual assistance and protection to each other" (*MPL* 55). Hume came to the conclusion that religious disputes were particularly pernicious.

Religious controversies, by inflaming political and social discontent, lay at the heart of the wars which convulsed Europe throughout the sixteenth and seventeenth centuries. But it was not simply the distant memory of religious warfare which concerned Hume. Eighteenth-century Scotland, although not in a state of civil war, continued to be divided into fierce religious factions which determined political allegiances and hindered Scotland's modernization. The Moderates of the Church of Scotland supported patronage, while the Popular Party (the Evangelicals) favored selection of ministers by church elders (earlier factions which endorsed selection by the congregation as a whole, such as the Covenanters, had by 1750 split off as Dissenters from the Church of Scotland). The Moderates embraced the modernization project advocated by the Select Society; for them, "the key issue was the creation and maintenance of a polite, enlightened Scottish clergy leading their nation out of the abyss of seventeenth-century fanaticism."[17] In 1766 William

Robertson, a prominent Moderate, argued that "the institution of patronage by enlightened members of the upper classes and representatives of the government had helped to improve the quality of the Scottish clergy."[18] The Moderates, while adhering to the Calvinist Westminster Confession of Faith, favored as an aspect of their modernization project an openness to natural religion, rational theology, and moral philosophy, opposed by the Popular Party as a hubristic denial of radical human fallenness. Moderates viewed Evangelicals as dogmatic and intolerant, and therefore dangerously close to seventeenth-century fanatics who were held responsible for Scotland's backwardness. Members of the Popular Party saw themselves as defending Presbyterian orthodoxy both in terms of church government and in their insistence on human depravity and the need for revelation.

The little we know about Hume's own religious upbringing suggests that it was pronouncedly Evangelical. The parish of Chirnside in which he resided had, in the late seventeenth century, been a center of Covenantism.[19] The minister during Hume's youth was George Hume, David's uncle, whose father had himself been a Covenanter. James Boswell has provided a revealing glimpse into Hume's early religious life. Recalling a conversation he had with Hume just days before the latter died, he reports:

He said he had never entertained any belief in Religion since he began to read Locke and Clarke. I asked him if he was not religious when he was young. He said he was, and he used to read the *Whole Duty of Man*; that he made an abstract from the Catalogue of vices at the end of it, and examined himself by this, leaving out Murder and Theft and such vices as he had no chance of committing, having no inclination to commit them. This, he said, was strange work; for instance, to try if, notwithstanding his excelling his schoolfellows, he had no pride or vanity.[20]

The *Whole Duty of Man*, a popular Calvinist treatise for edification and self-examination, detailed the many possible ways of failing in one's duty to God or fellow human beings, ranging from the sin of "despairing of God's mercy" or "presuming groundlessly upon it," "loving the pomps and vanities of the world, and following its sinful customs," to "using unlawful recreations, being too vehement upon lawful ones, spending too much time at them."[21]

The *Whole Duty of Man* was particularly insistent about the sinfulness of vanity, and urged that we must think of ourselves as "worms of the earth . . . polluted and defiled, wallowing in all kinds of sins, and uncleanness," in order to have "such a sense of our own meanness, and his excellency, as may work in us a lowly and unfeigned submission" to God's will and wisdom.[22] Hume was to write to Hutcheson with reference to the *Treatise* that "upon the whole, I desire to take my Catalogue of Virtues from Cicero's *Offices*, not from the *Whole Duty of Man*. I had, indeed, the former Book in my Eye in all my Reasonings."[23] Be that as it may, the latter is just as present in its absence; Hume's discussions of property, fame, beauty, and pride in the *Treatise* were developed in direct opposition to Calvinist denunciations of worldly goods. The Evangelical Presbyterianism in which he grew up was to remain the archetype of all religion for Hume, no matter how apparently generic and general the claims he went on to make concerning "theism" and "religion."

The conflict between the Moderates and the Evangelicals played itself out, in part, in heresy trials. All the cases which came before the General Assembly between 1717 and 1744 (including a charge against Francis Hutcheson) concerned the relationship between rational moral philosophy and Christian revelation.[24] Hume was threatened with charges of heresy several times, but a formal trial was averted through the efforts of several prominent Moderates whom Hume counted as friends. Nevertheless, Hume was thwarted from ever obtaining a university appointment.[25]

Religious factionalism and intolerance were therefore concrete and powerful realities for Hume, both in terms of his own attempt to speak his mind freely and in terms of his understanding of Scotland's predicament as a nation. While an understanding of the Scottish context is vital to understanding Hume's project, this is not to deny that Hume approaches his subject through a general inquiry which looks beyond local affairs. "Hume subsumed the case of Scotland within a consciously universal inquiry. As a philosopher of the progress of society in general, not simply a commentator on the condition of Scotland or even Britain in particular, he regarded an understanding of the common problems of developing, commercial societies as the prerequisite for dealing with the specific affairs of his own country."[26] It therefore made perfect sense to explore the history of England even if the primary motivating concern was with present-day Scotland.

In the *History of England*, Hume follows England's tortuous development into a peaceful, tolerant, and flourishing realm and explores the forces which had disrupted and continued to threaten this social peace and prosperity. He regarded the English mixed constitutional government, with its party system, as particularly prone to faction, the inevitable accompaniment to increased liberty.[27] While such liberty is to be prized, a free society of this sort could only be viable if it was possible thoroughly to understand and find some way of regulating party zeal. Hume addresses himself to factions and conflicts which arise, not only from religious disagreements, but also from conflicts of interest between different social groups as well as from personal animosities and loyalties. But he accuses religious factions of being the most zealous and violent and the most difficult to reconcile with one another, and moreover of infiltrating and infecting political parties and social life as a whole. In "Of parties in general," he argues that skillful legislation can prevent parties of interest from working at cross-purposes in society, but religious factions are almost impossible to reconcile with one another; "where the difference of principle is attended with no contrariety of action, but every one may follow his own way, without interfering with his neighbour, as happens in all religious controversies; what madness, what fury can beget such unhappy and such fatal divisions?" (*MPL* 60). Hume's project is thus twofold; to understand the sources and nature of religious disagreement and conflict, and to find a solution to religious conflict, thereby helping to secure the conditions for social peace and prosperity.

Unlike many thinkers of his day, who sought to eliminate religious conflict by securing uniformity of religious belief, Hume finds examples, from both the ancient and the modern worlds, of societies in which diversity of religious belief and practice is present without leading to violence or to deep social divisions. Polytheistic religions are, Hume argues in the *Natural History of Religion,* by nature more tolerant and less prone to religious faction, but we learn in the *History of England* that societies dominated by a monotheistic religion may approximate the conditions of polytheism by instituting a state church (in which ministers are government employees with no incentive to recruit members intensively) and enforcing toleration of religious dissenters. This, Hume believes, will tend to diffuse religious zeal and secure the peace.[28] As Donald Siebert notes, "in the example of what the Church of England had finally become in the eighteenth century after the policies of both ecclesiastical establishment and toleration had gradually been hammered out in the Restoration and Glorious Revolution, Hume found a desirable model . . . The church retained just enough ritual and liturgy – idolatry, if you will – to distract the worshiper from theogenic reverie and rivet his attention on the things of the world, but not to such a degree that he would be overwhelmed with superstitious fear."[29] Hume does not just provide an institutional prescription for tolerance, however. The *History of England* is, I shall argue, an attempt to increase awareness of the hypocrisy and self-deception of religious belief, thereby deflating factional bigotry, encouraging mutual sympathetic understanding, and enhancing concern for public welfare at the expense of factional interests.

The solution Hume envisioned did not require widespread religious skepticism. Hume's direct arguments on behalf of religious skepticism are directed at the philosophical elite. This aspect of the project was important because many thinkers continued to believe that an alliance between religion and philosophy would eventually render religious disagreement susceptible to final resolution. This hope spurred the development of both rationalist theology and natural religion. If religious doctrines can be rationally tested or derived from reflection on the world, then it seems that there is a determinate way to show to anyone that some religious beliefs should be accepted and others rejected. Hume regarded such philosophers, who hope to secure final agreement on religious matters, as dangerous, because they indirectly encourage dogmatism and hence religious conflict, even if they affirm the importance of free inquiry. On this issue, Hume found himself in opposition even to his friends among the Scottish Moderates, which may help to explain why he agreed not to publish the *Dialogues Concerning Natural Religion* during his lifetime.[30]

I do not mean to argue either that Hume's social concerns provide a rational justification of his skeptical religious epistemology or that he merely posed as a skeptic because he saw this as the only way to calm religious controversy. His arguments for religious skepticism (that no rational reflection, whether deductive or empirical reasoning, can give rise to religious knowledge), must be examined on their own grounds. My claim, rather, is that Hume's skepticism became more than a private matter, and that he found it important to develop arguments on its behalf, because of his concern about eliminating religious conflict and securing the conditions for peace and prosperity. In this sense, his epistemological concerns are derivative of his broader social concerns.

Given that Hume believed that only a few individuals are capable of maintaining religious skepticism, there were projects more important than arguing directly on behalf of skepticism; namely, to render disagreement about religious matters innocuous by showing that no religious premises are required for reasoning about human nature, morality, politics, or history. Hume sought to show, in fact, that disagreement about religious matters can be wholly irrelevant to life in human society. The masses could continue to believe their stories and myths, and philosophers could continue to speculate about first causes, but different stories or hypotheses would not be the occasion of zealous or violent conflict because they would not be seen as mattering in a practical way. Often, therefore, as in the *Treatise*, Hume simply does not mention God or Providence in his discussions of morality and politics, a sin of omission which modern readers are much more likely to miss than Hume's original readers, who were for the most part taken aback by his audacity. Sympathy lies at the heart both of Hume's attempt to show that moral beliefs and judgments need not rest on religious foundations and of his analysis of how religious belief distorts moral judgment and leads to bigotry and enthusiasm. Sympathetic understanding is essential to the capacity to understand the points of view of others, a capacity which in turn is requisite for good moral judgment, but the irrationalities of religious belief create obstacles to such sympathetic understanding and reinforce narrow factional points of view. I now turn to the background of Hume's attempt to show that moral beliefs require no religious assumptions and to the tradition of reflection on which he draws in developing his account of the role of sympathy in moral judgment.

CHAPTER I

Setting sympathy's stage

MODERN NATURAL LAW AND THE CONFLICT PROBLEMATIC

Although Hume's exclusion of religious presuppositions in his exploration of human nature and society is undeniably radical, it nonetheless stands within a long-standing tradition of inquiry which believed that it was possible to understand how we ought to live as moral and political beings by looking closely at human nature, apart from divine revelation. This is the tradition of modern natural law. Duncan Forbes argues persuasively that Hume's moral and political philosophy is linked with this tradition via Grotius, Hobbes,[1] Pufendorf, Carmichael, and, most immediately, Francis Hutcheson.[2] Forbes suggests that "the two main currents of advanced speculation in Scotland at that time: natural law teaching and Newtonian or Baconian experimental science came together, and allied to Hume's religious skepticism, produce his famous 'new scene of thought,' and one aspect of this was a modern theory of natural law."[3]

The modern natural lawyers, beginning with Grotius, emphasized the notion that the natural law governing human interactions in society can be derived from the salient features of human nature, which include both the tendency to pursue one's own well-being and the inclination toward sociability.[4] Modern natural law grew out of, but defined itself in part against, the classical natural law tradition associated with the sixteenth-century Spanish revival of Thomism.[5] Francisco da Vitoria, Francisco Suárez, and other thinkers drew on the Thomistic synthesis of Aristotle and Christian Stoicism in the context of articulating a response to Lutheran pessimism about the ability of human reason to perceive God's intentions and plans for human beings in the world.

According to classical natural law theory, God created and continues to govern the universe in ways which work toward the common good of all creation. God governs according to the eternal law of his nature, in which rational beings participate freely by following the natural law.

God does not issue a body of arbitrary and inexplicable commands to human beings; rather, God wills the fulfillment and perfection of all. There is, therefore, an intelligible connection between ethical precepts and human flourishing. God's will for human beings can be grasped not only by consulting divine revelation, but also by studying human nature. Natural law is the law of the perfection of our nature; given the sort of creatures we are, we must live and order society in certain ways in order to flourish and attain our true good, just as a tree must have sunlight and water and nutrients and space if it is to flourish and fulfill the potential inherent in the seed.

One of the key features of classical natural law was its understanding of the relationship between individual goods and the common good. According to Aquinas, true individual happiness cannot be defined apart from pursuit of the common good.[6] Happiness is the last end of human life, that toward which we are naturally inclined, and "since everything desires its own perfection, a man desires for his ultimate end, that which he desires as his perfect and crowning good."[7] Since the good for man is his perfection, perfection and happiness are identified with one another. Human beings are social beings, and are incomplete and unable to attain to perfection apart from society. Since each human being is part of a community and "it is manifest that the good of the part is for the good of the whole; hence everything, by its natural appetite and love, loves its own proper good on account of the common good of the whole universe, which is God."[8] In order to pursue our own individual happiness, we must pursue the common good, not because common goods are instrumental to the attainment of individual happiness, but because they are constitutive of true happiness, which, theologically understood, is fellowship in the enjoyment of God.[9] Of course, we may be mistaken about what will make us happy, but, as we increase in perfection, our understanding that our true individual good cannot be anything which conflicts with or undermines the common good will also grow. Ethics is simultaneously a matter of developing one's character toward perfection and of developing dispositions to act in ways which advance the common good. There is really no such thing as one's own private good or perfection or happiness, as something which might be defined wholly apart from all consideration of common goods. Although natural law, which guides us in the pursuit of the common good, is not learned from revelation, human nature and the human end are unabashedly theologically and ethically saturated terms.

Unlike the classical natural lawyers, the modern natural lawyers believed in the existence of real conflict between individual happiness and the common good. They no longer saw a coincidence or redundancy among happiness, perfection, and goodness, and began to conceive of individual goodness as something which could be defined prior to the common good. Grotius does not think that conflict arises out of individual misperceptions of personal good and the common good, conflict which can be eliminated with the mature realization that our good is to be found only in the common good. Rather, conflict can only be controlled, never eliminated, because my private advantage (that which is good for me) will often conflict with yours, and moreover because our desires for private advantage are often in conflict with our desire for society.

Hobbes' views reveal even more strikingly the distance between the classical and modern natural law theory. In Hobbes, the notion of "common good" has been supplanted by the notion of "common interests." Although for both Aquinas and Hobbes, it is fair to say that ethics has something to do with "a cooperative venture, in which agents join to produce a good that no one of them could produce alone,"[10] for Hobbes that cooperation is merely a means to an essentially private good, whereas according to the classical view the cooperation was constitutive of the good and the good was shared. According to Hobbes, we will the success of the cooperative venture only as a means, whereas according to Aquinas the success of the venture is an end in itself. So Hobbes states that "the finall Cause, End, or Designe of men, (who naturally love Liberty, and Dominion over others,) in the introduction of that restraint upon themselves, (in which wee see them live in Commonwealths,) is the foresight of their own preservation, and of a more contented life thereby; that is to say, of getting themselves out from that miserable condition of Warre, which is necessarily consequent . . . to the naturall Passions of men."[11]

Human beings are unlike the bees and ants, for whom "the Common good differeth not from the Private; and being by nature enclined to their private, they procure thereby the common benefit."[12] (Note that Aquinas does not simply claim that we are like Hobbes' bees and ants. It is not that in seeking our own good we automatically bring about the common good, but rather that, although we start out seeking our own good, as we grow in perfection we desire and seek the common good for its own sake, and end up finding in it our own good.) Hobbes sees our natural passions leading us into war, while Aquinas finds our natural appetites leading us to pursue the common good of creation. Hobbes was read as denying human sociability and as claiming that human beings are incurably and thoroughly selfish. Subsequent moral philosophers had to struggle to show that the human pursuit of self-preservation did not imply that ethics was merely an indirect expression of selfish interests.

The influence of Reformation ideas, in particular the revival of Augustinian–Stoic views of the nature of human beings, helps to account for many of the changes in natural law theory. This influence begins to be visible even in later Spanish Thomists such as Suárez and Luis de Molina who understood themselves to be defending Catholic orthodoxy. These thinkers "continue to insist on the capacity of all men at all times to apprehend the dictates of the law of nature. But they now go on to emphasise the implications of the fact that all men at the same time are inescapably fallen creatures."[13]

Luther insisted that human beings are utterly sinful. In our fallen state, we do not pursue the common good and are unable even to discern the relationship between it and our own good; instead, we are selfish and pursue only that which we see will benefit us personally.[14] With this Protestant insistence on the possibility of an utter break between what a person seeks on his or her own behalf and the common good, the nature of what the individual is seeking changes. Aquinas believed that even the most vicious person is striving to achieve perfection, just in a misguided way. But he had made, according to Luther and his followers, the crucial mistake of giving a description of the world as it would have been without the Fall (or had the Fall been less catastrophic). Luther believed that the Fall had opened up the possibility of a sort of self-seeking which is not a search for perfection at all, although it might perhaps still be considered a search for happiness. My selfish pursuit of happiness probably will conflict with yours, as we will be in competition for the same limited goods. Discussing the need for secular government, Luther wrote:

> Now since no one is by nature Christian or righteous, but altogether sinful and wicked, God through the law puts them all under restraint so they dare not wilfully implement their wickedness in actual deeds. . . In the same way a savage wild beast is bound with chains and ropes so that it cannot bite and tear as it would normally do, even though it would like to; whereas a tame and gentle animal needs no restraint, but is harmless despite the lack of chains and ropes.
>
> If this were not so, men would devour one another, seeing that the whole world is evil.[15]

Our "natural" desires are fallen and sinful. "Nature" no longer refers, as with Aquinas, to the way things were created, the way God intended them to be. To seek our own private good is still to be fundamentally mistaken about what really is good, yet that is what we *naturally* do. In seeking to obey God and serve fellow humanity, therefore, we must stifle or struggle to control or redirect our own selfish desires and interests, rather than discovering that only the common good can truly satisfy them. The notion of a private good defined apart from the common good is no longer simply a misperception – it has taken on a separate reality of its own.

The harsh reality of the religious wars of the sixteenth and seventeenth centuries also played a significant role in the transformation of natural law theory.[16] First, it made subsequent thinkers more pessimistic about the prospects for eliminating conflict from human society. Second, it impressed thinkers with the importance of showing that each individual has good reason to co-operate in creating and maintaining a peaceful society without appealing to contested theological concepts to provide such reasons. For Grotius, who sought to develop laws to guide international relations during a particularly turbulent period, this was of pressing importance.

This attempt to work without theological concepts can be illustrated by examining the change in the meaning of "natural." In Grotius, the status of "natural" is ambiguous. Like the classical natural lawyers, Grotius thinks that we can derive moral guidance from the proper understanding of our nature, but he has a truncated understanding of human nature, since he no longer sees it as tending toward good as perfection. The older, teleological view of human nature was normatively saturated, unlike Grotius' "thinner" view of human nature. In Hobbes' writings, "natural" has become thoroughly secularized – "natural" is just the way things happen to be. "Natural" thereby leaves theologically contested ground and stands neutrally among different understandings of the degree of our fallenness. To talk about what is natural to human beings is neither to discuss our final end nor to pass judgment on our sinfulness. It is not to trumpet a call for transformation, but simply to make observations about the conditions in which we find ourselves. For Hobbes, then, it is just "natural" to be self-seeking. It is true that we may have common interests – interests which coincide – and it is also true that we may need to co-operate in order to secure our own interests, but common goods and common endeavors are merely contingently connected to the private happiness of individuals as instrumental to it. Although we may be shortsighted about the best means to achieve our own good, we are no longer seen as fundamentally misguided in our understanding of it as something which can be pursued for ourselves as individuals irrespective of the common good. Even when the modern natural lawyers strive to show that interest and virtue are not opposed, therefore, they still treat the two as distinct and autonomous things.

In Grotius, moreover, the end of natural law is secularized and finitized – it is no longer God's glory or the common enjoyment of God, but rather the modest aim of living together in peace. Natural law, rather than playing a positive role in guiding us toward the common good, has a primarily negative role to play in controlling the conflict which inevitably arises in human interaction. Unlike Hobbes, however, Grotius did not think that sociability could be regarded as merely instrumental to private interest, for this would mean that the laws of nature are simply laws of expedience, and this was a skeptical conclusion which Grotius resisted forcefully. We ought to obey the laws of nature not because they are expedient, but because we see that they are in proper accordance with our nature.[17] In fact, Grotius claimed that the laws of nature would have some degree of validity even if God did not exist, because the laws show how social life *must* be regulated to manage conflict, given the facts of human nature.[18]

Although the modern natural lawyers "claimed to have established a science of law and morality without the aid of revelation, grounded on human nature and the 'nature of things' given to reason and experience," however, Duncan Forbes rightly warns against the "fallacy of premature secularization."[19] With the possible exception of Hobbes, the natural lawyers were not secular, but rather non-sectarian. They avoided making direct appeals to any particular conception of the deity in their science of law and morality, but they themselves held particular understandings of the nature of the deity, and their works rest on the assumption of the vague outlines of familiar Christian understandings of God. They regarded the laws of nature as the laws of God, though knowable without recourse to revelation. God commands us to obey the natural law and assigns rewards and punishments to secure our motivation to obedience, ensuring that we have good reason to comply, forbidding us to yield to contrary impulses, and making the moral law clear even to those with weak intellects. It is God, therefore, who finally solves the problem of the conflict between the pursuit of private happiness and the pursuit of the common welfare of all. Morality requires us to pursue the latter, but God guarantees that the former will follow. (According to Hobbes, the absolute sovereign takes the place of God in playing this role.)

All of the modern natural lawyers were agreed that conflict is real, not simply an illusion resulting from misperception of the good. The flip side of this new sensitivity to conflict was the widespread conviction, notably among Deists and Epicureans, of the order to be found in the world. "The principal thing that makes the entities in the world into an order is that their natures mesh. The purposes sought by each, the causal functions which each one exercises, interlock with the others so as to cohere into a harmonious whole. Each in serving itself serves the entire order."[20] In seeking our own best interest we automatically serve the general good. This picture of the individual fitting into the ordered whole may seem closer to Aquinas than to Hobbes, but only until we realize that the classical natural lawyers had regarded individual purposes as deriving from their place in the whole, rather than having their own inner purposes which are providentially harmonized in the whole.

Whether one stresses conflict or order, therefore, individual interests and purposes have acquired a new significance, which a classical natural lawyer could not have appreciated. Talk of interests now makes more sense than talk of the good, since interests are defined in terms of individuals in a way that goodness and perfection are not. Therefore, it is possible that two individuals' interests might conflict head-on without either of them being fundamentally mistaken about what his or her interests are. On the earlier view, there was in principle no barrier to understanding the good of another person – it was perfectly conceivable, in fact, that you might understand my good better than I myself, if your vision of the relationship of my individual good to the common good was less vitiated than mine. Ultimately, moreover, your good and mine are harmonized in the common good, so there was no fundamental disparity for us to strive to fathom. In the seventeenth and eighteenth centuries, in contrast, it began to seem obvious that the particularity of each person's physical, economic, cultural, and social location in the world makes a fundamental difference to that person's interests in a way that renders notions of common good always secondary. Point of view begins to seem a more relevant metaphor than clarity of vision.

An intimately related shift took place earlier with what has been called "the Renaissance rediscovery of linear perspective."[21] Medieval art sought to depict things in accordance with their significance, their place in reality. In order to do this, artists made more important things larger than less important things and depicted everything of relevance about an object, even if these things could only be seen by walking around the object or turning it over, or even if these things were not visible and had to be depicted symbolically or metaphorically. With the advent of linear perspective, however, artists sought to depict exactly what could be seen from a particular point of view, where circles become ovals and parallel tracks converge and people get smaller as they walk away from us. The medieval painter was unconcerned with physical point of view. What mattered was the painter's clarity of vision, the ability to grasp reality as such. In order to truly appreciate the medieval painting, to "see" the reality it depicts, one must share (or at least understand) the painter's whole world view. In a perspectival painting, in contrast, one is enabled to see what *anyone* would see, if, that is, he or she were to stand in a particular place and look in a particular direction. The medieval painter, like the classical natural lawyer, regarded the differences between points of view as mere illusions or distortions of reality. The perspectival painter, like later moralists, believed that access to reality could be obtained only by faithfully taking into account differences in points of view. Just as perspectival paintings came to be commonly referred to as more "realistic" than medieval paintings, later moralists treat the perspective from which individual interests are salient as the primary reality. Simultaneously, they become increasingly disinclined to talk about common good, a notion which seems to pay little heed to individual points of view.

INTERESTEDNESS AND INTELLIGIBILITY

This shift which I have been tracing from classical to modern natural law made ethics into a distinct sphere of constraints on acceptable action, rather than an all-embracing account of human action and the goods pursued in human action. Before, despite practical disagreements, there had been only one candidate for appropriate human action. This was action simultaneously directed toward individual happiness and perfection and fostering common good and perfection. Now, however, it seemed that one could appropriately act just in order to further one's own private interests and that the requirements of morality were something in competition with this line of action, something directing us to disregard our own interests and take others into account.[22] The new sense of the distance between persons made it difficult to understand why we should see the interests of others as something having a claim on us. The natural lawyers tried to affirm the traditional connection between individual and common good, but this was translated into a claim about private and public interests. The prima facie claim that private and public interests always coincide had several strikes against it, however. First, it seemed rather implausible. Second, when rendered more plausible, either by invoking otherworldly rewards and punishments or by arguing that private vices are, in the long run, public benefits (as did Bernard Mandeville's *Fable of the Bees*), this claim seemed to introduce a problem of interestedness into ethics.

Whereas the pursuit of perfection had not seemed problematically self-interested or selfish, the pursuit of one's own interests, particularly in the wake of Hobbes, did. Attempts to stress the connection between private and public interest only made matters worse, implying that even apparently disinterested actions are thoroughly selfish. One response to the problem of interestedness was to stress human sociability. Among the Latitudinarian divines, as I will discuss in greater detail below, this took the shape of insisting on a divinely given principle of natural benevolence within human nature, which enables us disinterestedly to pursue the interests of others.[23] Morality was thereby linked firmly with the interests of others and detached from one's own. Natural benevolence is presented as a naturalized version of sanctified humanity in order to counter Hobbes' naturalized version of fallen humanity. Both eliminate appeals to grace, but the former makes ethics instinctual, while the latter makes ethics both artificial and hypocritical.[24] Neither, that is, seems to leave room for the agent's deliberate choice of something as good to be pursued.

The problem of interestedness might seem to be less pressing for those who depicted morality as the following of rules without attempting to perceive any connection between them and one's own good or common goods. This was the route suggested by the ethical voluntarism of the Calvinists.[25] Their view opened up a gap between morality and human flourishing – for the human agent, the point of following moral rules was wholly contained in following the rules, rather than in contributing in some way to either one's own good or the common good of rational social beings. Any connection between the two was a contingent and arbitrary link arising out of God's will, which might instead call on us to reject all natural goods, rather than perfecting our earthly nature. Such a gap had existed in a less extreme form in the classical natural law view, which affirmed that while, from God's point of view, virtuous action always tended toward the perfection of nature, it might be difficult for human beings to discern God's grand plan. The link between virtue and perfection was not, however, regarded as a matter of the arbitrary whim of God, but as rooted in God's very nature as Creator of a natural order whose perfection he wills. The contingency of the relationship between morality and human flourishing, on the voluntarist account, was liable to create another problem, that of the intelligibility of morality. The point of moral action becomes nothing more than obedience itself, rather than being oriented toward the attainment of a good or goods. Why is moral action good, if it is not "good for" anything? The intelligibility problem was sometimes mitigated by appeals to the glory of God and thereby to the internal good of obedience to God.

For the most part, however, this austere Calvinist doctrine resorted to appealing to eternal rewards and punishments in order to motivate obedience to commandments which were unintelligible in terms of this-worldly human flourishing. This, of course, was the most purely self-interested motivation of all. So readers of the *Whole Duty of Man* are exhorted "to behave themselves in this world, that they may be happy forever in the next," and are told that their most general duty, without which "they will never think themselves much concern'd in the other," is "the consideration and care of their own souls."[26] This life is full of the Devil's snares, which wound the soul and distract us from keeping our attention fixed on the world to come. Not only is the flesh an enemy which resides within, but "the world is a vast army against us: There is no state or condition in it, nay scarce a creature which doth not at sometime or other fight against the soul: The honours of the world seek to wound us by pride, the wealthy by covetousness; the prosperity of it tempts us to forget God, the adversities to murmur at him," and even our nearest friends entice us to sinful pleasure.[27] The Devil's tactic, it appears, is to trick us into thinking that this world contains real goods.

Hume was suspicious of all efforts to conceive of morality apart from human flourishing, from living well and doing well in this world, which is the only one we know. It is not that he wanted to give a reductivist account of morals, equating moral judgments with descriptive statements reporting human pleasure or pain, but that he believed that human action becomes unintelligible if moral action is understood either as abstract rule-following or as directed toward the hypothetical goods of a form of existence we cannot truly comprehend, rather than as directed toward substantial goods.[28] This objection had force against not only voluntarist, but also rationalist, attempts to avoid the interestedness problem.

Rationalist thinkers such as Samuel Clarke and John Balguy overcame the interestedness problem by claiming that we are moved to act directly through rational insight into "eternal fitnesses" or the proper relations between different sorts of things, without any self-regarding motive whatsoever. We can act in a way that furthers general welfare without being self-interested at all. This solution to the problem of interestedness does not suffer from the problem of intelligibility; moral action is ordered toward general welfare. As the section in the *Treatise* entitled "Moral distinctions not derived from reason" indicates, however, Hume saw the rationalist view as failing to give an adequate account of how rational perception could hook up with the passionate nature of human motivation and response to the world. "Morals excite passions, and produce or prevent actions," he wrote. "Reason of itself is utterly impotent in this particular. The rules of morality, therefore, are not conclusions of our reason" (*T* 457).

The moral theory Hume went on to discuss in the *Treatise* can be understood as a continuation of the modern natural law project of securing agreement on morals in a world torn by sectarian strife. Hume shared the modern natural lawyers' concern with the problem of conflict in human society, as well as their conviction that it is by studying human nature that we learn how to live in peaceful society with others.[29] In opposition to the Calvinists, Hume wanted to show that there is an intelligible connection between morality and human flourishing, that ethics is not a matter of arbitrary fiat or mysterious essences, not something remote from human beings which calls upon us to stifle our desires and turn our backs on this life, but something which enables us to live our natural lives more fully and abundantly. Neither God the lawgiver nor God the providential Creator need be invoked to make sense of humans' approval and pursuit of virtue, and such invocations have only served to distort morals. Morality, he believed, has to do with living and doing well in human society, not with rejecting this world and preparing for the next.

The challenge which faced Hume was wholly to secularize modern natural law without undermining the acceptability of his account by making the mistakes Hobbes had been accused of – of depicting human beings as utterly selfish and morality as merely a hidden expression of self-interest. As I will discuss in greater detail in chapter 2, Hume's strategy in the *Treatise* is to appropriate Francis Hutcheson's moral-sense theory while introducing the principle of sympathy in order to radically, but subtly, secularize the theory. If Hume's links to the natural law tradition are rarely seen, despite the fact that Hutcheson's influence on him is widely recognized, it is in part because Hutcheson himself is rarely recognized as a natural lawyer. Hutcheson's most widely read books, *An Essay on the Nature and Conduct of the Passions and Affections*, and *An Inquiry into the Original of our Ideas of Beauty and Virtue*, are not treatises of natural law. They are, rather, something else which influenced Hume deeply, examples of the new experimental method in ethics, to which Hume refers at the outset of the *Treatise*. Although the natural lawyers were empiricists of sorts, since they took human nature as their starting-point, to Hume "this grounding of natural law in human nature must have seemed rudimentary, scarcely an experimental science of man at all."[30] Hutcheson, in contrast, delved more into what Hume regarded as the basic principles of the human mind.

Hutcheson's other works, notably *A System of Moral Philosophy*, however, show him more clearly to be a student of Gershom Carmichael, continuing the tradition of modern natural law. Carmichael, who translated the works of Pufendorf, was responsible for introducing the natural law tradition into Scotland. Carmichael was not an uncritical follower of Pufendorf; he thought that the secularizing trend in natural law was deplorable. Although he agreed that revelation has no part in natural jurisprudence, he held that natural religion was absolutely essential, and sought to deduce natural law from the existence and nature of the deity as known through natural religion.[31] The category of natural religion, which had not been available to earlier natural lawyers, allowed Carmichael to affirm the centrality of religion (including consideration of the prospect of bliss or misery after death) to natural law despite the irrelevance of revelation.

Hutcheson's *A System of Moral Philosophy* begins with a discussion of human nature and human happiness, and from this draws conclusions regarding morality and politics. "The intention of moral philosophy," Hutcheson begins, "is to direct men to that course of action which tends most effectually to promote their greatest happiness and perfection; as far as it can be done by observations and conclusions discoverable from the constitution of nature, without any aids of supernatural revelation."[32] The outline of the natural law project is clear. For Hutcheson, I shall argue, it is only through knowledge of divine Providence that we are finally able to understand the promptings of the moral sense and to reconcile private happiness with general welfare. Hume introduces the notion of sympathy in the *Treatise* in order to bridge this gap between private and public, giving an account of why we approve of things which do not redound to our personal benefit or serve our private interests while also maintaining an intelligible connection between human flourishing and morality. Sympathy as Hume uses it in the *Treatise* is thus designed to solve both the problem of interestedness and that of intelligibility, but without invoking at any point, as Hutcheson and the modern natural lawyers inevitably did, a providential deity. In later works, moreover, sympathy and related concepts will be crucial to Hume's analysis of what he regards as a much more threatening problem of interestedness, not private interest, but rather party prejudice and sectarian zeal.

THE SOLUTION OF SYMPATHY

Hume's appeal to the notion of sympathy is related to previous efforts, beginning with the Latitudinarian divines, to respond to the charge of interestedness, the "selfish hypothesis" of morals. Hume was not the first thinker to emphasize the moral importance of sympathy, although he did do something new with the notion by placing it at the core of his moral theory. Sympathy, understood generally as fellow-feeling with the passions or sentiments of others, became a near obsession for eighteenth-century thinkers. It is intimately associated with a cluster of concepts (including sensibility, sentiment, sensitivity, and moral sense) which pervaded French and English literature, criticism, and morals of the day. This widespread preoccupation with sympathy reflects the intensifying sense of the distance between persons, with their very different points of view, which made it difficult to understand not only why we saw their private interests as something having a claim on us, but even how it is possible for us to be drawn out of our individual worlds of private preoccupations and interests in the first place.[33] Charles Taylor writes that "the disengaged subject is an independent being, in the sense that his or her paradigm purposes are to be found within, and not dictated by, the larger order of which he or she is a part.[34] If "paradigm purposes" are found in some private world within, then the interiors of others become more important to us, and also more mysterious. We no longer understand what is important about someone by seeing how he or she fits into society, contributing to the perfection of the whole. Only once this gap between persons and these puzzles about ethics had come into existence could sympathy seem ethically important. The notion of sympathy seemed to offer a way of bridging the gap by connecting us with the "interiors" of others.

The first definition of sympathy given by the *OED* is "a (real or supposed) affinity between certain things, by virtue of which they are similarly or correspondingly affected by the same influence, affect or influence one another (esp. in some occult way), or attract or tend towards one another." The first citation for this definition dates from

1579. There were impersonal, mechanical overtones to the word "sympathy" from the outset, in contrast to the thoroughly personal connotations of the word "compassion," which dates back to the fourteenth century. Sympathy was, for example, said to exist between iron and a loadstone and between crabs and the moon. Sympathy was often used in a medical context; it was said to exist between two body parts when a disorder in one gave rise to a similar disorder in the other. Sympathy in the sixteenth century could also refer simply to agreement, harmony, or concord of nature, temperament, and disposition. This definition focuses on the affinity between two things, rather than on the phenomenon of the one being affected by the condition of the other. Sympathy was not used to refer to the communication of sentiments from one person to another until the mid-seventeenth century.

Positive views of sympathy in connection with ethics can be traced back to late seventeenth-century sermons of the Latitudinarian divines, particularly between 1660 and 1725.[35] Latitudinarian thought arose after the Restoration in England as a reaction against the Calvinist views of the Puritans, which had been dominant during the years of civil rebellion. The Puritans emphasized the wickedness of human nature and therefore of every merely human virtue, and God's incomprehensible judgment, which bestows eternal bliss on the Elect and eternal punishment on the damned. The Latitudinarians felt that both God's goodness and human virtue had thereby been maligned; instead, they insisted that God's benevolence is shown toward all his creatures and that human beings are naturally good and capable of emulating God's love by making themselves useful and beneficial to others.

The Puritans were not the only targets of Latitudinarian thought, however. The particular form that Latitudinarian claims about the goodness of human nature took cannot be fully understood unless they are also seen as a reaction against Hobbes' view of human nature, already referred to above. While the Puritans had argued that human beings, in their fallen state, act selfishly, Hobbes had provided a psychology of human action which made it difficult to see how human action, totally apart from the question of fallenness, could be anything but selfish. In *Leviathan*, which appeared in 1651, Hobbes had drawn a picture of all human action as inevitably driven by self-interested passions.[36] He defined good and evil solely in terms of what is pleasant to each individual, and claimed that we pursue what appears to us to be the greatest attainable good, that is, what will bring us either mental pleasure (glory), or sensual pleasure. He drew alarming conclusions from his psychology; unless all liberty is handed over to an absolute sovereign, human life will be nothing but a constant state of war of all against all. "Men have no pleasure," wrote Hobbes, "(but on the contrary a great deale of griefe) in keeping company, where there is no power able to over-awe them all."[37] We enter into society out of self-interested reasons, not out of love for others.

In order to show that benevolence and society were natural to human beings, therefore, the Latitudinarians had to exonerate the passions from the accusation of egoism, showing that human action could be accounted for on non-egoistic premises. It was Hobbes, and not the Puritans, who drove thinkers into the analysis of human psychology; "the powerful realism or apparent realism, of his demonstration that crass self-interest, however dressed up, is the true motive of all actions, could not be answered except by descending into the deep subrational drives of human nature. To answer Hobbes involved showing that this subrational part of our nature has more than one drive, that it can be good and 'social' instead of warring and chaotic."[38] Sympathy and pity were invoked as prime evidence that the passions are not directed solely to one's own private good. In keeping with his egoistic psychology, Hobbes had, however, already given a self-centered account of all apparently other-directed passions, including sympathy and pity. He deals with them in passing in the course of his discussion of the passions, writing that "Griefe, for the Calamity of another, is PITTY; and ariseth from the imagination that the like calamity may befall himselfe; and therefore is called also COMPASSION, and in the phrase of this present time a FELLOW-FEELING."[39] Latitudinarian thinkers argued that pity could not be reduced to imagination of harm to oneself, for this would not account for the associated impulse to help others.

Sympathy or fellow-feeling with others was regarded as a clear sign that benevolence is in accord with our nature; as one thinker wrote, "man only of all Creatures under Heaven, God has given this quality, to be affected with the Grief and with the Joy of those of his own kind; and to feel the Evils which others feel, that we may be universally disposed to help and relieve one another."[40] Sympathy could not *replace* dutiful obedience to the law of God, but it could challenge the Calvinist view that benevolence runs counter to our nature. In seeking to show that benevolence is natural, not merely a façade for selfish intentions, Latitudinarian preachers linked benevolent actions with involuntary responses to the plight of others. In the 1660s and 70s, for example, Isaac Barrow related stories of calamities intended to evoke compassion in the hearer "and thereby evidently signify that general sympathy which naturally intercedes between all men, since we can neither see, nor hear of, nor imagine another's grief, without being afflicted ourselves."[41] The immediacy of feeling was highlighted in order to preclude any hint of prudential calculation. According to these thinkers, sympathy, the fact of being moved and affected by the distress of others, evokes first compassion, that is, concern for the suffering person, and responses of active benevolence. Thus sympathy, pity or compassion, and benevolence were linked together, although the involuntariness and passivity of sympathy contrasted with the voluntary activity of benevolence (one thinker referred to "a kind of fatal and mechanical Sympathy").[42] In addition to combating Puritan depictions of sinful human nature and Hobbes' egoistic psychology, these thinkers explicitly rejected the Stoic view of sympathy as a form of weakness which the wise man ought to preserve himself from indulging in, and appealed to the example of Jesus, who had shown pity and sorrow at the plight of others. If Jesus had shown pity, it must be a virtue, not a moral weakness.[43]

In the eighteenth century, sympathy became a popular topic in edifying discourse and moral philosophy more generally.[44] In an article in the *Spectator* of 1714, Henry Grove provided what amounted to a neat summary of the Latitudinarian response to Hobbes. There are two principles of human action, self-love and benevolence, not just one, as Hobbes, following Epicurus, had maintained. The two principles are complementary, but cannot be reduced to one another. As Grove's comments indicate, stressing the automatic and unreflective nature of pity was increasingly seen as the only way to prove its disinterestedness:

The pity which arises on sight of persons in distress, and the satisfaction of mind, which is the consequence of having removed them into a happier state, are instead of a thousand arguments to prove such a thing as disinterested benevolence. Did pity proceed from a reflexion we make upon our liableness to the same ill accidents we see befall others, it were nothing to the present purpose; but this is assigning an artificial cause of a natural passion, and can by no means be admitted as a tolerable account of it, because children and persons most thoughtless about their own condition, and incapable of entering into the prospects of futurity, feel the most violent touches of compassion.[45]

The Third Earl of Shaftesbury wove the views of Latitudinarian divines into his own sentimentalist moral vision, which stressed the pleasures of the natural affections and of social life. Rather than focusing on the sympathetic communication of grief and sorrow in pity and compassion,

Shaftesbury saw the sympathetic communication of pleasant affections as a primary source of pleasure in society:

It will be considered how many the pleasures are of sharing contentment and delight with others; of receiving it in fellowship and company; and gathering it, in a manner, from the pleased and happy states of those around us, from accounts and relations of such happinesses, from the very countenances, gestures, voices and sounds, even of creatures foreign to our own kind, whose signs of joy and contentment we can anyway discern. So insinuating are these pleasures of sympathy, and so widely diffused through our whole lives, that there is hardly such a thing as satisfaction or contentment of which they make not an essential part.[46]

Since most of our pleasures derive from society, Shaftesbury concluded that Hobbes was utterly wrong to think we enter society only as a means to our own narrow self-interest.

Shaftesbury also saw a darker side to sympathy, however. "The very spirit of faction, for the greatest part," he claimed, "seems to be no other than the abuse or irregularity of that social love and common affection which is natural to mankind."[47] The real threat to human society is not individual self-interest, but rather faction, in which social love, though strong, is limited to one's own party or sect, rather than being extended to all. Such denunciations of faction are a common theme of civic republican or commonwealth thought, which defined virtue as public spirit or concern for public good over private interest.[48]

According to Shaftesbury, partiality is a sign that the various affections in the soul are disordered; "partial affection, or social love in part, without regard to a complete society or whole, is in itself an inconsistency, and implies an absolute contradiction."[49] Disorder and contradiction among the natural affections in one's soul eventually destroy the pleasures of society altogether. According to Shaftesbury, the moral task is, in the end, one of aesthetic creation; we must order our affections in such a way as to achieve inner harmony.[50] Shaftesbury's understanding of sympathy, both as the source of the pleasures of society and of faction and enthusiasm, is clearly reflected in Hume's characterization of the double-edged nature of sympathy. Hume does not, however, appropriate Shaftesbury's Stoic vision of the order of the soul and its place in the harmonious order of the universe, nor does he follow civic republicans in placing primary responsibility for the bigotry of factional prejudices on private interest. As we shall see, it is the self-deception of religious belief which enflames sects and parties, carrying them far beyond the rational bounds set by private interest.

Bernard Mandeville took Hobbes' place in the eighteenth century as the exponent of outrageous ideas by proclaiming that we are all utterly vicious, acting only to satisfy self-love, but that our vices are nonetheless indispensable to society. The true virtue of charity would be to love others, even mere strangers, as we love ourselves. Such love is, Mandeville strongly implies, chimerical, but

this Virtue is often counterfeited by a Passion of ours, call'd Pity or Compassion, which consists in a Fellow-feeling and Condolence for the Misfortunes and Calamities of others: all Mankind are more or less affected with it; but the weakest Minds generally the most. It is raised in us, when the Sufferings and Misery of other Creatures make so forcible an Impression upon us, as to make us uneasy.[51]

The pity we feel for others does not depend on the goodness of our characters, but only on the impact the object makes on our senses. Out of sight is out of mind, or at least, out of pity's range. The actions which we do out of pity we do in order to rid ourselves of the uneasiness which has been communicated to us through sympathy. Similarly, we may desire the good of others because it brings us sympathetic pleasure. These actions are, therefore, self-interested, even if they appear to show concern for others.

Mandeville, like the Latitudinarian divines, stresses that sympathy is wholly unreflective, but not in order to be able to conclude that it indicates the natural goodness of human nature. Pity, he insists,

is a thing of Choice no more than Fear or Anger. Those who have a strong and lively Imagination, and can make Representations of things in their Minds, as they would be if they were actually before them, may work themselves up into something that resembles Compassion; but this is done by Art, and often the help of a little Enthusiasm, and is only an Imitation of Pity; the Heart feels little of it.[52]

Those who have tried to refute Hobbes by arguing that pity cannot be self-interested, since it is instinctual and involves no reflection whatsoever, have therefore kicked the legs out from under their claim that pity demonstrates the fundamental goodness of human nature. Pity is nothing more than an amiable weakness, and, since it is something suffered, not something intentionally chosen, it has no true merit. Furthermore, "as it is an Impulse of Nature, that consults neither the publick Interest nor our own Reason, it may produce Evil as well as Good."[53]

Joseph Butler moved away from instinctive, unreflective sympathy in his account of compassion, insisting that we have an "affection to the good of our fellow creatures" which requires no reference to sympathy. Compassion is an intentional concern for the welfare of others which arises not out of an instinctive experience of sympathetically communicated pain, but out of an imaginative substitution in which we place ourselves in the situation of others and feel the same sorrow at their situation that we would feel in a similar situation. It is our prior affection for others which leads us imaginatively to put ourselves in their places and respond accordingly.[54] The theory of Hobbes does require reference to instinctive sympathy, Butler thinks, but such a phenomenon would be morally neutral and proves nothing about the nature of compassion.

If there be really any such thing as the fiction or imagination of danger to ourselves from the sight of the miseries of others . . . if there be anything of this sort common to mankind, distinct from the reflection of reason, it would be a most remarkable instance of what was furthest from his thoughts, namely, of a mutual sympathy between each particular of the species, a fellow feeling common to mankind. It would not indeed be an example of our substituting others for ourselves, but it would be an example of our substituting ourselves for others. And as it would not be an instance of benevolence, so neither would it be any instance of self-love; for this phantom of danger to ourselves, naturally rising to view upon sight of the distresses of others, would be no more an instance of love to ourselves, than the pain of hunger is.[55]

Butler's imaginative substitution is an intentional and reflective process, which makes no reference to the instinctive, automatic sympathy appealed to by previous thinkers. It arises out of benevolence, testifying to its existence and possessing true merit, unlike the mere "impulse of nature" characterized by Hobbes and Mandeville.

One final aspect of Butler's treatment of sympathy and compassion is worth noting. This is that Butler simply sidesteps what I have suggested was the original motivation for appeals to sympathy – the problem of understanding what is going on within the interiors of others. Human beings, he writes, "naturally compassionate all, in some degree, whom they see in distress; so far as they have any real perception or sense of that distress."[56] Butler does not grapple with the question of how we acquire a "real perception" or "sense" of someone else's distress, if not through sympathy in the first place. This is one of the questions that Hume's account seeks to address.

SYMPATHY AND THE "EXPERIMENTAL METHOD"

I have attempted to sketch the development of the late seventeenth- and early eighteenth-century discussion of sympathy in order to give a sense of the sorts of problems and questions which faced anyone who subsequently took up the subject of sympathy. I have been more interested in grasping the problems for which sympathy provided a solution, and the questions in turn raised about that solution, than in evaluating the relative merits of the arguments themselves, although I have hinted at the weaknesses of arguments insofar as they were perceived and provoked responses as the discussion developed. The thinkers I have discussed have disagreed about many things: How is sympathy as fellow-feeling related to pity as concern for, and benevolence as action on behalf of, someone else? Is pity a disguised manifestation of self-interest, or is it a sign of love and concern for others? Is sympathy intentional, active, and reflective, or unintentional, instinctive, and automatic? Is sympathy good, bad, or morally indifferent? While Hume provided his own answers to these questions in the course of his unprecedentedly detailed account of sympathy, he also introduced something entirely new into the discussion.

The conclusion to Book III of the *Treatise* makes it abundantly clear that Hume saw his own account of sympathy as something quite new and as one of his major contributions to the science of morals. He begins the conclusion by stating his hope that "nothing is wanting to an accurate proof of this system of ethics," since

We are certain, that sympathy is a very powerful principle in human nature. We find, that it has force sufficient to give us the strongest sentiments of approbation, when it operates alone, without the concurrence of any other principle; as in the cases of justice, allegiance, chastity, and good-manners. We may observe, that all the circumstances requisite for its operation are found in most of the virtues; which have, for the most part, a tendency to the good of society, or to that of the person possess'd of them. If we compare all these circumstances, we shall not doubt, that sympathy is the chief source of moral distinctions. (*T* 618)

What is so new about Hume's discussion of sympathy? Is he doing more than continuing the discussion on the relationships among sympathy, pity, and benevolence? The passage just quoted makes the strong claim that sympathy is a source of moral *distinctions*, not merely a source of *information* about what actions benefit others or an added *impetus* toward benevolent action.[57] Previous thinkers had given sympathy a role to play in ethical motivation, but not in making sense of the nature of moral approbation and disapprobation, that is in judgment.[58] Other evidence of Hume's conviction of the importance of sympathy to his "system of ethics" comes from manuscript amendments he made to the *Treatise*, probably in the year immediately following publication, while he still hoped to have the opportunity to bring out a new edition.[59] Since most of the amendments are not substantive, his addition of three references to sympathy testifies to his particular interest in highlighting the centrality of that principle to his theory.[60]

The rationale behind Hume's concluding spotlight on sympathy must be placed within his enterprise in the *Treatise* as a whole, which was conceived of as "An attempt to introduce the experimental method of reasoning into moral subjects,"[61] that is, an attempt to give an account of subjects related to human beings while limiting ourselves to experience and careful observation. This experimental method was closely linked to Hume's refusal to ask questions about final causes or God's providential designs. As J. B. Schneewind suggests, "the general aim of Hume's philosophical work was to show that we can explain every facet of human existence without appealing to anything beyond the realm of ordinary natural events related to one another in ways that can be discovered by means of scientific investigation . . . Hume tried to explain not only our political and social institutions but even our most basic thought processes and our scientific, moral, and religious beliefs without calling on God, or soul, or any unique mental substance different in kind from material substance."[62] Hume's goal in the *Treatise* was to arrive at a few simple explanatory principles from which all the observed phenomena of human minds derive. One of the principles to which Hume most often had recourse was the Lockean notion of the association of ideas, which he used in Book I to account for many of our complex ideas, including those of identity, space and time, and causality.[63] According to the principle of the association of ideas, when simple ideas are related by resemblance, contiguity, or cause and effect, the mind moves with great facility among them and tends to associate them together into complex ideas. In his abstract of the first book of the *Treatise*, Hume concludes by saying that the principles of association "are really *to us* the cement of the universe, and all the operations of the mind must, in a great measure, depend on them" (*T* 662). We cannot penetrate beyond to the ultimate cement of the universe, but we can nevertheless give a complete account of how our various beliefs arise.

When sympathy is first introduced, in Book II, it is as one more example of the results of association (this time of impressions), that principle which seemed to the young Hume to possess such wide-ranging explanatory power. Sympathy is explained by our fundamental resemblance to other human beings (*T* 318), and is further strengthened by contiguity and species of causation such as blood ties. But, in Book III, quite a different-looking sympathy, one that is extensive and corrected, is brought in to account for the moral approbation which attends the artificial virtues as well as for moral approbation of the natural virtues. Sympathy cannot remain a wholly instinctive and mechanical principle; the situations of others must be actively and intentionally entered into.[64] This differentiation of sympathy must be seen not only in light of Hume's own understanding of his enterprise, but also in terms of tensions within his theory which push his account of sympathy in directions which he had reason not to fully acknowledge. The significance of this transformation lies, I think, in the crucial role which sympathy comes to play in Hume's account of moral approbation. By the end of the *Treatise*, sympathy is no longer simply one more example of how complex human phenomena can be accounted for by pointing to different configurations of the same small set of principles, but rather has a much more direct role to play in making appeals to providence and final causes irrelevant to moral theory. This can be best understood by comparing Hume's view of sympathy with that of Hutcheson, whose moral theory was, in effect, an argument on behalf of God's Providence against what he regarded as the questionable moral views of the voluntarists and the Epicureans. In emphasizing sympathy in the conclusion to the *Treatise*, Hume is drawing attention away from extensive regions of overlap with Hutcheson to the differences between their theories, and is thereby implicitly highlighting the anti-providential thrust of his theory. Sympathy, in fact, replaces Providence in making sense of how we come to approve and disapprove as we do.

CHAPTER 2

Displacing Providence

SPECIES OF SYMPATHY

Hume's first mention of sympathy within the *Treatise* comes in Book II's discussion "Of the love of fame," which comes under the heading of the indirect passions of pride and humility. Here, the operation of sympathy is characterized as an involuntary, mechanical process by which sentiments are communicated from one person to another. The external signs (facial expressions and utterances) of, for example, someone's anger, convey to us the idea of the affection of anger. This idea of anger is associated with the lively impression of ourselves which is always present to us, and under this vivifying influence the idea of anger is converted into its corresponding impression, the actual affection of anger. The great resemblances among all human beings (and animals as well) facilitate the imagination's association of the impression of our self with the idea of the affection of the other person.

This convoluted model of sympathy makes more sense when it is seen as Hume's attempt to extend a model of the relationship of impressions and ideas which he has already developed in order to account for pride and humility, love and hatred, and which stems ultimately from his account of causality in Book I. There, Hume argued that the idea of necessary connection between two things can never be the result of an impression given to the senses made by any single instance of B following on A. If no impression of sensation can give rise to the idea of necessary connection, then some internal impression or impression of reflection must, since all ideas arise from impressions. This internal impression arises from custom, and is the mind's feeling of determination to pass from A to B when A has always been observed to be followed by B (*T* 165).

This inner determination of the mind to pass from one thing to another which is related to it by custom, contiguity, or resemblance, as well as the associated phenomenon of impressions of reflection giving rise to and enlivening ideas, are phenomena which Hume goes on to trace in his account of the passions. It is not the case that all the different things which produce pride, for example, are alike in possessing a single pride-eliciting quality. Rather, pride is a pleasurable impression which arises when an object which is related to oneself has a quality which itself gives one pleasure.[1] It involves a double relation of ideas and impressions which are intimately associated with one another and bring one another in train. The impression of pride resembles the impression of pleasure caused by the object, while the idea of the object is related to the idea of the self. Referring back to his account of causation, Hume writes that "In all judgments of this kind, there is always a present impression, and a related idea; and . . . the present impression gives a vivacity to the fancy, and the relation conveys this vivacity, by an easy transition, to the related idea" (*T* 290). Ultimately, the impression of pride reinforces the idea of the self (*T* 287).

When it comes to sympathy, Hume again claims an analogy with his account of judgments concerning causal connection; "What is principally remarkable in this whole affair is the strong confirmation these phenomena give to the foregoing system concerning the understanding, and consequently to the present one concerning the passions; since these are analogous to each other" (*T* 319). In this case, Hume claims, the present impression of self is able to lend vivacity to the idea of an affection belonging to someone else because of the relation between self and other which rests on our great resemblance to other human creatures.

He gets himself into a bit of a fix here, for in Book I of the *Treatise* he had argued that there is no such thing as a constant, simple impression of the self, but only a "bundle or collection of different perceptions, which succeed each other with an inconceivable rapidity, and are in a perpetual flux and movement" (*T* 251–252). How, then, can he appeal to an impression of the self in his account of sympathy? He himself equivocates in his explanation of how, in sympathy, the idea of someone's affection is enlivened into an actual impression: " 'Tis evident, that the idea, or rather impression of ourselves is always intimately present with us, and that our consciousness gives us so lively a conception of our own person, that 'tis not possible to imagine, that any thing can in this particular go beyond it. Whatever object, therefore, is related to ourselves must be conceived with a like vivacity of conception" (*T* 317). He first says "idea," then adds "impression," as though realizing both that an "impression" is needed to continue the analogy with other relations of ideas and impressions, but also that, according to Book I, no "impression" of self exists.

This problem can be mitigated by looking more closely at what Hume says about identity in Book I. He there insists on a distinction between "personal identity, as it regards our thought or imagination, and as it regards our passions or the concern we take in ourselves" (*T* 253). When it comes to the latter, "'tis evident, that as we are at all times intimately conscious of ourselves, our sentiments and passions, their ideas must strike upon us with greater vivacity than the ideas of the sentiments and passions of any other person" (*T* 339). While we have no simple impression of sensation of the self, our passions and concerns are able to create unity within the bundle of perceptions, "and in this view our identity with regard to the passions serves to corroborate that with regard to the imagination, by the making our distant perceptions influence each other, and by giving us a present concern for our past or future pains or pleasures" (*T* 261). Even more noteworthy is the fact that Hume *does* identify, not a simple impression of sensation, but a complex impression of reflection, of the self, when he writes that "nature has given to the organs of the human mind, a certain disposition fitted to produce a peculiar impression or emotion, which we call *pride*: To this emotion she has assign'd a certain idea, *viz.* that of *self*, which it never fails to produce" (*T* 287).[2]

If pride is the impression of self which is involved in sympathy, this has several related and potentially problematic implications. One, which Hume never explicitly addresses, is that it would seem that someone who lacks pride or self-esteem would not be capable of sympathy. A second, which Hume does confront, is that the involvement of an impression of self in sympathy, particularly if that impression is pride, seems to imply that sympathetically communicated affections would be felt as belonging to one's own self. I would not only come to share someone's sorrow or anger, but would myself become sad or angry, in a way that overshadows the connection of the ideas of the affections with the other person. As Hume admits, "when the affections are once directed to ourself, the fancy passes not with the same facility from that object to any other person, how closely so ever connected with us." But he is confident that "this difficulty will vanish, if we consider that in sympathy our own person is not the object of any passion, nor is there any thing, that fixes our attention on ourselves" (*T* 340). There is, therefore, an important contrast with felt pride in something, in which the idea of self is the object of passion. In sympathy, the impression of self must not be seen as the occurrent passion of pride caused by something in particular, but rather as a sort of ongoing background pride or self-awareness and esteem which, rather than distracting us from the experiences of those around us, enables us to be more sensitive and open to those experiences.[3] Just as the child with a secure and strong relationship with her mother is more friendly with strangers, while the insecure child clings to her mother, the person with healthy pride is able to sympathize with the sentiments and affections of others, while someone whose impression of self is in constant need of reinforcement is likely to be insensitive to those around her. The vice of pride and the virtue of humility switch places once sympathy is regarded as morally valuable.

Hume's associationist characterization of sympathy has come under fire by various critics who object to its omission of conscious imaginative activity. Páll Árdal complains that "the whole process of sympathizing is conceived of by Hume in very mechanical terms, and the impression of the self enters into the picture only as a source of vivacity or liveliness. There is no suggestion that in sympathizing one imaginatively puts oneself into the other person's place."[4] Philip Mercer suggests that "this notion of sympathy seems more akin to the instinctive response which is emotional infection than to the exercise involving imagination and self-consciousness" which Mercer regards as the only morally relevant sort of sympathy.[5] Hume's initial discussion of sympathy should not, however, be taken as his last word on the subject. One of the most remarkable aspects of Hume's discussion of sympathy is that, after having straitjacketed himself into an associationist account of sympathy, he immediately begins to refine his account and introduce significant new distinctions as he examines his account in light of actual human relationships and interactions. Again and again in what follows, I will be exploring ways in which Hume's practice complicates his theory.

When Hume first introduces sympathy, he invokes it to account for a range of phenomena which do not involve conscious intentional action. Many of these are examples of what we might call emotional infection. So, for example, sympathy accounts for the fact that "a good-natur'd man finds himself in an instant of the same humour with his company," as well as for the uniformity of national character (countering the theory that it arises from the influence of soil or climate) (*T* 317). Often, sympathy is at work without our even being aware of it; we think of the mood or the national character as truly our own, not communicated from others.[6] This sort of sympathy makes no distinction between self and other in the sympathetic communication of affections.

Our love of praise, the phenomenon which first impels Hume to introduce sympathy, is due to sympathy with others' opinions of us. If we always took exactly the same pleasure in praise of all sorts from all persons, this would indicate that we had an "original instinct" to be pleased by praise. As it is, we take more pleasure in praise from those we respect, agree with, or are close to. From these observations, says Hume, we may infer

that the uneasiness of being contemn'd depends on sympathy, and that sympathy depends on the relation of objects to ourselves; since we are most uneasy under the contempt of persons, who are both related to us by blood, and contiguous in place . . . Secondly, we may conclude, that relations are requisite to sympathy, not absolutely consider'd as relations, but by their influence in converting our ideas of the sentiments of others into the very sentiments, by means of the association betwixt the idea of their persons, and that of our own. (*T* 322)

Where the association between selves is closer, sympathetic communication of affections takes place more easily. Sympathy appears as something which we passively suffer or undergo; it happens to us in variable ways, and this variability is reflected in the differing ability of different persons' praise to cause us pleasure.[7]

The term "emotional infection," while it captures the passive element of sympathy in the phenomena mentioned thus far, is misleading if it implies that only emotions may be communicated. The love of praise, after all, is due to sympathy with *opinions*. Opinions are not only attitudes toward, but also beliefs about, as becomes clear when Hume remarks: "this is not only conspicuous in children, who implicitly embrace every opinion propos'd to them; but also in men of the greatest judgment and understanding, who find it very difficult to follow their own reason or inclination, in opposition to that of their friends and daily companions" (*T* 316). This may seem strange until we recall that Hume considers belief "more properly an act of the sensitive, than of the cogitative part of our natures" (*T* 183), and that beliefs are distinguished from their corresponding ideas by their vivacity. Therefore, if we acquire the mere idea of someone else's belief and this is sufficiently vivified, we would expect it to become a belief.[8] The broad range of applications of sympathy in the *Treatise* may be further hinted at by adding that it is also given as the explanation for the fact that we esteem the rich and powerful, even when we cannot expect to benefit from their riches or power (*T* 357, 365), and for our love of beauty, which Hume ties to the usefulness of objects to their possessors.

Some passages give a clear indication that sympathy is nothing other than Hume's attempt to give a truly scientific account of the human sociability which lies at the heart of Grotian natural law theory. At one point in Book II of the *Treatise*, Hume waxes rhapsodic, prompting the reader to

Take a general survey of the universe, and observe the force of sympathy thro' the whole animal creation, and the easy communication of sentiments from one thinking being to another. In all creatures, that prey not upon others, and are not agitated with violent passions, there appears a remarkable desire of company, which associates them together, without any advantages they can ever propose to reap from their union. This is still more conspicuous in man, as being the creature of the universe, who has the most ardent desire of society, and is fitted for it by the most advantages. We can form no wish, which has not a reference to society. A perfect solitude is, perhaps, the greatest punishment we can suffer. Every pleasure languishes when enjoy'd a-part from company, and every pain becomes more cruel and intolerable. Whatever other passions we may be actuated by; pride, ambition, avarice, curiosity, revenge or lust; the soul or animating principle of them all is sympathy; nor wou'd they have any force, were we to abstract entirely from the thoughts and sentiments of others. Let all the powers and elements of nature conspire to serve and obey one man: Let the sun rise and set at his command: The sea and rivers roll as he pleases, and the earth furnish spontaneously whatever may be useful or agreeable to him: He will still be miserable, till you give him some one person at least, with whom he may share his happiness, and whose esteem and friendship he may enjoy. (*T* 363)[9]

The pervasiveness of phenomena involving sympathy is testimony to the incomprehensibility of human beings, their passions, beliefs, and actions, apart from sociability. This must be firmly established before entering on moral and political topics. Yet Hume hopes also to appeal to sympathy to bolster his reiterated naturalistic (that is, anti-supernaturalistic) refrain of the resemblance between human beings and the rest of "animal creation."

Hume's discussion of pity is the occasion for two particularly telling modifications of his account of sympathy. The first involves the influence of general rules on sympathy, and the second is the distinction between "limited" sympathy and "extensive" sympathy. Before analyzing these modifications and exploring their significance, I should clarify what Hume means by "pity" and "compassion." He uses these two terms interchangeably to refer to a concern for the suffering of others, joined with a desire for their well-being like that desire found in love, but in the absence of actual love (*T* 368–369). Sympathy is not to be confused with pity or compassion, but it is intimately involved in them, for it is responsible for the initial communication of others' sufferings to us.

The first modification of Hume's account of sympathy is signalled by his comment that "there remains only to take notice of a pretty remarkable phenomenon of this passion; which is, that the communicated passion of sympathy sometimes acquires strength from the weakness of its original, and even arises by a transition from affections, which have no existence" (*T* 370). This is a remarkable phenomenon indeed – how can a communicated passion have no original? As examples, Hume suggests that our sympathetic rejoicing is intensified when someone graced by good fortune seems insensible to his prosperity, while our sympathetic dejection with someone plagued by troubles increases in proportion to his equanimity. These examples of sympathy are clearly not the same as the sort of emotional infection which affects us when we walk into a room of laughing people. In that case, the emotions affect us despite the fact that we know nothing about their context, whereas in this case we respond to the context despite the lack of expressed emotion. The explanation for this "remarkable phenomenon" lies in general rules:

When a person of merit falls into what is vulgarly esteem'd a great misfortune, we form a notion of his condition; and carrying our fancy from the cause to the usual effect, first conceive a lively idea of his sorrow, and then feel an impression of it, entirely overlooking that greatness of mind, which elevates him above such emotions, or only considering it so far as to encrease our admiration, love and tenderness for him. We find from experience, that such a degree of passion is usually connected with such a misfortune; and tho' there be an exception in the present case, yet the imagination is affected by the general rule, and makes us conceive a lively idea of the passion, or rather feel the passion itself, in the same manner, as if the person were really actuated by it. (*T* 370–371)

In appealing to general rules, Hume is in effect introducing a new variety of sympathy, one in which the idea of the passion or affection, rather than being conveyed by the external signs by which the other person expresses it, is a construction of the observer's mind. The fact that we sometimes blush when others act foolishly proceeds, for instance, from a *partial* sort of sympathy which "views its objects only on one side, without considering the other, which has a contrary effect, and wou'd entirely destroy that emotion, which arises from the first appearance" (*T* 371). If we were to sympathize not only with their foolishness, but also with their lack of awareness of it, we would feel no shame. Although the imagination is said to be obedient to the general rule, in fact, once it is given this creative role, sympathy begins to appear as a much more fluid phenomenon, involving both effort and selectivity in arriving at ideas of emotions in response to the complex characteristics of a situation. The appeal to general rules shifts the focus of the account away from occurrent states of sympathetic sentiment and toward stable dispositions to sympathize.

The second modification to Hume's account of sympathy arises out of his attempt to explain why we sometimes feel pity and other times derive malicious joy from the suffering of others. He suggests that "when our fancy considers directly the sentiments of others, and enters deep into them, it makes us sensible of all the passions it surveys, but in a particular manner of grief or sorrow. On the contrary, when we compare the sentiments of others to our own, we feel a sensation directly opposite to the original one, viz. a joy from the grief of others, and a grief from their joy" (*T* 381). It seems that comparison displaces sympathy when the reality of the other person is not fully present to us; distracted by the thought of ourselves, we fail to "enter deep" into their sentiments. This might suggest that the sort of sympathy a moralist would want to encourage would be one in which self is momentarily forgotten. This would be quite troubling if our self-forgetfulness made us unable to help the other person, as it might if we lost our awareness of the other person as the referent of the sympathetically felt affections.[10] As I have already indicated, however, apart from the cases of emotional infection, Hume thinks that although in sympathy we feel suffering (or joy), we know that it is that of another person or, rather, that which corresponds to the situation of another person. This will become increasingly clear in what follows. What is required for the sort of sympathy which enables compassion is not self-forgetfulness but a stable self-esteem which is capable of appreciating fully the reality of others. We are prone to comparison when our pride is wavering and in need of reinforcement.

Pity is not puzzling simply because it is sometimes displaced by malice; it is also surprising that pity is associated with benevolence and concern for the well-being of others, rather than hatred and avoidance of them, even though it arises from sympathetic pain and unpleasantness.[11] At this point, Hume introduces a crucial distinction between two sorts of sympathy:

I have mention'd two different causes, from which a transition of passion may arise, viz. a double relation of ideas and impressions, and what is similar to it, a conformity in the tendency and direction of any two desires, which arise from different principles. Now I assert, that when a sympathy with uneasiness is weak, it produces hatred or contempt by the former cause; when strong, it produces love or tenderness by the latter. (*T* 385)

What does Hume mean by these two causes of the transition of passions? This is perhaps best clarified by comparison to a case which is in some ways parallel to pity, but in which sympathy is not involved. Hume suggests that we imagine our reaction to the varying fortunes of a business partner (*T* 384). We will be saddened by our partner's misfortune, and will rejoice at his fortune, but in neither case will we hate our partner, rather, we will continue to love him, i.e. desire his well-being. In this case, our own actual interest and personal ties are involved. When we pity someone, we have no real interest at stake, but we sympathetically share not only the occurrent suffering of the person we pity, but his or her interests, hopes, and goals, which extend beyond that moment of suffering. It is this "extensive" sympathy that gives rise to the desire for the person's good fortune, which "counterfeits" love. When sympathy is weak, it remains "limited" to the double relation of ideas and impressions of the actual sufferings or joys of the moment. When it is strong it becomes "extensive," encompassing not only sufferings and joys, but also desires, which give context and meaning to whatever is being felt.[12]

The strength of sympathy is therefore correlated with its scope, in such a way that, while Hume presents the difference between weak and strong sympathy as merely quantitative, his account actually requires a qualitative distinction between limited and extensive sympathy. When we experience weak sympathy, we are aware of the communicated affection, but little else. If the emotion is unpleasant, therefore, we will try to get away from it in the most expeditious manner. Since, as Hume notes earlier, this phenomenon "depends, in a great measure, on the contiguity, and even sight of the object" (*T* 370), we can often rid ourselves of the unpleasant emotion simply by removing ourselves from the situation, rather than by attempting to do anything to change it. Thus we may hum to ourselves to drown out the angry, raised voices of our neighbors having an argument, or hurry past a street fight, for when we can no longer hear or see the commotion, we will cease to feel disturbed and uneasy.

In extensive sympathy, on the other hand, we are aware, not only of the other person's passion or sentiment, but of the other person as such:

When the present misery of another has any strong influence upon me, the vivacity of the conception is not confin'd merely to its immediate object, but diffuses its influence over all the related ideas, and gives me a lively notion of all the circumstances of that person, whether past, present, or future; possible, probable or certain. By means of this lively notion I am interested in them; take part with them; and feel a sympathetic motion in my breast, conformable to whatever I imagine in his. If I diminish the vivacity of the first conception, I diminish that of the related ideas; as pipes can convey no more water than what arises at the fountain. By this diminution I destroy the future prospect, which is necessary to interest me perfectly in the fortune of another. (*T* 386)

Although the sympathetically felt pain itself is unpleasant, in extensive sympathy we are occupied not only with the isolated emotion which is engendered in us, but move on to consider the other person as a whole, in the context of the situation being observed.[13] In particular, we come sympathetically to share not only his or her unpleasant emotion, but also his or her desire for relief or betterment. Hume concludes that "a strong impression, when communicated, gives a double tendency of the passions; which is related to benevolence and love by a similarity of direction; however painful the first impression might have been. A weak impression, that is painful, is related to anger and hatred by the resemblance of sensations. Benevolence, therefore, arises from a great degree of misery, or any degree strongly sympathiz'd with: Hatred or contempt from a small degree, or one weakly sympathiz'd with" (T 387). Pity, therefore, is the result of extensive sympathy and is accompanied by desire for the total well-being of the other, a sort of counterfeit benevolence which gives rise to love rather than arising from it (T 381).

Extensive sympathy, although in one sense involving greater identification with the other person, clearly does not destroy our awareness that we are concerned with "the fortune of another," rather than our own. If it did, it would not lead to efforts to help the other person. Just as our own identity is given coherence by our desires and interests, hopes and intentions, which extend through time and space, linking past, present, and future, distinguishing salient features and relationships in our environment, sympathy with the interests of another person allows us to see him or her as a person, having a similarly constituted identity as a center of desire and intention. We are not, as in emotional infection, deluded into regarding someone else's sentiments as our own, nor do we simply see the other person as a location from which sentiments and affections are expressed.

In discussing national character, catching the mood of one's companions, and the love of praise, Hume had stressed that the strength of sympathy varies with the closeness of the connection between individuals. "Closeness" can mean many things – genetic relationship, friendship, nationality, physical proximity – whatever is felt to be a salient form of connection or similarity. Pity excludes some of these forms of closeness, in that it occurs in the absence of love; "we pity even strangers, and such as are perfectly indifferent to us" (T 369). How then, can sympathy in the case of pity be strong enough to give rise to "extensive" sympathy? " 'Tis a great effort of imagination," writes Hume, to form such lively ideas even of the present sentiments of others as to feel these very sentiments; but " 'tis impossible we cou'd extend this sympathy to the future, without being aided by some circumstance in the present, which strikes us in a lively manner" (*T* 386). In attempting to define what sorts of circumstances meet this criterion, Hume invokes, not only the degree of suffering, but also the way in which suffering is presented to us: "A certain degree of poverty produces contempt; but a degree beyond causes compassion and good-will. We may under-value a peasant or servant; but when the misery of a beggar appears very great, or is painted in very lively colours, we sympathize with him in his afflictions, and feel in our heart evident touches of pity and benevolence" (*T* 387). The question is eventually begged, however, as Hume says "benevolence, therefore, arises from a great degree of misery, or any degree strongly sympathiz'd with: Hatred or contempt from a small degree, or one weakly sympathis'd with" (*T* 387). What makes sympathy strong, and therefore extensive, remains undefined, for it has to do, not only with how something is presented to us, but with how we apprehend what is presented. Whereas the distinction between weak and strong sympathy is based solely on the phenomenological character of the sentiments, the distinction between limited and extensive sympathy bears witness to the significance of context in shaping these sentiments. Once the mechanical connection between strong and extensive sympathy is problematized, as in these passages, the possibility emerges of an active form of sympathy which an individual can intentionally strive to "extend," rather than simply a fluctuating sympathy of which one is a passive subject. We can, so to speak, make sure to paint the misery of the beggar in "lively colours."

Thus far I have explored Hume's original associationist account of sympathy, as well as the important modifications introduced by general rules and the notion of extensive sympathy. The importance of the identity of both self and other to different varieties of sympathy have been discussed; extensive sympathy, I have suggested, is possible only for someone possessing stable self-esteem which is not threatened by apprehending the reality of the other as a person whose well-being as a whole can be taken into account. Limited sympathy, in contrast, is aware of the other only as a locus of present emotions and affections, while infectious sympathy may not even succeed in identifying the other as the source of the communicated affection. To begin to understand the operations of sympathy is, for Hume, to shed light on sociability, that salient feature of human nature which constrains and gives shape to human life in community. But what of sympathy as a source of moral distinctions? This is the subject to which I now turn. In order to indicate the significance of this new role for sympathy, I begin by contrasting it with Hutcheson's characterization of the moral sense.

THE HUTCHESON CONNECTION

One of the things which makes the relationship between Hume and Hutcheson crucial to understanding the role of sympathy in Hume's moral thought is that the conclusion to Book III of Hume's *Treatise*, in which sympathy figures so prominently, developed out of a correspondence between Hutcheson and Hume. In the autumn of 1739, Hume sent a draft of Book III of the *Treatise* to Hutcheson, which Hutcheson read and commented on.[14] Writing back to thank Hutcheson for his remarks, Hume reiterated his position on several points of disagreement, such as his role as "anatomist of morality," which make an appearance again in the *Treatise* conclusion.[15] In a postscript, Hume added:

> I cannot forbear recommending another thing to your consideration. Actions are not virtuous nor vicious, but only so far as they are proofs of certain qualitys or durable principles in the mind. This is a point I shou'd have established more expressly than I have done. Now I desire you to consider, if there be any quality, that is virtuous, without having a tendency either to the public good or to the good of the person, who possesses it. If there be none without these tendencys, we may conclude, that their merit is derived from sympathy.[16]

The fact that we approve of a quality as virtuous, in other words, is due to our sympathy with those to whose good it contributes. It is extensive sympathy, in particular, which Hume specifies is the sort of sympathy which is involved in moral evaluation (*T* 586, 619). This makes sense, because the capacity for moral judgment involves a sensitivity, not only to how people are immediately affected by actions, but also to how these affections fit in with their situation as a whole, and this is what is distinctive about extensive sympathy. If, for example, we saw a man give a delicious but deadly poison to a child, our sympathetic awareness of the child's pleasure in drinking the poison would be much less significant than our vivid awareness of the future suffering the poison will cause. If our sympathy were only with the child's pleasure, we would not judge the man to be wicked. If, however, we sympathize more extensively, having a sense of the child's total well-being, we will certainly judge the poisoner more harshly. Conversely, if a child's father refuses to allow her to watch television, her favorite activity, an adequate moral judgment would take much more into account than simply her present unhappiness, and would not necessarily conclude that the father is cruel.[17]

Unfortunately, we lack the benefit of Hutcheson's comments on Hume's *Treatise*, but, judging by the defensive nature of Hume's remarks in his letter, he anticipated resistance from Hutcheson on his point about the source of moral distinctions, as he clearly did on the other points discussed. What would Hutcheson have found objectionable?

In his classic biography of Hume, Ernest Mossner suggests that the principle of sympathy is one of the chief links between Hutcheson's thought and Hume's, writing that "both regarded [the principle of sympathy] as one of the strongest in the constitution of human nature and one of the foundation stones of ethics."[18] But this is a highly questionable claim. In his 1725 *Inquiry into the Original of our Ideas of Beauty and Virtue*, Hutcheson never mentions sympathy at all. He does discuss pity and compassion, but they play only a minor role in showing that benevolence is natural. Although compassion, being afflicted by the distresses of others, is painful, the fact that "we are not immediately excited by Compassion to desire the Removal of our own Pain . . . but we are excited directly to desire the Relief of the Miserable," serves, he thinks, to prove that benevolence is natural.[19] In his discussion of parental care and affection, moreover, Hutcheson effectively denies the existence of a general principle of sympathy. Responding to the charge that parents take care of their children only because their children's happiness makes them happy and their misery makes them miserable, Hutcheson insists that it is the antecedent love of parent for child which causes parents to be affected by the pleasures and pains of their children.[20] Sympathetic pleasures and pains are secondary phenomena, while benevolent impulses are basic and not derivative.

In his *Essay on the Nature and Conduct of the Passions and Affections*, published in 1728, Hutcheson adds to his original trio of senses (external, internal or the sense of beauty, and moral), a fourth and fifth – a "publick sense, viz. 'our determination to be pleased with the happiness of others, and to be uneasy at their misery', and a sense of honor."[21] Hutcheson's introduction of a public sense is his belated admission of the principle of sympathy.[22] But, while Hutcheson's public sense is superficially similar to what Hume will later call sympathy, Hutcheson regards the public sense as wholly distinct from the moral sense – there is no suggestion that the public sense "has force sufficient to give us the strongest sentiments of approbation" (*T* 618). In fact, there is no hint that the operations of the moral sense are in any way influenced by, or tied into, the operations of the public sense.

Although each sense is correlated with a set of desires (the public sense is correlated with our public desires, which include gratitude, compassion, natural affection, friendship, and universal benevolence), Hutcheson insists that the desires are "original" and "ultimate," not in any way derivative of the activity of the various senses.[23] The desires must be seen as original so that the sympathetic pleasures of the public sense cannot be regarded as the source of our motivation for seeking the happiness of others. Hutcheson argues at length against what he calls the Epicurean hypothesis (the usual way of referring to Mandeville) that the public sense produces a conjunction of interest whereby "the happiness of others becomes the means of private pleasure to the observer; and for this reason, or with a view to this private pleasure, he desires the happiness of another."[24] Hutcheson admits that this sort of subordinate desire of the happiness of others does exist, but claims that it cannot be equated with the virtuous affection of which we approve.

What the moral sense approves of is benevolent intentions "flowing from the love of others, and study of their happiness," "nor shall we find any thing amiable in any action whatsoever, where there is no benevolence imagin'd; nor in any disposition, or capacity, which is not suppos'd applicable to, and designed for benevolent purposes. Nay . . . the actions which in fact are exceedingly useful, shall appear void of moral beauty, if we know that they proceeded from no kind intentions toward others."[25] If our desire of the happiness of others derived merely from the pleasures and pains of the public sense, the fact that we approve of this desire, but do not approve of those who openly seek the happiness of others as a mere means to furthering their own interests, would be inexplicable.[26] Hutcheson has a bit of trouble finding an illustration of a situation in which it seems clear that a person's pursuit of the happiness of others is purely self-interested – he offers the rather unlikely example of a man who bets that he can make another person happy. Still, he remains confident that the moral sense is able accurately to detect the degree of disinterested benevolence, and to approve of it in proportion to its degree. To Hutcheson, then, Hume's conclusion about sympathy as a source of moral distinctions would have sounded like the Epicurean view that the happiness of others matters to us only as a means to sympathetically derived pleasure in it.[27] He would, therefore, have understood Hume to be claiming that morality is, at heart, self-interested. This was just the sort of reaction which, as I have argued, Hume was anxious to avoid, for it placed him in the despised company of Hobbes and Mandeville.

It is difficult to know how much Hume altered Book III after receiving Hutcheson's comments; it is known that he did not regard the changes as merely cosmetic, for he wrote Hutcheson in March of 1740 to say that "since I saw you [they had met for the first time in the winter of 1739], I have been very busy in correcting and finishing that Discourse concerning morals, which you perus'd; and I flatter myself, that the alterations I have made have improv'd it very much both in point of prudence and philosophy."[28] Hume is particularly concerned to avoid giving offense to religious readers, and he asks Hutcheson to read a revised version of the conclusion: "I have sent you the *Conclusion*, as I have alter'd it, that you may see I desire to keep on good terms even with the strictest and most rigid." We must read the conclusion in this light, as a document in which every idea is carefully packaged to avoid antagonizing readers on religious grounds, and all overt references to religious matters are excluded.

What Hume has to say in the conclusion about the advantage of his account of the sense of morals is that

All lovers of virtue (and such we all are in speculation, however we may degenerate in practice) must certainly be pleas'd to see moral distinctions deriv'd from so noble a source, which gives us a just notion both of the generosity and capacity of our nature. It requires but very little knowledge of human affairs to perceive, that a sense of morals is a principle inherent in the soul, and one of the most powerful that enters into the composition, but this sense must certainly acquire new force, when reflecting on itself, it approves of those principles, from whence it is deriv'd, and finds nothing but what is great and good in its rise and origin. Those who resolve the sense of morals into original instincts of the human mind, may defend the cause of virtue with sufficient authority; but want the advantage, which those possess, who account for that sense by an extensive sympathy with mankind. According to the latter system, not only virtue must be approv'd of, but also the sense of virtue: and not only that sense, but also the principles, from whence it is deriv'd. So that nothing is presented on any side, but what is laudable and good. (*T* 619)

Hume's stress on "the generosity and capacity of our nature" is clearly a denial of any affinity between his views and those of Hobbes and Mandeville, while the affirmation that "a sense of morals is a principle inherent in the soul" is a declaration of allegiance to Hutcheson. But this passage also contains an implied criticism of Hutcheson.

It is clearly Hutcheson whom Hume has in mind in referring to "those who resolve the sense of morals into original instincts of the human mind." In fact, as I indicated earlier, throughout the conclusion, Hume develops ideas already to be found in his letter to Hutcheson of September 17, 1739. Hume's emphasis on reflexive approval is also directed against Hutcheson, for, in the *Illustrations Upon the Moral Sense*, Hutcheson had explicitly denied the possibility of applying moral attributes to our moral sense faculty; "none can apply moral attributes to the very faculty of perceiving moral qualities; or call his moral sense morally good or evil, any more than he calls the power of tasting, sweet, or bitter; or of seeing, strait or crooked, white or black."[29] Hume here insists, in contrast, that the advantage of a system of morality which recognizes the role of sympathy is that it permits meta-levels of approbation. Approbation may be directed at something other than benevolence, since, through sympathetic reflection on the general beneficial effects of the sense of virtue and of sympathy itself, we may come to extend our approbation to these as well. What is at issue in this disagreement about reflexivity?

Hutcheson believes that to think we can apply moral attributes to our moral sense faculty is to join the rationalists, such as Samuel Clarke and, more locally, the jurist Sir James Dalrymple of Stair, who claimed that there are standards of morality perceived by a rational faculty prior to and independent of the activity of the moral sense. Hutcheson opposes the rationalist insistence that we are capable of passing moral judgment on our own moral sense, not only because it suggests that reason, rather than sense, is the ultimate arbiter of morality (and that some are therefore better equipped to be moral judges than are others), but also because he believes that many rationalists conflate moral evaluation and prudential or advantage-based evaluation.[30] When the rationalists got more concrete about the use of reason in morality than vague references to eternal fitnesses in the universe, they seemed to suggest that one could determine which action ought to be performed or approved of simply by employing reason to determine which action would contribute the most to total welfare. The latter, however, is a prudential, not a moral, issue. "What," asks Hutcheson, "is reason but that sagacity we have in prosecuting any End?"[31] Reason, to Hutcheson, is purely insturmental, and therefore it is excluded from moral evaluation, which is concerned with the quality of ends themselves. The rationalists, he claims, either presuppose the moral sense which tells us that it is *morally* best that all be happy, or presuppose that individual welfare is maximized when total welfare is maximized. The latter instance is not a moral determination at all, but a self-interested one, which places rationalists and Epicureans in the same boat, with Hutcheson's argument therefore dedicated to sinking both.

For Hutcheson, there is no way to mediate between the language of advantage or natural goodness and the language of moral goodness. We certainly do not first reason about what is most advantageous and then issue our moral approval of that.[32] Hutcheson's moral sense theory is therefore secured against insinuations that morality is merely a disguise for interested judgments and behavior. In securing the autonomy and disinterestedness of morality, however, Hutcheson has at the same time portrayed moral approval as an unconnected fact, only contingently related to human well-being or flourishing by the facts of what appeals to the moral sense.[33] He is thus confronted by one version of the problem of intelligibility discussed in chapter 1. The moral sense is not integrated into the activity of practical reason as a whole; our different senses and sets of desires are carefully detached from one another to ensure disinterestedness, with the result that human moral agency is fragmented. This isolation of the phenomenon of moral evaluation serves Hutcheson's enterprise as a whole, however, as will soon become clear.

In practice, Hutcheson concedes, we simply judge the affections and senses of others by our own, so that if we found someone with a sense which approved of malice, we would consider that sense perverted, while he or she would think that a sense which approved of benevolence was perverted. If someone without a moral sense observed both, he or she would be unable to judge one sense *morally* better than the other, although he or she could see that the sense which approves of benevolence is more *advantageous*, since it contributes more to the happiness of all concerned than a sense which approves of malice. Given Hutcheson's characterization of the moral sense, it is meaningless to complain that no one can morally approve of the moral sense, because it is not a benevolent affection, and only benevolent affections are a proper target for the activity of the moral sense.

Granting that we cannot approve of the moral sense itself, can we at least approve of human beings in their employment of the moral sense? If the moral sense is simply a natural instinct, it seems inappropriate to apply moral terms to its employment at all. After all, we do not condemn wild animals for their predatory instincts. The operation of instinct, writes Hutcheson's rationalist critic John Balguy, is "not voluntary, but necessary," and "it seems utterly impossible to reconcile Virtue with any kind of Necessity."[34] Balguy complains not only of the necessity of the operations of the moral sense, but also of their contingency: "it seems an insuperable Difficulty in our Author's Scheme, that Virtue appears in it to be of an arbitrary and positive Nature; as entirely depending upon Instincts, that might originally have been otherwise, or even contrary to what they now are; and may at any time be alter'd, or inverted, if the Creator pleases."[35] If we had been instilled with different instincts, we would simply have approved of different things. In that the connection between benevolence and the moral sense is purely contingent, Hutcheson's position is like the voluntarism he so detested, which made right and good dependent on the arbitrary will of God.

What Hutcheson particularly resisted about voluntarism was not so much the contingency of approval or of the good, however, but rather the notion that God's rewards and punishments bribe us into doing, for purely selfish reasons, whatever God commands. The only other option for the voluntarist seems to be to apply moral attributes by sheer force of will to whatever God names as right or good (including himself), and it is unclear what the motivational structure for such activity could be. Hutcheson's theory of moral sense showed that we are disinterested in our approval and pursuit of virtue. We find ourselves approving and disapproving – neither calculating advantages nor willing to find good what God says is good.

Hutcheson's theory also indicated that, while it is inappropriate to approve of the moral sense itself, some sort of higher-order approbation is possible – we approve of the benevolence of the deity which is responsible for the contingent connection between the deliverances of the moral sense and the enhancement of the general good. Most importantly, our possession of such a moral sense cries out for explanation, and in so doing functions as a sort of proof for the existence of a benevolent and providential deity.[36] As Knud Haakonssen remarks:

Our moral experience will show that individual moral phenomena, i.e. particular moral dispositions as judged by our moral sense, tend towards the general good . . . Our experience of this potential moral system of all humanity will, through a reasoning process analogous to the one which prepares our moral judgement of individual men, lead us to the conclusion that there is a superior moral motivation behind this system, namely the divine benevolence, which our moral sense will judge in the same way as it judges the moral qualities of men.[37]

The existence of a moral sense which approves of benevolence, but which is not internally connected with the rest of human psychology, is inexplicable, Hutcheson suggests, unless we have recourse to the designs of a benevolent deity. Hutcheson's efforts, it becomes clear, are not so much directed toward explaining ethics, but rather toward demonstrating that God need not be regarded as an avenging lawgiver (*pace* Evangelical clergy and Lockean voluntarists) in order to be appreciated as indispensable to ethics.[38] While it is true that Hutcheson makes a point of insisting that although "it has been often taken for granted in these papers, 'that the Deity is morally good' . . . the reasoning is not at all built upon this supposition," a few lines later he adds that "this very moral sense, implanted in rational agents, to delight in, and admire whatever actions flow from a study of the good of others, is one of the strongest evidences of goodness in the author of nature."[39] Hutcheson does not want to "suppose" what he is actually setting out to prove; his concern with providing a satisfactory defense of God and his goodness permeates his work.

Hutcheson's theory is also less independent of theological assumptions than he claims. His understanding of human nature is not arrived at simply by observation, but rather by working backwards from the divine scheme as a whole, and the place human beings are to play in it. This becomes even more clear in *A System of Moral Philosophy*, in which he claims that human beings are naturally benevolent and that the moral sense naturally determines us to approve of the most extensive benevolence, but then admits that "it must be obvious we are not speaking here of the ordinary condition of mankind, as if these calm determinations were generally exercised, and habitually controlled the particular passions."[40] What we "naturally" are is what we can be if we develop as we *ought* to. In a 1739 letter to Hutcheson, Hume complained that "I cannot agree to your sense of *Natural*. Tis founded on final Causes; which is a consideration, that appears to me pretty uncertain and unphilosophical. For pray, what is the End of Man? Is he created for Happiness or for Virtue? For this Life or for the next? For himself or for his Maker? Your definition of *Natural* depends upon solving these Questions, which are endless, & quite wide of my Purpose."[41] In *A System of Moral Philosophy*, Hutcheson ends up invoking Providence to keep his moral theory afloat, writing that "as the selfish principles are very strong . . . and the moral sense often asleep . . . our capacity, by reasoning, of arriving to the knowledge of a Governing Mind presiding in this world, and of a moral administration, are of the highest consequence and necessity to preserve our affections in a just order, and to corroborate our moral faculty: as by such reasoning and reflection we may discover a perfect consistency of all the generous motions of the soul with private interest."[42] The workings of the moral sense testify to the existence of a benevolent deity who arranges things so that we disinterestedly approve of benevolence, but we may, after all, need to reason back from the existence of such a deity in order to wake up our moral sense, pay attention to our benevolent impulses, and be confident that generosity will not, in the long run of eternity, be to the detriment of our own private interests. The providence of God plays a crucial role in this (admittedly circular) piece of moral reasoning, in solving the problem of intelligibility, making the connections between what we approve of as morally good and what contributes to natural good (comprised of general good or interests on the one hand and our own good or interests on the other). In making these connections, however, the problem of interestedness sneaks in again through the back door. As long as the inner gears of the moral sense remained below consciousness, accusations of self-interest were meaningless, but, having examined them in broad daylight, Hutcheson worries, despite himself, that the disinterested benevolence which evokes our moral approval may not function without a little grease of self-interest.

While Hume and Hutcheson are allied in their opposition to self-interested and rationalist accounts of morals, Hutcheson's enterprise in defense of Providence could scarcely have been more diametrically opposed to Hume's attempt to naturalize or secularize morality. If Hume could account for moral approval and disapproval without invoking either God's laws or God's benevolent designs, he could go a long way toward making the hypothesis of a providential deity superfluous. Just this, I argue, is what Hume regarded the principle of sympathy as accomplishing for his moral theory in the *Treatise*. Hume's assertion of the centrality of sympathy was therefore highly subversive of Hutcheson's attempt to show that human moral practices are inextricably linked with Providence and divine benevolence. But Hume could not claim outright that sympathy showed that the providence of God was wholly unnecessary to an account of morality, since this would be denounced as an avowal of atheism. Hence, he sought a less obtrusive way to convince readers of the advantages of his explanation of morality, one which might snare even unsuspecting religious believers and loosen their reliance on religious presuppositions.

Hume's stress on sympathy and reflexive approval does several things at once. First, it is intended to preempt the Hutchesonian worry that, if moral approval and disapproval are explained by the workings of sympathy, morality reduces to selfish interestedness. If it is absurd to say that we approve of someone in order to feel pleasure, it is yet more absurd to say that we disapprove of someone in order to feel pain. By focusing on moral approval and disapproval, Hume avoids making the Epicurean argument that we desire the happiness of others only because, sympathetically experienced, it contributes to our own private happiness. For Hume, morality begins with the human responses of approbation and disapprobation, and its influence on deliberation and decision, as I will discuss more fully below, is derivative, although no less powerful for that.[43] We cannot intend to act virtuously or to become virtuous until after "virtue" has come to mean something to us. Therefore, rather than focusing primarily on motivation and intention, he seeks to explain the phenomenon of moral *approval* and *disapproval* via our sympathetic experiences of the pleasure and pain of others, along with their extended contexts.[44] Hutcheson had shown the way in stressing the phenomena of moral response and evaluation as a way to capture the disinterestedness of morality, but he had failed to see that sympathy could be involved in these phenomena without rendering them self-interested.

In general, Hume resists the reduction of all motivation to selfish motivation, but he also resists the attempt to identify all approved-of actions with actions carried out for a single "moral" motive such as general benevolence (*T* 496–497). Hume was much less concerned with purity of intention or with specifically "moral" motivation than was Hutcheson. While it is of motives and stable principles that we approve, not of actions, the motivations which we call virtuous are various and multilayered (*T* 478–479). Neither caring for one's children nor respecting the property rights of others is done out of a motive of general benevolence, but both are nonetheless worthy of approbation. It is true that morality influences human passions and actions (*T* 457), but it does so not because we have an original instinct or motive directing us towards actions under a single denomination, whether "benevolent," or "dutiful," or "virtuous." Morality influences our actions through the complex of desires and responses which surround approbation and pride or self-respect.[45] Still, Hume stresses that moral approbation is natural, not artificial, at least in the sense that it is not something which scheming Mandevillian politicians dreamt up and deliberately designed.

Hume reunites the various features of human moral agency which Hutcheson had painstakingly isolated from each other. There is no need to wall off the "public sense" from the "moral sense" in order to preserve moral purity. Moral evaluation, for Hume, does not function in a vacuum – what we approve of is not a contingent matter of what sort of moral sense we are endowed with by our creator (nor is it a necessary truth of eternal geometrical fitnesses), but is intrinsically related to the sort of creatures we are, creatures to whom things can *matter*, and hence to the things that matter to us. Our approval of virtue has to do with our appreciation of its tendency to enhance human flourishing, which is brought home to us through extensive sympathy with others, not connected to our own self-interest by a system of rewards for good behavior nor by elaborate calculations which assure us that in serving others we serve ourselves. Hume's theory manages to solve the intelligibility problem without, like Hutcheson, invoking divine Providence, and it does so without uncovering a seamy selfish underside to morality.

Hume's conclusion is not just designed to point to the intelligible relationships between morality and human flourishing, private interest and general good, while deflecting worries about interestedness. It also allows him to claim that the moral sense is itself approved of, diffusing some of the worries which prompted charges of irrationalism against Hutcheson, without thereby joining the rationalist camp and undermining the priority of moral sentiments over deliverances of reason. The moral sense is not to be regarded as a mere instinct, with troubling consequences for human moral agency. Hutcheson's moral theory encouraged approval of God's benevolence, but the moral sense itself was regarded as a given and not subject to evaluation. Hume's emphasis on reflexive approval replaces (and camouflages the absence of) the higher-order approval of God's benevolence which was elicited by Hutcheson's theory. As we come to understand more fully the connections among our moral judgments and our desires and sentiments, the fact that we approve and disapprove as we do no longer requires references to providential design. Here in the conclusion to the *Treatise*, Hume drops his role as anatomist and, in a gentle parody of Hutcheson, introduces his own normative conception of human nature, one dependent not on final causes and God's providential plan, but on the sustained reflexivity of moral judgment, made possible by the continual operation of extensive sympathy. He makes the most of previous valorizations of sympathy in claiming that "nothing is presented on any side, but what is laudable and good" (*T* 619). As we have seen, sympathy as such is morally neutral, and, as subsequent chapters will argue, sympathy under some circumstances is pernicious and fosters sectarian zeal. But Hume is careful to specify that it is extensive sympathy which is laudable and good. Implicit in Hume's account is the possibility, once the importance of extensive sympathy to moral judgment is recognized, of beginning to cultivate and extend it intentionally, rather than being distracted from human affairs and practices by the search for reflection and confirmation of the deliverances of the moral sense in the deity. Reflexivity, importantly, implies the possibility of self-correction, not solely of self-approval.[46]

ACCOUNTING FOR APPROBATION

I have suggested that the principle of sympathy is a key element in Hume's strategy to render Hutcheson's religious assumptions superfluous. Although the accounts of morals given by the two thinkers have a great deal in common, by noting where Hume departs from Hutcheson's account we can begin to see how this divergence serves Hume's overall strategy. For both thinkers, approbation is a sort of love, and love is a response to pleasure (*T* 337). Hutcheson introduces his *Inquiry Concerning*

Moral Good and Evil with the claim that "by a superior sense, which I call a moral one, we perceive pleasure in the contemplation of such actions in others, and are determin'd to love the agent . . . without any view of further natural advantage from them."[47] Hume, similarly, insists that "an action, or sentiment, or character is virtuous or vicious; why? because its view causes a pleasure or uneasiness of a particular kind" (*T* 471). First, there is the immediate satisfaction, the pleasure elicited by the contemplation of character. Second, there is the moral approbation which is caused by the pleasure; "since every quality in ourselves or others, which gives pleasure, always causes pride or love; as every one, that produces uneasiness, excites humility or hatred: It follows, that these two particulars are to be consider'd as equivalent, with regard to our mental qualities, *virtue* and the power of producing love or pride, *vice* and the power of producing humility or hatred" (*T* 575). The twofold structure is even clearer in Hume's discussion of love and hatred, where he remarks that "the object of love and hatred is evidently some thinking person; and . . . the sensation of the former passion is always agreeable, and of the latter uneasy. We may also suppose with some shew of probability, *that the cause of both these passions is always related to a thinking being, and that the cause of the former produce a separate pleasure, and of the latter a separate uneasiness*" (*T* 331).

Hume also follows Hutcheson in seeking to determine what sorts of things consistently cause the peculiar sort of pleasure or agreeable sensation which both thinkers identify with approbation. Hutcheson concludes that the cause of the feeling of satisfaction which is moral approbation is in every case disinterested benevolence. Hume, in contrast, broadens the causes to include the view of a character "which is naturally fitted to be useful to others, or to the person himself, or which is agreeable to others, or to the person himself" (*T* 591). This difference is in line with Hume's movement away from the analysis of the purity of particular motivations and toward the evaluation of settled character traits – dispositions to act in certain ways which tend to have predictable effects on others – and also reflects Hume's denial of universal benevolence as a motive. He comments that:

In general, it may be affirm'd, that there is no such passion in human minds, as the love of mankind, merely as such, independent of personal qualities, of services, or of relation to ourself. 'Tis true, there is no human, and indeed no sensible, creature, whose happiness or misery does not, in some measure, affect us, when brought near to us, and represented in lively colours: But this proceeds merely from sympathy, and is no proof of such an universal affection to mankind. (*T* 481)

Benevolence cannot be the motive to all of the actions of which we approve, and it is particularly unsatisfactory to attempt to account either for our approval of traits which benefit their possessor or for the universality and impartiality of justice in this way.

The most significant point of divergence, however, is that Hutcheson makes no attempt to explain why benevolence causes pleasure in us. He simply observes that "the presence of some objects necessarily pleases us, and the presence of others as necessarily displeases us . . . by the very frame of our nature the one is made the occasion of delight, and the other of dissatisfaction."[48] The sole explanation for the pleasure which the mere observation of benevolence brings us lies in the benevolent intentions of the author of nature.[49] Hume, in contrast, after arguing that moral distinctions are derived not from reason but from a moral sense, writes that "thus we are still brought back to our first position, that virtue is distinguished by the pleasure, and vice by the pain, that any action, sentiment or character gives us by the mere view and contemplation. This decision is very commodious, because it reduces us to this simple question, *Why any action or sentiment upon the general view or survey, gives a certain satisfaction or uneasiness*, in order to shew the origin of its moral rectitude or depravity" (*T* 476).[50]

Since approbation is a form of love, it makes sense to turn to Hume's discussion of love for insight into the various pleasures and pains arising from characters and actions. In his discussion of the causes of love and hatred in Book II, Hume claims that:

nothing is more evident, than that any person acquires our kindness, or is expos'd to our ill-will, in proportion to the pleasure or uneasiness we receive from him, and that the passions keep pace exactly with the sensations in all their changes and variations. Whoever can find the means either by his services, his beauty, or his flattery, to render himself useful or agreeable to us, is sure of our affections: As on the other hand, whoever harms or displeases us never fails to excite our anger or hatred. (*T* 348)

The paradigm case of love, for Hume, is gratitude for benefits received. Hence, love is intrinsically related to our own personal interests, although it need not be self-interested in the sense of being a means to the satisfaction of our interests in the future.

Love which does not seem to be thus related to our interests requires special explanation. The love of relations, or indeed of acquaintances, may sometimes present just such a puzzle. Hume accounts for it by suggesting that "company is naturally so rejoicing, as presenting the liveliest of all objects, viz. a rational and thinking Being like ourselves, who communicates to us all the actions of his mind; makes us privy to his inmost sentiments and affections; and lets us see, in the very instant of their production, all the emotions, which are caus'd by any object. Every lively idea is agreeable, but especially that of a passion, because such an idea becomes a kind of passion, and gives a more sensible agitation to the mind, than any other image or conception" (*T* 353). Forms of love which are not simply cases of gratitude are to be explained, in other words, by invoking the principle of sympathy. Hume also notes that we tend to associate with those who resemble us, and he concludes that, as love arises from this resemblance, "we may learn that a sympathy with others is agreeable[51] only by giving an emotion to the spirits, since an easy sympathy and correspondent emotions are alone common to *relation, acquaintance*, and *resemblance*" (*T* 354).[52] Even this sort of love, which is not obviously a form of gratitude, is similarly a response to pleasure and is therefore self-referential, though not selfish. Of course, when it comes to friends and family, often we do have shared interests of various sorts, so our love is not purely disinterested.

Although on Hume's theory all love rests on a preceding experience of pleasure, he is intent on distinguishing between interested and disinterested sorts of love. While our motivations for action are not scrutinized for "purity," our moral judgments are. Hume's interest in the pleasures and pains we feel "upon the general view or survey," or "by the mere view and contemplation" of character and action testifies to his preoccupation with the necessity that judgments be unprejudiced in order to qualify as "moral." Hence, he writes that:

'Tis only when a character is considered in general, without reference to our particular interest, that it causes such a feeling or sentiment, as denominates it morally good or evil. 'Tis true, those sentiments, from interest and morals, are apt to be confounded, and naturally run into one another. It seldom happens, that we do not think an enemy vicious, and can distinguish betwixt his opposition to our interest and real villainy or baseness. But this hinders not, but that the sentiments are, in themselves, distinct; and a man of temper and judgement may preserve himself from these illusions. (*T* 472)

When we are trying to isolate the particular feelings of pleasure which cause moral approbation, we must eliminate the interference caused by other responses to character, such as those which relate to our own interests.

Since moral approbation is a sort of love elicited by the consideration of character without reference to our own interests, it presents an intensified version of the puzzle of why we love our relations and acquaintances and not solely our benefactors. Not surprisingly, Hume invokes the same solution he offered earlier, sympathy, in this case with the pleasures and pains of the person whose character we are considering and those affected by that person. Sympathy allows us to feel pleasure which is not interested, and love is always elicited by the experience of pleasure. So Hume, writing of our esteem for a good businessman, remarks that "The person is a stranger: I am no way interested in him, nor lie under any obligation to him: His happiness concerns not me, farther than the happiness of every human, and indeed of every sensible creature: That is, it affects me only by sympathy. From that principle, whenever I discover his happiness and good, whether in its causes or effects, I enter so deeply into it, that it gives me a sensible emotion" (*T* 588–589). Here Hume establishes a crucial distinction between the *emotions* we feel through sympathy, which are real, though not self-directed, and the *interests* of the stranger, which we share only imaginatively. It is necessary that the interest not be actual, or else moral approbation would not be disinterested. But it is also important that there be real feeling, since imagination alone cannot really move us. Simply having factual information about what sorts of character traits were beneficial or pleasant to others would not engender the affective response of moral approbation.

The principle of sympathy provides an answer to the puzzle of why we feel pleasure or pain at considering actions or characters even when our own interests are not directly involved, establishing an intelligible connection between moral judgment and the interests of others. Our pleasure at the mere observance of someone's generosity and benevolence are no longer merely brute facts prodding us into postulating a providential deity to set things up and give us a moral sense. At the same time, Hume avoids reducing morality to self-interest or prudential calculations. Perhaps those who reacted violently to "atheistic" theorists who seemed to relish exposés of the selfishness of morality would be more sympathetic to a theory which, while making references to the providence of God superfluous, explored the inner workings of morality without uncovering anything shameful.

Hume has created more puzzles for himself to solve, however. Since sympathy accounts for a wide range of species of love which are not simply gratitude – from love of relatives and fellow citizens to esteem of businessmen and amiable dinner conversationalists – we are left wondering how we arrive at something distinctively worthy of the name *moral* approbation. Despite Hume's emphasis on sympathy in the conclusion to Book III of the *Treatise*, sympathy as characterized thus far cannot be the whole story.

THE PROBLEM OF CONTRADICTION

In the opening sections of Book III, Hume describes moral approbation as a unique, simple, and irreducible sort of love caused by the pleasure felt when things are surveyed from general points of view. The affections we feel when we survey character from other points of view will cause various other sorts of love, but not moral approbation. Moral approbation, so understood, is apparently safe from reduction to selfish affections, safe from allegations that it has been instilled through the designs of crafty politicians. This characterization of moral approbation seems thoroughly Hutchesonian. I suspect, however, that Hume's attempts to undermine Hutcheson's overall religious intentions have rendered this and other related aspects of Hutchesonian theory problematic. For Hutcheson, the moral sense is an original instinct specially formed to take pleasure solely in benevolence, and moral approbation is a sort of love directed toward those who are benevolent. Moral approbation is distinguished from other sorts of love in that it is directed toward someone under the aspect of benevolence. Hume is forced to find some other way of characterizing the distinctiveness of moral approbation because he refuses to be content with simply accepting that something as wholly unrelated to us as the virtuous character of a twelfth-century king could simply be constituted a necessary cause of pleasure (since this gap makes an appeal to divine Providence tempting), and because he believes that approbation is not solely directed toward the benevolent, but rather has several causes. As we saw above, in attempting to give a naturalistic account of these features of morality, Hume makes the kinship between various sorts of sympathetically engendered love obvious, thereby rendering the need to differentiate moral approbation from other responses to character more acute.[53]

Hume accomplishes this differentiation by introducing the notion of a general view or survey, particularly steady and unprejudiced points of view from which alone moral sentiments can be felt. Technically, this position is consistent with Hutcheson's view that there is a distinct moral sense, which is activated only under special circumstances (for Hutcheson, mere reflection on character; for Hume, an especially general and unprejudiced reflection on character). This moral sense does not develop or change, and it is found universally throughout the human species. Hume seems to try to hold on to this view of things, insisting that "had not men a natural sentiment of approbation and blame, it cou'd never be excited by politicians; nor wou'd the words *laudable* and *praise-worthy*, *blameable* and *odious*, be any more intelligible, than if they were a language perfectly unknown to us" (*T* 579).[54] In reality, however, the moral sense proper comes close to dropping out of Hume's account, as the emphasis of the account shifts to the question of how we develop the capacity to take up these special points of view.[55] Moral approbation is not specifiable apart from its location in the social and linguistic framework as a whole, and as a result it is opened up to the possibility of development and change and interaction with human artifacts of various sorts.[56] The uniformity of sentiments is no longer a biological fact which guarantees moral objectivity, but rather something which arises out of historical and cultural particularity.[57]

Hume's discussion of the variability of sympathy and its correction can be seen as an embryonic developmental account of moral evaluation.[58] In it, Hume traces the development of the capacity to take up steady, general points of view, even if he resists concluding that the moral sense itself develops. I quoted earlier from Hume's discussion of the causes of love and hatred, where he writes that "nothing is more evident, than that any person acquires our kindness, or is expos'd to our ill-will, in proportion to the pleasure or uneasiness we receive from him, and that the passions keep pace exactly with the sensations in all their changes and variations" (*T* 348). Since moral approbation and disapprobation are forms of love, we would expect them to vary in proportion to the intensities of the pleasures and pains which cause them. Will this be an appropriate variation, corresponding to degree of vice and virtue? Hume admits that it will not, in part because our sympathetic pleasures and pains may vary in intensity independently of the intensity of the pleasures and pains of those from whom they are communicated to us:

As this sympathy is very variable, it may be thought, that our sentiments of morals must admit of all the same variations. We sympathise more with persons contiguous to us, than with persons remote from us: With our acquaintance, than with strangers: With our countrymen, than with foreigners. But notwithstanding this variation of our sympathy, we give the same approbation to the same moral qualities in China as in England. They appear equally virtuous, and recommend themselves equally to the esteem of a judicious spectator. (*T* 580–581)

The very characteristics of sympathy which allowed it to account so capably for preferential love of family and neighbors are handicaps when it comes to making sense of the disinterestedness of moral judgments.

It is because of this problem of the variability of sympathetically acquired affections that Hume introduces the notion of point of view into his account of moral sentiment.

Our situation, with regard both to persons and things, is in continual fluctuation; and a man, that lies at a distance from us, may, in a little time, become a familiar acquaintance. Besides, every particular man has a peculiar position with regard to others; and 'tis impossible we cou'd ever converse together on any reasonable terms, were each of us to consider characters and persons, only as they appear from his peculiar point of view. In order, therefore, to prevent those continual contradictions, and arrive at a more stable judgement of things, we fix on some steady and general points of view; and always, in our thoughts, place ourselves in them, whatever may be our present situation. (*T* 581–582)

This passage makes it obvious that the capacity to take up steady and general points of view is not something with which we are born, but something which develops in response to our experiences of conflict and contradiction with the views of others.

Hume is not entirely consistent about whether we feel actual moral sentiments which vary according to our situation and therefore need to be corrected for certain purposes, or whether it is impossible to feel moral sentiments at all until we have taken up a proper point of view.[59] At times, he seems to endorse the latter view, as when he says that "'tis only when a character is considered in general, without reference to our particular interest, that it causes such a feeling or sentiment, as denominates it morally good or evil" (*T* 472). This implies that the moral sense is activated only under special conditions. In his discussion of the role of different points of view in moral judgment, however, he seems to lean toward the former view, saying that "all sentiments of blame and praise are variable, according to our situation of nearness or remoteness, with regard to the person blam'd or prais'd, and according to the present disposition of our mind" (*T* 582). But are these *moral* sentiments? Or are they other forms of love, which do not really merit such a designation?

This may seem like a semantic question, or one which foists a post-Kantian understanding of "moral" onto Hume. In one sense, of course, Hume does straightforwardly regard these sentiments as moral. Thus, we find him saying in his discussion of the artificial virtues that "our first and most natural sentiment of morals is founded on the nature of our passions, and gives the preference to ourselves and friends, above strangers" (*T* 491). "Moral" here corresponds best to the seventh definition offered by the *OED* – "pertaining to, affecting, or operating on the character or conduct, as distinguished from the intellectual or physical nature of human beings." But Hume certainly recognizes differences among various sorts of responses to character, and in his discussion of the necessity of steady and general points of view he comes close to isolating something even post-Kantians would call moral.[60] What I particularly want to take note of is that it seems that the only sentiments which are "original" (hard-wired, to use a rather painful metaphor, into the organism), rather than developing (naturally) through social interaction, are preferential and interested sorts of loves and affections. Whether or not we choose to call these moral sentiments, Hume admits that they are not adequate for moral discourse – "'Twere impossible we cou'd ever make use of language, or communicate our sentiments to one another, did we not correct the momentary appearances of things, and overlook our present situation" (T 582).[61] The capacity for moral evaluation has thus become something which develops only out of social interaction and the need for social lubrication, although it develops naturally, without anyone sitting down to design it. Both the benevolent designs of God and the stratagems of politicians are superfluous.

We need not invoke sympathy at all in order to account for our initial, interested sentiments of praise and blame. We will simply praise those who benefit us and blame those who hurt us. But sympathy *is* necessarily involved in an account of corrected, properly moral, sentiments. When it comes to issuing moral judgments, Hume says, "'tis therefore from the influence of characters and qualities, upon those who have an intercourse with any person, that we praise or blame him. We consider not whether the persons, affected by the qualities, be our acquaintance or strangers, countrymen or foreigners" (T 582). It is not simply a matter of embarking on a disinterested fact-finding expedition about the influence of characters and qualities, however, for that would never result in love, and moral approbation is, after all, a form of love. Our passions must be engaged somehow, if only through "that reason, which is able to oppose our passion; and which we have found to be nothing but a general calm determination of the passions, founded on some distant view or reflexion" (T 583). Once we are driven from our first, interested point of view in search of a more steady point from which to make judgments, "we cannot afterwards fix ourselves so commodiously by any means as by a sympathy with those, who have any commerce with the person we consider. This is far from being as lively as when our own interest is concern'd, or that of our particular friends; nor has it such an influence on our love and hatred: But being equally conformable to our calm and general principles, 'tis said to have an equal authority over our reason, and to command our judgment and opinion" (T 583–584). Moral approbation and disapprobation are sentiments caused by the sympathetic pains and pleasures we feel with those affected by the person whose character we are considering.

Since we may not have any bond or connection with these persons, our ability to sympathize with them may not be great, but it is apparently enough for a calm determination of the passions.

Occasionally, as in the passage just quoted, Hume suggests that moral judgments are a matter of reason, rather than sentiment. At first sight, this seems to conflict with his insistence that moral judgments cannot be determinations of reason, since they are "supposed to influence our passions and actions, and to go beyond the calm and indolent judgments of the understanding" (*T* 457).[62] It is true that Hume is not consistent in his employment of the word "reason." At times he uses "reason" in the vernacular way which confuses it with what he calls "calm desires." So, for example, he writes that "when we consider any objects at a distance, all their minute distinctions vanish, and we always give the preference to whatever is in itself preferable . . . This gives rise to what in an improper sense we call *reason*" (*T* 536; see also *T* 417). Our moral judgments are not discoverable merely through the comparison of ideas, deduction, or demonstration – reason in the strict sense, but are rather what Hume calls impressions of reflection, which encompass all passions which are caused by ideas (*T* 276). There *are* feelings which are produced even by the general views of things (*T* 587).[63]

Although the accusation of inconsistency is unfounded, the question of how the "calm" moral sentiments provide an effective motive to virtue which manages to prevail even over the violent "selfish" passions remains. Having begun to understand the practice of moral approbation, we are now in a position to inquire into the question of motivation to virtue. Since Hume spends quite a bit of time talking about the original motivations to virtue and very little talking about the nature of motivation once the practice of approbation has matured, I will to some extent be putting words in Hume's mouth, expanding on the clues he drops here and there. The original motivation to do those things which are the usual actions performed by those possessing the character traits we come to call virtues varies from case to case. For the natural virtues, the original motivation is some sort of natural instinct such as gratitude or natural affection, while for the artificial virtue of justice, the original motivation is self-interest. Specifically moral motivation, which supplements or in some cases supplants the original motive, can arise only once the practice of moral approbation gets off the ground.[64] Such a practice could emerge only among the sort of creatures who yearn for the love and respect of others and who are therefore sensitive to the opinions of others.[65] So Hume asks:

Who indeed does not feel an accession of alacrity in his pursuits of knowledge and ability of every kind, when he considers, that besides the advantage, which immediately result from these acquisitions, they also give him a new lustre in the eyes of mankind, and are universally attended with esteem and approbation? And who can think any advantage of fortune a sufficient compensation for the least breach of the social virtues, when he considers, that not only his character with regard to others, but also his peace and inward satisfaction entirely depend upon his strict observance of them; and that a mind will never be able to bear its own survey, that has been wanting in its part to mankind and society? (*T* 620)

The esteem of others becomes, through sympathy, a source of pride or self-respect (*T* 316ff.). But, in order for our sympathy with others' opinions of ourselves to be complete, their opinions must concur with our own. Hence, it does no good to deceive others with regard to our character (unless we can also deceive ourselves, and this creates a highly unstable situation).[66] In order to possess a mind capable of bearing its own steady survey, we must not only possess the love and respect of others, but be conscious that we are worthy of such esteem.[67] Once the practice of moral approbation has come into its own, new motivational possibilities are created – it is now possible for us to be motivated by the desire to be loved and respected *qua* virtuous. Virtue emerges as a good in its own right – it is not simply an instrumental good used to obtain love and respect, but rather a good internal to or constitutive of a life worth living.[68]

Although we cannot make sense of the notion of virtue without recourse to the intercourse of human sentiments, we certainly can and do pursue virtue regardless of whether we thereby receive the esteem of others.[69] Admittedly, the virtues are dispositions which enable us to more fully "bear our own survey," but this is because the relationship between virtue and this sort of integrity or self-respect is not contingent, but rather constitutive. Although it is true that there is a certain pleasure attendant on being able to withstand one's own self-survey, this pleasure is not the end at which self-survey aims. Rather, "the enjoyment supervenes upon the successful activity in such a way that the activity achieved and the activity enjoyed are one and the same state. Hence to aim at the one is to aim at the other; and hence also it is easy to confuse the pursuit of excellence with the pursuit of enjoyment *in this specific sense.*"[70] This sort of pleasure or satisfaction cannot be sought as an external good. Although Hume does not express himself in such terms, I think it makes sense to say that, according to his account, it is the notion of self-respect which lends human life the sort of unity which is necessary if the virtues as a whole are to have a point.

It is not our own occurrent moral sentiments, our own specific approvals of virtue and disapprovals of vice, *per se*, which motivate us in the pursuit of virtue. It is, rather, the whole intersubjective practice of moral approval and disapproval which generates and continually reinforces the motivation to be virtuous, by ensuring that virtue is the sort of thing in which we may take pride. Ultimately, our pursuit of virtue becomes independent of the contingencies and blindnesses which affect others' approval, and becomes constitutive of our ability to withstand our own moral scrutiny.

The *Whole Duty of Man* proclaimed humility, the prime virtue, to be of two sorts; "the first is the having a mean and low opinion of our selves, the second is the being content that others should have so of us," which involves caring nothing for the opinion of others.[71] We need humility "to keep us from any high conceits of our performances, which if we once entertain, it will blast the best of them, and make them utterly unacceptable to God."[72] On Hume's account, such habitual self-depreciation and depreciation of the esteem of others (refusing to discriminate between the approval of those we respect and that of those we do not) would make impossible the emergence of the love of virtue for its own sake and warp the development of moral judgment.

SYMPATHY AND THE *ENQUIRY*

Up to the point at which Hume introduced the notion of corrected sympathy, it seemed that there was a simple one-to-one correspondence between pleasure (or pain) and the love (or hatred) it caused, whether that was gratitude, or affection, or esteem, or moral approbation. Since the connection between pleasure or pain and love or hatred was automatic, conscious reflection about the pleasure or pain was irrelevant. No deliberation or practical reason seemed necessary. Now, however, things have become more complicated. In order to arrive at a proper moral judgment, we must disregard a whole range of interested passions. We must sympathize with certain specific persons who might not be related to us in any way. Hume suggests that the point of view the spectator must take up is that of the one being evaluated and those closely connected with him or her (*T* 591). This suggests that the point of view which enables moral judgments to be made is not a perspective equally remote from all real perspectives, but rather an attempt to grasp the points of view of those most affected by a person's character or action. It is a point of view which must, therefore, constantly shift in

order to consider different characters and different actions.[73] This shows
Hume's distance from contemporary "moral point of view" theories,
despite remarks by commentators such as Árdal, who claims that Hume
is trying to show that judgments of value are "objective" because they
take into account "only those features of a situation which would be
common to any spectator."[74] It is better to say that, for Hume, there is no
single "moral point of view," but rather various perspectives which must
be taken into account in order to arrive at any moral judgment. He
speaks, in fact, in the plural of "some steady and general points of view"
(*T* 581–582). What is needed is not a moral point of view, but sympathetic
understanding of the various points of view of other individuals. Our
responses to a number of sympathetic pains and pleasures must be
balanced against one another before a final judgment or sentiment of
approbation or disapprobation issues forth.[75]

Hume continues to imply that this balancing act occurs wholly
automatically and subconsciously. In fact, in the three references to
sympathy which Hume wished after first publication to insert into the
Treatise's discussions of justice, allegiance, and chastity, he obscures the
complexity of the operation by calling it simply "sympathy with *public
interest*" (*T* 670), or "sympathy for the general interests of society" (*T* 671).

Hume's talk of sympathy with public interest might be regarded as a
sort of summary statement, for sympathy as Hume characterizes it in the
Treatise must always be sympathy with something particular, not
anything as vague as the general interests of society. It would seem that
we would be unable to know what the general interests of society are
until after we have taken into account the whole range of particular pains
and pleasures felt by members of society as a result of such conventions,
particularly since a single act of justice taken out of context may be
unintelligibly harmful.

The fact that the phrase "sympathy with public interest" is shorthand
for individual sympathetic affections seems clear in Hume's discussion of
the origin of justice and property, where he remarks that:

> when the injustice is so distant from us, as in no way to affect our interest, it still
> displeases us; because we consider it as prejudicial to human society, and
> pernicious to every one that approaches the person guilty of it. We partake of
> their uneasiness by *sympathy*, and as every thing, which gives uneasiness in
> human actions, upon the general survey, is call'd vice, and whatever produces
> satisfaction, in the same manner, is denominated virtue; this is the reason why
> the sense of moral good and evil follows upon justice and injustice. (*T* 499)

There are several possible motivations for Hume to insist that sympathy
with public interest issues out of a subconscious and passive process of

equilibration of various particular sympathetic pains and pleasures. First, it is, I think, part of Hume's attempt to differentiate himself from Mandeville and his ilk. As I discuss below, this becomes even more clear in the subsequently published *Enquiry*. If the process were conscious, it would be seen as more liable to infection by selfish calculation.[76] It would seem less "natural" and more like something which politicians might have dreamt up to accomplish their own ends.

Second, Hume's theory, like Hutcheson's, is democratic in tendency, in that it suggests that everyone, in the natural course of things, becomes a capable moral judge whose judgments agree with those of other persons who have undergone the same process. There is no need to discern which of competing moral authorities deserve obedience and there is no need to possess a prodigious intellect, capable of long trains of deduction resulting in the moral law, or to be confident that one has discerned the ultimate purpose of human existence.[77] The capacity for moral judgment is supposed to develop behind the scenes out of standard raw responses. To suggest that the process is not automatic after all would threaten to move moral knowledge once again out of universal reach and to reintroduce the specter of stubborn disagreement, disagreement which cannot be resolved by some element of the theory or by reference to deviation from the process whereby raw sentiments are corrected.

A third reason for maintaining the unconscious nature of the process is that Hume is attempting in the *Treatise* to provide a causal description of what goes on in the practice of moral judgment. He observes that these judgments are, for the most part, immediate, and not preceded by an elaborate active process on the part of the evaluator. He does not seek to give an exact account of how various pains and pleasures should be weighted against one another or try to show how we might enhance our ability to sympathize with others. Hume distinguishes his enterprise from that of the practical moralist, who must paint morality in beautiful colors. He calls himself an anatomist of morality, saying that "there is even something hideous" in the view of things he presents (*T* 621). A more accurate understanding of anatomy may improve a painting's "elegance" and "correctness," but the anatomist never provides more than this superficial sort of corrective. Hume denies, in fact, that a moral theory is the sort of thing which is applied directly to practical deliberation and moral evaluation.[78]

Despite Hume's insistence in the *Treatise* that he is doing pure moral anatomy, his account of what is supposed to be going on behind the scenes as moral judgments are generated (taking up a special point of view, sympathizing with certain specific persons, weighing sympathetic pains and pleasures against one another), provides suggestions of things which may potentially be brought into conscious moral life.[79] Theory and practice are mutually informing. If we believe that moral judgments involve a specially disinterested point of view, perhaps we can deliberately strive to take up such a point of view. Kant's moral theory gives an indication of what might result from this move, but one which threatens to render morality unintelligible in terms of what we actually *care* about. If we believe that moral judgments require us to balance pains and pleasures against one another, we might seek formulas or general balancing principles which, when applied, will guarantee the correctness of moral judgment. This is the road taken by the utilitarians. Finally, if we believe, as Hume's account suggests, that morality requires sympathetic understanding of the pains and pleasures and hopes and desires of others, we may actively seek to extend our sympathy with others and to identify impediments to sympathy.

Although extensive sympathy seems to be the most appropriate candidate for playing a central role in moral evaluation, acknowledging its role in this capacity presents Hume with a problem. Moral judgments are issued in a wide range of circumstances, including those in which we would expect our degree of sympathy to be quite weak, either because we are not being confronted by horrendous suffering or because we share very little in common with those being evaluated. Yet extensive sympathy, as Hume describes it in Book II's discussion of pity, requires a strong degree of sympathy in order to carry our attention beyond the immediate sympathetically felt affections.[80] The capacity for stable and reliable moral judgment begins to seem unattainable, unless our ability to sympathize extensively can be developed and strengthened, and the forces which weaken or block extensive sympathy are identified.[81] It is noteworthy, therefore, that as Hume moves from sympathy as a sort of emotional infection to extensive sympathy which identifies with all of the desires and interests of the other person and even projects emotions which are either not expressed or not felt at all, he speaks of the imagination in increasingly active terms.[82] Whereas at first the role of the imagination seemed to be merely as a mechanical converter of ideas into impressions, now the imagination seems capable not only of great effort, but also of selectivity in certain situations and broadened compass in others.[83] Within the *Treatise*, Hume continues to regard the imagination as a faculty over which we have no conscious control, but the language he uses is that of activity, and he opens the door to thinking of sympathy as something we might engage in intentionally.[84] It seems, in particular, that we might strive to extend our sympathy beyond its initial, limited form, even if that first sympathy is basically involuntary.[85]

Hume's *Enquiry Concerning the Principle of Morals*, published in 1751 as a recasting of Book III of the *Treatise*, does not move in this direction, however. Instead, the tendency to speak simply of sympathy with "public interest," rather than considering how this complex sympathy is formed, is even more pronounced. In addition, Hume frequently speaks there of a "principle of humanity" or "sentiment of humanity." This has often been read as a repudiation of his earlier assertions about the role of sympathy in moral judgment. This is an overstatement; Hume continues to discuss the importance of sympathy to moral judgment (*E* 185–186, 260), but he refers to the "sentiment of humanity" or to "social sympathy" rather than to "extensive sympathy," and distances himself somewhat from the psychological mechanism of his original associationist account.[86]

In looking at the contexts of Hume's talk of the "sentiment of humanity" in the *Enquiry*, it becomes increasingly clear that the changes which Hume here introduces come in response to a fear (perhaps substantiated by the reception of the *Treatise*) that Hume's readers will place him in the Hobbesian camp and take him to be expounding a selfish account of morals. Although I have suggested that Hume's account of sympathy can in fact avoid the problem of interestedness, it was not so read by his contemporaries. Hume's response is twofold: to downplay the role of imagination and to redefine and then concede the existence of "general" benevolence, which in the *Treatise* he had said was just an illusion.

Hume's associationist account of sympathy in the *Treatise*, which held that in the operation of sympathy the idea of another person's sentiment is enlivened by its association with the lively impression of one's own self, seemed to some to trace sympathy back to self-love after all. So Hume here strives to clarify his position by insisting that "it can never be self-love which renders the prospect of [personal advantages] agreeable to us, the spectators, and prompts our esteem and approbation. No force of imagination can convert us into another person, and make us fancy, that we, being that person, reap benefit from those valuable qualities, which belong to him" (*E* 234; see also *E* 217). The import of this remark is not to deny the role of sympathy in moral approbation, but to distance Hume's view from the Hobbesian notion that sympathetic phenomena involve imagining that something which happened to another person really happened to us.

In the *Treatise*, as we have seen, Hume denied the existence of general benevolence, while in the *Enquiry* he insists on it, but a closer look reveals that in both works he claims that general benevolence arises out of sympathy. It may be helpful to place the two statements alongside one another. In the *Treatise*, Hume argued that general benevolence could not be the original motive to justice, for:

In general, it may be affirm'd, that there is no such passion in human minds, as the love of mankind, merely as such, independent of personal qualities, of services, or of relation to ourself. 'Tis true, there is no human, and indeed no sensible, creature, whose happiness or misery does not, in some measure, affect us, when brought near to us, and represented in lively colours: But this proceeds merely from sympathy, and is no proof of such a universal affection to mankind. (*T* 418)

That which often gets dignified by the name "love of mankind" is just a result of sympathy, and one which in reality occurs only in concrete situations, not in the abstract; "Perhaps a man wou'd be belov'd as such, were we to meet him in the moon," but *only* if we met him there (*T* 482). And Hume underlines his conclusion by pointing to his associationist mechanism – we would love the man on the moon solely because he is human, "but this proceeds only from the relation to ourselves; which in these cases gathers force by being confined to a few persons" (*T* 482).

Hume's damage repair in the *Enquiry*, coming notably within the appendix "Of self-love," states that:

Benevolence naturally divides into two kinds, the *general* and the *particular*. The first is, when we have no friendship or connexion or esteem for the person, but feel only a general sympathy with him or a compassion for his pains, and a congratulation with his pleasures. The other species of benevolence is founded on an opinion of virtue, on services done us, or on some particular connexions. Both these sentiments must be allowed real in human nature: but whether they will resolve into some nice considerations of self-love, is a question more curious than important. The former sentiment, to wit, that of general benevolence, or humanity, or sympathy, we shall have occasion frequently to treat of in the course of this enquiry; and I assume it as real, from general experience, without any other proof. (*E* 298)

Hume is now willing to say that general benevolence exists, but he clearly points out the qualitative differences between general and particular benevolence, and continues to insist that the former arises from sympathy. The difference seems largely to be one of rhetorical emphasis – in the *Treatise*, he tends to suggest that, since sympathy accounts for what is termed benevolence, we should not continue to invoke benevolence, whereas in the *Enquiry*, he suggests that we might as well concede the existence of "general benevolence," and not worry about the precise mechanisms by which it arises out of sympathy (*E* 298–302). Hume's *Enquiry* definition of general benevolence is given in terms of a particular individual, and is therefore perfectly compatible with Hume's earlier insistence that the so-called love of mankind must be reducible to particular instances of sympathy with the Englishman in Italy, the European in China, or the man on the moon. Elsewhere in the *Enquiry*, however, Hume is more interested in the "sentiment of humanity" as the general outcome of sympathetic acts than in its particular instances.

The thrust of my comments here is not to imply that Hume ought to have been providing a calculus of sympathy. What is problematic about identifying the moral point of view as the position from which the general "sentiment of humanity" is felt, rather than presenting it as the position which is reached when the many particular acts of sympathy are properly weighed against one another, is not that the latter makes a moral calculus possible while the former does not. A moral calculus is not – and Hume seems to have shared this sentiment – either a feasible or desirable goal. What is troubling is that speaking solely of a "sentiment of humanity" obscures the complexity of the moral sentiments and of moral judgment, implying that the proper judgments are automatically generated or appear ready-made on the scene.

But, if the "sentiment of humanity" is too static a notion to be very useful for purposes of moral education, does it nevertheless represent a genuine advance in a theoretical account of the origin of moral distinctions *qua* moral? This is similar to the work which some thinkers seem to hope to get done by the concept of a "moral point of view," the work of filtering and somehow transforming non-moral sentiments and judgments into moral ones.[87] I suspect this work is done no better by a sentiment of humanity than by multiple acts of sympathy which must somehow be balanced against one another. The same basic – and quite familiar – problem plagues both. Invoking a "sentiment of humanity" to account for the origin of moral distinctions begs the question of how this sentiment obtains its distinctive ethical status. Even if it were true to state that it is a sentiment common to all and applying to all, or to state that in fact it takes precedence over all the others, this would not answer the question of why it *ought* to take precedence over all others. If, as in the *Treatise*, we talk instead of a process in which natural sympathetic sentiments are equilibrated with one another, a similar problem arises – how do we know what the *proper* process of equilibration should be?

It might help to step back a bit to note that within his moral philosophy, Hume can be taken to be doing several things at once. He is giving an account of the *origin* of moral distinctions, of the difference between vice and virtue, of how the idea of virtue first came to be "annexed" to particular natural and artificial traits of character. He is also describing the psychological processes by which each individual comes to feel moral approbation and disapprobation – the immediate *causes* of the moral sentiments. And he is exploring the processes by which individuals come to approve and disapprove *appropriately* – what we might call moral development. It would be misleading to say that Hume is "trying" to do all of these things, since he does not distinguish among them, and might well disavow them under the description I have given. The claim that "sympathy is the chief source of moral distinctions" (*T* 618) can mean many different things. Still, separating out the various ways in which Hume's aims can be understood by the contemporary reader is a helpful interpretive tool.

I suggested above that Hume's discussion of the variability of sympathy and its correction form an embryonic developmental account of moral evaluation, of the capacity for corrected sympathy and the moral point of view. To the extent to which this is seen as an attempt to give an account of the origin of moral distinctions, of the way in which moral distinctions first developed out of pre-moral distinctions, rather than an account of how the capacity for good moral judgment can be formed, it is misguided. Tempting as it may be to ground the moral in the natural in this way, all such accounts are fundamentally question-begging.[88] There will always be a point at which some hand-waving and muttering takes place, a point at which normative elements are slipped in and "natural" sentiments are exchanged for moral sentiments. Sympathy comes onto the scene as something purely natural, but the corrected sympathy at work in moral judgment is moral. In reality, we are never getting back beyond the normative to the purely natural – how would we escape the normative in order to do so?

Annette Baier's interpretation of Hume's moral philosophy helps to bring this issue into sharper focus. She calls Hume's moral theory a form of "critical or corrective naturalism."[89] This does not mean that moral distinctions are simply a matter of conventional practices; "for ... 'natural' and conventional obligations to get any moral force, they must be endorsed by the the moral sentiment – that is, by pleasure taken from an impartial point of view – after sympathy has been felt, or attempted, with the feelings of each person (or each representative person) that the

cooperative scheme involves or concerns."[90] Now, this may well be our
best way of getting at moral truths in particular cases, but such a
procedure should not be taken to be an account of the *ultimate origin* of
moral distinctions. What constitutes impartiality, if not the ability to give
due weight to all of the various factors involved? Thus impartiality cannot
be defined in a pre-moral way. Moral distinctions are already presupposed
within the description of the emergence of moral distinctions. They
cannot, therefore, simply be the product of a mechanical equilibration.

The most we can say is that there are certain capacities, including the
capacity to sympathize with the sufferings and joys of others, which are
necessary conditions of human moral agency, but if we try to tell a story
of how out of such conditions morality was first generated, we end up
begging the question of why one particular aspect of our nature is
morally important while others are not. All attempts to describe the
"state of nature" have said much more about the concerns of those
writing the description than about the reality they sought to describe.

Baier recognizes that "our biological inheritance is ambiguous," and
that we must fight our worse tendencies with our better.[91] She worries a
bit over whether it is consistent for Hume to recognize that some of the
institutions he wishes to condemn (she suggests religious and sexist
institutions as examples) are statistically normal. Obviously, she says,
there is more moral disagreement than Hume admits. I would argue that
the central concession which must be made is to recognize that the
"critical" or "corrective" aspect of Hume's naturalism is actually
normative, and that Hume is not moving and cannot move from a purely
pre-moral factual starting point to a normative outcome.

Hume catches this problem, of course, when it comes to attempts to
argue deductively from factual premises to normative conclusions. But it
applies as well to that strand within his own moral philosophy which,
conflating the emergence of moral distinctions with development of an
individual's capacity to make moral distinctions, attempts to give an
account of the natural origins of moral distinctions.[92] Hume is not wrong
to say that our moral judgments reflect things which are of benefit to
others, but this is not a purely natural, pre-moral benefit, and it is not by
apprehending such benefits through the lens of corrected sympathy that
they mysteriously become the source of *moral* approbation. This means
that he cannot utterly avoid the sort of normative account of human
nature which he rejects in Hutcheson as being dependent on "final
causes." Instead, he must provide his own.[93] An automatic process of
equilibrating natural responses seemed appealing as an account of the

ultimate origin of moral distinctions because it made unnecessary both
Providence and Mandeville's scheming politicians. But by now it should
be clear that invoking either one or the other does nothing to remove the
fact that normative distinctions must be presupposed in any account of
the origin of normative distinctions. No such account, providential or
non-providential, can be satisfactory, since no such account is possible –
or needed. Human existence, *qua* human, is normative through and through.

When we look, however, at Hume's account of moral judgment not as
an attempt to delve into the origins of moral distinctions, but as an
exploration of the development of moral judgment, we can appreciate
the way in which Hume has in fact succeeded in displacing Providence.
Hume's solution to the problem of intelligibility appears, if anything, in a
stronger light; it is clear that there is an intrinsic connection between
moral judgments and human flourishing, since moral goods are traced
back not to pre-moral flourishing, but to moral flourishing. And sympathy
is enough to prod us out of self-interested concerns; we do not need divine
threats or promises which end up entangling us even more hopelessly in
self-interested pursuits. In continuing to explore the role that religious
allegiances play in the development of the capacity for moral judgment,
Hume will argue not merely that it is possible to do without Providence
while continuing to show moral concern for others, but that appeals to
Providence tend positively to distort moral judgment. As we shall see,
sympathetic capacities will continue to play a central role here.

After the *Enquiry*, however, the term "sympathy" is used infrequently
in Hume's writings. When the term explicitly appears, it tends to refer
not to corrected, extensive sympathy, but simply to the immediate sort of
limited sympathy which Hume first discussed in the *Treatise*. Hume
would quite understandably have wished to avoid the association with
"selfish" systems of ethics which seemed to haunt his *Treatise* account of
the role of sympathy in moral judgment. Yet he continues to appeal to
activities and sentiments which are intimately related to corrected
sympathy in his subsequent works, particularly, I shall argue, in his
writings on tragedy, taste, and religion, and in his historical writings. He
speaks of "entering into" the sentiments of others, of placing oneself "in
the same situation" as an audience, of taking on "enlarged views" or
"enlarged principles." His discussions shift from attempting to provide
an analysis of how sympathetic sentiments give rise to moral distinctions
to understanding how the development of a capacity for what we might
term "sympathetic understanding" helps in the formation of good
judgment, and to understanding, conversely, how sympathetic sentiments

gone awry can interfere with good judgment. Having understood these workings, "corrected sympathy" becomes something which may be intentionally cultivated, rather than something which is produced automatically behind the scenes, accessible only to the moral anatomist.

In the previous chapter, I suggested that the concept of sympathy came into its heyday in response to a conceptual need – a heightened sensitivity to the distinctiveness of individual points of view or ways of being situated in the world which understood this distinctiveness as threatening the possibility and coherence of morality. In the *Treatise*, the phenomenon of extensive sympathy is seen as creating the possibility of moral discourse, and moral discourse is seen as an important way of transcending the limited view of things in terms of competing interests ("every particular man has a peculiar position with regard to others; and 'tis impossible we cou'd ever converse together on any reasonable terms, were each of us to consider characters and persons, only as they appear from his peculiar point of view," *T* 581).[94] As long as it was regarded as automatic and instinctual, sympathy was reassuring testimony to *already existing* resemblance and connection. But this passive sympathy reinforces factional divisions and partial judgment. In the *Treatise*, Hume begins to confront the need for a sympathy which responds to the sense of a lack of resemblance and connection, and prepares the ground for his later reflections on how something akin to extensive sympathy may be actively striven for, rather than passively undergone.[95] Sympathy in the *Treatise* provides the connection of intelligibility between morality and human flourishing without making ethical judgment self-interested or invoking a connection made by divine Providence. This renders superfluous attempts by religious factions to insist on their own opposing insights into God's providential designs or God's laws. Hume's later writings wrestle with the fact that factional religious strife does, in fact, infect moral discourse and practice. Hume seeks to understand these influences with a view to eliminating them. For this to be possible, of course, it would be necessary for moral distinctions to survive the demise of notions of Providence, but no particular account of the ultimate origin of moral distinctions is needed. What is needed, however, for morals to outlive Providence, is that something akin to sympathy be actively cultivated, not simply taken for granted as part of the hidden gear mechanism of morals.

CHAPTER 3

"Poetical systems" and the pleasures of tragedy

SPECTATORS AND SYMPATHY

In this chapter and the one that follows, I turn to Hume's contributions to two important debates of his century: the problem of the "unaccountable pleasures" of tragedy, and the search for a standard of taste in aesthetic judgment. Although both problems fall within the realm of what eighteenth-century thinkers termed "criticism," they are in some ways quite different – the former is an ethical problem associated with a puzzle in the aesthetic realm, while the latter concerns the nature of aesthetic (and, on some accounts, moral) judgment. The tragedy problem is concerned with spectators' immediate, unreflective response to tragic drama, while the problem of the standard of taste is concerned with the final judgment of a work of art, a character, or an action, rendered by a special sort of spectator, one who qualifies as evaluator or judge. Yet the two problems are closely related, since both focus on the effects of a work of art on spectators, making central art's capacity to "move" and to "touch" the soul.[1] And both are, in important ways, explorations of the nature of sympathetic understanding of different points of view. Hume's discussion of the pleasures of tragedy leads him into a consideration of the nature of belief and the differences between sympathetic responses to reality and to fiction. He shows that, contrary to Evangelical convictions, there is no reason to be suspicious of pleasure in tragic *drama*, but that the artificiality of Evangelical beliefs distorts believers' sense of reality and leads to pathological indifference to, and sometimes even enjoyment of, *real life* tragedy.

The neoclassical school of criticism which dominated the seventeenth and early eighteenth centuries dedicated itself to the classification of aesthetic genres and to the elucidation of rules governing various genres of art. But these attempts to bring rational coherence into the realm of criticism backfired, as rules seemed to multiply endlessly while great works continued to defy them or obey them only under obviously strained interpretations. This pervasive disagreement over the content of the rules and their application led some thinkers to accuse neoclassicism of a dry rationalism which was out of touch with the concrete immediacy of aesthetic reaction and evaluation. These critics hoped to find the basis for greater agreement in aesthetic judgments by turning away from the abstract dissection of works and genres to the emotions aroused by art. What is new in eighteenth-century aesthetics, therefore, is the focus on the experience of the spectator, rather than the work of art itself and its genre.[2] This is parallel to the contemporaneous movement in moral philosophy, from categorizing actions according to their moral species or describing morals as knowledge of the eternal relations of things in the universe, to analyzing the phenomenon of moral evaluation, approaching the virtues via our response to seeing them in others. In both cases, there is a reaction against a hierarchical view, in which the many are supposed to submit to the authoritative judgments of a few, in favor of a more democratic view. Only an elite can puzzle through rules of genre, but everyone finds some performances (and some characters and actions) enjoyable and others distasteful.

When these thinkers (whom I shall rather freely call sentimentalists) do address the nature of the creative process in art, the pressing question concerns what the poet or actor must do in order to move the audience. Most theorists held that the artist had first to be moved in order to be able to move others.[3] Hence, what goes on in the poet during the composition of the work and what goes on in the actor during the performance of the work are identified with what goes on in the spectator during the performance.[4] In the moral realm, similarly, even when the moral agent is the focus of attention, the preoccupation is still with the way in which dramatic scenes call forth moral responses from spectators, hence with the relationship between moral agency and spectatordom. This is taken to an extreme by the literature of sensibility, which displays a trend toward treating helpless pity as the sole, or most valuable, moral response.[5] In this case the actor collapses back into a mere spectator and feelings become the only moral actions. What moves us as spectators to horror and pity is linked, on the one hand, to moral condemnation and judgment and, on the other, to active benevolence and attempts to relieve the suffering of others; when the active element is lost, moral evaluation and moral response are conflated.

Both moralists and literary thinkers, therefore, were occupied with the relationship between spectator and spectacle, with moving and being moved, both on a theoretical and on a practical level. The eighteenth-century notion of sympathy unites all of these concerns, so it should not come as a surprise to find it at the heart of the debate over the pleasures of tragedy. "There is no spectacle so fair and beautiful," writes Hume, "as a noble and generous action; nor any which gives us more abhorrence than one that is cruel and treacherous . . . A very play or romance may afford us instances of this pleasure, which virtue conveys to us; and pain, which arises from vice" (*T* 471). He describes virtuous action as a bit of theater, which moves us even when we are disinterested spectators, whose private interests are unaffected by the spectacle. The moral life is intrinsically theatrical. Conversely, theater can teach us about our responses to character and action. David Marshall comments that:

The experience of sympathy may be presented as a figure for the ideal experience of (for example) reading a novel; but sympathy itself finally must be seen as a theatrical relation formed between a spectacle and a spectator, enacted in the realm of mimesis and representation . . . [N]ot only must works of art touch or move their readers or beholders; people in the world must regard each other as spectators and spectacles, readers and representations. At the same time that the experience of novels and plays and paintings is transported into the realm of affect, sentiment, and sympathy, the experience of sympathy itself seems to be uncomfortably like the experience of watching a play.[6]

In both the theater and the moral life, we find that we have entered a hall of mirrors, for "the minds of men are mirrors to one another, not only because they reflect each others emotions, but also because those rays of passions, sentiments and opinions may be often reverberated, and may decay away by insensible degrees" (*T* 365). We find theater in sympathy and sympathy in theater.

The protagonist of a tragedy is subject to suffering and distress; her hopes are dashed, his plans go awry. We might expect the audience to be upset by this spectacle of suffering – certainly they would be distressed if they themselves had to suffer in like fashion, and they *do* become emotionally involved with the protagonist and his or her plight. Yet audiences actually *enjoy* watching tragedies; they do not avoid them as we would expect them to avoid suffering. On one level, this is simply a puzzle about why people enjoy watching depictions of suffering. On another level, it quickly raises ethical problems. How does the fact that we enjoy depictions of suffering reflect on us as moral beings? In the theater, we sympathetically suffer with the protagonist, and pity him or her, but this sympathy and pity are detached from any sort of active response to suffering. What can the gap in the realm of fiction between being *moved* and being moved to *act* teach us about the times when such a gap opens up in reality? Does the passivity of the theater inculcate bad moral habits, smothering active responses to real distress? In the theater we seem actually to relish our own sympathetic suffering. Do we similarly delight in our pity for real suffering? Depending on how the puzzle of the pleasure of tragedy is explained, the associated ethical worries are either exacerbated or eased.

The terms in which eighteenth-century thinkers discussed the problem of the pleasures of tragedy were inherited from Aristotle.[7] The eclipse of neoclassicism in the early eighteenth century did not mean that Aristotle was thrown out, only that he was (sometimes drastically) reinterpreted. Sentimentalist claims both about the pleasure of representation as such and about the value of the pity and fear aroused by tragedy invariably gesture toward Aristotle as an authority. Aristotle had noted that "we delight in looking at the most proficient images of things which in themselves we see with pain," but, rather than being troubled by this phenomenon, he believed that it was a valuable form of moral education. Human beings delight in all sorts of representations, including representations of painful things, because we learn from them, and learning is always pleasant. We learn from representations because they contain some of the features of the objects they represent, though in a simplified – hence clarified – way. Our recognition of these features helps us subsume particulars under more general concepts; we become able to see not merely individuals, but also different kinds of things or different sorts of human character.

While Aristotle did appeal to this delight in learning in order to account for human pleasure in representations of painful or troubling things, he also held that tragedy has a special role to play which is distinct from the educative function which all representations have in common, because the sort of pleasure particular to tragedy is that which arises from pity and terror. While some forms of poetry chiefly involve the depiction of character and are to be used straightforwardly for moral education, the primary function of those, like tragedy, which are more about action than about character, is catharsis.[8] Aristotle's term catharsis has been variously interpreted, sometimes as a means of cleansing ourselves of the dangerous and disturbing emotions of pity and terror, sometimes as allowing the harmless release of pent-up emotions.[9] Eighteenth-century sentimentalists, who viewed the passions in a positive light, began to interpret catharsis as a kind of emotional healing;

emotions, such as pity and terror, which are often felt in a disproportionate way in real situations, are aroused in a harmless way by poetic representations, exercised, and thereby brought into due proportion.[10] Catharsis is ethically relevant, on this interpretation, because our emotional responses to situations are morally important. "Since ... virtue," writes Aristotle, "is concerned with feeling delight correctly and loving and hating [correctly], clearly one should learn, and become habituated to, nothing so much as judging correctly, i.e. feeling delight in decent characters and fine actions ... Habituation to feeling pain and delight in things that are like [the truth] is close to being in the same state regarding the truth [itself]."[11] The sentimentalists often interpreted this to mean that virtue is *nothing but* feeling delight in certain things and pain in others.

The response to tragic drama might appear to be a sort of *akrasia*, since our emotional response to the disturbing events on stage is not followed by responsive action. How can the right sort of emotional reaction to a situation be detached from taking the proper action in response? The quick answer, for Aristotle, is that there is more to the virtuous person's perception of a situation than an emotional response, and practical wisdom involves making relevant distinctions between reality and representation. (Aristotle is not of much help, however, when it comes to defining how such relevant distinctions are to be made.) At any rate, eighteenth-century thinkers who focused more narrowly on emotional states did not have this quick answer.

The pleasures of tragedy are liable to seem more morally problematic if the distinction between reality and fiction becomes fuzzy. This is likely to happen when focus is on the immediate emotional impact of events, since the emotional response to something fictional may well be indistinguishable from the emotional response to something real. Ethical concerns about the pleasures of tragedy will therefore be particularly troubling when emotions are regarded as the core of the moral life. Since such a focus on emotional impact was typical both of ethics and of aesthetics in the eighteenth century, the fact that debate about the pleasures of tragedy was so intense is hardly surprising. Hume's explorations move in the direction of denying that the effects of artistic representation on audiences can be adequately understood solely in terms of the emotional states they engender. Despite the subjectivism of his "official" theory of belief as articulated in the *Treatise*, Hume's attempt to grapple with the pleasures of tragedy points to the importance of looking at connections among beliefs and at the intersubjective context of our beliefs, not merely at the subjective intensity of isolated emotional or attitudinal states, if we are to understand the impact fiction has on us and the moral differences between the impact of fiction and reality. We cannot afford to neglect the broader framing context which links present events with events in the past and expectations about the future, and which links emotions with judgments and actions.

THE "DOUGLAS" CONTROVERSY

Hume's most systematic thoughts on the problem of the pleasures of tragedy are found in a short essay "Of tragedy," which was one of the *Four Dissertations* published in 1757, along with "Of the standard of taste," "Of the passions," and the "Natural history of religion," which not surprisingly received the lion's share of attention at the time and to this day. Hume had originally planned a volume on criticism as part of the *Treatise of Human Nature* (*T* xii), but, when the initial volumes of the *Treatise* had the misfortune to fall, in Hume's unforgettable expression, "deadborn from the press," the young writer abandoned the project of writing the remaining volumes. Instead, he turned his attention to shorter, less systematic books and essays, finding for these an appreciative and expanding audience.[12] Hence, the collected *Essays Moral, Political, and Literary* are our primary source for Hume's thoughts on criticism and literary subjects, although there are also valuable comments in the *Treatise* and in the *Enquiries*.

Although the *Four Dissertations* appeared in 1757, we don't know exactly when "Of tragedy" was written. When Hume first mentions them to his publisher in 1755, he writes that "there are four short Dissertations, which I have kept some Years by me, in order to polish them as much as possible."[13] Mossner speculates that "Of tragedy" was written sometime in the years 1749–51, which would make it coincide with the publication of the *Enquiries*.[14] Yet its publication in 1757 was, by coincidence, quite timely, as it coincided with Hume's neck-deep involvement in one of the most notorious eighteenth-century controversies over theater.[15] This controversy sheds light on the bitter sectarian conflict which characterized Hume's religious and political context, a context which the writings themselves tend to obscure.

John Home, a good friend as well as a relative of David Hume, had written a tragedy, *Douglas*, based on an old folk-tale of a Scottish hero. He hoped to see it performed on the London stage, but David Garrick refused to put it on in Drury Lane. This was felt by Home's intimates, among them Lord Kames, Hugh Blair, Alexander Carlyle, Adam Ferguson, and David Hume, to be a snub not only to Home's genius, but also to Scottish letters, and they decided to sponsor a performance of the tragedy in Edinburgh. The theatrical performances were still officially under the strict control of the 1737 Licensing Act. This was easily evaded, however; following the usual practice, the advertisement for *Douglas* read "A Concert of Music. After which will be presented (gratis) The New Tragedy Douglas. Taken from an Ancient Scots Story and Writ by a Gentleman of Scotland."[16]

In their eagerness to promote homegrown talent, Home's friends failed to take into account the strong current of anti-theatrical opinion which remained in Scotland. What is striking about attitudes toward theater in Scotland at this time is that radically divergent views coexisted with utter complacency in each camp about the soundness of their own views. Thus, the flagrant wickedness of the theater was so obvious to Evangelicals that condemnation of it seemed to require no justification, while at the same time, among the Moderate clergy, the theater was regarded as wholly innocent, a view which to its adherents seemed equally self-evident.

When news of the upcoming performance reached the Evangelicals, they were outraged, and issued an official *Admonition and Exhortation*, containing the strong statement that "The opinion which the Christian church has always entertained of stage plays and players, as prejudicial to the interest of religion and morality, is well known; and the fatal influence which they commonly have on the far greater part of mankind, particularly the younger sort, is too obvious to be called into question."[17] What made the appearance of *Douglas* particularly intolerable to the Evangelicals was the fact that its author was a member of the clergy of the Scottish church. Charges were brought against Home and several other members of the Moderate clergy, although the Evangelicals could do nothing to prevent the performances of *Douglas* from taking place, and by responding so violently seem only to have contributed to the play's success.

Since neither side was particularly interested in arguing on behalf of their own position, much of the uproar and controversy surrounding *Douglas* took the shape of satire and lampoon in broadsides, ballads, and skits, rather than calm reasoning. Even the serious pieces are sometimes difficult for the modern reader to take seriously; John Haldane, for example, wrote "Players Scourge; or, A Detection of the Ranting Prophanity and Regnant Impiety of Stage Plays, and Their Wicked Encouragers and Frequenters; and Especially against the Nine Prophane

Pagan Priests, Who Countenanced the Thrice Cursed Tragedy Called Douglas."[18] David Hume was often targeted for abuse, aimed both at his skeptical, "atheistical" views and at his corpulent body. Some real argument in defense of the theater was attempted, including Ferguson's "The morality of stage-plays seriously considered," which used references from scripture to justify the permissibility of theater, and a tract by Robert Wallace, which helped to avert an attempt at interdiction of the theater by Evangelical clergy by calling attention to the negative repercussions of such a step. Wallace pointed out that "The Nobility and gentry will not incline to be totally Deprived of the entertainment of the theater which they consider not only as innocent but improving. Whatever regard the laity in Generall have for the pious and morall instructions of the clergy, they do not choose to be Dictated to in their amusements and Diversions which they do not believe to be unlawful."[19]

A weighty contribution from the opposite camp came from John Witherspoon, in his *A Serious Inquiry into the Nature and Effects of the Stage*. Witherspoon's essay reveals that at the heart of the Evangelical rejection of the theater lay a deep distrust of the passions as such and of pleasure in particular.[20] This pessimistic view of fallen human nature, according to which all sources of enjoyment are guilty until proven innocent, can be traced back to Augustine. Augustine, too, was troubled by the pleasures of tragedy. He queried:

Why is it that a person should wish to experience suffering by watching grievous and tragic events which he himself would not wish to endure? Nevertheless he wants to suffer the pain given by being a spectator of these sufferings, and the pain itself is his pleasure. What is this but amazing folly? For the more anyone is moved by these scenes, the less free he is from similar passions. Only, when he himself suffers, it is called misery; when he feels compassion for others, it is called mercy. But what quality of mercy is it in fictitious and theatrical inventions? A member of the audience is not excited to offer help, but invited only to grieve. The greater his pain, the greater his approval of the actor in these representations.[21]

Augustine takes note of the technical puzzle of the link between pleasure and pain in tragedy, but only insofar as it raises the ethical issue, a fact which is true also of the anti-theatrical tradition extending to Witherspoon which takes its cue from him. Although it is good to commiserate with those who suffer, the truly compassionate person should always wish that there were no call for commiseration. Theater is dangerous because it creates the desire for new occasions to feel pity and compassion, and this desire might carry over into real life. For Augustine, the fact that in the theater we see a representation of suffering rather than real suffering is irrelevant if our emotional response to both is the same. Emotional responses are regarded as among the inner dispositions which must be carefully scrutinized for their purity. They are morally important even when they do not affect outward action.[22]

Witherspoon observes that "recreation and amusement enter into the nature of the stage, and are, not only immediately and primarily, but chiefly and ultimately, intended by it."[23] The spectator derives pleasure from the imitation or representation itself, regardless of the moral nature of the actions presented on stage. Unlike Aristotle, who took this pleasure as a sign that imitation is educative in and of itself, Witherspoon insists that this pleasure cannot be morally educative, since it is independent of the didactic content or lack thereof of stage plays. Hence, theater remains mere recreation rather than a true form of moral education.

Although recreation is permissible, it is so only when absolutely necessary. "Recreation," writes Witherspoon, "is an intermission of duty, and is only necessary because of our weakness; it must be some action indifferent in its nature, which becomes lawful and useful from its tendency to refresh the mind and invigorate it for duties of more importance."[24] To be a Christian is to be dedicated to a highly strenuous mode of existence, so even an "innocent" pastime can be a pernicious distraction from one's duty. Witherspoon goes on to argue that stage plays are impermissible because they are not a necessary form of recreation and are, indeed, counter-productive. Unlike social interaction and exercise, they are not truly restful; the stage "agitates the passions too violently, and interests too deeply, so as, in some cases, to bring people into a real, while they behold an imaginary distress."[25] Theatrical presentations, he goes on, "fix the mind so very deeply, and interest the affections so very strongly, that, in a little time, they fatigue themselves."[26] Theater runs counter to the Christian spirit of self-denial and mortification, of heavenly-mindedness and weaning from earth; the Christian "ought to set bounds to, and endeavour to moderate his passions as much as possible, instead of voluntarily and unnecessarily exciting them."[27]

Even if plays were morally instructive, therefore, they would remain primarily a form of unnecessary and therefore morally pernicious recreation. But Witherspoon also insists that it is impossible for most plays to be instructive, since in order to be successful, they must appeal to the taste of those who attend, and most of these will be wicked, since most people are wicked. Moreover, in order to be realistic, most of the characters represented on the stage must be wicked, and these bad examples will have considerable influence on spectators, especially since "every person attending the representation of a play, enters in some measure himself, as well as the actors, into the spirit of each character, and the more so the better the action is performed."[28] Witherspoon asserts that "frequently seeing the most terrible objects renders them familiar to our view, and makes us behold them with less emotion. And from seeing sin without reluctance, the transition is easy, to a compliance with its repeated importunity, especially as there are latent remaining dispositions to sinning in every heart that is but imperfectly sanctified."[29] Witherspoon's dissertation returns unfailingly to the theme of the inherent sinfulness of man and the resultant necessity for constant vigilance in the face of apparently innocent pursuits. Although his essay reflects the most current discussions of the pleasures of tragedy, Witherspoon is troubled by pleasure taken in *all* theater, not just in tragedy. He alludes to the pleasures of imitation, tragedy's ability to "fix the mind" and "interest the affections," and spectators' sympathy with the characters on stage (theories which I take up below), but all of these theories have been taken out of a context in which rehabilitated passions play a positive role in the moral life, and are filtered instead through Witherspoon's dark view of the passions as sin's stronghold in human nature.[30] His tract gives us a glimpse of what the champions of *Douglas* were up against.

Hume's involvement in the *Douglas* controversy was not limited to his support of the performances in Edinburgh. Resolving to do all he could in advocacy of his friend, he decided to break a long-standing policy of not prefacing his works with dedications by dedicating the *Four Dissertations* to Home. Friends who realized that the public endorsement of a notorious skeptic would only hurt defenders of the theater among the Moderate clergy advised him to suppress the dedication, and he did so temporarily, but he later regretted his failure of nerve and had the dedication published in a number of papers and weeklies both in Edinburgh and London. As a result, of course, the dedication was far more widely read than it would ever have been if published with the *Four Dissertations*. It not only served as fuel for the fires of debate in Edinburgh, but also helped to pave the way for the play's successful performance, not long thereafter, in London. By this time, Hume had acquired the reputation in England of a leading man of letters, and his critical opinion carried a good deal of weight.

Amidst all of the uproar and controversy, very little attention was paid to the actual content of *Douglas*. The drama is a "pathetic tragedy," carefully observing neoclassical strictures while at the same time striving to evoke a maximum of pity and compassion. The familiar device of concealed identity is used to structure the plot. Lady Randolph joyfully discovers her long-lost son, but her current husband, tempted into jealous suspicion by an Iago-like character, suspects her of having an affair with this strange young man. Lord Randolph kills the young Douglas before the matter can be explained, thereby driving Lady Randolph to suicide.

What gives added interest to the story is the running conflict throughout the play between the warlike virtues of Lord Randolph and Douglas, and the peace-loving maternal virtues of Lady Randolph.[31] This tension, which is never fully resolved within the play, would surely have struck a chord with Hume, who himself pondered the relationship between the "great," heroic virtues and the "good," agreeable virtues in the *Treatise* (*T* 592–604). Another significant theme of the play is its attack on concealment and hypocrisy. Lady Randolph blames her first act of dissimulation, of failing to confess to her father her secret marriage, for all her subsequent woes:

> . . . Sincerity
> Thou first of virtues, let no mortal leave
> Thy onward path! althou' the earth should gape
> And from the gulph of hell destruction cry
> To take dissimulation's winding way.[32]

The tragedy stemming from hidden identity is therefore seen not simply as a matter of fate, but as the result of human weakness, and of a failure of that key eighteenth-century virtue, sincerity.

Despite the fact that its author was a member of the clergy, *Douglas* is remarkably non-Christian in its basic orientation. Several of the minor characters in the play are conventionally religious, making reference to the ministrations of God's angels, to God's judgment, and to God's all-seeing eye. But when Lady Randolph expresses her anguish at the thought of her son going into battle, his response to her has the ring of a pagan, not a Christian:

> What shall I say? how can I give you comfort?
> The God of battle of my life dispose
> As may be best for you![33]

Lady Randolph, moreover, ends her life in suicide, and this act is designed to elicit pity, not condemnation, from the audience. The focus of the play is entirely on this-worldly affections, and Lady Randolph goes to her death in noble, defiant despair, with no suggestion that consolation lies in the world to come. It is worth noting that Hume proposed to group "Of tragedy" with an essay in defense of suicide in the *Four Dissertations*, though the essay on suicide was eventually set aside as too inflammatory.[34] *Douglas* helps to make Hume's argument on the this-worldly charms of tragedy, as well as lending support to his silenced argument in defense of suicide.

Hume's dedication to Home does not enter the lists of the general debate about tragedy, nor does it defend the notion of a clergyman as author. The dedication is primarily an expression of personal friendship (Hume admits that "it is less my admiration of your fine genius, which has engaged me to make this address to you, than my esteem of your character and my affection to your person"), along with somewhat exaggerated praise for the tragedy, which Hume calls "one of the most interesting and pathetic pieces, that was ever exhibited on any theater" (*FD* iv-v). Hume does make an indirect allusion to the acrimonious debate in Edinburgh by slipping in a contrasting reference to Hume and Home's mutual tolerance of their religious differences, mentioning that "another instance of true liberty, of which antient times can alone afford us an example, is the liberty of thought, which engaged men of letters, however different in their abstract opinions, to maintain a mutual friendship and regard; and never to quarrel about principles, while they agreed in inclinations and manners" (*FD* ii). Most of his attention here is directed, not toward the Calvinist foes of theater, however, but is rather focused on disarming English prejudice toward Scottish letters. Hence, he talks of *Douglas* as "interesting" and "pathetic," and adds that "the unfeigned tears which flowed from every eye, in the numerous representations which were made of it on this theater; the unparalleled command, which you appeared to have over every affection of the human breast: These are incontestable proofs, that you possess the true theatric genius of *Shakespear* and *Otway*, refined from the unhappy barbarism of the one, and licentiousness of the other" (*FD* iv-v).[35]

Hume's praise of the play's capacity to touch and move its audiences would certainly do nothing to disarm such critics as Witherspoon, for whom this power to move was precisely the focus of concern, rather than proof of literary greatness. To *endorse* theater on the basis of its capacity to move the spectator was to defy openly Evangelical distrust of pleasure and emotional spartanism and to deny that the main role of the passions is to encourage sin and licentiousness. Yet Hume does not simply point to the theater's capacity to move and delight spectators with sympathetic grief without also exploring the attendant moral dangers. His essay "Of tragedy" can be interpreted as an attempt to wrestle with ethical issues which not only responds to concerns about the pleasures of tragedy, but also goes on the offensive against Evangelicals, implying that their rejection of theater is symptomatic of pervasive pathology.

Hume's comments on *Douglas* suggest that the pleasure we derive from tragedy comes directly from the suffering depicted therein – we are moved by the suffering, and this movement of the soul is a source of pleasure. The best tragedy is that which gives us the most pleasure, and that in turn is the one which moves us with the most sympathetic suffering and pity. Consistent with this, Hume elsewhere implies that poets attain greatness specifically through their ability to touch and move spectators, rather than as a result of anything else about their works – "can it possibly be doubted, that this talent itself of poets, to move the passions, this pathetic and sublime of sentiment, is a very considerable merit; and being enhanced by its extreme rarity, may exalt the person possessed of it, above every character of the age in which he lives?" (*E* 259).

To point to theater's ability to move the soul was to evoke the Cartesian-derived solution to the intellectual puzzle of why watching tragedy is a source of pleasure. According to Descartes, the movement of our animal spirits is always a potential source of harm to us, but it is felt as pleasurable as long as the movement is harmonious and does not damage our nerves. "All that we call pleasurable sensation or agreeable sentiment is simply due to the fact that objects of sense excite some movement in the nerves which would be capable of harming them had they not strength sufficient to resist the movement, or were the body not well disposed; and this produces in the brain an impression which, being instituted by nature to give evidence to this good disposition and this strength, represents that to the soul as a good pertaining to it."[36] Lassitude and lack of stimulation are the most disagreeable states of being, so in general we enjoy having our emotions aroused.

In real situations, pity and fear are felt as inharmonious, rather than as pleasurable, and real situations in which our emotions are highly aroused also tend to be situations in which we are exposed to potential external harm. Theater, in contrast, is depicted as arousing the emotions in a harmonious and harmless fashion. Descartes also believed that the virtuous soul possessed such inner harmony and stability that "none of the troubles that come from elsewhere have any power to harm it, but rather serve to increase its joy, inasmuch as seeing that it cannot be harmed by them, it is made sensible of its perfection."[37] This Stoic outlook implies that the virtuous soul experiences life in much the same way that most people experience theater; whether one experiences sadness, joy, love, hatred or any other passion, everything serves as a source of pleasure, as the nerves are excited and moved without being harmed. The virtuous person, of course, has not only this pleasure of the body, but the added pleasure of the soul which comes from the knowledge that the pleasure is due to its own perfection, rather than to the fictitiousness of what is being experienced. Although Descartes, like Witherspoon, is suspicious of the unruly passions, he sees them not as lures to sinfulness but rather as sources of damage to the self. The virtuous soul is able to render the passions innocuous without suppressing or eradicating them. Theater, since it makes it possible for the soul to be excited and moved without risk of damage, is not regarded as a threat, but neither is its exercise of the passions seen as morally valuable, since its separation of passion from harm is external and has nothing to do with the state of the soul.

It was the widely read Abbé Dubos, a French critic writing in the early part of the eighteenth century, who was largely responsible for popularizing Descartes' physiological explanation of the pleasures of tragedy, although he simplified the theory and wholly detached it from Descartes' Stoic attitude toward the passions. In his *Réflexions critiques sur la poesie et la peinture*, Dubos insists that "one of the greatest wants of man is to have his mind incessantly occupied," and that "those passions, which are attended with the highest pleasures, are likewise productive of the most durable and acutest pains; nevertheless, man has still a greater dread of the heaviness which succeeds inaction, and finds in the bustle of business, and in the tumult of his passions, a motion that amuses him."[38] Dubos often suggests that the end of theater is nothing other than to move and to please the soul; "since the chief end of poetry and painting is to move us, the productions of these arts can be valuable only in proportion as they touch and engage us."[39]

Dubos comes much closer than Descartes to suggesting that the emotions of pity and fear are always in themselves enjoyable. Dropping Descartes' central concern for the internal harmony and stability of the soul, Dubos displays concern only for the undesirable *external* dangers which are attendant on emotions such as pity and fear when these are aroused by real rather than fictitious situations. In a way, this approach entirely dissolves the puzzle of the pleasures of *theatrical* tragedy, but in doing so the initial puzzle becomes transformed into a much broader problem about the pleasures of watching spectacles of suffering in general. Dubos insists, for example, that human beings enjoy watching public executions, noting that "that natural emotion, which rises, as it were, mechanically within us, upon feeling our fellow creatures in any great misfortune or danger, hath no other attractive, but that of being a passion, the motions whereof rouse and occupy the soul; nonetheless, this very emotion has charms capable of rendering it desirable, notwithstanding all the gloomy and importunate ideas that attend it."[40] Occasionally, as in his review of *Douglas* and in his discussion of curiosity in the *Treatise*, Hume seems to follow Dubos in this respect; "human life is so tiresome a scene, and men generally are of such indolent dispositions, that whatever amuses them, tho' by a passion mixt with pain, does in the main give them a sensible pleasure" (*T* 452). We shall see presently, however, that Hume resists the conclusion that passion (i.e. movement of the soul) is, even when accompanying dangerous circumstances are disregarded, always pleasant. Dubos, however, goes so far as to state that people of the greatest humanity also have the most heightened pleasure in suffering, since they are the most moved by such dismal spectacles. "Thus," he says, "the pleasing charm of emotion cancels the first principles of humanity in the most polite and most tender-hearted nations; and obliterates, in people of the greatest Christianity, the most evident maxims of their religion."[41] Paradoxically, those said to possess the greatest humanity may also be the least likely to act to ease suffering, since they enjoy the sight of it the most and are hence less motivated to eliminate it. Hume may not, as we shall see, be disposed to call these the people of greatest humanity!

Dubos, however, turns this observation into an ethical argument in defense of fictional representation. Art manages to give us nearly the same amount of pleasure without any of the bad consequences; it manages to "separate the dismal consequences of our passions from the bewitching pleasures we receive in indulging them . . . Might not art contrive to produce objects that would excite artificial passions, sufficient to occupy us while we are actually affected by them, and incapable of giving us afterwards any real pain or affliction?"[42] Art will, he implies, take care of our desire for arousal so that we will be less likely to enjoy spectacles of suffering in real life.

Dubos couples this with the not quite compatible, but similarly ethically-motivated argument that art is a good thing because it can excite our compassion or move our humanity without leaving us overly afflicted. Here the suggestion is that we are so drawn to and so caught up in spectacles of real suffering that we are unable to respond compassionately.

What was depicted earlier simply as pleasure is now seen as a sort of fascination which transfixes us and renders us incapable of acting, rather than undermining our *desire* to act.[43] So he says that "Nature . . . has thought proper to form us in such a manner, as the agitation of whatever approaches us should have the power of impelling us, to the end, that those, who have need of our indulgence or succor, may, with greater facility, persuade us."[44] This theory assumes that pain must somehow please or attract us in order to move us to help – otherwise we would remain indifferent to suffering or flee from it.

Although Dubos offers these arguments on behalf of the moral value of tragedy, his conceptualization of the nature of the movement of the soul simultaneously undermines these claims. Dubos viewed the soul's movement in terms of delicate fibers highly susceptible to damage, rather than on analogy with muscular fibers, which are strengthened through exercise. Hence, he holds that repeated exposure to spectacles of suffering blunts the emotional response to them. An artist, similarly, is unable to render good judgments of artistic merit, since his sensibility "has been blunted by the necessity of occupying himself with verses and painting, especially as he must have been frequently obliged to write and paint, as it were, against his will, in particular moments, when he felt no inclination for his work. He has become therefore insensible to the pathetic of verses and pictures."[45] Doctors, similarly, become callous and lose their ability to be tender and compassionate towards their patients. Given such a view, tragedy's arousal of emotion threatens to erode spectators' capacities for moral response to suffering in the real cases when such response is crucial. This would severely limit tragedy's potential to play a positive moral role.[46] Witherspoon, too, held that overexposure would blunt our natural responses, but with a crucial difference – the problem is not merely that we become indifferent to the spectacles of suffering, but that once we cease to be horrified by them, we will be unable to suppress our ineradicable urges to commit our own shocking deeds. Our capacity to feel horror is blunted, but the flames of our unruly passions are only fanned by repeated exposure.

Edmund Burke made even more radical claims along the lines of Dubos' suggestion that we derive pleasure from watching both real and fictional suffering in his *Origin of our Ideas of the Sublime and Beautiful*, which was, like Hume's *Four Dissertations*, published in 1757. Burke claims that the fact that we are drawn to the pains and misfortunes of others means that we delight in them, both in reality and when represented on the stage, as long as we are not ourselves in any immediate danger. He writes, for example, that "Terror is a passion which always produces delight when it does not press too close, and pity is a passion accompanied with pleasure, because it arises from love and social affection."[47] Delight for Burke is the peculiar sort of pleasure associated with the sublime, a sort of fascinated horror or awe which causes tension (excitement) without actual pain.[48] Burke adds a new twist to the theory of pleasure in tragedy by suggesting that the delight we feel is mixed with uneasiness, and gives to each a moral role: "[T]he delight we have in such things, hinders us from shunning scenes of misery; and the pain we feel, prompts us to relieve ourselves in relieving those who suffer; and all this antecedent to any reasoning; by an instinct that works us to its own purposes, without our concurrence."[49]

The more closely a tragedy imitates real suffering, the more pleasure we derive from it, but we would always leave the theater for a chance to witness a live public execution. Tragedies are not, as with Dubos, a non-destructive way of sating the desire to see spectacles of suffering, a desire which derives from our soul's morally indifferent need for movement, nor are they preferable to a reality which transfixes us so much that we are incapable of action. They are morally valuable only to the extent that they approach reality and create in us exactly the same pleasure mixed with uneasiness. Because the delight we feel is mixed with pain, Burke does not worry, as did Dubos, that the pleasure taken in suffering might feed a desire to witness more and more spectacles of suffering, both fictional and real.

"OF TRAGEDY"

Despite the extent to which Hume's dedication to *Douglas* makes him sound like a disciple, with Burke, of Descartes and Dubos, Hume resists valorizing the movement of the soul caused by pity and fear to the extent of any of these thinkers. At the outset of "Of tragedy," he writes:

> It seems an unaccountable pleasure, which the spectators of a well-written tragedy receive from sorrow, terror, anxiety, and other passions, that are in themselves disagreeable and uneasy. The more they are touched and affected, the more are they delighted with the spectacle; and as soon as the uneasy passions cease to operate, the piece is at an end. (*MPL* 216; see also *E* 259)

This statement of the puzzle clearly indicates that certain passions or movements of the soul are "in themselves," apart from the situations in which we usually feel them, unpleasant. Elsewhere, Hume queries, "Who would live amidst perpetual wrangling, and scolding, and mutual reproaches? The roughness and harshness of these emotions disturb and displease us: we suffer by contagion and sympathy; nor can we remain indifferent spectators, even though certain that no pernicious consequences would ever follow from such angry passions" (*E* 257–258). It is not even, as with Descartes, that certain movements of the soul are antagonistic to one another, and therefore inharmonious, but that motion of the soul is, quite simply, not always pleasant.

It comes as no surprise, therefore, to find Hume, in "Of tragedy," consider Dubos' solution to the question of why tragedy causes pleasure only to reject it, because "it is certain, that the same object of distress, which pleases in a tragedy, were it really set before us, would give the most unfeigned uneasiness; though it be then the most effectual cure to languor and indolence" (*MPL* 218). Hume is willing to admit that we are attracted to scenes of high passion, in the sense that we are drawn to them and our attention is fixed by them – thus we run to the gaming table with the highest stakes, and are most spellbound by tales of high danger. But he refuses to identify this sort of attraction with pleasure.

There *are* cases in which we do derive pleasure from watching real scenes of suffering, but in these cases the pleasure does not derive from an inherently pleasurable movement of the soul, as becomes clear when Hume challenges Dubos' acceptance of the Lucretian claim that we find it pleasant to watch a ship sink, as long as we are safe on the shore. Hume asks his reader to

Suppose the ship to be driven so near me, that I can perceive distinctly the horror, painted on the countenance of the seamen and passengers, hear their lamentable cries, see the dearest friends give their last adieu, or embrace with a resolution to perish in each others arms: No man has so savage a heart as to reap any pleasure from such a spectacle, or withstand the motions of the tenderest compassion and sympathy. (*T* 594)[50]

If the ship is so far away that we do not perceive any of the suffering, we might derive some pleasure from the sight when we compare the danger with our own safety; the pleasure derives from how well we come out on the basis of the comparison. This notion of comparison, which derives from Hobbes, could potentially be extended from the Lucretian example to account for the pleasures of tragedy.[51] Hume, however, is content to use it to refute the view that it is always pleasant to witness suffering.

Hume's refusal to accept the notion that motion of the soul is, as such, pleasant, coheres with his understanding of the nature of the immediate sympathetic response to spectacles of distress and suffering. When we sympathize with others, our idea of their suffering is enlivened into actual suffering. Hence, sympathy with pain and suffering is unpleasant. Other thinkers, such as Dubos or Burke, could simply claim that our response to suffering is pity and that pity is felt as pleasurable, since they were not committed to the view that the emotional valence of our response is the same as that in the spectacle before us. This disagreement also appears in Hume's response to Smith's *Theory of Moral Sentiments*. Hume suggests that the claim that all kinds of sympathy are necessarily agreeable is the "hinge" of Smith's system, but that Smith has failed to make a case for this claim. "Now it would appear," writes Hume, "that there is a disagreeable Sympathy, as well as an agreeable: And indeed, as the Sympathetic Passion is a reflex Image of the principal, it must partake of its Qualities, & be painful where that is so . . . It is always thought a difficult Problem to account for the Pleasure, receivd from the Tears & Grief & Sympathy of Tragedy; which woud not be the Case, if all Sympathy was agreeable. An Hospital woud be a more entertaining Place than a Ball" (*LDH* 1:169, p. 313).[52]

In Hume's theory, in contrast to these others, a further account is needed to explain why we don't simply flee from such spectacles of distress. As we saw in the previous chapter, our response to scenes of suffering and pain will depend on whether our sympathy is limited or extensive. Are we aware of nothing more than the communicated affection? Then we will try to escape the discomfort it brings us. If we also become interested in the other's well-being as a whole, however, we will be unable to escape the discomfort simply by averting our gaze from the other's suffering. It is not pleasure in the sight of suffering which engenders a benevolent response. Benevolence is due rather to recognition of the place of that suffering in the context of the other's life as a whole and his or her desires and potential for good. Hume's theory eliminates the rather disconcerting claim that pain somehow pleases or attracts us, and the even stronger claim that it must do so in order to motivate us to help one another.

If we attempt to apply this to Hume's discussion of tragedy, it becomes clear that tragic theater would have to involve extensive rather than limited sympathy, since if we felt only limited sympathy we would find the experience quite disagreeable. We would be swept up in a succession of strong emotions, many of them negative, without becoming involved in the narrative which gives it all direction and sense and makes us care intensely about the outcome. We would be indifferent to the sufferer or perhaps resent him or her for being the occasion of our own discomfort. When we take pleasure in tragedy, in contrast, we become caught up in the story and root for the protagonist. This is an instance of extensive sympathy, for "in considering the sufferer we carry our view on every side, and wish for his prosperity, as well as are sensible of his affliction" (*T* 389). It is an immediate response, which varies along with our prior predilections, rather than the corrected general sympathetic understanding of foreign points of view required for good moral judgment. But since it is extensive rather than limited sympathy, it moves beyond the disturbing passions themselves. Still, extensive sympathy with real suffering, though it gives rise to love and benevolence, is not *pleasurable*, in contrast to our response to suffering depicted in tragedy.

In "Of tragedy," Hume suggests that "as soon as the uneasy passions cease to operate, the piece is at an end. One scene of full joy and contentment and security is the utmost, that any composition of this kind can bear; and it is sure always to be the concluding one. If, in the texture of the piece, there be interwoven any scenes of satisfaction, they afford only faint gleams of pleasure, which are thrown in by way of variety, and in order to plunge the actors into deeper distress, by means of that contrast and disappointment" (*MPL* 216). This implies that poetry primarily seeks to raise in us the inherently disagreeable sympathetic emotions, and that it is precisely these which interest us in the fate of the characters on stage; "The whole art of the poet is employed, in rouzing and supporting the compassion and indignation, the anxiety and resentment of his audience. They are pleased in proportion as they are afflicted, and never are so happy as when they employ tears, sobs, and cries to give vent to their sorrow, and relieve their heart, swoln with the tenderest sympathy and compassion" (*MPL* 217). This emphasis on sorrow seems merely to exacerbate both aspects of the problem of the pleasures of tragedy – why is it that we feel pleasure at tragedy, and why isn't this pleasure morally problematic?

Having rejected Dubos' account of the pleasures of tragedy, Hume goes on to consider that of Fontenelle. This explanation, too, rests ultimately on the notion that the soul finds it pleasant to be moved, but allows that some movements are painful. Like Descartes, Fontenelle held the knowledge of fiction to be central to audiences' enjoyment of tragedy, but, rather than pointing to the harmoniousness of fiction-aroused passions, or to the lack of dangerous consequences, Fontenelle claims that "the movement of pleasure, pushed a little too far, becomes pain; and that the movement of pain, a little moderated, becomes pleasure. Hence it proceeds that there is such a thing as a sorrow, soft and agreeable: It is a pain weakened and diminished."[53] The idea of falsehood, which always remains with us as we watch a fictional representation, "suffices to diminish the pain which we suffer from the misfortunes of those whom we love, and to reduce that affliction to such a pitch as converts it into a pleasure."[54] Fontenelle goes on to suggest that we feel a mixture of sentiments – sympathetic suffering along with relief at the knowledge that we are seeing only fiction – rather than a simple reduction of pain. The mixture of sentiments is what composes "une douleur agréable," an "agreeable sorrow." Fontenelle also insists that the net emotion remains sorrowful, rather than being simple pleasure, claiming that "as that affliction, which is caused by exterior and sensible objects, is stronger than the consolation which arises from an internal reflection, they are the effects and symptoms of sorrow, that ought to predominate in the composition."[55] Fontenelle's "douleur agréable" differs from the mixed emotion which Burke discussed, in which the delight was not a reflection of a scene's lack of reality, but rather an intrinsic fascination with scenes of misery. Fontenelle's second theory seems to involve something much like Hume's principle of comparison, as he puts it to work in the Lucretian shipwreck example, although here the comparison is between fictional suffering and knowledge of the real state of affairs, rather than between the distant suffering of someone else and one own's safety. The reality – fiction contrast is central.

Rather than discussing Fontenelle's second, more complex, theory, with its seeming affinity for his own thinking, Hume focuses on Fontenelle's initial suggestion that the pleasure of tragedy is simply a softened pain resulting from the accompanying idea of fiction. Hume had earlier embraced a similar hypothesis, one which regarded "soft" pain as a sort of pleasure. In the *Treatise*, for example, Hume wrote that "in the common affairs of life, where we feel and are penetrated with the solidity of the subject, nothing can be more disagreeable than fear and terror; and 'tis only in dramatic performances and in religious discourses, that they ever give pleasure. In these latter cases the imagination reposes itself indolently on the idea; and the passion, being soften'd by the want of belief in the subject, has no more than the agreeable effect of enlivening the mind, and fixing the attention" (*T* 115). Or in a discussion of belief:

There is no passion of the human mind but what may arise from poetry; tho' at the same time the feelings of the passions are very different when excited by poetical fictions, from what they are when they arise from belief and reality. A passion, which is disagreeable in real life, may afford the highest entertainment in a tragedy, or epic poem. In the latter case it lies not with that weight upon us: It feels less firm and solid: And has no other than the agreeable effect of exciting the spirits, and rouzing the attention. (*T* 630–631)

In "Of tragedy," however, Hume claims that there must be a distinct source of positive pleasure; pain does not become pleasant simply by virtue of being softened. He identifies at least two such sources of pleasure in poetry – eloquence and imitation. Similar explanations of the pleasures of tragedy had preceded the Cartesian physiological explanation of which both Dubos' and Fontenelle's theory were offshoots.[56] They were current in the fifteenth and sixteenth centuries, and were endorsed by neoclassicists, who were especially preoccupied with the role of imitation in art.[57] Hume explains that "this extraordinary effect proceeds from that very eloquence, with which the melancholy scene is represented. The genius required to paint objects in a lively manner, the art employed in collecting all the pathetic circumstances, the judgment displayed in disposing them: the exercise, I say, of these noble talents, together with the force of expression, and beauty of oratorial numbers, diffuse the highest satisfaction on the audience, and excite the most delightful movements" (*MPL* 220). Hume claims that "the same principle takes place in tragedy; with this addition, that tragedy is an imitation; and imitation is always of itself agreeable" (*MPL* 220). The central point is that there must be an unambiguous source of pleasure; pain cannot simply be softened or toned down into pleasure. The claim that imitation is always agreeable is clearly a reference to Aristotle, but this comment is actually more reminiscent of Plutarch. Plutarch had traced our enjoyment of representations of suffering and pain to the human love of artistry, our love for the human ability to shape things of all sorts, including representations of natural things.[58] Aristotle's claim about delight in representation, in contrast, was not a claim about human appreciation for human-made things, but rather derived from a more general claim about the pleasure human beings have in learning. Hume's discussion of imitation, like Plutarch's, does not refer to the educative value of theater.

Hume does not rest content with a simple endorsement of neoclassical doctrine, however. He proposes a modification, one which makes sympathetic passions central to the pleasures of tragedy. Hume suggests that something must first arouse and interest the mind in order for it to appreciate the beauties of eloquence and imitation. "The same force of oratory," he insists, "employed on an uninteresting subject, would not please half so much, or rather would appear altogether ridiculous; and the mind, being left in absolute calmness and indifference, would relish none of those beauties of imagination or expression, which, if joined to passion, give it such exquisite entertainment" (*MPL* 220). If the mind is calm, eloquence will seem melodramatic, not beautiful, whereas if the mind is aroused, we will truly appreciate the artistry. The reason poets tend to employ pain and distress in order to arouse the mind is that "nothing can furnish to the poet a variety of scenes and incidents, except distress, terror, or anxiety. Compleat joy and satisfaction is attended with security, and leaves no farther room for action" (*MPL* 220). The point is not to deny that the agreeable passions affect the soul as much as the disagreeable passions, but to point out that they generate only the wish to remain in that agreeable state. Hence, while painters, who depict only one moment, can seek to arouse an agreeable passion, poets, who must keep the plot moving, must focus on something distressing or conflict-ridden.

Artistry is not, moreover, the sole source of pleasure in tragic drama. Another source of pleasure in tragedy comes from the depiction of heroic and steadfast responses to misfortune. Although even disagreeable passions can, given artistic presentation, bring us pleasure,

the great charm of poetry consists in lively pictures of the sublime passions, magnanimity, courage, disdain of fortune; or those of the tender affections, love and friendship; which warm the heart, and diffuse over it similar sentiments and emotions. And though all kinds of passion, even the most disagreeable, such as grief and anger, are observed, when excited by poetry, to convey a satisfaction, from a mechanism of nature, not easy to be explained: Yet those more elevated or softer affections have a peculiar influence, and please from more than one cause or principle. Not to mention that they alone interest us in the fortune of the persons represented, or communicate any esteem and affection for their character. (*E* 259)

Both the explanation in terms of artistry and this account which identifies the pleasure as pleasure in human *response* to distress, have important ramifications for the ethical concerns raised by the pleasures of tragedy, for they refuse to identify the pleasure as pleasure in the sight of human distress itself.

Hume does not portray the response to tragedy as a mixed emotion – distress aroused by the tragedy plus distress-enhanced pleasure in creative artistry and virtuous resistance to evil. Instead, he claims that "the uneasiness of the melancholy passions is not only overpowered and effaced by something stronger of an opposite kind; but the whole impulse of those passions is converted into pleasure, and swells the delight which the eloquence raises in us" (*MPL* 220). The passions are conceived of as vectors, possessing both force and directionality. But, when the violent passions of tragedy are united with the calm sentiments of beauty, the result is not simple vector subtraction, although the vectors do have opposite directionalities. Rather, the direction of the less forceful vector is reversed and adds to the force of the other; "The impulse or vehemence, arising from sorrow, compassion, indignation, receives a new direction from the sentiments of beauty. The latter, being the predominant emotion, seize the whole mind, and convert the former into themselves" (*MPL* 220). At this point Hume seems to sense that this picture of a 180-degree change in direction does not do justice to the complexity of our emotional response to tragedy, for he switches metaphors and adds that the sentiments of beauty "at least tincture them [the violent passions] so strongly as totally to alter their nature" (*MPL* 220).[59] Rather than presenting the picture of pain "softened" into pleasure or a reversal of pain's vector, this portrays the passions and sentiments as watercolor paints which yield new colors when mixed. But this suggestion is only a momentary apostasy, which Hume fails to integrate into his reversal theory.

FICTION, REALITY, AND BELIEF

Although Hume's reversal theory differs from Fontenelle's softening theory, both seem to rely on a clear distinction between reality and art. For Hume, appreciation of artistry ("eloquence" and "imitation") serves as a positive source of pleasure, and the knowledge that tragic events are real prevents pleasure in human struggle against suffering, while, for Fontenelle, the contrast between reality and art softens pain into pleasure. This suggests that there is an important difference between reality and representation, such that our knowledge of the fact that we are not being confronted with actual suffering allows us to see it as art, and this makes our pleasure both possible and innocent. Our response to reality is then clearly distinct from our response to fictional representation; our pleasure in tragedy on stage does not encourage pleasure in real-life tragedy.

Fontenelle's theory, certainly, required a clear distinction between our state of mind when what we observe is accompanied by an "idea of falsehood" and when it is not. But such a claim is problematic for Hume because of his understanding of belief as "nothing but *a more vivid and intense conception of any idea*" (*T* 119–120).[60] Indeed, Hume developed his theory of belief in intentional contradistinction to Descartes' understanding of belief as involving the addition of an idea of the existence of A to the idea of A, and it is this Cartesian theory of belief which Fontenelle is following. Hume was suspicious of Descartes' theory of belief because of its voluntarism-if we can, as Hume agreed with Descartes, "mingle, and unite, and separate, and confound, and vary our ideas in a hundred different ways" (*T* 96), and if there are separate ideas of truth and falsehood, we would be able to add them to any ideas we wished, thereby producing belief.[61] Hume's theory is designed to capture the impossibility of believing at will.

On Hume's theory of belief, however, our intense response to poetry seems bound to undermine our ability to distinguish between fiction and reality and confound our moral responses to each, exacerbating the problem of the pleasures of tragedy. There are intimate links, therefore, between Hume's understanding of belief and his response to the problem of the pleasures of tragedy. In fact, it is in the course of puzzling over the differences between reality and fiction in the *Treatise* that Hume betrays some uneasiness with his official characterization of belief and begins to venture in a different direction, one which has repercussions for understanding his response to the problems of tragedy in "Of tragedy."[62]

Hume's definition of belief as a "vivid and intense conception" makes belief and passion mutually reinforcing, even mutually causally effective; Hume writes that "as belief is almost absolutely requisite to the exciting our passions, so the passions in their turn are very favourable to belief; and not only such facts as convey agreeable emotions, but very often such as give pain, do upon that account become more readily the objects of faith and opinion" (*T* 120). Having said this, Hume has a very difficult time denying that the vivacity of our passions in the theater will lead us to conceive of the related ideas in a manner indistinguishable from belief. Poetry does present us with many affecting objects, and "when any affecting object is presented, it gives the alarm, and excites immediately a degree of its proper passion . . . This emotion passes by an easy transition to the imagination; and diffusing itself over our idea of the affecting object, makes us frequently assent to it, according to the precedent system" (*T* 120). Moreover, he admits that "'tis difficult for us to withhold our assent from what is painted out to us in all the colours of eloquence; and the vivacity produc'd by the fancy is in many cases greater than that which arises from custom and experience" (*T* 123).

Yet Hume does try to account for the impact of poetry while distinguishing it from reality. He says that poets have formed a "poetical system" which links ideas together in a way that "makes them enter into the mind with facility, and prevail upon the fancy, without influencing the judgment" (*T* 121). Poets also mingle fiction with fact in order to make a deeper impression on the affections:

[T]he several incidents of the piece acquire a kind of relation by being united into one poem or representation; and if any of these incidents be an object of belief, it bestows a force and vivacity on the others, which are related to it . . . This, indeed, can never amount to a perfect assurance; and that because the union among the ideas is, in a manner, accidental: But still it approaches so near, in its influence, as may convince us, that they are deriv'd from the same origin. (*T* 122)

The vivacity of belief is due, Hume suggests, to our customary experience of the connections among our beliefs, and their connection with our current impressions, which constantly reinforce our confidence in them. Poetry mimics the effects of this reinforcement by creating an artificial union among ideas.

In the Appendix to the *Treatise*, Hume wrestles with these problems further. While he still seeks to distinguish belief by its peculiar feeling, the notion of the different sorts of connection among ideas begins to do more work in his explanation. In both poetry and madness, we may observe that "the vivacity they bestow on the ideas is not deriv'd from the particular situations or connexions of the objects of these ideas, but from the present temper and disposition of the person" (*T* 630). Artificial or peculiarly subjective sources of vivacity are admitted as possibilities. Hence, Hume backs off from the equation of vivacity with belief, writing that "how great soever the pitch may be, to which this vivacity rises, 'tis evident, that in poetry it never has the same feeling with that which arises in the mind, when we reason . . . The mind can easily distinguish betwixt the one and the other; and whatever emotion the poetical enthusiasm may give to the spirits, 'tis still the mere phantom of belief or persuasion" (*T* 630). A bit further on, he reinforces the suggestion that the peculiar feeling of belief cannot be equated with its violence or agitation. "Where the vivacity arises from a customary conjunction with a present impression [as in usual cases of belief]; tho' the imagination may not, in appearance, be so much mov'd; yet there is always something more forcible and real in its actions, than in the fervors of poetry and eloquence. The force of our mental actions in this case, no more than in any other, is not to be measur'd by the apparent agitation of the mind" (*T* 631). He concludes that "the vigour of conception, which fictions receive from poetry and eloquence, is a circumstance merely accidental, of which every idea is equally susceptible; and that such fictions are connected with nothing that is real" (*T* 631).

Hume began by characterizing belief simply as a more intense conception of an idea, with the customary association with present impressions serving as a possible source of intensity. Yet his attempts to account for the intensity of mental movement caused by fictional representations lead him to focus on connections between ideas not primarily as sources of intensity, but rather as the crucial factor in distinguishing reality from fiction. Vivid conception becomes something accidental, sometimes linked to the real and sometimes not. This turn towards the relational rather than intrinsic features of belief is precisely the direction in which Antony Flew argues Hume should have gone in order to avoid the pitfalls of his psychological theory of mental images. Rather than following Locke in an approach which "begins with the logically private realm of one man's experience," Hume would have done better to start "from the common public world of physical things and events, the world of 'the reality of things' and of transactions between people."[63] To my mind, Hume went much further in this direction than Flew recognizes, despite remaining within the constraints of Lockean psychological assumptions.

Flew claims not only that Hume's official account has trouble explaining the process of belief formation, but further that it is unable to distinguish between rational and irrational beliefs. Hume treats belief simply as "the automatic result of the operation of a sort of existential computing machine" and therefore forfeits the ability to distinguish good from bad reasons for belief.[64] It is clear, however, that in his discussions of the relationship between experience and belief, Hume is striving to develop criteria of reasonable belief. His avoidance of the language of reasons should, I think, be put down to his antipathy to Cartesian rationalism. It should not be interpreted as a thoroughgoing mechanism, but rather as an attempt to naturalize the language of reason and to move it away from the dominant deductive model.[65]

Hume thus approaches a holistic understanding of belief, in which beliefs are neither certified by a special feeling attached to them (whether a special clarity and distinctness or a special emotional intensity), nor justified exhaustively by deduction or induction. Rather, our beliefs form an interdependent web, and when we question the truth of one we rely on the truth of others. Our belief in something falters when the connections with other beliefs are absent or dissolve.[66] I may wake up with a strong sense of grief and a vivid conviction that my close friend has died, but when I cannot remember how I found out about her death, and no one else seems to know about it, I begin to have doubts, and when I dial her number and she answers the phone, I conclude that I only dreamt that she died. Similarly, although Scarlett O'Hara may seem very real to me, I do not find her mentioned in any history books, I cannot locate her birth certificate in any archive, and if I were to tell friends that I am her great-great granddaughter they would think I was mad. The connections and reinforcements which would lead me to consider Scarlett a real person are lacking, regardless of the vividness of my conception of Scarlett.[67] In her discussion of Hume's account of association, Baier writes that "were mental representations our only representations, their accuracy could not be investigated . . . All our talk of true images, and of relative accuracy, derives from our social interpersonal world . . . Not just the vividness of the memory, but also the coherence of the memory report with all the other evidence we together take ourselves to have, goes into our judgment of whether this is a remembering or a misremembering."[68] As Baier's interpretation suggests, the sorts of "connexions" which distinguish reality from fiction are to a great extent due to the interpersonal world in which we make sense of others and ourselves. It is also with reference to this interpersonal world that criticism of belief and articulation of reasons for belief become possible.

Although he ventures in the direction of a holistic understanding of belief, Hume remains preoccupied with isolated emotional/mental states and hence convinced that fiction must *feel* different to the mind than does belief. He ends up with an uneasy compromise, summarized in the *Enquiry Concerning Human Understanding*: "Let us, then, take in the whole compass of this doctrine, and allow, that the sentiment of belief is nothing but a conception more intense and steady than what attends the mere fictions of the imagination, and that this manner of conception arises from a customary conjunction of the object with something present to the memory or senses" (*E* 50).[69] He still attempts to identify belief by the way it feels to the mind, although he isolates this particular feeling by reference to the framing context of beliefs. What is characteristic both of the official theory and of the emergent alternative, however, is the stress on experience. Beliefs become increasingly "artificial" as the connection between the idea believed and our own experience becomes increasingly tenuous.

If we read Hume's attempts to resolve the tragedy problem in light of his exploration of belief, the emphasis of his account of the pleasures of tragedy falls in a new place. It becomes clear that his explanation of the pleasures of tragedy does not depend on a black-and-white distinction between fiction and reality, nor between reality and representation, but rather on the connections among ideas and the way these ideas are framed. While Hume initially seeks to resolve the problem of the pleasures of tragedy by finding a simple way to make distinctions between reality and fiction, his focus on the connections among ideas creates a more complex and context-dependent picture of what counts as "reality" and what as "fiction," not in this case for purposes of theoretical knowledge, but for purposes of practical response. Although his point against Fontenelle ostensibly has to do with the need for a source of positive pleasure and does not directly address the role of the "idea of fiction," the example which Hume employs is a case in which the artistic representation which causes pleasure is of real rather than fictional events. Cicero's eloquent epilogues, accounts of real suffering and brutality, produced, at least according to Hume, the same sorrowful pleasure in Cicero's audience as paintings or theatrical depictions of imaginary tragic events. Since "the audience were convinced of the reality of every circumstance," it is impossible to claim that the sorrow is here "softened by fiction" (*MPL* 219). In this case, the response to something fictional seems not to differ from the response to something true or real.

Of course, Cicero's audience is enjoying a *representation* of something real, not the sounds of actual suffering. Still, the example of Cicero's epilogues calls to mind Hume's discussion of the shipwreck example taken from Lucretius. Pleasure derived from the eloquent recitation of horrible real events is like pleasure taken in watching a distant shipwreck safely from shore in that the spectators, in both cases, feel distanced from the reality of the events. They do not feel personally called on to respond to the suffering (to be fair, the implication in these examples is that they would not be able to help even if they tried). The suffering is, although they "know" it to be real, unreal *to the spectators*, and hence it does not engage their moral responses or enter into their deliberations about what to do. Just as fictional representations can mimic many of the connections which reinforce our beliefs in things as real, reality can mimic fiction when we interpret something in what we hear or see as a distancing or disconnecting element, something which disturbs the usual close connection between what we see and hear and what enters into our deliberations.[70] This last comment may seem rather vague, since it suggests a pervasive indeterminacy about what is interpreted as a distancing element and hence what is regarded as real or fictional. But to say that what is taken to be real rests ultimately on an interpretation does not mean that an individual is under no constraints, that he or she may simply decide that something is or is not real (either in an abstract or in a practical, deliberatively relevant sense). There are many constraints, some physical and some social. Take, for example, Lucretius' shipwreck. If it became physically possible for the spectators to help the drowning passengers and someone noticed this and pointed it out, then the fact that people were drowning would begin to enter into the deliberations of the spectators, if for no other reason than that it would become necessary to justify to others or to themselves why they were not trying to save the victims.

Were it not for this sense of distance and unreality, the pleasure, whether it arises from the spectator's comparison of the idea of danger with his or her own safety or from appreciation of the speaker's eloquence, would be overwhelmed or cut off entirely. Comparison or appreciation of eloquence might even result in feelings of guilt and intensified grief. Hume recognizes that the presence of a source of pleasurable sentiments will not necessarily result in overall enjoyment, for he notes that if an action represented in tragedy is too "bloody" or "atrocious," then "the greatest energy of expression, bestowed on descriptions of that nature, serves only to augment our uneasiness" (*MPL* 224). Similarly, an eloquent speech on the loss of a child will only deepen the grief of the child's parents. Hume accounts for these phenomena by claiming that these are cases in which the disagreeable passions preponderate over the agreeable sentiments, but this is little more than a restatement of the question. What Hume's choice of examples makes clear, however, even if his interpretation does not, is that the abstract belief in the fictionality of the events being watched or heard about is not what determines whether pleasure or pain will predominate in a particular case, since all combinations are possible – pleasure in fictional suffering, pain in fictional suffering, pleasure in real suffering, and pain in real suffering. The determining factor in the examples Hume gives is rather the way in which the spectacle concretely relates to the audience's existence – the child is one's own, Verres is responsible for the brutal acts Cicero describes, Lord Clarendon's hearers are "too deeply concerned" in the downfall of the royal party. Rousseau eloquently bemoans the "false pity" evoked by theater, explicitly linking it with theater's distancing effect. He writes:

I hear it said that tragedy leads to pity through fear. So it does; but what is this pity? A fleeting and vain emotion which lasts no longer than the illusion which produced it; a vestige of natural sentiment soon stifled by the passions; a sterile pity which feeds on a few tears and which has never produced the slightest act of humanity . . . In giving our tears to these fictions, we have satisfied all the rights of humanity without having to give anything more of ourselves; whereas unfortunate people in person would require attention from us, relief, consolation, and work, which would involve us in their pains and would require at least the sacrifice of our indolence . . . The more I think about it, the more I find that everything that is played in the theater is not brought nearer to us but made more distant.[71]

Rousseau suggests that theater distances things from us because it gives us no role to play in the actions on stage – we have no influence on or responsibility for the outcome. Hume presses even further, showing how real situations for which we feel no responsibility or necessity to respond are accompanied by the same sense of distance.

Hume's discussion not only shows that this sense of detachment is requisite to the pleasures of tragedy, but reveals at the same time that tragic drama's employment of artistry and imitation is not requisite to tragedy's capacity to bring us pleasure, since potential sources of mental pleasure abound; "the force of imagination, the energy of expression, the power of numbers, the charms of imitation; all these are naturally, of themselves, delightful to the mind" (*MPL* 222). Reality itself offers many delights to the mind, even when not mediated by eloquent representation, and some of these are bound up with suffering or cruelty or horror. What determines our overall response depends, as Hume claims, on whether the horror enhances the beauty or whether the beauty intensifies the horror, and this in turn (as can be gleaned from Hume's examples and his discussion of belief) depends on our sense of detachment from or involvement in the spectacle before us, and its resultant concrete reality or lack of reality for us.

What limited sympathy and pleasurable sympathy in tragic drama have in common is the presence of distancing elements which result in a lack of involvement on our own part. When sympathy is limited, we are not even emotionally engaged on behalf of those in distress, or sensitive to the context of the unpleasant emotions which we experience sympathetically. When we take pleasure in sympathy with distress, we are caught up in the spectacle and emotionally involved in the action, but the presence of an aesthetic frame or some other distancing element prevents us from experiencing the spectacle as something which makes moral claims on us, something under the ethical categories of "horrifying," "outrageous," "cruel," etc., and frees us to enjoy the excitement of the spectacle under aesthetic categories, as "beautiful" or "moving." Our wish for the prosperity of the sufferer remains nothing but a wish. We are emotionally involved without being involved on the level of deliberation – we feel no sense of responsibility, for we do not conceive of our narratives interacting with the narratives before us. As long as the spectacle from which we feel aesthetic detachment is a theatrical tragedy, there is no reason to fear, and the ethical problem dissolves. It would be rather inappropriate to leap on stage in defense of the protagonist of a tragic drama. Recall that Hume insisted, against Dubos and Burke, that real life tragedy is not usually a source of pleasure but rather of distress – when we are not aesthetically detached from the spectacle presented to us, it is not virtue's inspiring fight, but the suffering itself, which has the preponderance of force.

RELIGION AND POETRY: THE DANGERS OF DETACHMENT

What sort of a response does Hume provide to Evangelical condemnation of theater? He refuses to pander to Calvinist worries about the wickedness and flammability of the passions. Our passionate response to tragic theater roots us in this world, reminding us of the hopes and fears which we share with other human beings, keeping us from deluding ourselves into thinking that we are indifferent to this existence and do not care about whether our lives go well or do not. We do not take pleasure in suffering itself, but rather in human beings' indomitable struggle against suffering; "the mere suffering of plaintive virtue, under the triumphant tyranny and oppression of vice, forms a disagreeable spectacle, and is carefully avoided by all masters of the drama. In order to dismiss the audience with entire satisfaction and contentment, the virtue must either convert itself into a noble courageous despair, or the vice receive its proper punishment" (*MPL* 224).

Hume contrasts this involvement in the spectacle of the display of strength of human character and struggle against misery with the manifestation of Calvinist hatred of the world. "Most painters," he writes, "have been very unhappy in their subjects. As they wrought much for churches and convents, they have chiefly represented such horrible subjects as crucifixions and martyrdoms, where nothing appears but tortures, wounds, executions, and passive suffering, without any action or affection" (*MPL* 224). The insistence that humility is the highest virtue and that this life is without value robs these depictions of suffering, claims Hume, of any source of pleasure – martyrs are not supposed to be courageous and defiant, but are expected to yield to suffering in the conviction that nothing of value is being taken from them. There is nothing to convert the painful emotions to pleasure, and the overall effect is dismal and depressing. To understand how tragic drama can be a source of pleasure is also to gain insight into Evangelical religious psychology, for Hume insists that "the same inversion of that principle, which is here insisted on, displays itself in common life, as in the effects of oratory and poetry" (*MPL* 224). He ends the essay with what one can easily construe as an oblique reference to Evangelical sermons and devotional literature: "What so disagreeable as the dismal, gloomy, disastrous stories, with which melancholy people entertain their companions? The uneasy passion being there raised alone, unaccompanied with any spirit, genius, or eloquence, conveys a pure uneasiness, and is attended with nothing that can soften it into pleasure or satisfaction" (*MPL* 225). The pursuit of Calvinist virtues induces a habitual melancholy which robs life of pleasure, and the promise of pleasure which theater holds out is only a temptation to soil these virtues.

But sometimes even more troubling distortions of personality and psychology result from religious belief.[72] Sometimes, Hume believes, it leads to indifference to real life suffering, or even creates a disposition to enjoy such suffering. This is due to the fact that religion has the capacity to induce a sort of aesthetic detachment from, not tragic drama, but real life tragedy. In the *Natural History of Religion*, it becomes clear that Hume sees religious doctrine as a sort of "poetical system." Like poetry, religious doctrine forms an artificial union among ideas, using familiar terms in unfamiliar ways in order to make plausible incomprehensible or incoherent doctrines such as the immortality of the soul and the justice and loving kindness of a God who predestines people to everlasting torment in hell.[73] It builds up an alternative picture of reality which competes with the everyday world, in which living beings simply die, and terms of approbation, if they are at all meaningful, must be applied consistently. It claims, moreover, that its true picture of reality shows the everyday world to be insubstantial, because fleeting, and only a doorstep to eternity. It therefore encourages a sense of detachment from the everyday world and its happenings except insofar as they are a preparation for the next.

This is like the aesthetic detachment which makes pleasure in tragic drama possible, except that in this case it is not dramatic fiction which is felt to be unreal, but rather mundane existence. One result is that the only social bonds which retain any force are those among members of one's own religious sect – these are the individuals who share, and thereby reinforce, the connections among one's beliefs, one's "poetical system" of reality. One's sense of reality requires blind loyalty to one's sect. Thus religious zealots persecute those who do not share their beliefs, and are indifferent to the anguish they perpetrate. In fact, they may feel no emotional involvement whatsoever with the object of persecution; since immediate, unreflective sympathy is confined to those with whom we perceive some bond of connection, the sympathy of zealots will be confined to members of their own sect. The zealot is detached from the suffering of his or her victims, and does not regard it as truly real. Hume's account in the *History of England* of the Crusaders' assault on Jerusalem dwells on just these features of religious zeal:

They put the numerous garrison and inhabitants to the sword without distinction. Neither arms defended the valiant, nor submission the timorous; no age or sex was spared: infants on the breast were pierced by the same blow with their mothers, who implored for mercy: even a multitude ... who had surrendered themselves prisoners, and were promised quarter, were butchered in cool blood by those ferocious conquerors. The streets of Jerusalem were covered with dead bodies; and the triumphant warriors, after every enemy was subdued and slaughtered, immediately turned themselves, with the sentiments of humiliation and contrition, towards the holy sepulchre. They threw aside their arms, still streaming with blood: they advanced, with reclined bodies, and naked feet and heads, to that sacred monument: they sung anthems to their Saviour, who had there purchased their salvation by his death and agony: and their devotion, enlivened by the presence of the place where he had suffered, so overcame their fury, that they dissolved in tears, and bore the appearance of every soft and tender sentiment. (*H* I, VI, 128)

The humiliation and contrition that the Crusaders feel are not a sense of guilt at having committed such outrageous acts, but the habitual humiliation which was the crowning Calvinist virtue, a sense of shame at their sinful inclination to continue to value worldly existence. They weep over the death of their Savior, but feel no responsibility for the horrible anguish they themselves have just caused. All that human suffering is not really real to them; caught up in religious zeal, the human beings they slaughtered were little more to them than physical obstacles blocking their approach to the sacred places which were infinitely more real. Murder may even become a source of pleasure, when the enemy is pictured as the embodiment of evil and killing takes on metaphysical significance as a victory of the good principle.

What is morally problematic about tragedy, therefore, is not the fact that we take pleasure in tragic drama, but that a distorted sense of reality and fiction may lead us to be indifferent, or even to take pleasure in, real life suffering. The solution to this problem is certainly not to ban theater;

by offering a "poetical system" which stresses the goods of worldly existence, theater may even hold out some promise of combating the poetical system of Calvinism and revivifying appreciation for these goods. Hume recognizes that pleasure at tragic drama will seem problematic, even to those who were not suspicious of passion across the board, as long as there is no hard and fast way to distinguish reality from fiction. Nevertheless, he refuses to take refuge in a rationalistic distinction between reality and fiction, seeking instead to develop a distinction based on an associationist model made richer by including connections which derive from the social world. Hume's solution to the problem of the pleasures of tragedy has the potential to relieve some of the fears of those who oppose tragic drama by refusing to focus solely on isolated emotional states and turning instead to a comprehensive context-sensitive view.

Hume's response to the problem of the pleasures of tragedy shows why the phenomenon of pleasure in tragic drama need not raise ethical concerns, but it also sheds light on the way in which a sense of unreality or detachment may short-circuit extensive sympathy and appropriate moral responses in real life situations, a phenomenon which certainly is ethically troubling. The connection between belief and response to tragic spectacles implies that sympathetic appreciation for alien points of view, if it is to be a resource for good moral judgment, cannot be understood solely in terms of islolated emotional responses, but that it reflects entire webs of belief. Hume's discussion of tragedy thus reveals, from a different perspective than the *Treatise*, both the need for and the possibility of a more active way of extending sympathy to others, one which does not simply follow previous predilections and conform to prejudice and sect, but which is steady, general, and reflective, as well as critical of prior beliefs. In chapter 4, I turn to Hume's attempt to develop a standard of taste, which gives a more positive indication of sympathetic understanding as a principle which is actively developed and employed in the moral life.

Sympathetic understanding and the threat of difference

IN SEARCH OF A STANDARD OF TASTE

Seventeenth-century neoclassicism, modeling itself after Cartesian rationalism's emphasis on the mathematically demonstrative, emphasized a sharp separation between rational appraisal and emotional response. This translated into an increasing preoccupation with the codification of aesthetic rules which could be rationally applied to works of art, while "taste" was confined to explicitly non-rational elements of aesthetic response and generally disregarded.[1] With the emergence of the sentimentalist reaction against rigid neoclassical rationalism, however, taste was given a primary role in aesthetic evaluation; "the restriction of 'reason' to logical abstraction, accompanied by the exclusion of other concepts of mind which had found a place in the broad classical conception of ethical insight, was counter-balanced by an increasing emphasis upon feeling, sentiment, or instinct as the basis of taste."[2] Among the sentimentalists, attention shifted away from elucidating the rules adhered to by works of true beauty and classifying genres according to their several purposes to considering how the average spectator responded to a work of art. Since different individuals react in different ways to the same painting or performance, the extreme skeptic might well conclude that no agreement in matters of taste is possible; "a thousand different sentiments, excited by the same object, are all right: Because no sentiment represents what is really in the object . . . [E]very individual ought to acquiesce in his own sentiment, without pretending to regulate those of others" (*MPL* 230). The search for a standard of taste attempts to answer the skeptic by locating "a rule, by which the various sentiments of men may be reconciled; at least, a decision, afforded, confirming one sentiment, and condemning another" (*MPL* 229).

In the course of the search for a standard of taste, the concept of taste underwent a transformation intimately related to the shift from sympathy to more active, intentional moral capacities which I am tracing in Hume's thought. While taste remains a capacity which is exercised immediately, it comes to be seen as an active rather than a passive faculty, and to encompass reflective elements that are rational in a broad sense. Walter Jackson Bate writes that "this moderately empirical conception of 'judgement,' with its varying nuances which its very indefiniteness admitted . . . took on as well a capacity for instinctive and immediate application which continental neo-classic rationalism had tended to divorce from abstract reason. The word 'taste' itself became broadened to include, not an unschooled and innately trustworthy feeling, but a far wider capacity of judgment, which is augmented and directed by experience and by learning, and which in time may acquire an almost intuitional sagacity in its objective insight."[3] Greater sensitivity to the pervasive influence of different contexts and points of view, which was encouraged by the empirical focus on audience reaction, remained a feature of this broader notion of "taste" or judgment, however, distinguishing it from rationalistic conceptions of ethical judgment.

What sort of response is an aesthetic judgment? Modern aesthetic orthodoxy insists on the distinction of aesthetic judgments from other sorts of judgments.[4] Jerome Stolnitz articulates this view when he argues that the autonomy of aesthetics which begins to take shape in the eighteenth century is one of the most important ideas separating modern from traditional aesthetics; it is an idea "now so much taken for granted that it seems almost banal to mention it, viz., that the work of art must be evaluated in respect of its intrinsic structure and significance, not as a moral vehicle or a source of knowledge. It is worth reminding ourselves that in traditional thought, moral edification, 'truth,' or the dignity of the 'real life' model 'imitated' in the work, legislate for the value of the art-object."[5]

Many eighteenth-century thinkers did not characterize the point of view of aesthetic evaluation by contrasting it with a moral point of view, but rather explored both in tandem in the course of their search for the standard of taste. The influence of Shaftesbury's notion of intuitive judgments of beauty can be discerned in many eighteenth-century attempts to think through the relationship between ethics and aesthetics, but his followers neglected his Neoplatonic vision of the grand harmony of the world and the soul, transforming his complex theory into the stripped-down notion that beauty and virtue are both matters of sense rather than reason, to be identified through their immediate pleasurable effect on the beholder.[6] Beauty and virtue coalesce, not because both are names for harmony in the world, but rather because both are distinguished from their opposites by the fact that they are "fitted to give a pleasure and satisfaction to the soul" (*T* 299). It is hardly surprising, therefore, to find Hume referring to virtue as "moral beauty" or "beauty of the mind," just as he refers to "natural beauty" or "beauty of the body" (*T* 300; *E* 265, 244). Of course, not every eighteenth-century thinker who was interested in taste was convinced that beauty and virtue were so similar. Edmund Burke, for example, claimed insistently that morals were *not* a matter of taste, but rather of reason. Taste he restricted to the realm of aesthetic judgment, writing that "I mean by the word Taste no more than that faculty, or those faculties of the mind which are affected with, or which form a judgment of the works of imagination and the elegant arts."[7] For Hume, however, taste refers to ethical as well as aesthetic judgment (*E* 165), and both have need of a standard by which to judge sentiment.

Whereas some thinkers, such as Kames and Blair, thought that if the imagination was not absorbed in the object and dominated by passion, it became a mere spectator who could not give a vivid representation, but only a description, Hume, as I shall argue in this chapter, suggests that it is the spectator's perspicuous description which alone makes understanding possible.[8] Hume's spectator does not futilely try to deny his or her exteriority. According to Leo Braudy, Hume's ideal history readers are those "who can view the events of history with detachment and sympathy."[9] Insofar as "detachment" is characteristic of all judgments of taste, it is not the sense of unreality characteristic of immediate pleasure in poetry, but rather a heightened degree of reflexivity. When it comes to evaluation, it is not enough to be a passive feeler, absorbed in the spectacle; we must become observers of the immediate emotional effects of a work on us. This heightened reflexivity loosens us from our private interests and prejudices; it need not unhook ethical reflection and responsibility. Disinterestedness was pursued not in order to eliminate moral concerns from the realm of art, but rather in order clearly to define the point of view of the beholder, eliminating private idiosyncrasies and prejudices in order to make agreement possible, both in aesthetic and in ethical judgments.

Although Hume does not explicitly invoke the notion of sympathy in his essay "Of the standard of taste," it is here and in a few related writings I will be discussing in this chapter that I find the further development of the sympathetic understanding which was adumbrated in the *Treatise*. We begin to encounter, as one of the central characteristics of good judgment, a capacity akin to extensive sympathy. Like extensive sympathy, it possesses a lively appreciation of all the details and circumstances of others' situations, but it exceeds the scope of extensive sympathy by reaching beyond prior affinities to alien points of view. Finding a standard of taste therefore involves discussing the "correction" of sympathetic sentiments, or, perhaps more precisely, articulating the need for a particular sort of sympathetic activity.

In order to sharpen the outlines of the Humean form of sympathetic understanding, I contrast it with concurrently emerging Romantic notions of the projective sympathetic imagination and from Adam Smith's theory of sympathy. In Humean sympathetic understanding, unlike these other forms, a spectator or judge recognizes and seeks to understand those who differ from him- or herself without either dismissing the other persons as incomprehensible or ending up in an extreme skepticism or (what we would call) relativism that simply acquiesces in the other's own self-evaluation. Good judgment cannot simply take into account the pleasures and pains of others; the need to evaluate works of art written by and for distant cultures and societies makes clear the importance of understanding others' beliefs, goals, desires, and self-understanding as well. My discussion of the significance of Hume's focus on assuming foreign points of view highlights its affinities with the hermeneutic notion of *Verstehen*. A full exploration of this connection lies beyond the scope of this work. I do hope, however, that discerning the outlines of an active form of sympathetic understanding in Hume's thought will add complexity to our picture of eighteenth-century conceptions of sympathy.

This chapter also explores the links between Hume's advocacy of sympathetic understanding of foreign points of view and his continuing assault on Scottish Evangelicals. Evangelicals epitomize for Hume the moral dangers inherent in an approach which tries artificially to derive or deduce ethical standards (or aesthetic rules), whether from a speculative religious system or through a priori reason. Within Hume's moral universe, in contrast, we must always begin with historically contingent standards which we encounter in our social world, even if we can then go on to criticize these standards. Hume argues that the artificiality of religious morals renders them inaccessible to sympathetic understanding, but we shall have reason to be suspicious of the way Hume tries to draw a priori limits to the extent of this sympathetic capacity.

In the *Treatise* and the *Enquiry Concerning the Principles of Morals*, Hume explores the phenomenon of moral evaluation without directly addressing moral disagreement and hence without raising the problem of the standard of taste. He discusses variations in sympathy, but not in moral judgments, and he implies that sympathy is automatically corrected as conflicting viewpoints bump up against one another in the course of social interaction. In these early works, as I have indicated, Hume's account of the development of the capacity for moral evaluation aims at pure description. But he can pretend to be describing a natural, universal process of moral development only because he overlooks the existing variety of moral sentiments and the lack of agreement in moral evaluations. When he does allude to the problem of the standard of taste, it is only to dismiss it as a pseudo-problem. So, for example, he writes in a footnote of the *Treatise* that "in what sense we can talk either of a right or a wrong taste in morals, eloquence, or beauty, shall be consider'd afterwards. In the mean time, it may be observ'd, that there is such an uniformity in the *general* sentiments of mankind, as to render such questions of but small importance" (*T* 547n). No standard for taste is needed if no disagreement in taste is recognized.

When Hume finally returns to the subject in "Of the standard of taste," however, he seems disposed to take disagreement much more seriously. Now he claims that uniformity in *general* sentiments is misleading, because "when critics come to particulars, this seeming unanimity vanishes; and it is found, that they had affixed a very different meaning to their expressions" (*MPL* 227). He points out subtle differences in taste noticeable within small circles of close friends as well as greater differences which strike us when we consider the long ago or far away – hence, the need for a standard of taste is now apparent. His account becomes openly normative, not in the sense of providing a general formula which when applied will deliver correct moral judgments in particular cases, but in the sense of attempting to characterize the nature of *good* judgment. The relevant contrast is not between descriptive and normative accounts, since what Hume offers here, too, is a sort of description, though one which acknowledges that not all judgment is automatically good and which takes this fact to be relevant to the task of description.[10] Hume draws our attention to the things which distinguish good taste from bad, and the nature of his account leaves room for intentional efforts to develop better judgment, since he does not conclude that good taste is solely a result of genetic endowment, social circumstances, or other forms of luck. We can call his account a normative description, even if that seems at first glance to be an oxymoronic expression.

In the introductory paragraphs of the essay "Of the standard of taste," Hume seems eager to make his remarks applicable to both morals and criticism, since both, he says, are founded on sentiment rather than abstract reason and have a tendency to cloak disagreement by using "thin" normative terms which seem universally applicable until they are filled out with a more particular "thick description."[11] Yet, once he has defined the object of his search, the standard of taste, he confines himself to the criticism of poetry, and the field of morals is not allowed to appear overtly again until the final pages of the essay. Reflections on moral disagreements, closely linked with reflections on religious intolerance, form a frame for reflection on a standard for aesthetic judgments. Later in this chapter, I return to consider the significance of this frame, but for the time being I take up in some detail Hume's discussion of taste in the field of criticism, highlighting similarities and differences between the account of taste and his account of moral evaluation in the *Treatise*.

Hume begins by rejecting the relativism about sentiments which the extreme skeptic professes. Hume's notoriety as a skeptic might have led many of his readers to expect him to embrace this position, so he is careful to distance himself from it at the outset. Not all sentiments are on an equal footing, although we can afford to pretend that they are when considering insignificant differences in taste. Hume is confident that "whoever would assert an equality of genius and elegance between OGILBY and MILTON, or BUNYAN and ADDISON, would be thought to defend no less an extravagance, than if he had maintained a mole-hill to be as high as TENERIFE, or a pond as extensive as the ocean. Though there may be found persons, who give the preference to the former authors; no one pays attention to such a taste; and we pronounce without scruple the sentiment of these pretended critics to be absurd and ridiculous" (*MPL* 230–231). Hume is not attempting to give an account of differences in aesthetic judgment while remaining neutral among them; he speaks unabashedly from his own viewpoint and his own substantive critical judgments. One does not develop a standard by starting from nowhere, but by beginning in one's own location and critically reflecting on it.

Disagreements in taste cannot be resolved by deducing rules of composition a priori; such a rationalistic procedure would only manage "to reduce every expression to geometrical truth and exactness," with a highly artificial, wooden result which "has been found the most insipid and disagreeable" (*MPL* 231). Such rules as there are, are nothing "but general observations, concerning what has been universally found to please in all countries and in all ages" (*MPL* 231). Here Hume seems momentarily to slip back into the idiom of the *Treatise* and the *Enquiries*, simply denying disagreement and dissolving, rather than solving, the problem of the standard of taste. If there really *is* disagreement, then someone's taste is being excluded from the scope of "universal" agreement about what pleases. But Hume goes on to clarify his claim by saying that "we must not imagine, that, on every occasion, the feelings of men will be conformable to these rules" (*MPL* 232). Only certain responses to poetry count and are tallied up with the general observations of mankind – the circumstances and the disposition of the mind must be just right. Hume does not simply overlook observers whose substantive judgments disagree with his, therefore. Rather, what he is groping after are the aesthetic attitudes or points of view which are characteristic of the qualified observer.

Hume's attempt to define the standard of taste is a restatement and further elaboration of his *Treatise* account of the way variations in sympathy are corrected by distancing oneself from one's own interested and prejudiced viewpoint and assuming more stable and general points of view. The extensive parallels between these two accounts provide crucial support for the claim that there is a continuing role for sympathetic capacities in Hume's later writings, despite the fact that the term "sympathy" fades into the background. At the same time, there are important differences between the *Treatise* account of the correction of sympathy and the later account of the standard of taste. In the *Treatise*, Hume maintained that a steady and general point of view emerges naturally and automatically as an equilibration of our experiences of contradictions between our views and those of others, as well as between our views at one moment and at another (although as I argued in chapter 2, certain strands of his discussion press in the direction of a more intentional or active understanding of this process). In "Of the standard of taste," in contrast, Hume treats critical judgment as an activity which requires the exertion of effort in taking up an appropriate point of view, and which may be developed and refined with practice and attention. When we "would try the force of any beauty or deformity," for example, "we must choose with care a proper time and place, and bring the fancy to a suitable situation and disposition. A perfect serenity of mind, a recollection of thought, a due attention to the object; if any of these circumstances be wanting, our experiment will be fallacious, and we shall be unable to judge of the catholic and universal beauty" (*MPL* 232–233).[12]

The admission of reflective faculties into the realm of taste and sentiment is already marked in the *Enquiry Concerning the Principles of Morals* by the conciliatory claim that "*reason* and *sentiment* concur in almost all moral determinations and conclusions." In order to pave the way for proper moral judgment, he continues:

It is often necessary, we find, that much reasoning should precede, that nice distinctions be made, just conclusions drawn, distant comparisons formed, complicated relations examined, and general facts fixed and ascertained ... [I]n many orders of beauty, particularly those of the finer arts, it is requisite to employ much reasoning, in order to feel the proper sentiment; and a false relish may frequently be corrected by argument and reflection. (*E* 172–173)

In this attempt to unite reason and sentiment in taste, Hume backs away from the wholehearted antirationalism of the Abbé Dubos, to whose influential work "Of the standard of taste" is in other respects quite indebted. Dubos held that "if there is any subject, in which reason ought to be silent when opposed to experience, 'tis certainly in those questions which may be raised concerning the merit of a poem. 'Tis when we want to know, whether a poem pleases or not; whether generally speaking, it be an excellent or indifferent performance."[13] According to Dubos, "the way of discussion and analysis . . . is indeed very proper, when the point is to find out the causes why a work pleases or not, but this method is inferior to that of the sense, when we are to decide the following questions: Does the work please, or does it not? Is the piece good or bad in general? For these are both the same thing."[14] Hume's critical writings rehabilitate "the way of discussion and analysis" while preserving a central role for feeling and sentiment. Bate's description of late eighteenth-century British associationists' notion of the faculty of imagination is equally true of Hume's understanding of judgment; "whatever is gained from such conscious efforts – if the gain is to be made essential and intrinsic – becomes ultimately a part of the unconscious mind, and is thus capable of being utilized with instinctive immediacy."[15] Moreover, since it "is founded directly upon an associational union and concert of many aspects or 'faculties' of thought, it is able to bring the mind to focus, as it were, from several positions at once," and is therefore not only regarded as more immediate, but also as more comprehensive and more able to deal with flux and change than is abstract reason.[16] Hume seeks to preserve the concreteness and immediacy of judgment while allowing some room in it for active reflection.

　　Why not read Hume simply as elaborating the conditions under which the right response is obtained while stressing that the actual judgment of taste is purely a matter of feeling, akin to the deliveries of a moral sense? As in my chapter 2 discussion of the differences between Hume and

Hutcheson on the moral sense, my concern here is not so much with Hume's intentions, but with what is really doing the work in Hume's account. Once again, it seems to me that if we look at what is pulling full weight in Hume's account, it is not a special faculty, a "sense" of taste, but the "nice distinctions" and "distant comparisons," the intentional, in a broad sense rational, activities of the judge.[17] The immediate relish or revulsion is just as likely to be false as true. This will, I hope, become more clear in the course of discussing "Of the standard of taste."

As in his discussion of moral sentiment, Hume insists that "some particular forms or qualities, from the original structure of the internal fabric, are calculated to please, and others to displease" (*MPL* 233). In particular instances, however, they may fail to have the expected effect. The reason Hume gives for this failure is "some apparent defect or imperfection in the organ." He compares aesthetic taste with the organs of external sense – taste-buds and eyes – which are affected by the health of the organism. A judgment rendered by someone whose organs are diseased is rightly disregarded. Hence, the description of the sound state of the organ becomes crucial to arriving at the true standard of taste. Perception may be distorted not only by internal defects, but also by external circumstances, in which case the defect in the sense organ is really only "apparent." Hume recognizes this distinction, for he says not only that "many and frequent are the defects in the internal organs, which prevent or weaken the influence of those general principles, on which depends our sentiment of beauty or deformity," but also that "particular incidents and situations occur, which either throw a false light on the objects, or hinder the true from conveying to the imagination the proper sentiment and perception" (*MPL* 234). But, after enumerating the characteristics of the true critic, one whose "organ of taste" is in good health, he mentions two sources of variation which do not stem from defects in taste; one due to differences in "internal frame," the other to differences in "external situation" (*MPL* 244). These are "the different humours of particular men" and "the particular manners and opinions of our own age and country" (*MPL* 243). In practice, therefore, the important distinction is not between internal defect and external distortion (which turn out to be impossible to distinguish from one another, since we cannot distinguish what is really "internal" from the external forces which shape or create it) but rather between differences in judgment which reflect good or bad taste and differences to which the true standard of taste should remain neutral.

Before confronting these differences of judgment directly, it is worth discussing the five characteristics of the true critic, in order to situate Hume both against his earlier account of moral judgment and against contemporary understandings of critical appraisal. The first defect in taste which results in failure to feel the proper sentiment of beauty is "the want of that delicacy of imagination which is requisite to convey a sensibility of those finer emotions" (*MPL* 234). Delicacy involves the ability to "perceive every ingredient in the composition" (*MPL* 235), to separate out every beauty or deformity, every excellence or blemish, in a work, no matter how minute nor how mixed up with one another they are. Hume conceives of delicacy of taste as one of those virtues which are qualities immediately agreeable to ourselves, for he maintains that this taste "must always be a desirable quality; because it is the source of all the finest and most innocent enjoyments, of which human nature is susceptible . . . Wherever you can ascertain a delicacy of taste, it is sure to meet with approbation" (*MPL* 237). In a person with such taste "the perfection of the man, and the perfection of the sense or feeling, are found to be united" (*MPL* 236). Does Hume mean to suggest not only that delicacy of taste is always regarded as an element worthy of approbation, but also that taste cannot be perfected without perfecting one's other virtues? While this view would contrast with the one in the *Treatise*, which suggested that the capacity for proper moral judgment may exist in a less-than-virtuous character (*T* 583), such a change in view would be consonant with the overall shift from a descriptive account which disregards differences in judgment if not differences in actual character to a normative account which recognizes and attempts to resolve disagreement. If the capacity for proper moral or critical discernment or judgment is held to be universal, as in the *Treatise*, then of course the capacity for such discernment must not require the perfection of all other virtues. If the unity of the virtues had been insisted on in the earlier work, vice would have been conjured wholly out of existence. In "Of the standard of taste," in contrast, the virtues are linked together, while the claim that good taste is universal is abandoned.

Hume conforms to dominant eighteenth-century conceptions of taste in regarding delicacy of taste, like the sensitivity of sense organs, as part of a person's natural endowment, but he modifies this view substantially by refusing to treat the degree of delicacy as something fixed once and for all in each individual. When he considers this issue, rather, he switches from the metaphor of sense organs to that of talents which must be cultivated if they are to be of any worth, claiming that "though there be naturally a wide difference in point of delicacy between one person and another, nothing tends further to encrease and improve this talent, than *practice* in a particular art, and the frequent survey or contemplation of a particular species of beauty" (*MPL* 237). In insisting on a positive role for practice, Hume takes a stand in the debate, alluded to in the last chapter, over whether aesthetic responses are blunted by overexposure or strengthened by practice. Dubos, for one, had worried that the delicate nervous sensibility requisite for judgments of taste was highly susceptible to damage. Since Dubos regarded aesthetic judgments solely as a matter of passive receptivity and immediate feeling, practice could contribute nothing positive to countervail what he saw as the inevitable deadening of sensitivity. Only if some active discernment is involved, as Hume here claims, can practice be regarded as valuable.

Hume suggests that the value of practice is evident even when a single work is concerned; multiple attempts to assess a work will refine our judgment of it. This is because "there is a flutter or hurry of thought which attends the first perusal of any piece, and which confounds the genuine sentiment of beauty" (*MPL* 238). This is reminiscent of his insistence, quoted previously, on the importance of bringing "the fancy to a suitable situation and disposition" in order to ensure, among other things, "a perfect serenity of mind" (*MPL* 232). It also echoes Dubos' suggestion that "to be a good spectator, one must have that peace of mind, which rises not from the exhausting, but from the serenity of the imagination."[18] The danger to judgment stems from the risk that our senses will be "seduced by pleasure. The more a work pleases, the less we are capable of detecting and computing its faults."[19] Dubos had wavered on this question, however, for he also writes that the works of the masters must not be judged coldly; had a judge "that vivacity and delicacy of sentiment, which are the inseparable companions of genius, he would be so struck with the beauties of celebrated pieces, that he would fling away his scales and compasses to judge of them, as other people have always done, that is, by the impression made by those works."[20] The latter view seems more consistent with Dubos' thoroughgoing sentimentalism. What is the danger of being seduced by pleasure if the question of what pleases and the question of what is a good work of art are the same? There is tension between the sentimentalist belief that a good work of art is one which is able to move and touch the soul, and the nagging worry that good judgment is impaired when one is carried away by a spectacle. Hume's resolution of this problem leads him away from the simple equation of the good work of art with that which pleases. It also plays a role, as we shall see, in Hume's preference for history over poetry.

The third requirement of good taste is the ability to form comparisons among different works and different kinds of works of art. Only this allows us to assign a work to its proper rank. Even primitive or vulgar works contain elements which please and are therefore beautiful, but the low degree or lack of delicacy of these elements will become apparent only when we have something with which to contrast them. "The coarsest daubing contains a certain lustre of colours and exactness of imitation, which are so far beauties, and would affect the mind of a peasant or Indian with the highest admiration" (*MPL* 238). "Peasants" and "Indians" have not been able to benefit from the comparison of their works of art with those of ancient Greece or modern Europe. Here Hume assumes that the same basic elements are felt to be beautiful by all – lustre of colour, exactness of imitation, harmony, etc. He does not entertain the possibility that the taste of an Indian might be radically different, so that he or she might point to dull colors or dissonance and discord as reasons for the beauty of something. While Hume's assumptions about what may be considered beautiful seem somewhat parochial, some sort of coincidence or overlap in taste does seem necessary, for, if disagreement went all the way down, we would not take the Indian or peasant to be talking about what is "beautiful" at all, but would seek for a translation which would be a better match for one or more of our other concepts.

The good critic must also

> preserve his mind free from all *prejudice*, and allow nothing to enter into his consideration, but the very object which is submitted to his examination. We may observe, that every work of art, in order to produce its due effect on the mind, must be surveyed in a certain point of view, and cannot be fully relished by persons, whose situation, real or imaginary, is not conformable to that which is required by the performance. (*MPL* 239)[21]

What "situation," then, is required by the performance? Hume seems to have two different sorts of things in mind. First, if I stand in some special relationship to the author or the work, I must endeavor to set aside that relationship, or else it will affect my response to the work. "When any work is addressed to the public," for example, "though I should have a friendship or enmity with the author, I must depart from this situation; and considering myself as a man in general, forget, if possible, my individual being and my peculiar circumstances" (*MPL* 239). The critic must be disinterested insofar as he "forgets his interest as a friend or enemy, as a rival or commentator" (*MPL* 239). Second, although Hume urges the critic to consider himself as "a man in general," this apparently does not mean that the critic achieves a sort of "view from nowhere," or even a single location from which any work may be evaluated, for Hume also insists that "a critic of a different age or nation . . . must place himself in the same situation as the audience, in order to form a true judgment of the oration" (*MPL* 239). The person of prejudice, in contrast, "obstinately maintains his natural position, without placing himself in that point of view, which the performance presupposes. If the work be addressed to persons of a different age or nation, he makes no allowance for their peculiar views and prejudices; but, full of the manners of his own age and country, rashly condemns what seemed admirable in the eyes of those for whom alone the discourse was calculated" (*MPL* 239). The critic must not only free himself from the particularity of his own point of view, but must also enter into the point of view of the audience for which the work was originally intended.

This discussion of "prejudice" recalls the *Treatise* account of the way in which sympathy and its correction creates the possibility of proper moral evaluation. In both cases, our tastes are based on our sentiments, but the development of a standard of taste or judgment requires the correction of these sentiments as we strive to achieve a more steady and general point of view. In both cases, the inevitable multiplicity of points of view threatens agreement in judgments – "every particular man has a peculiar position with regard to others; and 'tis impossible we cou'd ever converse together on any reasonable terms, were each of us to consider characters and persons, only as they appear from his peculiar point of view" (*T* 581–582). The solution to this problem lies in the assumption of a special point of view which is particularly suited to the situation in question. In effect, the sentiments of immediate sympathy are displaced by a new, intentional form of sympathetic understanding of other points of view. In both "Of the standard of taste" and the *Treatise* discussion of point of view, moreover, the critical point of view is not a fixed point which can be determined once and for all a priori, for Hume simultaneously presses for a viewpoint of "a man in general" and for sympathy with concrete and particular viewpoints which are not one's own but which are especially relevant to judgment in the case under consideration. It is not simply that we must forget our own interests and take up viewpoints which are foreign to us, for these foreign viewpoints are not a single final viewpoint from which judgment is made. They are perspectives which we must appreciate before arriving at final judgment, but good judgment must consider them along with other considerations. Just as my responses to a number of sympathetic pains and pleasures must be balanced against one another before I finally approve or disapprove, my sympathetic assumption of the point of view of a warrior in an honor-based society will help me appreciate the original fascination of the *Iliad*, but my final judgment will also take into account the whole range of my own beliefs about what makes a poem (and a life) great. Hume never gives a formula for weighing these different viewpoints against one another; there is a gap here which can only be filled in concrete cases by practical judgment, not in advance by some sort of general rule.

By describing variation in critical judgment as a result of prejudice, Hume is able to imply that our "natural" sentiments are those of the critical point of view, whereas prejudice distorts the natural play of sentiments. He writes, for example, that "it is well known, that in all questions, submitted to the understanding, prejudice is destructive of sound judgment, and perverts all operations of the intellectual faculties: It is no less contrary to good taste; nor has it less influence to corrupt our sentiment of beauty" (*MPL* 240). Similarly, he suggests that where the critic "lies under the influence of prejudice, all his natural sentiments are perverted" (*MPL* 241). By labeling our unreflective personal viewpoint one of distortion, Hume reserves the term "natural" for *good* taste. We must clear obstacles away from the path of aesthetic judgment, but the genuine and proper sentiments of beauty are immediate and non-arti-factual.[22] Proper aesthetic sentiments are the sentiments felt "naturally" and "universally" by the unprejudiced observer, where naturalness and universality are terms of praise for such sentiments, though they appear in the guise of sources of the authority for them.[23]

For my purposes, however, what is perhaps of greatest significance in Hume's discussion of prejudice is the suggestion that one's own assumptions and manners may be inappropriate standards against which to judge the artistic productions of those of different ages or nations. This implies that not all differences carry normative weight; they should not always be regarded as better or worse. Moreover, an *active* effort is required to overcome prejudice; even if the correct sentiments come naturally to the unprejudiced person, one must work hard at being unprejudiced. I will return to this issue in what follows.

The final characteristic of the good critic is "good sense." Good sense allows the observer to perceive all the parts of a work and understand their relationships with one another. Good sense is also required to ascertain whether a work can attain the end for which it is calculated, and to judge whether the characters act in ways consistent with themselves. Here Hume lumps several neoclassical doctrines together, simply parroting standard views without bringing new insights to bear. In fact, he slips into claims which he is not in a very good position to defend, such as the statement that "where good sense is wanting," the critic "is not qualified to discern the beauties of design and reasoning, which are the highest and most excellent" (*MPL* 241). He says nothing to indicate why beauties of design and reasoning should be regarded as any higher or more excellent than any others, nor does he indicate what it means to say such a thing.

In the end, the true critic must be identified pragmatically – there is no failsafe seal of authenticity to look for. Hume seems to think that we are able to recognize beauty when it is pointed out to us even when we cannot discern it on our own.[24] When disagreement erupts, "men can do no more than in other disputable questions, which are submitted to the understanding: They must produce the best arguments, that their invention suggests to them; they must acknowledge a true and decisive standard to exist somewhere, to wit, real existence and matter of fact; and they must have indulgence to such as differ from them in their appeals to this standard" (*MPL* 242). Hume combines this insistence on the pursuit of truth with a faith that, when it comes to matters of sentiment, truth cannot be effaced as completely as in speculative matters, which are not rooted in concrete practices. Radical skepticism about our ability to discern true beauty or goodness is a nonsensical reaction to specific areas of disagreement in ethics or aesthetics, since disagreement only makes sense against a backdrop of agreement, and error against a background of truth without which these practices would break down and be incoherent.

Having discussed the prerequisites of good taste, Hume turns to consider differences in critical sentiments and judgments which cannot be settled by appeal to a single standard of taste. He identifies, as mentioned above, two sources of such variation – "the one is the different humours of particular men; the other, the particular manners and opinions of our age and country" (*MPL* 243). He labels the former a "diversity in the internal frame" and the latter a difference in "external situation" (*MPL* 244). They roughly coincide with what someone today might label differences in personality and differences in culture, although Hume also includes variations we find among different age groups. When it comes to these, the differences are "entirely blameless on both sides." It is inappropriate to speak of a "defect" or "perversion" of judgment. There is no reason for dispute, Hume argues, when there is no standard available for resolving the dispute, and this is the case when individual variations of temperament and personality are at issue. Differences in personality need not reflect differences in moral character.

This section of the essay deals with some of the same sources of disagreement treated earlier under the heading of "prejudice," but it makes no allusion to that discussion and puts a different spin on the issues. In discussing prejudice, Hume insisted on the necessity of putting oneself in the position of the intended audience, making allowances for their peculiar views and prejudices, in order to judge a work of art. The critic who fails to do so is influenced by prejudice and his or her judgments do not conform to the standard of taste. In this later section, in contrast, Hume describes these differences in situation not as sources of prejudice which require careful adjustment, but rather as natural differences which inevitably colour our appreciation of a work and which cannot be wholly expunged – "vainly would we, in such cases, endeavor to enter into the sentiments of others, and divest ourselves of those propensities, which are natural to us" (*MPL* 244). The inability to do so is not seen as a failure. The tension between the two sections can be relieved in part by recognizing that they are directed toward different concerns – we might say that while the earlier section stressed the necessity of sympathy with alien points of view, this section stresses the inevitable limits of such sympathetic efforts. Just as in the *Treatise* discussion of sympathy, Hume suggests that perceived similarities and felt affinities are bound to influence our passive aesthetic responses; "we choose our favourite author as we do our friend, from a conformity of humour and disposition. Mirth or passion, sentiment or reflection; whichever of these most predominates in our temper, it gives us a peculiar sympathy with the writer who resembles us" (*MPL* 244).

Yet Hume continues to insist, and more distinctly than in the *Treatise*, that we should somehow strive to enter into the viewpoints of others despite our natural predilections for the similar. Indeed, such efforts are required, not so that we will enjoy a work as much as the intended or "similar" audience, but so that we will not be caught in an error of judgment. We must resign ourselves to not sharing the intensity of their emotional response to the work, but we must strive to ensure that we do not mistake our own parochial responses to such works for judgments according to the universal standard of taste. As Hume says in the *Treatise*, "we sympathize more with persons contiguous to us, than with persons remote from us: With our acquaintance, than with strangers: With our countrymen, than with foreigners. But notwithstanding this variation of our sympathy, we give the same approbation to the same moral qualities in China as in England" (*T* 581). So in "Of the standard of taste," Hume writes that "it is not without some effort, that we reconcile ourselves to the simplicity of ancient manners, and behold princesses carrying water from the spring, and kings and heroes dressing their own victuals. We may allow in general, that the representation of such manners is no fault in the author, nor deformity in the piece; but we are not so sensibly touched with them" (*MPL* 245). In another example, modern Europeans will not be pleased by ancient plays in which the central female character never appears on stage, although "a man of learning and reflection can make allowances for these peculiarities of manners" (*MPL* 245). We have less immediate, passive sympathy with the ancients than with fellow moderns, but good judgment requires us to strive actively to enter into their situation, to attain a sympathetic understanding of their point of view.

Thus far, the most prominent difference between the account of the nature of judgments of taste given in the *Treatise* and that given in "Of the standard of taste" is that in the latter Hume acknowledges that the capacity for good judgment does not develop automatically, and that only a few individuals are likely to develop it fully. As the partial overlap between Hume's discussion of prejudice (which perverts one's taste) and of "innocent differences" (which affect one's taste but do not pervert it) indicates, Hume cannot quite make up his mind about how much to require from the critic or the standard of taste by way of impartiality and correcting for differences in point of view. The overall conclusion seems to be that judgments of taste should not precede active sympathetic understanding of alien points of view, although we must recognize that such understanding does not wholly displace our passive emotional reactions.

THE PROBLEM OF "VICIOUS MANNERS"

Despite the fact that the body of the essay "Of the standard of taste" confines itself to the area of criticism, up to this point the account has seemed applicable to both moral and aesthetic judgment. In fact, given that both beauty and virtue are defined by Hume as things which are pleasing to the spectator "upon the general view or survey," moral approbation of elements of a poetic work cannot be clearly distinguished from aesthetic appreciation of them. At the end of the essay, however, Hume reintroduces moral subjects in a way that implies that all he has said about correcting for alien points of view applies to poetry only when "innocent peculiarities of manners are represented" (*MPL* 245):

The poet's monument more durable than brass, must fall to the ground like common brick, or clay, were men to make no allowances for the continual revolution of manners and customs, and would admit of nothing but what was suitable to the prevailing fashion. Must we throw aside the pictures of our ancestors, because of their ruffs and farthingdales? But where the ideas of morality and decency alter from one age to another, and where vicious manners are described, without being marked with the proper characters of blame and disapprobation, this must be allowed to disfigure the poem, and to be a real deformity. I cannot, nor is it proper I should, enter into such sentiments; and however I may excuse the poet, on account of the manners of his age, I can never relish the composition. (*MPL* 246)

Does Hume mean to claim that when we perceive *moral* differences, it is inappropriate to try to identify with the point of view of the audience? Does this mean that our judgment of the work as morally (and therefore aesthetically) flawed precedes and precludes the act of sympathetic understanding? Would not this be a case of what Hume earlier called prejudice, of criticism which "rashly condemns what seemed admirable in the eyes of those for whom alone the discourse was calculated" (*MPL* 239) rather than appreciating their distinctive point of view?

Hume presents this caveat about moral differences as a solution to the longstanding Quarrel of the Ancients and Moderns, which stimulated reflection on the difficulty of justly evaluating the works of distant times and cultures. This quarrel associated aesthetic judgment with historical judgment in a way which gives further testimony to the fact that aesthetic evaluation was not clearly distinguished from ethical evaluation. Partisans of both ancients and moderns are guilty of excess, according to Hume, for "we often find the one side excusing any seeming absurdity in the ancients from the manners of the age, and the other refusing to admit this excuse, or at least, admitting it only as an apology for the author, not for the performance" (*MPL* 245).[25] Dubos, for example, a stalwart defender of the ancients, wrote that:

The prejudice therefore which the greatest part of mankind have for their own times and country, is a fertile source of false remarks as well as of wrong judgments. They take what is practised there for a rule of what ought to be always and everywhere observed. And yet there is only a small number of customs, or even of virtues and vices, that have been praised or condemned in all times and countries. Now poets are in the right to practise what Quintilian advises orators, which is to draw their advantages from the ideas of those for whom they compose, and to conform to them. Wherefore we should transform ourselves, as it were, into those for whom the poem was written, if we intend to form a sound judgment of its images, figures and sentiments. The Parthian, who after being repulsed in the first charge, flies back full gallop . . . ought not to be looked upon as guilty of cowardice; because this manner of fighting was authorized by the military discipline of that nation, founded on the idea they had of courage and real valour. (II, 393)

Dubos, then, explicitly advocates sympathetic identification (or something more mysterious – "transformation") even when it comes to alien virtues and vices. He also assumes that our own moral beliefs are wholly irrelevant to our consideration of the Parthian. Only Parthian moral beliefs are relevant to our judgment of his character (for Dubos moves from talking of our judgment of the poetic work in which the soldier makes his energetic retreat to talking of our judgment of his character). Dubos embraces a sort of moral relativism, at least when it comes to considering the poetry of the ancients.[26] To be sure, we judge the Parthian soldier, not according to his own private evaluation of himself, but according to the moral standards operative in his culture. Dubos is not a skeptic; he does not consider all subjective preferences to be equally valid. But he does imply that the moral standards of a given cultural-historical context should determine our own evaluation, not simply be important information about whether the Parthian's moral beliefs were justified given his context. Dubos' remarks indicate that he regards moral truth, not merely justification, as context-relative. Hume's comments may be read as a reaction against the moral relativism which accompanied attempts, such as that of Dubos, to defend the ancients at all costs. But must Hume undermine his own conviction of the importance to judgment of sympathetic understanding of alien points of view in order to stave off moral relativism? Must he make a sharp distinction between the way in which we evaluate aesthetic and moral features of a work?

One thinker who took such an approach in order to avoid relativism in morals was Edmund Burke, whose response to "Of the standard of taste" appeared in the second edition of *Of the Sublime and the Beautiful*.[27] In some respects, Burke sounds much like Hume, as when he suggests that defects in taste arise most commonly "from a want of proper and well-directed exercise, which alone can make it strong and ready. Besides that ignorance, inattention, prejudice, rashness, levity, obstinacy, in short, all those passions, and all those vices which pervert the judgment in other matters, prejudice it no less in this its more refined and elegant province." But Burke, unlike Hume, follows the rationalist neoclassicists in drawing a sharp distinction between two components of taste – imagination and judgment.[28] He assumes that "the imagination is . . . affected according to some invariable and certain laws,"[29] and hence that "so far then as Taste belongs to the imagination, its principle is the same in all men; there is no difference in the manner of their being affected, nor in the causes of the affection."[30] The fact that we do not find universal agreement in taste is due to the fact that works of art do not merely affect the imagination. Rather, "as many of the works of imagination are not confined to the representation of sensible objects, nor to efforts upon the passions, but extend themselves to the manners, the characters, the actions, and designs of men, their relations, their virtues and vices, they come within the province of the judgment, which is improved by attention and by the habit of reasoning."[31] Where moral matters are concerned, a wholly different faculty, judgment, is brought into play. For Hume, in contrast, judgment does not operate separately from feeling; rather, the possibility of good judgment is created by achieving a point of view from which our feelings and responses reflect proper judgment rather than personal prejudice or blind provincialism. Both our rational and our emotional capacities are employed in the process of interpretation, reflection, and judgment. It is not through reason alone that we attain sympathetic understanding of others, because sympathetic understanding has everything to do with desires and ends and creaturely responses. Although "Of the standard of taste" makes clear that judgments of taste are not a matter of simple feeling, Hume would never conclude with Burke that "so far as the imagination and passions are concerned, I believe it is true, that the reason is little consulted; but where disposition, where decorum, where congruity are concerned, in short wherever the best Taste differs from the worst, I am convinced that the understanding operates and nothing else."[32]

It would be a mistake, I think, to conclude that Hume is now contradicting his earlier account of moral and aesthetic judgment and erecting at this juncture a Burkean barrier against moral skepticism and relativism. Hume does not say that it is impossible and improper to try to enter into the alien *point of view*, but rather that "I cannot, nor is it proper I should, enter into such *sentiments*" (my emphasis). Sentiment is always a slippery word, as I have earlier indicated, but here I take it to refer to the moral beliefs of the poet. To enter into the sentiments expressed in the poem would be to share the moral *judgments* of the poet. Sympathetic appreciation for the poet's point of view does not, however, require us to give up our own moral beliefs and accept those of the poet. The fact that we "excuse the poet, on account of the manners of his age" or grant him some indulgence "on account of his prejudices" (*MPL* 246) already indicates that we are sensitive to his point of view; we recognize that, given his context, he was justified in holding the moral beliefs he held.[33] We have not neglected to make sense of his moral reactions. Hume's claim that we do not embrace what we judge to be vicious moral sentiments in evaluating a work does not, therefore, amount to an attempt to create a sharp distinction between the way in which we approach foreign morals and manners in a work and the way in which we approach other features of a work.

While this section of "Of the standard of taste" does not contradict what Hume has said earlier in the essay and in the *Treatise* about the importance of active sympathetic appreciation of foreign points of view, it does suggest that the potential for moral transformation inherent in these acts of sympathy is severely limited. Our moral beliefs seem to be so entrenched that they are immune to any real challenge arising from our attempts to grapple with difference. He contrasts speculative opinions with moral principles, saying that:

There needs but a certain turn of thought or imagination to make us enter into all the opinions, which then prevailed, and relish the sentiments or conclusions derived from them. But a very violent effort is requisite to change our judgment of manners, and excite sentiments of approbation or blame, love or hatred, different from those to which the mind from long custom has been familiarised. And where a man is confident of the rectitude of that moral standard, by which he judges, he is justly jealous of it, and will not pervert the sentiments of his heart for a moment, in complaisance to any writer whatsoever. (*MPL* 247)

Hume regards the inherent conservatism of moral beliefs as something positive – it provides a measure of security against efforts to introduce radical reforms by making morals conform to speculative principles. Such efforts would be radically destabilizing and most probably pernicious.[34] But there is also a downside to this conservatism, at least as it is characterized above, for it seems to leave no chance that our encounter with difference could give us any unexpected moral insights, or make us realize the falsity of any of our moral beliefs.

If we turn, however, to "A dialogue," the short piece appended to the *Enquiry*, we find Hume reaching quite different conclusions about the morally transformative possibilities of sympathy with alien points of view. "A dialogue" purports to be an account of a conversation between the well-traveled and well-educated Palamedes and the author Hume. Palamedes describes his experiences in the country Fourli, where the inhabitants are civilized and intelligent, but hold radically unfamiliar moral beliefs. They are in favor of homosexual liaisons and incest, do not value marital fidelity, are indifferent to insults to their honor, and praise parricide, instances of treachery and assassination, and suicide. Hume initially expresses disbelief; "such barbarous and savage manners are not only incompatible with a civilized, intelligent people, such as you said these were; but are scarcely compatible with human nature" (*E* 328).

Hume exclaims that he can hardly conceive of the possibility of such a people, and he calls their manners "barbarous" and "savage," that is, hardly recognizable as human.[35]

Palamedes then reveals that he has been talking all along about the Ancients, and he proceeds to give specific instances of the sorts of behavior he had described, from the assassination of Caesar to the meekness of Themistocles. Hume responds by evoking, as he does in "Of the standard of taste," the Quarrel of the Ancients and Moderns, here extending it specifically to the field of morals. Hume accuses Palamedes of being "the only man I ever knew who was acquainted with the ancients, and did not extremely admire them. But instead of attacking their philosophy, their eloquence, or poetry, the usual subjects of controversy between us, you now seem to impeach their morals, and accuse them of ignorance in a science, which is the only one, in my opinion, in which they are not surpassed by the moderns" (*E* 330). Hume complains that "your representation of things is fallacious. You have no indulgence for the manners and customs of different ages. Would you try a Greek or Roman by the common law of England? Hear him defend himself by his own maxims; and then pronounce" (*E* 330). It is clear here, as it perhaps was not in "Of the standard of taste," that attempts to sympathetically identify with alien points of view may in fact have an influence on our moral evaluations of others' actions.

Hume's first objection is that Palamedes has not given a just description of the Athenians and their practices. He did not mention, for instance, that Caesar was a usurper. It is easy to make manners look despicable by describing them in one way rather than another, "especially, if you employ a little art or eloquence, in aggravating some circumstances, and extenuating others, as best suits the purpose of your discourse" (E 330). This Hume illustrates by describing French manners in a way which makes them appear equally odious. His preoccupation with description reveals an awareness that "the critical problem of understanding already arises at the level of observation and description . . . of identifying or describing a series of movements as an action of a certain sort."[36]

Palamedes is delighted, rather than dismayed, by Hume's facility at redescription, and now reveals himself as what Hume would consider an extreme skeptic: "I had no intention of exalting the moderns at the expence of the ancients. I only meant to represent the uncertainty of all these judgments concerning characters; and to convince you, that fashion, vogue, custom, and law, were the chief foundation of all moral determinations" (*E* 333). Like the extreme skeptic who appears in "Of the standard of taste," Palamedes questions the very possibility of fixed standards in this realm. "What wide difference . . . in the sentiments of morals, must be found between civilized nations and Barbarians, or between nations whose characters have little in common? How shall we pretend to fix a standard for judgments of this nature?" (*E* 333).

Hume, however, is unwilling to surrender to relativism. He suggests, rather, that a standard can be found "by tracing matters . . . a little higher, and examining the first principles, which each nation establishes, of blame and censure. The Rhine flows north, the Rhone south; yet both spring from the same mountain, and are also actuated, in their opposite directions, by the same principle of gravity. The different inclinations of the ground, on which they run, cause all the differences of their courses" (*E* 333). The same underlying principles can account for very different sorts of things, given different contexts. This suggestion is in line with Hume's endeavor to develop a "science of man" which accounts for the wide diversity of human phenomena by reference to the smallest possible number of basic phenomena. Hume goes on to reiterate his claim that "there never was any quality recommended by any one, as a virtue or moral excellence, but on account of its being useful, or agreeable to a man himself, or to others" (*E* 336). Differences in morals are to be explained by differences in point of view; they "may be reduced to this one general foundation, and may be accounted for by the different views, which people take of these circumstances" (*E* 336). People may have different beliefs about what is useful, or their differing circumstances may render different things useful.

Does this imply that Hume's solution to the threat of relativism is just a barefaced re-assertion of the uniformity of human nature which accounts for and excuses all differences in ethical judgment by reference to differences of cultural context? There is a long-standing dispute over whether Hume believed in a uniform, unchanging human nature and was therefore blind to radical cultural and ethical differences, or whether Hume was actually a cultural or moral relativist, very sensitive to differences in manners and inclined to excuse them.[37] This antithesis is much too stark, however, for the uniformity of human nature is not for Hume a substantial constant content, but rather a formal principle of hermeneutic charity, while his "relativism" recognizes the importance of context by allowing judgments which regard the moral beliefs of others as justified but false.[38]

Just as Hume's theory, as presented in the *Treatise*, does not give us an exhaustive decision procedure to follow in deciding how to act, it also does not constitute a theory according to which we could assemble a list of virtues, given appropriate information about an alien context or point of view. The theory is so general, and what might possibly be regarded as useful or agreeable so various, that it does not really even paint more than the barest sketch of a universal human nature underlying all apparent differences. This is equally true of the oft-cited passage from the *Enquiry*, where Hume claims that "there is a great uniformity among the actions of men, in all nations and ages, and that human nature remains still the same, in its principles and operations . . . Would you know the sentiments, inclinations, and course of life of the Greeks and Romans? Study well the temper and actions of the French and English: You cannot be much mistaken in transferring to the former *most* of the observations which you have made with regard to the latter" (*E* 83; emphasis in original). On the next (and less-cited) page, which is reminiscent of Hume's discussion with Palamedes in "A dialogue," it becomes clear that this "uniformity" of human nature exerts only minimal constraints on the conceivable (and possible) range of difference:

Should a traveller, returning from a far country, bring us an account of men, wholly different from any with whom we were ever acquainted; men, who were entirely divested of avarice, ambition, or revenge; who knew no pleasure but friendship, generosity, and public spirit; we should immediately, from these circumstances, detect the falsehood, and prove him a liar . . . And if we would explode any forgery in history, we cannot make use of a more convincing argument, than to prove, that the actions ascribed to any person are directly contrary to the force of nature, and that no human motives, in such circumstances, could ever induce him to such a conduct. (*E* 84)

If we were told that these aliens praised everything we condemned, and condemned everything we praised, we might well conclude that we had misunderstood what was meant by praise and condemnation. Had Hume insisted on a full-blown universal human nature, he would have restored the universal scope of moral judgment, but on a purely contingent basis. On my reading, what Hume's theory gives him is rather a hermeneutic of charity.[39]

When we are confronted by those who hold moral beliefs different from our own, our task is not simply to list the traits which they approve and disapprove of and to compare that with a similar list of our own. Rather, we must try to understand how these traits which they praise fit in with the alien way of life as a whole, so that we can understand how they contribute to or are constitutive of the goods pursued by individuals in that community. So, for example, in discussing infanticide, Hume writes that "Had you asked a parent at Athens, why he bereaved his child of that life, which he had so lately given it. It is because I love it, he would reply; and regard the poverty which it must inherit from me, as a greater evil than death, which it is not capable of dreading, feeling, or resenting" (*E* 334). We have moved beyond the externally applied label "infanticide" to consider the agent's own description of the act and the reasons he or she gives in justification. The act is no longer incomprehensible to us, since we now see how it could be taken to avoid the evil of life in poverty. As Donald Livingston writes, "the unifying principle of human nature, for Hume, is not a set of regularities modeled on the principle of gravity, but the original principle of sympathy: all that is necessary is that people be able to recognize the goods that other people pursue."[40]

Seeing actions in light of the evils avoided or the goods pursued by those who do them does not mean, however, that we automatically approve of them. Of "Greek loves," Hume writes:

I shall only observe, that, however blameable, they arose from a very innocent cause, the frequency of the gymnastic exercises among that people; and were recommended, though absurdly, as the source of friendship, sympathy, mutual attachment, and fidelity; qualities esteemed in all nations and all ages. (*E* 334)

Understanding has not excluded the possibility of blame. Here Hume implies that the moral error rests in an "absurd" assumption about the sources of good things like friendship and fidelity. The advocacy of homosexual love makes sense in light of these beliefs, although one who holds the beliefs to be false will still judge the moral views to be in error.

Hume also applies this hermeneutic of charity to practices closer to home, both in time and in space:

Nothing surely can be more absurd and barbarous than the practice of duelling; but those, who justify it, say, that it begets civility and good-manners. And a duellist, you may observe, always values himself upon his courage, his sense of honour, his fidelity and friendship; qualities, which are here indeed very oddly directed, but which have been esteemed universally, since the foundation of the world. (*E* 335)

Hume can understand the justifications given of duelling while still condemning the practice himself. In order even to make sense of it as something which might be seen as evidence of virtue, however, he must be able to identify broad areas of agreement between himself and those with whom he disagrees. Only against this background of agreement can he even see the disagreement as a disagreement about what is virtuous. In this case, there is agreement, Hume thinks, about the praiseworthiness of courage, honour, fidelity and friendship.

Different goods may not be compatible with one another, and some disagreements in moral beliefs are to be accounted for as a sacrifice of one good in order to obtain another. So, Hume says, "The consequence of a very free commerce between the sexes, and of their living much together, will often terminate in intrigues and gallantry. We must sacrifice somewhat of the *useful*, if we be very anxious to obtain all the *agreeable* qualities; and cannot pretend to reach alike every kind of advantage" (*E* 339). Having penetrated beneath the surface fact of disagreement to the trade-off between mutually recognized goods, we are in a better position to understand and evaluate each position. Perhaps it will be the views of our own society which are ultimately called into question, rather than the alien views. The imaginative exercise in "A dialogue" need not simply reinforce the views current among our contemporaries – Hume certainly wishes to challenge the view that suicide is wrong and betrays some doubts about the so-called military virtues (*MPL* 577–589; *T* 601).[41] Our attempts to understand difference may well lead to identifications of moral error, but we will be in a position to do more than condemn. Hume is confident that "erroneous conclusions can be corrected by sounder reasoning and larger experience" (*E* 336). Our attempt to make sense of alien moral beliefs involves, in part, the construction of explanations of moral error, explanations which could form the basis of attempts to persuade the others of their error, or, alternatively, to realize our own error.

Our appreciation for alien points of view does not involve shedding or suspending our own moral beliefs. In fact, the only way in which we can understand the views of others is by triangulating from our own. It is only in becoming aware of the goods we pursue and the evils we avoid that we can understand the actions and moral beliefs of others as, similarly, efforts to pursue such goods and avoid such evils. Learning from alien points of view *requires*, therefore, that we not lose our own moral bearing.[42] This resonates with Clifford Geertz's insistence that we can apprehend the outlook of another people or period "at least as well as we apprehend anything else not properly ours; but we do so not by looking *behind* the interfering glosses that connect us to it but *through* them."[43] We come to understand things from the native's point of view, Geertz asserts, not "through some sort of extraordinary sensibility, an almost preternatural capacity to think, feel, and perceive like a native," but rather "by searching out and analyzing symbolic forms – words, images, institutions, behaviors – in terms of which, in each place, people actually represented themselves to themselves and to one another."[44] It is this sort of active hermeneutic process of sympathetic understanding which is needed to overcome the biases of immediate extensive sympathy.

DIVERGENT SYMPATHIES

Hume's notion of the way sympathetic understanding is involved in our evaluation of alien manners comes into clearer focus when contrasted with the range of opinions on the subject held by his forerunners and contemporaries. Dubos, as I indicated above, believed that sympathy with the manners of the ancients involved an imaginative transformation into the original audiences of the works we read or watch, a transformation so thorough that our own moral beliefs are left behind as wholly irrelevant to the evaluative task. This view has been traced back to Shaftesbury, who "lightly assumed that we continually observe other minds, recreating their experience as our inner sense observes the 'scenes' representing their characteristics and qualities." Poetry is capable of "carrying observers, so to speak, into the very minds of other personalities."[45]

Rousseau's conception of sympathy is quite close to Dubos', although his position on the scope of sympathy is almost the reverse of Dubos'. Rousseau thinks that sympathy with the ancients is impossible, since "we would be unable to put ourselves in the places of men who are totally dissimilar to us."[46] Therefore, he writes, "let no one then attribute to the theatre the power to change sentiments or morals [manners] which it can only follow and embellish."[47] While we cannot sympathize with the alien morals of the ancients, it seems that we almost irresistibly sympathize with vice; "Who does not himself become a thief for a minute in being concerned about him? For is being concerned about someone anything other than putting oneself in his place?"[48] Although the theater cannot play a positive role in increasing our understanding of alien ways of life, it is nonetheless a potent source of moral corruption. In this sense, the theater *can* change our manners after all; "it is impossible that the opportunity of going every day to the same place to forget oneself and becoming involved with foreign objects should not give other habits to the citizen and form new morals [manners] for him."[49]

Both Dubos and Rousseau, despite their different beliefs about the value and scope of sympathy, regard it as a sort of transformation into another being, which involves the temporary loss of one's own identity and moral bearing. Hume, in contrast, insists that "no force of imagination can convert us into another person, and make us fancy, that we, being that person, reap benefit from those valuable qualities, which belong to him. Or if it did, no celerity of imagination could immediately transport us back, into ourselves, and make us love and esteem the person, as different from us" (*E* 234; see also *E* 217).[50] There is no deception or illusion involved in sympathy, no mysterious transformation into the other, and hence no loss of self. As I argued in chapter 2, this is true even of sympathy as it is first introduced in the *Treatise*, although sympathy there does imply a sort of direct experience of the feelings of others. It is no less true of the sympathetic understanding by which one enters into the situations of others, not by a mysterious identification and loss of identity, but by a process of translation and interpretation.[51]

Nineteenth-century Romantic notions of sympathetic imagination perpetuate and accentuate the divergence between the Humean principle of sympathetic understanding and conceptions of sympathy fostered by the remarks of Dubos and Rousseau. Romantic notions of sympathy linked it closely with increasingly active and creative understandings of the imagination.[52] Eighteenth-century sentimentalism, with its preoccupation with sympathy and pity, had succeeded in raising awareness of suffering and sensitivity to the less fortunate, but it had also, as I have mentioned, valorized a passive, paralyzed, response – the spectator is overcome with sympathetic emotion. This was perhaps not surprising in an era in which (despite its optimism about gradual progress) radical social change intentionally enacted by human agents was unthinkable.[53] This was no longer the case in the next generation, however, and "sympathy" took a back seat to "sympathetic imagination," "moral imagination," and "imaginative identification," terms which seemed to do greater justice to the active, creative power of the human mind. Bate writes that "it is one of the common tenets of English romantic criticism that the imagination is capable, through an effort of sympathetic imagination, of identifying itself with its object; and, by means of this identification, the sympathetic imagination grasps, through a kind of direct experience and feeling, the distinctive nature, identity, or 'truth' of the object of its contemplation."[54] Radner also links the emergence of an active view of sympathy with the rise of Romanticism, suggesting that "this view of compassion therefore suggested new defenses of poetry: that it takes a person's mind off his own concerns and interests him in others; that it gives him practice in fleshing out situations; and that it exercises and strengthens the projective imagination."[55]

While these characterizations highlight the activity of Romantic sympathy, they obscure internal disagreements over the place of the self in the activity of sympathy. Wordsworth and the other Lake School

Poets claimed a universal sympathy with all things but were criticized for being capable only of seeing themselves everywhere. Keats, among the critics of this "egotistical sublime," in his early years went to the other extreme, that of trying to escape the self entirely, in his eagerness to sympathize with everything that lay outside of himself. In the end, these two extremes (seeing oneself in everything else and losing sight of oneself entirely) tended to collapse into one another, the stable alternative to which was the Humean option of increased self-awareness as the indispensable accompaniment to sympathetic understanding. This option, however, tended to be eclipsed by Romantic exuberance; Hazlitt, perhaps not accidentally a writer of prose rather than poetry, was probably the one to carry it on most faithfully.

Wordsworth's *Preface* to *Lyrical Ballads* reflects his early intoxication with the ideals of the French Revolution, and his hope of creating a revolution in poetry which would not only mirror, but inspire, political revolution. He sought to write a radically democratic poetry which took as its subjects common people and common aspects of life, rather than cultural elites and their exalted environs. Wordsworth made it his practice to employ ordinary language rather than elevated forms of expression in his poetry,[56] claiming that "such a language, arising out of repeated experience and regular feelings, is a more permanent, and a far more philosophical language, than that which is frequently substituted for it by poets, who think that they are conferring honour upon themselves and their art, in proportion as they separate themselves from the sympathies of men, and indulge in arbitrary and capricious habits of expression, in order to furnish food for fickle tastes, and fickle appetites, of their own creation."[57] By eliminating artificial distinctions and focusing on the common, this new sort of poet promises to secure the completest sympathy with others; "it will be the wish of the poet to bring his feelings near to those of the persons whose feelings he describes, nay, for short spaces of time perhaps, to let himself slip into an entire delusion, and even confound and identify his own feelings with theirs."[58] But Hazlitt's sharp criticism of the Lake School is telling:

They were for bringing poetry back to its primitive simplicity and state of nature . . . so that the only thing remarkable left in the world by this change, would be the persons who had produced it. A thorough adept in this school of poetry is jealous of all excellence but his own. He does not even like to share his reputation with his subject; for he would have it all proceed from his own power and originality of mind. Such a one is slow to admire any thing that is admirable; feels no interest in what is most interesting to others, no grandeur in any thing grand . . . He tolerates only what he himself creates; he sympathizes only with what can enter into no competition with him, with "the bare trees and mountains bare, and grass in the green field." He sees nothing but himself and the universe.[59]

So the zealous attempt to feel one's way into the experiences of others can easily degenerate into a preoccupation with one's own experiences in the delusion that they reflect what is truly common to all. It is most clear in the phenomenon of sympathy with nature that the projective imagination is merely finding itself in all that it contemplates. In the case of the Lake School Poets, the lapse back into self was accompanied by a lapse into political apathy, and poetry became an escape rather than a stimulus to action. Brissenden comments that "the myth of the unloved, misunderstood, agonised and alienated artist is a romantic myth; and it is intimately related to, is in part perhaps a variant of, the myth of the virtuous but impotent man of sentiment."[60]

Keats tried to learn from Hazlitt's critique of the Lake Poets and the egotistical sublime, but tended to try to escape egotism by escaping the self. "As to the poetical Character itself," he wrote, "(I mean that sort of which, if I am any thing, I am a Member; that sort distinguished from the wordsworthian or egotistical sublime. . .) it is not itself – it has no self – it is every thing and nothing – It has no character – it enjoys light and shade; it lives in gusto, be it foul or fair, high or low, rich or poor, mean or elevated – It has as much delight in conceiving an Iago as an Imogen. What shocks the virtuous philosopher, delights the camelion Poet."[61] Yet Hazlitt's critique of Keats' 1818 poem "Endymion" is that "he painted his own thoughts and character; and did not transport himself into the fabulous and heroic ages. There is a want of action, or character, and so far, of imagination."[62] Escaping the self is a hard thing to do!

David Bromwich's assessment is that Keats, in his later odes, came to recognize the self as "a necessary thing, in charge of the daylight world which Keats no longer regrets, and which has its own sympathies to ask of us."[63] In a more extended comment, worth citing because it focuses on the ethically important issue of whether sympathy should involve loss of self-consciousness or a heightening of it, Bromwich writes:

The narrator of a Keats ode is always on the verge of becoming not quite himself, and he makes us believe that to remain so is to widen experience. But this sounds like what English critics have sometimes called "empathy" – translating the German *Einfühlung* – and I need to say why it is closer to what Hazlitt all along had been calling "sympathy." Empathy is the process by which a mind so projects itself into its object that a transfer of qualities seems to take place. Keats, on the other hand, was looking for a capability of so heightening the imagination's response to anything that the identities of both the mind and its object would grow more vivid as what they are.[64]

If this interpretation is on the mark, then Hazlitt and the later Keats stand with Hume in affirming that sympathetic understanding of others requires greater awareness of one's own self, one's feelings and beliefs, rather than forgetfulness or loss of self. Egotism and self-absorption cannot be avoided by trying to lose the self altogether. By talking of sympathy as a mysterious sort of transformation which leaves the self behind and eschews the nitty-gritty details of translation and understanding, moreover, the Lake School Poets encouraged relativism. They implied that sympathy precludes critical appraisal of the moral sensibilities of those different from ourselves, rather than enabling productive engagement with difference. This sense that appraisal was an impossible or inappropriate companion to sympathy was encouraged by the links being forged between sympathy and the imagination, as well as between imagination and creative poetic genius, and by the emerging "autonomy" of the aesthetic realm. While understandable as a reaction to the overly simplistic moralism of much eighteenth-century art, claims of aesthetic autonomy have, I believe, proven crippling to both ethics and art.

Some of the other eighteenth-century discussions of sympathy do not fit so neatly as those of Dubos and Rousseau into the proto-Romantic category. Here I will consider only two other thinkers: Samuel Johnson and Adam Smith. While sympathetically entering into others' situations, according to Hume, involves neither transformation into the other nor loss of self, it also is not simply a matter of trying to think about what one would feel in the circumstances of another person. Samuel Johnson, despite his overall neoclassical bent, makes room for a certain sort of sympathetic identification, asserting that "all joy or sorrow for the happiness or calamity of others is produced by an act of the imagination, that realizes the event however fictitious, or approximates it however remote, by placing us, for a time, in the condition of him whose fortunes we contemplate; so that we feel, while the deception lasts, whatever notions would be excited by the same good or evil happening to ourselves."[65] A deception takes place, but rather than allowing us to feel what the other feels, it enables us only to feel what we ourselves would feel in such a situation; "we can only know what others suffer for want, by considering how we should be affected in the same state; nor can we proportion our assistance by any other rule than that of doing what we should then expect from others."[66] This leaves us with a very limited capacity to understand alien manners and points of view, which Johnson both recognizes and discounts.

Our passions are therefore more strongly moved, in proportion as we can more readily adopt the pains or pleasures proposed to our minds, by recognizing them as once our own, or considering them as incident to our state of life. It is not easy for the most artful writer to give us an interest in happiness or misery, which we think ourselves never likely to feel, and with which we have never yet been made acquainted.[67]

Hence, if we wish to extend the range of our sympathy, we should avoid seeking to make sense of differences by focusing on them, but rather seek to ignore differences and focus on existing commonalities. In *Rasselas*, Johnson suggests that the writer "must divest himself of the prejudices of his age and country; he must consider right and wrong in their abstracted and invariable state; he must disregard present laws and opinions, and rise to general and transcendental truths, which will always be the same."[68] The aim is not to understand concrete instances of otherness, but rather the abstraction of universal truth.

The differences between ages and countries, Johnson thinks, fall primarily into the public realm, while the commonalities lie in the domestic sphere. In the private, domestic sphere, we discover universal human nature: "There is such a uniformity in the state of man, considered apart from adventitious and separable decorations and disguises, that there is scarce any possibility of good or ill, but is common to human kind."[69] This becomes an argument for the priority of biography over other sorts of writing, since "the business of the biographer is often to pass slightly over those performances and incidents, which produce vulgar greatness, to lead the thoughts into domestic privacies, and display the minute details of daily life, where exterior appendages are cast aside, and men excel each other only by prudence and by virtue."[70] Johnson's promotion of biography stands in telling contrast with Hume's advocacy of history, which I take up in the following section. As this last quotation indicates, Johnson locates morals in the domestic realm, and therefore seems to assume universality of moral beliefs and standards, and variation only in the extent to which these standards are approximated by individuals. Yet morals seem neither to lie obediently in the private realm nor to be as untouched by disagreement as Johnson's comments suggest. Sympathy, as he portrays it, does not enable us to fathom alien morals, since it does not involve seeking to identify those things sought as good and avoided as evil by others, but rather sees in a situation only what we would regard as goods or evils. As Bate comments, "sympathy, like any other emotional capacity, was regarded by Johnson as at best a means of enforcing the rational grasp of the universal."[71]

Adam Smith begins his *Theory of Moral Sentiments* by affirming, like Johnson, that sympathy involves imagining what we would feel in the situation of another:[72]

[A]s we have no immediate experience of what other men feel, we can form no idea of the manner in which they are affected, but by conceiving what we ourselves should feel in the like situation. Though our brother is upon the rack, as long as we ourselves are at our ease, our senses will never inform us of what he suffers. They never did, and never can, carry us beyond our own person, and it is by the imagination only that we can form any conception of what are his sensations. Neither can that faculty help us to this any other way, than by representing to us what would be our own, if we were in his case.[73]

This statement firmly denies that sympathy is a mysterious transformation into the other with a concomitant loss of self.[74] Sympathy, for Smith, does not involve feeling what another person is actually feeling, but is rather a matter of *imagining* what we observers would feel in a counterfactual situation.

Like Hume, Smith believed that sympathy could account for moral approbation – the postulation of an original instinctive moral sense was unnecessary. But the way the two thinkers incorporate sympathy into their moral theories is only superficially similar. According to Smith:

When the original passions of the person principally concerned are in perfect accord with the sympathetic emotions of the spectator, they necessarily appear to this last just and proper, and suitable to their objects; and, on the contrary, when, upon bringing the case home to himself, he finds that they do not coincide with what he feels, they necessarily appear to him unjust and improper, and unsuitable to the causes which excite them.[75]

As he describes this process, Smith begins to use "sympathy" to refer, not to the imaginative act, but rather to the coincidence of feeling which is (only sometimes) the outcome of the imaginative act. His double use of "sympathy" can be somewhat confusing. "To approve of the passions of another, therefore, as suitable to their objects," he says, "is the same thing as to observe that we entirely sympathize with them; and not to approve of them as such, is the same thing as to observe that we do not entirely sympathize with them."[76] The very *fact* of sympathizing – in the second sense, that is – constitutes our approval. Sympathy of this sort seems to provide nothing more than a litmus test for determining whether others' motives and sentiments accord with our own; "the coincidence or opposition of sentiments, between the observer and the person observed, constitutes moral approbation or disapprobation."[77]

Smith goes on to refine this notion by claiming that we compare the sentiments of the other not directly with our own, nor with what we would feel in the other's situation, but with what we would feel if we *were* the other person:

[T]hough sympathy is very properly said to arise from an imaginary change of situations with the person principally concerned, yet this imaginary change is not supposed to happen to me in my own person and character, but in that of the person with whom I sympathize. When I condole with you for the loss of your only son, in order to enter into your grief, I do not consider what I, a person of such a character and profession, should suffer, if I had a son, and if that son was unfortunately to die; but I consider what I should suffer if I was really you; and I not only change circumstances with you, but I change persons and characters.[78]

Philip Mercer suggests that "perhaps Smith's most serious confusion stems from his failure to clarify whether sympathy involves imagining what one would feel if one were in the other's situation or whether it involves imagining oneself as the other person."[79] What is more important than accusing Smith of inconsistency or confusion is understanding why he wavers on this point. It seems to me that Smith increases the demands on the imagination as he begins to grapple with the difficulty of distinguishing between a person's *situation* and a person's *identity*. Smith seems at times to assume that a man and a woman, a professor and a lawyer, a lord and a peasant, will all have the same feelings and the same sentiments if placed in the same situation (if, for example, they had a child who died or were victims of a robbery). Or rather, the sole differences in their feelings and sentiments would be *moral* differences, reflecting degrees of vice or virtue. But, at other times, Smith implies that there is a range of differences which may affect sentiments without reflecting vicious character traits. Therefore, he suggests that the ideal imaginative act of sympathy must not only consider the immediate external situation, but must also imaginatively reproduce all of the relevant non-moral variables. He gestures toward this in the quote above by speaking not simply of "circumstances," but also of "person" and "character" and "profession."[80]

Smith, like Hume, seems to be trying to create room for the possibility of recognizing *some* differences in feeling or sentiment as morally indifferent while retaining our capacity to judge other such differences as reflective of vicious character. Once such a distinction is made, how do we determine which differences fall into which category? Smith hopes, perhaps, that the imaginative act of sympathy will separate out these two categories, since I carry my own moral sensibilities into the imaginative act with me while seeking to leave everything else behind. This is crucial for Smith's moral theory, for, if I left *everything* behind, then there would never be any difference between how I imagine I would feel if I were the other person and how that other person really feels, and I would approve of everything that the other person did.[81]

Although all eighteenth-century theorists of sympathy are, I believe, concerned in some way with overcoming the gap between different individuals' experience of the world, the object of Smith's imaginative act of sympathy is neither to *recreate* nor to *merge* with the other's experience, leaving oneself wholly behind (as in Romantic sympathetic identification), nor to *understand* the other's experience prior to evaluating it, without trying to leave oneself behind (as with Hume's interpretive sympathetic principle), but rather to create for ourselves as moral beings an imaginary experience which gives rise to sentiments which we can hold up against the actual sentiments of another person.[82] While the first sort of sympathy precludes the possibility of judgment of those who differ from ourselves, and the second creates the possibility of judgment across difference by seeking understanding without losing hold of the self, Smith's imaginative sympathy seems to me to take a shortcut through the problem of understanding, thereby reaching judgment prematurely.

In Smith's theory, grasping and making sense of the actual sentiments of the other person, those sentiments with which we compare our imaginatively manufactured sentiments, is seen as unproblematic – these sentiments are not what we seek to understand through sympathy, but rather the things with which we compare our imaginary sentiments. In fact, Smith assumes that the only variations among individuals will be in the degree of affections, not in their kind. The sentiments of others are almost always immediately accessible and transparent to observers. The exception that Smith notes is a telling one: the passions of hatred, anger, and resentment "are the only passions of which the expressions . . . do not dispose and prepare us to sympathize with them, before we are informed of the cause which excites them."[83] We do not sympathize with anger without knowing something about what caused it, although we *will* sympathize immediately with those to whom the anger is directed, since their fear or resentment is immediately comprehensible to us.[84] The ideal objects of sympathy are passions or emotions which purportedly possess context-free comprehensibility, and Smith seems to think that most passions, unlike those of anger and resentment, conform closely to this ideal.

Given the assumption that the actual sentiments of others are obvious to us, our own description and understanding of the situation can unproblematically determine our imaginative task and hence our judgment. We need not try to identify and understand the other's description of the situation, the way in which she conceives of the good pursued or the interests at stake, in order to make sense of her sentiments or actions. We simply observe the person and the situation and think, "She is ashamed" or "he is angry." The imaginative act (which is distinct from this simple observation of other's sentiments) gives us information, not about what the other person is feeling, but about whether what the other person is feeling is appropriate or not.

While Smith assumes that the passions of others are transparently comprehensible to us, he does think that our capacity to imagine how we would feel if we were someone else is limited by the extent and kind of differences which separate us. These limits to our imagination in turn restrict the range of passions with which we can sympathize, as well as the range of persons whose feelings we can enter into and sympathize with. Smith does not say that we will be wholly unable to imagine how we would feel in certain situations or if we were someone quite different from ourselves, but he stresses that in many cases there will be a huge discrepancy between the intensity of our imaginary passions and the intensity of the passions we observe in the other person. As a result of the limits of our imagination, we may not be able to "enter into" someone else's sentiments despite the fact that they are not vicious, because our imaginary conception of what it would be like to be such a person is not vivid enough. In such cases, our capacity to sympathize would not seem to be a just determinant of moral approval or disapproval. When we are confronted with the sight of someone in great sorrow and dejection, for example, "we cannot bring ourselves to feel for him what he feels for himself, and what, perhaps, we should feel for ourselves if in his situation. We therefore despise him! unjustly, perhaps, if any sentiment could be regarded as unjust, to which we are by nature irresistibly determined."[85] On the one hand, then, Smith takes the sentiments of others to be transparent to us, which is to deny the possible depths of difference. On the other hand, however, Smith recognizes that difference is a barrier to the imagination, but then finds no resources with which to encounter it and simply resigns himself to the impossibility of sympathy (of either sort) in such cases.[86] We seem fated to unjust moral sentiments and judgments, although Smith confesses that he is unable on his own account to justify regarding these sentiments as unjust.

Smith's observations about sympathy's failures feed directly into his Stoic moral theory. Much like Johnson, he suggests that sympathy is to be achieved by eliminating or concealing differences as much as possible, not by attempting to develop the capacity for sympathy across differences. Sympathy with the sentiments of others is not something we can really *try* to have. At times, "we may . . . inwardly reproach ourselves with our own want of sensibility, and perhaps, on that account, work ourselves up into an artificial sympathy, which, however, when it is raised, is always the slightest and most transitory imaginable; and generally, as soon as we have left the room, vanishes, and is gone for ever."[87] The places where sympathy fails mark the places where we should tone down our idiosyncrasies or be stoic about our pains. If we desire the sympathy of others (and we all do), then we would do well not to show how much our broken arm is hurting, or allow our particular attachments and affections to influence us very much:

A certain reserve is necessary when we talk of our own friends, our own studies, our own professions. All these are objects which we cannot expect should interest our companions in the same degree in which they interest us. And it is for want of this reserve, that the one half of mankind make bad company to the other. A philosopher is company to a philosopher only; the member of a club to his own little knot of companions.[88]

The desire for sympathy gives rise to a twofold equilibration process, in which the agent moderates the degree of his or her passions while spectators intensify theirs, both seeking to approximate the response level of an "impartial spectator."

As Smith develops the notion of the impartial spectator, actual sympathy with others becomes much less important than approximating the responses of the impartial spectator; in evaluating someone's interests, for example, "we must view them neither from our own place nor yet from his, neither with our own eyes nor yet with his, but from the place and with the eyes of a third person who has no particular connection with either, and who judges with impartiality between us."[89] While we can never really view things through the eyes of others, Smith thinks that we can, at least temporarily, view things through the eyes of the impartial spectator; "the man of real constancy and firmness does not merely affect the sentiments of the impartial spectator. He really adopts them. He almost identifies himself with, he almost becomes himself that impartial spectator, and scarce even feels but as that great arbiter of his conduct directs him to feel."[90] The moral point of view, therefore, is distanced from all real viewpoints, rather than issuing from attempts to understand distinct concrete viewpoints. What one ought to feel in a given situation is what the impartial spectator feels. Since Smith assumes that we can immediately perceive the sentiments of the others, he also assumes that we can determine a priori what constitutes impartiality. Although the impartial spectator is supposed to have a God's eye point of view, which gives equal credit, so to speak, to the viewpoints of all individuals, our own description of the situation, our own understanding of the interests of the various participants, is smuggled into our sense of what constitutes impartiality in any given case. This contrasts with Hume, who says that the moral judge must try to understand the feelings of those closely involved in the situation under consideration, seeking "sympathy with the person himself, whose character is examin'd; or that of persons, who have a connection with him" (*T* 591, also *T* 583), just as the critic must place him- or herself in the same situation as the original audience of the work. The moral point of view is not one of abstraction. As I pointed out earlier, there is for Hume, no single constant point of view for the judge or critic, and therefore no a priori determination of what constitutes impartiality. The concrete reality of other viewpoints must *first* be understood. Smith unifies the moral point of view, but at the cost of eliminating fruitful encounters with difference.

Smith's shortcut through the challenge of understanding difference results in a conservative and provincial moral theory. Our desire for sympathy, our attempts to please the impartial spectator, lead us to conform with the moral values of our society, not to question them. Basic economic and educational parity are requisite for mutual sympathy, and this encourages the perpetuation of distinctions of rank and order in society.[91] Although Smith deplores the fact that people tend to have greater sympathy with economic good fortune and social distinction than with the lack thereof, he writes that "Nature has wisely judged that the distinction of ranks, the peace and order of society, would rest more securely upon the plain and palpable differences of birth and fortune, than upon the invisible and often uncertain difference of wisdom and virtue."[92] In our desire for sympathy, we will reinforce the status quo by pursuing wealth and honoring it. Mercer charges that Smith cannot account for moral disagreement and that "for Smith morality is something given and static," concluding that the primary value of

Smith's account is its ability "to suggest to us something of value about how sympathy functions as to perpetuate and stabilize particular attitudes and beliefs within a society and how in doing this it helps to preserve the identity of that society."[93]

Smith recognizes the variability of morals from age to age and country to country, and recognizes furthermore that his moral theory simply indicates that the morals of each society will be effectively perpetuated by attempts to gain sympathy; each of us will strive to approximate the sentiments of the impartial spectator who embodies the moral ideals of our own society. There is no reason to think that we will be able to imagine what it would be like to be a person in a different society than our own, and furthermore we have no mandate to judge those who are approximating the ideals represented by a different impartial spectator.[94] It is when he thinks about the issue of moral differences between cultures that Smith is most tempted to lapse into the Hutchesonian language of moral sense. He refers, for example, to "the natural principles of right and wrong," with which custom and fashion may or may not coincide, and suggests that "the sentiments of moral approbation and disapprobation are founded on the strongest and most vigorous passions of human nature; and though they may be somewhat warpt, cannot be entirely perverted."[95]

In the end, however, Smith embraces the relativistic alternative, suggesting that we recognize that the sentiments of the impartial spectator will vary from society to society and simply proceed on the assumption that the practices of societies different from our own are blameless; "every age and country look upon that degree of each quality which is commonly to be met with in those who are esteemed, among themselves, as the golden mean of that particular talent or virtue; and as this varies according as their different circumstances render different qualities more or less habitual to them, their sentiments, concerning the exact propriety of character and behaviour, vary accordingly."[96] Beliefs about propriety are hence contingent on what is *habitual* in an age or country. As Glenn R. Morrow suggests, "if the moral sentiments of the individual are the expression of the general sentiments of the society of which he is a member, it is to be expected that moral standards will vary according to the conditions of the different societies in which they arise," and this implies "the relativity of the moral consciousness to the state of society."[97] Smith does not find these differences too troubling, since he trusts that the "natural" workings of sympathy reflect the wise plans of the Deity, and this faith undergirds his confidence that "in general the style of manners which takes place in any nation may commonly, upon the whole, be said to be that which is most suitable to its situation."[98] He always keeps in mind the tribunal "of the all-seeing Judge of the world, whose eye can never be deceived, and whose judgments can never be perverted."[99] It is God who achieves the truly impartial viewpoint, rather than simply representing the idealization of the moral views of a given society. His sentiments assure the existence of an absolute standard, no matter how unable we are to fully discern it.

While Hume and Smith can both be understood as grappling with the problem of differentiating morally relevant versus morally indifferent changes and differences, Smith's theory of the sympathetic imagination seems to me to provide fewer resources for dealing with this problem than does the principle of sympathetic understanding found in Hume's writings. One fundamental difference between them is that Hume's discussions are aimed at developing the capacity for sympathetic understanding of differences, not at concealing or repressing differences in order to ensure that we will always receive sympathy. Hume's discussions, unlike those of Smith, suggest that our capacity to imagine how we would feel if we were someone else is dependent on our prior development of the ability to understand the terms in which the other person understands him- or herself and the situation. The imagination does not possess a special power that allows us to see things differently. We can only see things differently if we have grasped the categories in which a different life is lived, and that is not a matter of the imagination (at least as "imagination" is usually understood). We may not be able to say immediately whether a person is ashamed or angry, taking vengeance or carrying out a ritual cleansing. In gaining internal understanding of the person's experience, by understanding the terms in which they would describe their experience, situation, and actions, we slowly develop the capacity to imagine what it would be like to be such a person. But this capacity to imagine cannot precede our understanding of the different traditions, virtues, practices, and categories in which the other's life is lived. We cannot separate our ability to identify and name what the other person is feeling from our ability to imagine what it would be like to be that other person. Finally, Hume's account, unlike Smith's, shows that understanding of the other, rather than leading to relativism, creates the possibility of learning from our encounter with difference, of changing our moral views, rather than blindly perpetuating our moral errors through our efforts to please the "impartial spectator" who perfectly reflects the ideals of our own society.

BEYOND POETRY — HISTORY, SPECULATION, AND RELIGION

There is still one tension in Hume's work which remains to be taken up in this chapter: bearing in mind all that "A dialogue" indicates we stand to learn from sympathetic understanding of foreign points of view, how can we account for the moral conservatism evinced in "Of the standard of taste?" Why does Hume there suggest that our encounter with foreign morals is accompanied by no real understanding, no encounter which might possibly influence our own beliefs? Why must we so quickly condemn what we take to be vicious manners when they are depicted in poetry? Why is it necessary to be "jealous" of our moral standards, if we are truly confident of their rectitude? One clue lies in the fact that, in "Of the standard of taste," Hume is considering a special subclass of our encounters with foreign manners, those which are mediated by poetry rather than, say, a traveler's face-to-face encounter or a prose account. In the essay "Of the study of history" (1741), Hume contrasts poetry with history:

There is also an advantage in that experience which is acquired by history, . . . that it brings us acquainted with human affairs, without diminishing in the least from the most delicate sentiments of virtue. And, to tell the truth, I know not any study or occupation so unexceptionable as history in this particular. Poets can paint virtue in the most charming colours; but, as they address themselves entirely to the passions, they often become advocates for vice . . . But . . . the historians have been, almost without exception, the true friends of virtue, and have always represented it in its proper colours, however they may have erred in their judgments of particular persons. (*MPL* 567)

It is true of poetry, as of history, that it "extends our experience to all past ages, and to the most distant nations; making them contribute as much to our improvement in wisdom, as if they had actually lain under our observation" (*MPL* 566). What we expect from poetry, however, is that we will be moved, caught up in the spectacle, in the alternate life-possibility which is being presented. We encounter poetry as something unreal. Since we regard it as unreal, we do not see it as something which is relevant to our deliberation about what to do, nor as an appropriate object of evaluation. Our evaluation would have no impact on poetic characters. An event in poetry, unlike an event in history, does not connect in time with the events which make up the reality which surrounds us. As a result, the event does not *matter* in the same way. Even if the robber gets away with the cash from the store, or the husband abandons his wife and children, when we finish reading the book or watch the final curtain fall, nothing that transpired in the poetic action will have changed anything in our usual surroundings. These characteristics of poetry encourage us to leave our deliberative and evaluative capacities behind us and simply become passively immersed in the desires and hopes and projects of the fictional characters. The reflective processes of moral judgment (as well as the practical reasoning of deliberation), would, in fact, lessen our absorption in poetry. Just as evaluation of our own actions and those of those around us requires us to gain some distance from our own desires and interests, evaluation of characters in a play or novel would require us to acquire critical distance from their hopes and schemes.

When it comes to resources for moral education, Hume gives history pride of place over not only poetry, but also real life and philosophy.[100] When we are engaged in life and action, our own interests are involved and warp our judgment. A philosopher's vision, on the other hand, is not corrupted by prejudice, but when he "contemplates characters and manners in his closet, the general abstract view of the objects leaves the mind so cold and unmoved, that the sentiments of nature have no room to play, and he scarce feels the difference between vice and virtue." "History," in contrast, "keeps in a just medium betwixt these extremes, and places the objects in their true point of view. The writers of history, as well as the readers, are sufficiently interested in the characters and events, to have a lively sentiment of blame or praise; and, at the same time, have no particular interest or concern to pervert their judgment" (*MPL* 568; also *E* 223–224). We must be engaged enough to understand sympathetically and to care about the character's desires and projects, but we must not have abandoned our critical faculties as irrelevant. Hume's advocacy of history expresses his confidence that sympathetic understanding of different points of view is possible, rather than resting content with an understanding based on whatever we already identify as points of resemblance. It is history, Hume thinks, which gives the most promise of cultivating extensive sympathy in a way which contributes to the capacity for moral evaluation.

Hume's approach to history combines elements of both philosophical history and what Megill, following Meineke, has called historism.[101] Philosophical history was "strongly rooted in the uniformitarianism of the Enlightenment, [and] was characterized by a belief in the basic constancy of human nature, with historical change appearing in the guise of a struggle between the opposing forces of reason and unreason, and with the value of history attributed not so much to its provision of a record of objective events as to its ability to tell us about the historical agent, man himself."[102] Historism, in contrast, was characterized by a conviction of the importance of contextual evaluation. Historists "argued that the historian must pay attention to the particularity of the historical object. And they further argued that to take proper account of this particularity the historian must self-consciously attempt to evaluate every historical object in terms of the context to which it belongs."[103] According to Cassirer, "Hume agrees as little with the general type of philosophy of history of the Enlightenment as he does with its theory of knowledge or its philosophy of religion. In him the static approach to history, which is oriented to the knowledge of the permanent properties of human nature, begins to relax; he looks more to the historical process as such than to the solid substratum presupposed by the process."[104] John Burke suggests that "the distinction between the past as it was and the past as it appears to have been led Hume to introduce a new criterion into his account of English history – the *situation*, a notion not unlike that of the *Zeitgeist* favored by later historians."[105] I have argued at length in this chapter for Hume's conviction of the importance of sensitivity to context in considering both history and poetry. Just as Hume's solution to the Quarrel of the Ancients and Moderns maintains the importance of sympathetic understanding of alien contexts while holding on to the possibility and importance of moral evaluation across contexts, his approach to history gives context its due while maintaining that the historian's role extends beyond the mere description of past events to the education of the capacity for moral judgment. Wellek observes of Hume's time that "dogmatism was being undermined by some sort of recognition that other ages had standards and viewpoints of their own. But 'relativism' as such was not necessarily a preparation for the historical approach, though obviously it removed obstacles from the way. It frequently led rather to barren scepticism, to a mere assertion of despair, to the old and essentially vicious maxim of *De gustibus non est disputandum*."[106] Hume manages to avoid both "dogmatism" and "barren skepticism," affirming that we can learn more from studying the past than its difference and separation from our own time.[107]

While Hume champions history for its potentially transformative role in moral education, John Witherspoon was only slightly less suspicious of history than he was of poetry. Although Witherspoon believed that history was necessary for proving the truths of natural religion and for confirming the truths of revealed religion, he nevertheless suspected that "it had been better for the world that several ancient facts and characters, which now stand upon record, had been buried in oblivion."[108] History is dangerous because it, like stage plays, seeks to be "a picture of human life, and must represent characters as they really are. An author for the stage is not permitted to feign, but to paint and copy."[109] As Barish writes, "Witherspoon makes it a fault that they aim at a lifelike portrayal, since this means acquainting their audiences too convincingly with the true facts of life."[110] This fear of truth is not unconnected with Witherspoon's fear of sympathetic identification. In response to the suggestion that the stage educates, gives knowledge of the world, and broadens the mind, Witherspoon responds that "it is certainly the greatest madness to seek the knowledge of the world by partaking with bad men in their sins."[111] Witherspoon sees in sympathy only a sort of vicarious vice; he does not see the possibilities of an active interpretive principle of sympathetic understanding. Encounters with difference, both in poetry and in history, are potential sources of corruption; they are not an occasion for moral education, since there is no room for fallibilism when moral beliefs have been certified once and for all by Christian revelation.

Hume's comments in "Of the standard of taste" do testify to the recognition that poetry tends to uncouple sympathy from moral judgment, in contrast to history, which is able to link expanded sympathetic understanding to the development of moral judgment in a more reliable way. I have argued, however, that they do not sound a retreat from the advocacy of active sympathetic understanding of foreign points of view. Hume does try to set limits to the scope of sympathetic understanding, but in order to see where these limits lie it is necessary to know something about the context in which "Of the standard of taste" was written, and to pay attention to what I have called the frame of the essay. The stark contrast between Hume's advocacy of active sympathetic understanding and Witherspoon's fear of the polluting threat of difference turns out to be significant.

"Of the standard of taste" was not one of the original four essays whose publication Hume proposed to Millar in 1755, nor was it one of the two essays Hume proposed as replacements for the essay on "some Considerations previous to Geometry & Natural Philosophy," which Hume decided was not worth publishing. The two essays which were to take the place of the Geometry essay were "Of suicide" and "Of the immortality of the soul," but these were suppressed as a result of persuasion from Adam Smith and intimidation from the powerful Evangelical leader William Warburton. Warburton, Mossner surmises, saw an advance copy of the *Five Dissertations* and sought to use it to prosecute Hume's publisher before the Church of England.[112] These events coincided with a campaign against Hume among the Evangelical Scottish clergy; in May of 1756 the General Assembly of the Church of Scotland set a committee to work on the question of whether Hume ought to be censured or even excommunicated from the church.[113] A letter Hume wrote to Allan Ramsay at the time takes the investigation as an occasion for wit rather than foreboding, yet excommunication would certainly have made life in Edinburgh rather uncomfortable for Hume.[114] He withdrew the two offending essays, and wrote "Of the standard of taste" to fill their place.[115]

With this context in mind, the frame of the essay takes on greater significance. Hume returns in the end to the contrast with which he begins the essay – that between speculative and practical sorts of disagreement. In this end frame, Hume looks beyond the realm of critical judgment once more to consider morals and speculation. Whereas our moral judgments are relevant to our contemplation of alien manners, and we do not, therefore, necessarily admire characters which we judge to be vicious even if they were judged admirable by their contemporaries, speculative judgments are different. When it comes to speculative systems, "there needs but a certain turn of thought or imagination to make us enter into all opinions, which then prevailed, and relish the sentiments or conclusions derived from them" (*MPL* 247). This flexibility in viewpoint goes along with a lack of stable criteria of judgment. Although at the outset of the essay Hume affirms that disagreement in matters of science and opinion is usually more apparent than real, he now says that "though in speculation, we may readily avow a certain criterion in science and deny it in sentiment, the matter is found in practice to be much more hard to ascertain in the former case than in the latter" (*MPL* 242). At any given moment science may seem to have very stable standards of judgment, but, when we look back through time, we discover that "theories of abstract philosophy, systems of profound theology, have prevailed during one age: In a successive period, these have been universally exploded: Their absurdity has been detected: Other theories and systems have supplied their place, which again gave place to their successors: And nothing has been experienced more liable to the revolutions of chance and fashion than these pretended decisions of science" (*MPL* 242).

These remarks echo Dubos, who wrote that "those opinions whose extent and duration are founded on sense, and on the inward experience, as it were, of such as have always adopted them, are not subject to be exploded, like philosophical opinions, whose extent and continuance are owing to the facility with which they are received upon other men's credit and authority."[116] Dubos bases his contention on the immediacy and privacy of the judgments of sense – it is as though a thousand people were to perform the same experiment and get the same results, rather than one person performing the experiment and all the others accepting the result on faith. There is much more experience backing up aesthetic judgments than speculative judgments, Dubos believes. While Hume's basic claim parallels that of Dubos, he does not offer the same sort of justification. Having distanced himself from Dubos' wholesale irrationalism, Hume cannot simply rely on the uniformity of immediate sentiments. Instead, his defense of the critical judgments which survive through time rests on an argument to the effect that time removes some of the barriers to good judgment which exist when we consider things closer to ourselves. Foreigners and posterity are able to render the best judgments, by virtue of their lack of prejudice or partiality. Hume focuses on the instability of speculative systems in contrast with the stability of judgments of taste, expressing confidence that "just expressions of passion and nature are sure, after a little time, to gain public applause, which they maintain for ever" (*MPL* 242). Hume has faith that "nature" and "just sentiment" will out.

Differing speculative opinions are in general much less momentous and important than differing moral opinions. They are to be expected, are probably ineliminable, and seem to have had relatively little impact on daily life, which has remained fairly constant through numerous speculative revolutions. But Hume does not confine himself to talking about speculative opinions in general. Rather, he goes on to assert that "of all speculative errors, those, which regard religion, are the most excusable in compositions of genius; nor is it ever permitted to judge of the civility or wisdom of any people, or even of single persons, by the grossness or refinement of their theological principles" (*MPL* 247). Since even believers insist that religious matters, despite their speculative nature, are beyond the reach of reason, there is no reason to expect agreement here, and no way to decide between competing versions of true religion. Disagreement in religious belief should be granted indulgence. Here, in an essay on the standard of critical taste, Hume is offering his own personal defense of religious toleration against the imminent threat of censure or excommunication.

Hume does not simply defend nonconformity in religious belief, however. He also goes on the offensive against the Evangelicals, suggesting that "no religious principles can ever be imputed as a fault to any poet, while they remain merely principles, and take not such strong possession of his heart, as to lay him under the imputation of *bigotry* or *superstition*. Where that happens, they confound the sentiments of morality, and alter the natural boundaries of vice and virtue. They are therefore eternal blemishes, according to the principle abovementioned; nor are the prejudices and false opinions of the age sufficient to justify them" (*MPL* 247). Although his examples of such bigotry and superstition are taken from Roman Catholicism, the implied rebuke to the Evangelical Scottish clergy is obvious. Bigots are unable to tolerate disagreement in religious matters, and persecute dissenters and skeptics. The Evangelical persecution of Hume's religious skepticism therefore merits them the title of bigots. They also deserve to be accused of superstition, since "religious principles are also a blemish in any polite composition, when they rise up to superstition, and intrude themselves into every sentiment, however remote from any connection with religion" (*MPL* 248). Censure and excommunication are evidence of superstition, for they are an example of religious principles intruding into daily life. Hume ends the essay by urging condemnation of bigotry and superstition in poetry, but his more immediate attack is on his own persecutors among the Evangelical clergy.

"A dialogue" ends on a similar note, with a contrast between "maxims of common life and ordinary conduct" and "artificial lives and manners" (*E* 341). Palamedes calls Hume's attention to the fact that, in ancient times, religion was a matter for speculation which left ordinary life alone. "After men had performed their duty in sacrifices and prayers at the temple, they thought, that the gods left the rest of their conduct to themselves, and were little pleased or offended with those virtues or vices, which only affected the peace and happiness of human society" (*E* 341). Philosophy, on the other hand, was thought to be highly relevant to daily deportment and "it acquired a mighty ascendant over many, and produced great singularities of maxims and conduct" (*E* 341). Now, however, philosophy

seems to confine itself mostly to speculations in the closet [and] . . . its place is now supplied by the modern religion, which inspects our whole conduct, and prescribes an universal rule to our actions, to our words, to our very thoughts and inclinations; a rule so much the more austere, as it is guarded by infinite, though distant, rewards and punishments; and no infraction of it can ever be concealed or disguised. (*E* 341–342)

Artificial lives advocated by ancient philosophy or modern religion differ radically from one another, and there seems to be no reasonable way to decide among them. Hume's concluding reply to Palamedes is that:

> When men depart from the maxims of common reason, and affect these artificial lives, as you call them, no one can answer for what will please or displease them. They are in a different element from the rest of mankind; and the natural principles of their mind play not with the same regularity as if left to themselves, free from the illusions of religious superstition or philosophical enthusiasm. (*E* 343)

Since there is no reliable way to decide once and for all among competing speculative systems, there is no way to decide among the virtues which ancient philosophy or modern religion advocates. When such speculation invades ordinary life, it flouts the usual connections which link moral sentiments with human flourishing. This does not mean, of course, that the natural workings of the mind eliminate *all* moral error, including errors which arise from false beliefs or inconsistencies in belief, moral or otherwise. But a fallibilism about one's inherited moral views can be combined with a general trust in them, as long as they evolve from within, responding to growing experiential knowledge of the goods of human existence and of the means to secure such goods. Moral judgment involves a continuing process of reflection on our moral responses, and is not just raw feeling, but abstract deductive reason should never be allowed to dictate morals. When an attempt is made to derive morals from speculative systems, one's immediate moral responses are regarded as irrelevant and one's internally developing capacity for moral judgment is discounted. Moral views artificially derived from without will tend to be regarded by their adherents as final and infallible, and hence will fail to respond to internal changes in circumstances and will be intolerant of variations in manners.

Livingston suggests that Hume's remarks in "Of the standard of taste" about not entering into alien moral sentiments are specifically about perverse and malicious acts which are done for no good at all, either from the agent's or the historian's point of view. It is not possible to achieve sympathetic understanding of such acts. While I am hesitant to affirm that Hume believed that there are acts "done not for the sake of what is thought, however confusedly, to be some good but for the sake of evil," I do think that Livingston has put his finger on something. When people's manners become artificial, deduced from or dictated by speculative philosophical or religious beliefs, Hume does think that it is particularly difficult to fathom their moral sentiments or the ends they pursue in their daily activities; "no one [approaching them from a foreign standpoint] can answer for what will please or displease them" (*E* 343). At the outset of the essay on taste, Hume takes as an example of radical differences in moral beliefs the Alcoran, which "bestows praise on such instances of treachery, in humanity, cruelty, revenge, bigotry, as are utterly incompatible with civilized society. No steady rule of right seems there to be attended to; and every action is blamed or praised, so far only as it is beneficial or hurtful to the true believers" (*MPL* 229). Artificial manners are incomprehensible because they are often self-defeating in the long run, since they are, in Hume's view, out of touch with the basic need for survival and destructive of human flourishing. Although claims are made of their goodness, they are not "good for" anything. The ends they pursue may be arbitrarily imposed from without, or so distant from concrete existence that the shared basics of concrete existence do not furnish the outsider with a basis for sympathetic understanding of goods pursued and evils avoided. Artificial manners may also, Hume suggests, fail to achieve the freedom from prejudice which characterizes good moral judgment, and hence their moral views may not even appear to the outsider to be moral views at all. If there is ever a barrier to sympathetic understanding, it is where artificial manners are concerned.

Hume argues in favor of toleration by promoting a skepticism about the possibility of speculative knowledge which renders religious questions unanswerable and their answers inapplicable to daily existence.[117] This skepticism is combined with an insistence that morals not only need not rely on speculative claims, but in fact that morals will be better off when freed from the distortions imposed externally by speculative systems. Unlike those whose dogmatic morals derive from speculative beliefs, those whose morals are free of this artificial influence need not have recourse to warfare in order to cope with moral disagreement. Hume believes not only that we will find greater existing agreement when speculative distortions are removed, but also that "ordinary life" possesses resources for understanding, evaluating, and learning from alien moral beliefs. It remains to be seen whether Hume is right to draw the limits of sympathetic understanding at religious belief. His distinction between "speculative" beliefs and "artificial" manners, on the one hand, and "natural" manners, on the other, seems too neat and simple, given his own recognition of the complexity and variability of cultural forms. His appeal to the "natural boundaries" of vice and virtue and to the regularity with which the natural principles of the mind play when left to themselves seems to lapse into a more substantial view of universal human nature, something which can be invoked in order to exclude certain things from the task of understanding, rather than as an assumption which guides interpretation along inclusive lines.

In chapter 2 I traced the way in which Hume's moral theory created a need for a more active principle of sympathy. An automatic and instinctive sympathy simply reinforces pre-existing similarities and connections, but proper moral judgment requires extensive sympathy in circumstances under which we would expect our degree of immediate sympathy to be quite weak, as when we are mostly aware of a *lack* of resemblance and connection. There is a very general sort of similarity, at the level of our recognition of other people as fellow human beings (or our recognition of other forms of life as fellow living beings), which is a prerequisite of our ability to recognize and respond to suffering as suffering, rather than simply as a state of being which the organisms under observation tend to avoid.[118] Hume recognizes this in his initial discussion of sympathy by suggesting that similarity facilitates the conversion of the idea of someone else's affection into the affection itself. "Tis obvious," he writes, "that nature has preserv'd a great resemblance among all human creatures, and that we never remark any passion or principle in others, of which, in some degree or other, we may not find a parallel in ourselves . . . [T]his resemblance must very much contribute to make us enter into the sentiments of others, and embrace them with facility and pleasure" (*T* 318). Hume does not consider this level of resemblance sufficient, however, to ensure extensive sympathy with all those we recognize as fellow human beings, to enable us to penetrate into alien points of view when these are embedded in ways of life whose symbolic cultural forms are radically different from our own. Extensive sympathy will be expected as a matter of course only when there is some additional salient resemblance, when, "besides the general resemblance of our natures, there is any peculiar similarity in our manners, or character, or country, or language" (*T* 318).

While the need to be able actively to extend the range of extensive sympathy became painfully obvious in the *Treatise*, the nature and source of such a principle remained rather unclear. If sympathy is basically involuntary and passive, how can we strive to extend it beyond its initial limited form? In the *Treatise*, Hume begins to move toward an answer by granting a more active role to the imagination, speaking of its "efforts" and describing its occasional selectivity or broadened scope. But it seems like mere sleight of hand to suggest that, if we just try hard enough, we will mysteriously find ourselves able to understand how people very different from ourselves react to the situations in which they find themselves, being "moved" and "touched" in concert with them. We need more of an account of what is actually going on in such sympathetic activity. It is "Of the standard of taste" and "A dialogue," I believe, which have given us the key to understanding how it is possible actively to engage in extensive sympathy. We cannot magically produce sympathy, transporting ourselves imaginatively into other people and intuiting their passions. Even in the *Treatise*, Hume states clearly that "no passion of another discovers itself immediately to the mind. We are only sensible of its causes or effects. From *these* we infer the passion: And consequently *these* give rise to our sympathy" (*T* 576). But this still implies that sympathy must involve a replication of the passions and sentiments of others. What the latter writings suggest we *can* actively strive to achieve is not this replication of passions, per se, but, rather, sympathetic understanding of the points of view of others. This involves extending our capacity to recognize similarities with others by discerning the ends they seek, rather than observing them as a behaviorist would. We must identify the goods they pursue and the evils they avoid, rather than simply noting that the behavior they praise and condemn does not correspond with what we praise and condemn, finding their moral beliefs therefore incomprehensible and "barbarous." We must learn about the context of their moral beliefs, the context in which their catalogue of vices and virtues makes sense, if we are to understand and be able to anticipate their responses (their moral reactions in the broadest sense) to what goes on around them.

CHAPTER 5

Religion and irrationality in history

In the previous chapter, I argued that Hume holds out the possibility of sympathetic understanding even of those whose customs and beliefs are very different from our own, and that he does so without falling into a relativism which would make ethical evaluation of these customs and beliefs impossible. While it is true that "Of the standard of taste" does limit the scope of sympathetic understanding, Hume draws the limit at religious beliefs and the moral practices which arise out of them, and not, as has often been assumed, at alien ideas of morality and decency *per se*. Religious or "artificial" manners, as I briefly indicated, were accused of blocking attempts at sympathetic understanding because they involve pursuing ends which seem to frustrate, or to be disconnected from, the shared goods of human life. These shared goods and ends are conditions for the possibility of understanding the complex whole of customs and beliefs of those who strike us as foreign or alien.

There is much more to be learned about the possibilities and limits of sympathetic understanding of different points of view by reflecting on what Hume regards as the greatest barrier to such understanding, and much to be learned about Hume's views of religion by considering it under this description. Hence, in this chapter, I turn to Hume's analysis and critique of religion, looking first at the *Natural History of Religion*'s account of the insinuation of irrationality into religious belief as theism emerges out of polytheism. I discuss Hume's appropriation and redirection of the tradition of Christian reflection on sin as self-deception by comparing and contrasting Hume and Pascal. I then turn to the *History of England*, discussing irony and sentimentality as rhetorical techniques which Hume employs to disengage readers from their party prejudices and encourage them to take up more enlarged views. In the *History of England*, Hume's critique of religion as irrational takes more concrete form in his discussions of both sincere and hypocritical professions of religious belief, religious factions, and related violence.[1] "Sincere hypocrisy," (which we might term self-deception), along with wishful thinking and related forms of irrationality, emerge as the factors responsible for frustrating sympathetic understanding. If we grant that certain kinds of irrationality do stymie sympathetic understanding, is it truly blocked by irrationalities of religious belief in general or Christian theism in particular? Is Collingwood right to say of Hume (along with Voltaire) that "with their narrow conception of reason they had no sympathy for, and therefore no insight into, what from their point of view were non-rational periods of human history" in which everything was "superstition and darkness, error and imposture"?[2] Or is Hume able to engage sympathetically with religious believers while differentiating between different sorts of irrationality which influence their beliefs and actions?

In "A dialogue," Palamedes chooses two exemplars of "*artificial* lives and manners" to contrast with one another. The Cynic Diogenes (413–327 BCE) is chosen as a representative from ancient philosophy, while Blaise Pascal (1623–62) is chosen as a representative from modern religion. In order to encourage skeptical or relativistic conclusions about morality, Palamedes points out that each was held up as an ideal by his contemporaries, but that they stand in stark contrast to one another. But Hume insists that the practices of these two men cannot fairly be proposed as evidence for such a conclusion, since the artificiality of their lives impedes the regular operation of the natural principles of their minds.

Pascal is characterized as the prototypical embodiment of the "monkish virtues":

The aim of Pascal was to keep a perpetual sense of his dependence before his eyes, and never to forget his numberless wants and infirmities . . . [He] made constant profession of humility and abasement, of the contempt and hatred of himself; and endeavoured to attain these supposed virtues, as far as they are attainable. The austerities . . . of the Frenchman were embraced merely for their own sake, and in order to suffer as much as possible . . . The saint refused himself the most innocent [pleasures], even in private . . . [He] endeavoured to be absolutely indifferent towards his nearest relations, and to love and speak well of his enemies . . . The most ridiculous superstitions directed Pascal's faith and practice; and an extreme contempt of this life, in comparison of the future, was the chief foundation of his conduct. (*E* 342–343)

Pascal seems, on Hume's description, to have acted in a way which runs directly counter to individual and communal flourishing, and which might even threaten bare survival. Rather than seeking self-preservation, he held himself in self-contempt and embraced suffering. Moreover, he denied the goods of community, since he disregarded the claims of familial bonds on him. Pascal's virtues, far from being either "useful" or "agreeable" to himself or others, seem to be "good for" nothing and as unpleasant as possible. Sympathetic understanding, which requires recognizing the goods that others pursue, is – at least according to Hume – stymied.[3]

When sympathetic understanding is frustrated, a distinct sort of question presses itself on us. How can we account for the emergence of artificial lives like that of Pascal? How do practices which undermine human flourishing come to be characterized as virtuous? How can we account for the very existence of "artificial" lives? Since there seems to Hume to be no *reason* to live in such a way, he begins to look for an external causal account.[4] When it comes to artificial lives, the effort to enter sympathetically into the situations of others must be supplemented by a search for historical and psychological explanation, an attempt to come up with a narrative which makes sense of the fact that people don't act the way we would expect them to act, given the beliefs they avow, or act in ways that seem self-defeating. There is no need for any such special explanation of behavior which we can understand as motivated by the pursuit of recognizable goods or ends of human action, but where, even after our best effort to sympathize with their point of view, people seem to be acting in pursuit of no good at all, some further account of their actions is called for. When Hume ends "A dialogue" by saying that "no one can answer for what will please or displease" those who lead artificial lives, it is this sort of question about religious belief and practice which he wishes to plant in his reader's minds, and it is this sort of question he seeks to answer in the *Natural History of Religion,* where he searches out religion's origin in human nature (*E* 343). The very project of writing a "natural history" of religion suggests that Hume will not be considering religious beliefs as straightforward truth-claims; a natural history is not a story about the accumulation of good reasons for taking something to be true, but a story about how, apart from such good reasons, beliefs come into being and change over time.[5]

A central thrust of Hume's theory of belief in both the *Treatise* and the *Enquiry* was that, since there is no impression which corresponds to the idea of God, no full-fledged belief in God is possible. In broader terms, his claim was that human beings utterly lack direct experience of the reality of a personal God. Just as Hume's official theory of belief was complicated by his concrete reflections on the vivid intensity of the mental impressions aroused by fiction and theatrical representations (as discussed in chapter 3), his theory is developed and deepened through his attempt to grapple with the concrete reality of religious belief. If the idea of God does not arise from an impression of God, if it is experience of something other than God that leads people to believe in God, what are those impressions or experiences which nevertheless bring belief into existence and allow it to persist? In the *Treatise*, Hume attempted to answer this in general terms by reference to the influence on the imagination of frequent repetition of an idea (*T* 116) and by the impact of contiguous or resembling ideas (*T* 109). Within the *Natural History of Religion*, a more fully developed account is given.

VARIETIES OF RELIGIOUS BELIEF

One of the most striking things about Hume's account of polytheism (which he believes emerged prior in history to theism) is that it is intimately connected with and quite straightforwardly intelligible in light of what Hume regards as basic goods of human life – in this sense, Hume does not consider polytheism irrational. Polytheism arises out of the ordinary concerns of human life:

It must necessarily, indeed, [Hume says] be allowed, that, in order to carry men's intention beyond the present course of things, or lead them into any inference concerning invisible intelligent power, they must be actuated by some passion, which urges their first enquiry . . . No passions . . . can be supposed to work upon such barbarians, but the ordinary affections of human life; the anxious concern for happiness, the dread of future misery, the terror of death, the thirst of revenge, the appetite for food and other necessaries. (*NHR* 29)

Because the "true springs and causes" of events in the world were not visible to them, these unknown causes, which had the power to determine whether or not they achieved their goals, became the focus of human hopes and anxieties. "No wonder, then," Hume suggests:

that mankind, being placed in such an absolute ignorance of causes, and being at the same time so anxious concerning their future fortune, should immediately acknowledge a dependence on invisible powers, possessed of sentiment and intelligence. The unknown causes which continually employ their thought, appearing always in the same aspect, are all apprehended to be of the same kind or species. Nor is it long before we ascribe to them thought and reason and passion, and sometimes even the limbs and figures of men, in order to bring them nearer to a resemblance with ourselves. (*NHR* 30)

In terms of the *Treatise* theory of belief, Hume might say that although there are no existing objects which correspond to these various deities, the idea of these deities, conceived by the imagination, is enlivened by the resemblance which we perceive between human actions and natural events, as well as by the anxious passions of these peoples.

Belief is not rooted in direct experience of personal deities, and therefore lacks strong justification, but it is also not contradicted by any experiences available to primitive peoples. A number of powerful but limited beings, often working at cross-purposes, seems to account quite nicely for the unexpected twists and turns of events. Once we conclude that intelligent agents and their active intentions lie behind all the spring rains and famines, earthquakes and epidemics, which so profoundly influence the course of our lives, we are no longer at a loss when it comes to dealing with these "unknown causes." We can begin to try to influence the activities of the deities as we would try to influence powerful human agents – by offering them gifts and praise, by threatening or pleading with them.

The initial emergence of religion is thus itself to be seen as an attempt at sympathetic understanding, an attempt, that is, to understand the workings of the world as intentional action performed for intelligible reasons, in the pursuit of recognizable goods or ends. It is because events seem to be so disordered and unpredictable that human beings seek this sort of understanding so urgently. The mere fact that fear stimulates thinking about hidden causes doesn't by itself render religious belief irrational, any more than we are forced to conclude that modern science is irrational because it is motivated by the desire to understand and control natural forces. As with any theoretical account of the world, the plausibility of this one is linked to our perception of the world, and this perception in turn is linked to our interests and concerns and our prior knowledge of the world.

A shift in perception, or an expanded range of experience, might make the theory lose its hold on us. "Could men anatomize nature," Hume remarks, "according to the most probable, at least the most intelligible philosophy, they would find, that these causes are nothing but the particular fabric and structure of the minute parts of their own bodies and of external objects; and that, by a regular and constant machinery, all the events are produced, about which they are so much concerned" (*NHR* 29). This recognition of order and regularity, of constant conjunction of events in the world, would not *eliminate* questions concerning the ultimate reasons for things being as they are, but such questions would be pushed back from the level of particular events to that of an ultimate source of order. We would no longer ask why this particular famine was visited upon us, since we would be able to trace the regularities in nature which issued in famine at this particular time and place, but we could still ask why the world is such that famines occur at all. As Livingston remarks, all "constant-conjunction regularities . . . are equally intelligible or unintelligible; that is, they are simply brute facts. To render them understandable, we should have to uncover the rationale or 'cause' behind them which would show us in an intuitively satisfying way why they must be as they are. A more general regularity including them all will not do because it too would have constant conjunction *form* and so would be in need of explanation."[6] We have no real idea of what such an ultimate cause would be like (and Hume's *Dialogues Concerning Natural Religion* reveals the illegitimacy of Deist attempts to give this bare-bones concept some flesh), although inherent mathematical necessity and intelligent power are proposed candidates.

The most "intuitively satisfying" account of the way things are would be the sort with which we are familiar from the human practice of justifying action; "for moral explanation . . . the principle of intelligibility is that an act is intelligible just in case it can be covered by a good reason the agent had for acting."[7] But, unlike the realm of human action, we cannot observe the agent acting, cannot ask for reasons, cannot come to perceive what constitutes living well or doing well on the part of the unknown agent. Fortunately, the recognition of regularity in the operations of the world calms the demand for an account of each isolated event. Prosperity, along with social and political order, go even further toward distracting the urge to ask unanswerable questions (*NHR* 30–31).

Hume's "barbarians," however, did not perceive the order and regularity lying behind the accidents governing their existence, and hence did not conclude that a *single* power lay behind all unknown causes of events. They were impressed not by general laws but by singular events. Nevertheless, in the course of attempts to influence the gods, polytheism tends naturally, according to Hume, to be transformed into theism, and a single power comes to be seen as responsible for all of the operations of the world. The god who is regarded as having particular jurisdiction over one's home territory, or the god who is regarded as ruler of the other gods, is given particular attention:

his votaries will endeavour, by every art, to insinuate themselves into his favour; and supposing him to be pleased, like themselves, with praise and flattery, there is no eulogy or exaggeration, which will be spared in their addresses to him. In proportion as men's fears or distresses become more urgent, they still invent new strains of adulation; and even he who outdoes his predecessor in swelling up the titles of his divinity, is sure to be outdone by his successor in newer and more pompous epithets of praise. Thus they proceed; till at last they arrive at infinity itself, beyond which there is no farther progress. (*NHR* 43)

Theism, therefore, quite unlike philosophical Deism, is the end result of a practice of flattery spurred on by fear and anxiety. Prior to the emergence of theism, we have no difficulty understanding the reasons people had for their religious beliefs and practices. Given the belief that invisible powers are responsible for unexpected events which affect our lives, it is sensible to try to influence these powers in every way possible so that they will act in ways conducive to our individual and communal flourishing. Even if this belief is false, we can nevertheless perceive the reasons for the actions which follow from it, and the belief itself is a reasonable one.[8] While Hume objects mildly to it because "it is not ascertained by any just reason or authority" (*NHR* 53), he does not claim that it is "absurd" or "contradictory" or suggest that these polytheists had any good reason to question their beliefs about the powers controlling the world. With the emergence of theism, however, the character of religious belief and practice strikes Hume as much more complex and perplexing, since, "rather than relinquish this propensity to adulation, religionists, in all ages, have involved themselves in the greatest absurdities and contradictions" (*NHR* 139). It is, in fact, these "absurdities and contradictions" which indicate to Hume that these individuals had no *reasons* for arriving at their theistic beliefs. He surmises that when it comes to theism, fear is no longer just a stimulus to reflection on the nature of unknown causes, but has itself become the cause of belief.

Prominent among the contradictions in theistic beliefs are those having to do with the deity's natural and moral attributes. Religious believers praise the deity in terms which render him (or recognize him as) increasingly transcendent, infinite, and powerful, yet they also continue, seeking to make sense of the deity's actions, to conceive of the deity anthropomorphically. Having conceived of the deity as infinite, Hume says, "it is well, if, in striving to get farther, and to represent a magnificent simplicity, they run not into inexplicable mystery, and destroy the intelligent nature of their deity, on which alone any rational worship or adoration can be founded" (*NHR* 43). The problem with divine simplicity, as Cleanthes reveals in the *Dialogues Concerning Natural Religion*, is that "a mind whose acts and sentiments and ideas are not distinct and successive, one that is wholly simple and totally immutable, is a mind which has no thought, no reason, no will, no sentiment, no love, no hatred . . . is no mind at all" (*D* 29). Divine simplicity conflicts with divine intelligence. Moreover, as Demea argues in the *Dialogues*, "all the *sentiments* of the human mind, gratitude, resentment, love, friendship, approbation, blame, pity, emulation, envy, have a plain reference to the

state and situation of man, and are calculated for preserving the
existence and promoting the activity of such a being in such circumstances.
It seems, therefore, unreasonable to transfer such sentiments to a
supreme existence or to suppose him actuated by them" (*D* 27). In the
absence of such sentiments, however, it is hard to make sense of the idea
of intentional action on the part of the deity.

Since the development of religious theories is stimulated and later
caused by fear and anxiety concerning future events, there is, according
to Hume, a tendency to conceive of the invisible powers which control
human destiny as malicious. "Every image of vengeance, severity,
cruelty, and malice must occur, and must augment the ghastliness and
horror, which oppresses the amazed religionist. A panic having once
seized the mind, the active fancy still farther multiplies the objects of
terror" (*NHR* 65). We could perhaps attribute terrible events to
competition among the gods or the limited power of our patron gods.
Once a single, all-powerful deity is held responsible for everything,
however, it becomes increasingly difficult to conceive of him as anything
but evil. Yet the deity is not only regarded as omnipotent, but also as
omnibenevolent; "our natural terrors present the notion of a devilish
and malicious deity: Our propensity to adulation leads us to acknowledge
an excellent and divine" (*NHR* 68). Hence the contradiction which
emerges when the terrors of existence are placed alongside the deity's
supposed omnipotence and benevolence.

But Hume is less concerned with contradictions among beliefs about
the natural and moral nature of the deity as such, than with the
psychological and moral consequences of attempting to hold these
beliefs. He argues that believers' real ideas of the deity do not correspond
to their exalted conceptions of the infinite perfections of the deity: "we
may observe, that the assent of the vulgar is . . . merely verbal, and that
they are incapable of conceiving those sublime qualities, which they
seemingly attribute to the Deity. Their real idea of him, notwithstanding
their pompous language, is still as poor and frivolous as ever" (*NHR* 45).
The lack of congruence between their verbal assertions and their real
ideas is shown by the senselessness of their practices. Why, for example,
would the first principle of all things be displeased by someone's dousing
a fire, as the Magians believe? Why would circumcision be of any
concern to an infinite and transcendent deity (*NHR* 45–46)?

Moreover, Hume argues, religious beliefs are different in quality from
ordinary beliefs:
The conviction of the religionists, in all ages, is more affected than real, and

scarcely ever approaches, in any degree, to that solid belief and persuasion, which governs us in the common affairs of life. Men dare not avow, even to their own hearts, the doubts which they entertain on such subjects: They make a merit of implicit faith; and disguise to themselves their real infidelity, by the strongest asseverations and most positive bigotry. But nature is too hard for all their endeavours, and suffers not the obscure, glimmering light, afforded in those shadowy regions, to equal the strong impressions, made by common sense and by experience. The usual course of men's conduct belies their words, and shows, that their assent in these matters is some unaccountable operation of the mind between disbelief and conviction, but approaching much nearer to the former than to the latter. (*NHR* 60)

The mind's inability to give true assent to their religious beliefs is intimately related, not solely to the lack of impressions derived from experience of the reality of the deity, but also to inherent inconsistencies among these beliefs. To affirm one aspect of the nature of the deity too firmly would bring into the foreground its tension with other divine attributes. Hence, religious beliefs are held with a foggy tenuousness which masks contradiction. The absurdity inherent in theistic belief is ultimately converted from a lurking threat to the crowning glory of faith. It contributes to an aura of exaltation and mystery which surrounds religious beliefs; faith in such absurdities eventually becomes a source of merit, a way of subduing the tendency of reason to pridefully challenge inscrutable divine wisdom (*NHR* 54).

The acceptance of some contradictions among one's religious beliefs paves the way for the emergence of more, as the mind loses its capacity to distinguish truth from falsehood and doubt from conviction.[9] This corruption of the capacities of the mind is a consequence of its developing habit of what we might call self-deception.[10] The dynamics of self-deception are described most clearly in Hume's discussion of problems having to do with divine morality – or lack thereof. These problems are given special attention throughout Hume's account of the emergence of theism.

The flattery of the gods is at first a prudential measure, since one might anger the gods by pointing out their limitations and failings:

Will you say that your deity is finite and bounded in his perfections; may be overcome by a greater force; is subject to human passions, pains, and infirmities; has a beginning, and may have an end? This they dare not affirm; but thinking it safest to comply with the higher encomiums, they endeavour, by an affected ravishment and devotion, to ingratiate themselves with him. (*NHR* 45)

This is initially a purely *affected* devotion, expressed during public worship in the temple or wherever the deity resides. In private one might curse him for wickedly sending the plague which carried off one's children, but when the deity might be listening one is careful not to betray such sentiments. As their notions of the power and knowledge of the deity become more exalted, however, people no longer feel safe in entertaining any critical opinions of the deity, even in their innermost thoughts.

In proportion to the supposed extent of his science and authority, their terrors naturally augment; while they believe, that no secrecy can conceal them from his scrutiny, and that even the inmost recesses of their breast lie open before him. They must then be careful not to form expressly any sentiment of blame and disapprobation. All must be applause, ravishment, extasy. And while their gloomy apprehensions make them ascribe to him measures of conduct, which, in human creatures, would be highly blamed, they must still affect to praise and admire that conduct in the object of their devotional addresses. (*NHR* 67)

Worshippers must affect admiration even of a God who sentences people to *eternal* damnation, and must do so not solely publicly, but privately – they attempt to deceive themselves, since it is no longer possible to deceive the deity by professing one thing while believing something else. "Among idolaters," comments Hume, "the words may be false, and belie the secret opinion: But among more exalted religionists, the opinion itself contracts a kind of falsehood, and belies the inward sentiment. The heart secretly detests such measures of cruel and implacable vengeance; but the judgment dares not but pronounce them perfect and adorable. And the additional misery of this inward struggle aggravates all the other terrors, by which these unhappy victims to superstition are for ever haunted" (*NHR* 67). While polytheism encourages hypocrisy, only theism encourages self-deception.

Self-deception has often been analyzed in terms of intentionally coming to believe something which contradicts something else one already believes, for example, theists convince themselves that God is good although they really believe that God is wicked. It is difficult to give a non-paradoxical account of self-deception, but the paradox can be partially diffused by allowing for some sort of separation among beliefs, so that the person is not said to be avowing the conjunction of two contradictory statements.[11] The Freudian suggestion is that this separation is accomplished by permitting only one of the beliefs to be conscious, but Donald Davidson, among others, argues persuasively that the boundaries keeping related but opposed beliefs apart need not be permanent and need not correspond to a boundary between consciousness and subconsciousness.[12] The concept of the subconscious is not, of course, available to Hume, but he does speak, in the passage just quoted above, of a division between heart or sentiment and judgment or opinion. (The implication is that heart or sentiment are somehow more reliable, less capable of insincerity.) The division or boundary is a theoretical postulate which makes it easier to talk about self-deception; it is not clear that it does more than that.

Self-deception as it is commonly understood is not simply a matter of the dirt-common state of holding logically incompatible beliefs, however. What makes self-deception something special is the element of intentionality involved in acquiring a belief which conflicts with a belief one already has or in actively suppressing awareness or recognition of the conflict between the two beliefs.[13] Hume's account of the development of self-deception, as theism emerged out of polytheism, certainly characterizes the phenomenon as intentional, but as he is giving an account of a change occurring over many generations, rather than in the lifetime of a single individual, it is unclear whose intentions he could be talking about. Are persons who are socialized into a theistic religion guilty of self-deception? It hardly seems fair to charge them with acquiring their beliefs irrationally, since they could hardly begin by failing to trust their own intellectual and religious authorities. Are they perhaps only guilty of a hardened conservatism of belief, which does not easily question beliefs which are already firmly held?[14] Hume makes a stronger claim than this, for he asserts that theistic belief is never full-fledged belief. Theists must continually attempt to believe theological propositions that they can never wholly accept. They are therefore involved in an unending process of self-deception.

Jon Elster argues that the concept of self-deception is incoherent, asking "how does one manage to *forget intentionally* what one 'really' (somehow, somewhere) believes? And, having achieved this impossible feat, how does one achieve that of *believing at will* what one also believes that there are no adequate grounds for believing?"[15] Neither forgetting nor believing are subject to direct intentional control. Most analyses of self-deception seem to assume a voluntaristic theory of belief. Elster suggests, in contrast, that purported instances of self-deception be explained in a number of different ways: as unsuccessful attempts at self-deception, as unsuccessful attempts at character modification, and as cases of wishful thinking, since "I may bring it about now that I come to believe something at a later time, if I can also and simultaneously bring about forgetfulness of the process itself."[16] I must forget, that is, that I intended to deceive myself. I see no reason to refrain from calling at least this last phenomenon self-deception, however.

Hume's emphasis on the weakness and instability of religious belief leads me to conclude that he is characterizing an unsuccessful attempt at self-deception. Hume, as I argued in chapter 3, understands belief as a function of customary connection, not at all as a result of voluntary decisions of the will. In that earlier discussion, I suggested that Hume saw religious faith as a sort of "poetical system," an artificial web of connected beliefs which competes with the real, natural, this-worldly web of belief. But how can we distinguish "poetical systems" from reality? This is largely a matter of the comprehensiveness of the web of belief, its capacity to find internal resources with which to mend breaks and to fill gaps. In the case of religious belief, Hume thinks, the breaks are such that individuals are driven to the extreme of adopting a voluntaristic attitude toward belief and responding to their recurrent doubts by seeking to will themselves into believing religious doctrines. It is fear that spurs them on, providing an artificial source of "vivification" to religious ideas. Many of the dangers Hume associated with religion he linked with unsuccessful attempts by believers to believe at will or to deny the failure of their attempts at self-deception.[17] Indeed, Hume's term "hypocrisy," unlike "deceit," points to pretenses which may not be successful. I will continue, however, to use the more familiar modern term "self-deception" to refer even to the unsuccessful attempt to deceive oneself by ignoring or improperly weighting evidence or by acting as though one believed something.

The self-deception of theists has wide-ranging ethical ramifications; "even though superstition or enthusiasm should not put itself in direct opposition to morality; the very diverting of the attention, the raising up a new and frivolous species of merit, the preposterous distribution which it makes of praise and blame, must have the most pernicious consequences, and weaken extremely men's attachment to the natural motives of justice and humanity" (*D* 84). One's capacity for moral judgment is eventually undermined by the constant effort to praise God's goodness and benevolence in the face of his unappeasable appetite for punishment.[18] Believers seek to apply the same moral terms to human beings and to God, claiming an analogy but insisting that the terms are inadequate to God. In reality, according to Hume, the application of these terms to the deity begins in dishonesty and ends in confusion. In their efforts to exalt the deity, theists become hesitant to praise human virtues, since to do so seems to question God's superiority. "Where the deity is represented as infinitely superior to mankind," writes Hume, "this belief, though altogether just, is apt, when joined with superstitious terrors, to sink the human mind into the lowest submission and abasement, and to represent the monkish virtues of mortification, penance, humility, and passive suffering, as the only qualities which are acceptable to him" (*NHR* 52). The exaltation of the deity goes hand in hand with the denigration of finite, this-worldly existence, along with denigration of the virtues which are those habits of character constitutive of living well and doing well within this life. The "monkish virtue" of humility is especially obnoxious to Hume because it is so seldom genuine – not surprisingly, since it is a state which is essentially a by-product. The direct pursuit of humility is therefore self-defeating – the more I try to be humble, the more likely I am to become self-absorbed or prideful.[19]

Spiritual virtues, on Hume's account, always compete with natural virtues, since "it is certain, that, in every religion, however sublime the verbal definition which it gives of its divinity, many of the votaries, perhaps the greatest number, will still seek the divine favor, not by virtue and good morals, which alone can be acceptable to a perfect being, but either by frivolous observances, by intemperate zeal, by rapturous extasies, or by the belief of mysterious and absurd opinions" (*NHR* 70). It is only practices which are disagreeable and useless, or even positively harmful, which can claim to be performed solely out of religious devotion, without the tincture of any other motive. Moral duties do not fit into this category of practices at all, since

The duties, which a man performs as a friend or parent, seem merely owing to his benefactor or children; nor can he be wanting to these duties, without breaking through all the ties of nature and morality. A strong inclination may prompt him to the performance: A sentiment of order and moral obligation joins its force to these natural ties: And the whole man, if truly virtuous, is drawn to his duty, without any effort or endeavour. Even with regard to the virtues, which are more austere, and more founded on reflection, such as public spirit, filial duty, temperance, or integrity; the moral obligation, in our apprehension, removes all pretension to religious merit; and the virtuous conduct is deemed no more than what we owe to society and to ourselves. In all this, a superstitious man finds nothing, which he has properly performed for the sake of the deity, or which can peculiarly recommend him to the divine favour and protection. (*NHR* 71–72)

Morality is much more likely, therefore, to be subverted by religion than upheld by it. It is not only concrete ideals of character which are affected; the very understanding of what virtue is becomes clouded by the sustained identification of frivolous or harmful practices as virtuous. Religious believers no longer understand that the virtues are traits of character which contribute to the flourishing of human life, that they are, broadly speaking, "useful" and "agreeable." Instead, they connect virtue with approval of the deity, and this approval is arbitrary and mysterious, like the deity himself. The self-deception of religious belief leads to moral blindness and confusion.

THE CHARGE OF SELF-DECEPTION: HUME VS. PASCAL

Hume had a rich tradition of reflection on self-deception upon which to draw in developing his critique of theistic belief. Ironically, however, given the target of Hume's charge of self-deception, this tradition of thought emerges out of Christian attempts to make sense of human responsibility for the Fall and continuing sinfulness.[20] Christian thought on self-deception reaches back to Augustine's introduction of the will as a power of the soul which spontaneously turns away from true knowledge of God and self.

One Christian thinker whose reflection on self-deception is likely to have influenced Hume is the British moralist and bishop, Joseph Butler (1692–1752).[21] Butler was particularly concerned with the role self-deception plays in immoral conduct, with the way in which people conceal their own wrongdoing from themselves and continue to avow religious faith and devotion. "If there be any such thing in mankind as putting half-deceits upon themselves, which there plainly is," Butler writes, "either by avoiding reflection, or (if they do reflect) by religious equivocation, subterfuges, and palliating matters to themselves; by these means conscience may be laid asleep, and they may go on in a course of wickedness with less disturbance." Such a person "deliberately contrives to deceive and impose upon himself, in a matter which he knew to be of the utmost importance."[22]

Butler calls this phenomenon "hypocrisy" (although he acknowledges that this word is usually used to refer to pretending before others, not before oneself) since he claims that "in scripture, which treats chiefly of our behaviour towards God and our own consciences, it signifies not only the endeavour to delude our fellow-creatures, but likewise insincerity towards him, and towards ourselves."[23] Hume, too, uses the word "hypocrisy" in order to talk about such phenomena.[24] He was, however, less interested in self-deception with regard to the moral character of one's actions than in a more all-encompassing self-deception about the way the world is, a self-deception which does not just redescribe one's evil actions as good, but which spurs one to perform new actions, such as fasting, joining the Crusades, or persecuting a heretic.

In this respect, Hume's reflections on self-deception resonate more closely with those of Pascal, a figure who – as we have already seen – simultaneously intrigued and repelled Hume. Like Hume, Pascal conceived of self-deception as a phenomenon affecting one's perception and activity as a whole, not simply one's view of the morality of one's actions. It is likely that Hume first read Pascal's *Pensées*, along with the works of the Port-Royalists Arnauld and Nicole, in the library of the Jesuit college of La Flèche where he wrote the *Treatise of Human Nature*.[25] At any rate, Pascal was apparently on Hume's mind a few years later when he was writing "A dialogue." Pascal's diagnosis of the human situation and the dire need to renounce the world in pursuit of eternal happiness are scarcely distinguishable from Evangelical Presbyterian orthodoxy, but a French Catholic was a much safer overt target for Hume's criticism than the Evangelicals at home. In "A dialogue" Hume appropriates Pascal's analysis of the human proclivity toward self-deception in order to portray Pascal as himself an instance of the self-deception of artificial religious lives and the way in which such lives block sympathetic understanding. Whereas Pascal used the notion of self-deception in his religious critique of secular lives, Hume uses the notion of self-deception to develop his secular critique of religious lives. Hume does not, however, simply invert Pascal's analysis; he appropriates a criticism which members of one Christian sect have directed at members of other sects and takes the bold step of directing it against theists in general.

"We are nothing but lies, duplicity, contradiction, and we hide and disguise ourselves from ourselves," says Pascal.[26] Why do we hide from ourselves? Because we cannot bear to look at the radical contingency and impermanence of our lives. Instead, we distract ourselves with a round of diversions so as to escape despair, pursuing things which can never make us happy, seeking "rest by way of activity." To admit that these activities are empty and vain would be to come to truly know ourselves, to know of human beings that "they simply want a violent and vigorous occupation to take their minds off themselves, and that is why they choose some attractive object to entice them in ardent pursuit."[27] We cannot bear to be alone with ourselves, because we cannot bear to think of the uncertainty, finitude, and misery of our existence. Self-deception, moreover, is linked to the deception of others, for we want their love and esteem and cannot admit the vices and imperfections that make us unworthy of it. We do our utmost to fool them so that they in turn will reinforce our own delusions about ourselves and our lives.[28] Human community is first and foremost a locus for mutually reinforcing façades and distractions and hence a barrier to self-knowledge and knowledge of God. "While the present never satisfies us, experience deceives us, and leads us on from one misfortune to another until death comes as the ultimate and eternal climax."[29]

Pascal concludes from this, not that we are miserable creatures, doomed to perpetual unhappiness, but rather that the fact of our perpetual dissatisfaction and unrest point beyond worldly goods and finite existence.

What else does this craving, and this helplessness, proclaim but that there was once in man a true happiness, of which all that now remains is the empty print and trace? This he tries in vain to fill with everything around him, seeking in things that are not there the help he cannot find in those that are, though none can help, since this infinite abyss can be filled only with an infinite and immutable object; in other words by God himself. God alone is man's true good . . . Since losing his true good, man is capable of seeing it in anything, even his own destruction, although it is so contrary at once to God, to reason and to nature.[30]

The Fall was the result of our unwillingness to recognize our lack of self-sufficiency, our need to be centered in God. We willfully blinded ourselves by closing our eyes to our dependence on God. Henceforth, to be in sin is to be blind to the nature of our true good, and to seek in finite goods a satisfaction which only God, who is infinite good, can provide.

For Pascal, human beings and human existence are full of contradictions, of which only this Christian understanding of reality can make sense. Unless we recognize the simultaneous greatness and wretchedness of human beings, we can never know ourselves and acknowledge our proper relationship of dependence on God.[31] Once we recognize that God is our true good, we will despise the things of this world and our own self-love, which has led us to deny our true relationship to God. The truth of Christianity is shown by its comprehension of our nature. "No other religion has proposed that we should hate ourselves. No other religion therefore can please those who hate themselves and seek a being who is really worthy of love."[32]

From Pascal's perspective, it is irrational not to be concerned about eternity, not to recognize that the only good thing in this life is the hope for another better one. Indifference to eternity is the height of self-deception:

Of all their aberrations it is no doubt this which most convicts them of folly and blindness, and where they can most easily be confounded by the first application of common sense and by natural instincts. For it is indubitable that this life is but an instant of time, that the state of death is eternal, whatever its nature may be, and thus that all our actions and thoughts must follow such different paths according to the state of this eternity, that the only possible way of acting with sense and judgment is to decide our course in the light of this point, which ought to be our ultimate objective.[33]

Although the usual state is one of ignorance and self-deception, Pascal is confident that anyone is capable of seeing the truth about themselves and the world, and that indeed anything else is unreasonable. *(The Whole Duty of Man* echoes this diagnosis and prescription, although its vocabulary is that of witchcraft rather than self-deception: "none knows, perhaps the next hour, the next minute the night of death may overtake them; what a madness is it then for them to defer one moment to turn out of that path, which leads to certain destruction, and put themselves in that, which will bring them to bliss and glory? Yet so are men bewitched, and enchanted with the deceitfulness of sin, that no intreaty, no persuasion can prevail with them, to make this so reasonable, so necessary a change."[34])

Hume and Pascal agree that self-deception is rooted in human fear, more specifically, in the fear of not being in control of one's own being and destiny. They disagree radically, however, in their understanding of the implications of and remedies for this fear. According to Pascal, our fear is first and foremost fear of death and of the eternity which lies beyond it. Our fear of eternity is so great, in fact, that we conceal it from ourselves by pursuing earthly delights, willfully distorting our vision of their true value relative to eternal life. According to Hume, however, what we fear most is that our current plans and projects will be frustrated and our earthly happiness destroyed. It is the theist whose vision of the value of things is distorted, since the theist places a high value on the illusory notion of eternal life and downgrades the goods of this life, which are the only true goods.

Hume argues that the concern about one's eternal state is artificially induced. In the *Dialogues*, Philo develops a critique of invocations of fears and desires associated with eternity, in the context of arguing that eternal rewards and punishments are unnecessary to motivate right action:

The inference is not just, because finite and temporary rewards and punishments have so great influence that therefore such as are infinite and eternal must have so much greater. Consider, I beseech you, the attachment which we have to present things, and the little concern which we discover for objects so remote and uncertain. When divines are declaiming against the common behaviour and conduct of the world, they always represent this principle as the strongest imaginable (which indeed it is), and describe almost all human kind as lying under the influence of it, and sunk into the deepest lethargy and unconcern about their religious interests. Yet these same divines, when they refute their speculative antagonists, suppose the motives of religion to be so powerful that, without them, it were impossible for civil society to subsist; nor are they ashamed of so palpable a contradiction. (*D* 83)

Hume is willing to admit that "there arise, indeed, in some minds, some unaccountable terrors with regard to futurity: But these would quickly vanish, were they not artificially fostered by precept and education" (*D* 92).[35] We are incapable of steadily maintaining a concern which reaches beyond the present life.[36] It is contrary to common sense to seek to drown out our real finite concerns for the sake of a shadowy concept of life beyond the grave.

Underlying Hume's convictions about the focus of our fears is a skepticism about the coherence of some of the concepts employed by Christian thinkers like Pascal. While Pascal wants us to weigh the brief span of mortal life against eternal life, Hume questions our very capacity to put the latter notion on the scale, since it is not clear that we can make sense of what it would mean for us to possess "eternal life." How could the soul live on after the death of the body, when "every thing is in common between soul and body[?]. The organs of the one are all of them the organs of the other. The existence therefore of the one must be dependent on the other" (*D* 95). As Elster points out, if an end-state is not logically coherent, all action toward it will be self-defeating.[37] If eternal life is incoherent, those who pursue it cannot help but act irrationally. Far from indicating that we are destined for eternal life, moreover, Hume proposes that our fear of death is nothing but an instinct which is straightforwardly in the service of our present life – "Death is in the end unavoidable; yet the human species could not be preserved, had not nature inspired us with an aversion towards it" (*D* 96).

So Pascal's sinner hopelessly seeks ultimate satisfaction in finite earthly goods, while Hume's theist equally hopelessly seeks happiness in the hereafter. Hume cannot appeal to the pride and self-centeredness of sin in order to account for this widespread self-deception, however. The *Natural History of Religion* is an attempt to give a secularized version of the Fall, the emergence of superstition and self-deception out of fear of the unknown. The remedy for sin is repentance; Pascal advises that we give up our search for control and acknowledge our utter dependence on God. Then we would no longer need to fear and disguise the finitude and contingency of our earthly existence. Hume, in contrast, argues that holding God responsible for what goes on in the world leads eventually to greater internal dishonesty. Instead, we should strive for greater knowledge of the workings of the world so that, recognizing that things occur in an orderly fashion, we will have less fear of unknown causes. More importantly, given the severe limits of our capacity for knowing the ultimate causes of the workings of the world, we should strive to create ordered communities which will bring peace and security and a measure of control over our existences (*NHR* 30). Fear will then diminish, and with it the impetus for self-deception. Hume rejects Pascal's harsh Augustinian evaluation of human community, and regards it instead as a source of security and the locus of most of the true enjoyment in life. Religious zeal and bigotry are to blame for disrupting community and robbing it of both security and enjoyment.

The charge of self-deception is a powerful, if ultimately unproductive, weapon. By invoking self-deception, Pascal can account for the widespread prevalence of apparent indifference toward eternal rewards and punishments. Those, like Hume, who claim that eternity isn't even worth thinking about, are the most self-deceived. Hence, their claims and arguments are explained away as pathological and need not be taken seriously at face value. Hume, likewise, can invoke self-deception in order to account for Pascal's insistence both on the benevolence of God and on the justice of eternal punishment, as well as to account for Pascal's claims about the infinite importance to human beings of eternity. Hume and Pascal can continue to trade accusations of self-deception, and hence discount the opponent's position a priori, without considering each claim and criticism on its own terms. From then on, they can attend only to each other's behavior, while discounting avowed beliefs and intentions. One point of asymmetry in the battle is worth noting, however, for it seems to place Hume in a stronger position than Pascal. In his famous wager, Pascal advocates a voluntaristic therapy for religious skeptics.[38] For Hume, however, such attempts to will oneself into believing something are always a telltale sign of self-deception. His therapy for religious self-deception, as we shall see, is not a voluntaristic one.

It is not simply a matter of claiming that one's opponent has made a mistake, as, for example, Hume claims with respect to primitive polytheists. They were wrong, he thinks, in their beliefs about the nature of the unknown causes they feared, but their beliefs were not contradictory or self-deceptive. Their beliefs were straightforward theoretical beliefs about the way the world is, and can be criticized and defended as such. We may be interested in investigating how they arrived at particular false beliefs, but we can understand their beliefs as a coherent whole, and see the relationship between their actions and beliefs, apart from such an account, since we can make sense of the goods they were pursuing and hence their reasons for acting as they did.

If theists' beliefs were utterly incoherent and contradictory, by contrast, then sympathetic understanding of their beliefs and practices would be beside the point, even if it were possible. Anything may follow from a contradiction, after all. But it is true that Hume is at least able to *identify* the goods that Pascal was seeking – the goods of eternal life. If these goods can somehow be made intelligible in terms of the goods of human life and flourishing, then the point of view from which Pascal's manners are lived out can be sympathetically understood even by one who does not share his "artificial life." Pascal is in pursuit of a life which he believes will contain all and only true and secure goods, goods that most people mistakenly try to pursue in this life. These goods can be understood by analogy with earthly goods. Yet Hume's criticism goes deeper, since he doesn't think that the good of eternal life is a coherent notion, and therefore it cannot really be pursued. Pascal's "virtues," according to Hume, undermine the very conditions for the pursuit of any goods at all.

In treating theistic belief as incoherent and self-deceptive, Hume is moving away from accepting religious beliefs as straightforward common-sense beliefs about the way the world is. This is a movement which has had long-lasting repercussions for the study of religion, and perhaps also the human sciences more broadly, insofar as their development has been shaped by the study of religion. Once the study of religion leaves the realms of theology and apology for one's own religious community, sympathetic understanding is often also left behind. Sociological and anthropological approaches to the study of religion, in particular, have not treated religious beliefs as straightforward truth claims, nor religious actions as actions flowing from such truth claims. They have instead been treated as requiring special explanation because of their irrationality or self-evident falsity.[39] Such approaches have, ironically, treated religious belief in general the way that religious groups have often treated the beliefs of outsiders, whether non-believers or members of competing religious communities. (Given the close historical relationship between missionary work and anthropology, this is hardly surprising). There are circumstances under which causal explanations of human behavior ought to or must replace, rather than simply complementing, sympathetic understanding. The more difficult question is not whether there is a place for causal explanations which sidestep actors' internal reasons, but rather, when is such causal explanation necessary and appropriate? How appropriate is Hume's boundary line?

Does he define it more fairly and with greater self-criticism than do rival religious groups who trade accusations of self-deception among themselves? This question will be easier to answer when we turn from the context of natural history to that of social and political history.

IRONY AND SENTIMENTALITY IN THE "HISTORY OF ENGLAND"

Hume's *History of England* secured fame and material ease, if not fortune, for its author.[40] In this work, Hume's project is not just to give a description of events, nor primarily to give an external explanation of why they happened the way they did, but rather to portray events and persons in a way which presents them either as negative or positive models for his readers. Unlike the *Treatise* and the *Enquiry*, it is thus necessarily a project of understanding and evaluation. In addition, to a much greater extent than the critical essays, it presses Hume to turn from theorizing about the possibility of entering sympathetically into different points of view to put his ideas into practice, applying them to particular persons and events. With respect to the beliefs and actions of theists, however, the charges of self-contradiction and absurdity appear to excuse Hume from any further attempt at sympathetic understanding.[41] After all, we can expect from them "no steady rule of right" (*MPL* 229), and "no one can answer for what will please or displease them. They are in a different element from the rest of mankind; and the natural principles of their mind play not with the same regularity, as if left to themselves, free from the illusions of religious superstition or philosophical enthusiasm" (*E* 343). Despite these avowals of the incomprehensibility of religious attitudes, however, Hume does try to shed light on the actions of religious believers, unearthing their reasons for action and their intended ends. He does not as a rule treat them as insane or regard their actions as random events. In the final section of this chapter, I will try to account for the different ways in which Hume treats religious believers by arguing that Hume distinguishes between different levels of increasing "absurdity" or irrationality of religious belief.[42] Only a careless use of the broad category "irrational" gives rise to the impression that all sorts of irrationality block sympathetic understanding. At that point I pause to ask, however, whether Hume was able to extend sympathetic understanding to its final limit. In the current section, I consider the aims and rhetoric of Hume's *History*, asking in particular how this influences the treatment of religion.

In the *History of England*, the concrete social and political concerns which prompt Hume's theoretical reflections become impossible to ignore. His attempt to develop a natural history of religion, to give an admittedly idealized explanation of the emergence of polytheistic belief and its transformation into theism, grows out of his concern with how religious belief had played itself out in the messy reality of the preceding few centuries. In the *History of England*, Hume wrestles with the complex phenomena of religion in the world. Here it is not easy to determine what someone's motives for starting a war or defying the pope or persecuting a religious minority really were. The clean air of theory is left behind, although the concepts of self-deception and irrationality developed in the "ideal," theoretical narrative of the emergence of theism play an important role in the *History of England* as well. Hume's overriding concern is with the violence of religious factions and with the way in which religious controversies threaten to destroy the social fabric.[43] If religious belief is so faint and uncertain, how can it unleash such powerful forces in the world? And how can his readers learn from the negative examples of these forces doing their devastating work? His interest in the contradictions and self-deceptions of theistic belief is not bloodless and theoretical, nor is it confined to the level of the individual religious believer. Rather, he suggests that there is a link between self-deception and religious zeal, between irrational beliefs and intolerant persecution. The irrationality of belief makes itself felt, with devastating results, in the social and political world.

Here we see a stark contrast with Pascal, for whom self-deception is of concern almost exclusively at the level of the self-deceiving individual whose eternal happiness is thereby gravely threatened. The social and political ramifications of self-deception are uninteresting to Pascal, since social and political phenomena in general have so pale a significance. Here Hume's views are more in tune with Butler's. Butler, like Hume, suggested that there was a link between "hypocrisy" and destructive zeal. In a sermon commemorating the anniversary of the execution of Charles I at the hands of Puritan enthusiasts, Butler proclaimed that "in the history which this day refers us to, we find our constitution, in Church and State, destroyed under pretences, not only of religion, but of securing liberty, and carrying it to a greater height. The destruction of the former was with zeal of such a kind, as would not have been warrantable, though it had been employed in the destruction of heathenism."[44] Religious zeal provides agents with a justification for evil actions which they must see as good and, more dangerously, as sanctioned by God. Hume, as I will argue below, gives an added twist to his account of the relationship between religious zeal and "hypocrisy."

In chapter 4, I contrasted Hume's sense of the morally ambiguous role of sympathetic understanding in poetry with his confidence in the morally educative role of sympathetic understanding in history. History's advantage had to do with the possibility of writers and readers of history actively entering into the situations and points of view of historical characters and events while remaining untouched by particular interests or concerns which might prejudice judgment. These historical points of view are therefore a prototype for the point of view which we strive to achieve in all moral judgments, since "'tis only when a character is considered in general, without reference to our particular interest, that it causes such a feeling or sentiment, as denominates it morally good or evil" (*T* 472). The ideal historian cultivates an active and extensive sympathetic understanding of characters and events in the past, just as the good moral judge does toward all characters and events, past or present. The same corrected extensive sympathy which provides a solution to the internal strife of contradictory and fluctuating sentiments (*T* 581–582) is also needed to overcome political and religious civil war and faction.

Hume took pride in his approximation of the ideal of impartiality in the *History of England*, although his authorial stance was never recognized as a virtue by his contemporaries.[45] In "My own life," Hume recounts:

I was, I own, sanguine in my expectations of the success of this work. I thought, that, I was the only historian, that had at once neglected present power, interest, and authority, and the cry of popular prejudices; and as the subject was suited to every capacity, I expected proportional applause: But miserable was my disappointment: I was assailed by one cry of reproach, disapprobation, and even detestation: English, Scotch, and Irish; Whig and Tory; churchman and sectary, free-thinker and religionist; patriot and courtier united in their rage against the man, who had presumed to shed a generous tear for the fate of Charles I, and the Earl of Stafford. (*H* I, vi)

Many interpreters have failed to appreciate that for Hume, to be disinterested is not to avoid evaluative judgments of historical actors, but to seek to understand and evaluate actors and events on a case-by-case basis, according to their own merits, rather than simply lauding (and whitewashing) those people whose actions led to the ascendancy of one's own faction while denouncing those of other parties.[46] Impartiality is not an attempt to recount the past with pure objectivity. Hume would not have seen the point of such an enterprise, even if it were possible. Moreover, for Hume, the unapologetically normative enterprise of history is neither relativistic and skeptical about the possibility of trans-historical evaluation, nor blind to relevant differences of context.

Although he prides himself on being disinterested, in the sense of not allowing his judgment to be prejudiced by factional interests, Hume clearly is seeking to shape and influence the judgments of his readers.[47] The reflections on religion in the *History* are not a series of journal entries containing Hume's attempts to make sense of religious belief and its ramifications for himself alone. They are carefully crafted in an attempt to engage the sympathies and enlarge the views even of those readers who are zealous factionalists when they begin reading.

Irony and sentimentalism are among the rhetorical strategies Hume employs to achieve these aims.[48] Wayne Booth has written eloquently about the way in which irony builds a bond of sympathy between author and reader, implying that they are in on a secret which others do not get. Hume encourages his reader to join him in a private laugh at the expense of benighted superstitious and enthusiastic believers of days gone by. Hence, the reverse side of the bond between Hume and his readers is alienation from the targets of Hume's irony. As Booth writes, masters of irony "convince us that we are brothers and sisters under the skin,"[49] but this "we" can also be an exclusionary "we." Hume wants his readers, whether or not they are religious believers, to feel more kinship with his skepticism than with rabid crusaders, cranky monks, or zealous reformers. Hume's irony does not, however, permit his readers to lapse into the sort of detachment which engenders the aesthetic pleasure in tragedy discussed in chapter 3; he constantly reminds his readers of the concrete relationships between themselves and the characters and events about which they are reading. The irony is effective because it is directed towards the readers' own tradition, something with which their own identity is bound up.

One example of Hume's use of irony is his report that, during the thirteenth-century civil conflicts in England, "the bishop of Chichester gave a general absolution to the army [marching against Henry III], accompanied with assurances that, if any of them fell in the ensuing action, they would infallibly be received into heaven, as the reward of their suffering in so meritorious a cause" (*H* I, xii, 263). The promise is mentioned without comment, yet it is clear that Hume does not think much of the merit of the cause, since he elsewhere discusses the senselessness and destructiveness of these conflicts. The disproportion between the pettiness of the conflicts and the sublimity of the bishop's promise is blatantly obvious. The reader who seconds Hume's judgment here is also a little more likely to be suspicious of other promises of religious rewards in exchange for temporal services.

Hume's discussion of Henry III of France is another case in point. Henry was urged by the Catholic league to seek the exclusion of the next heir to the crown, a professed Huguenot:

Henry himself, though a zealous Catholic, yet, because he declined complying with their precipitate measures, became an object of aversion to the league; and as his zeal in practising all the superstitious observances of the Romish church was accompanied with a very licentious conduct in private life, the Catholic faction, in contradiction to universal experience, embraced thence the pretext of representing his devotion as mere deceit and hypocrisy. (*H* II, XLI, 49–50)

Hume defends the sincerity of Henry's religious belief against the Catholics who attacked it, but at a cost – his religious beliefs, regardless of their sincerity, aren't expected to be reflected in virtuous conduct. The reader must either continue to accuse him (and, by implication, many others) of hypocrisy, or must admit that adherence to the speculative tenets of a particular sect doesn't justify any predictions about conduct. Similarly, Hume allows the faith of Charles II to be sincere, but only when Charles is fearful and unhealthy:

During his vigorous state of health, while his blood was warm and his spirits high, a contempt and disregard to all religion held possession of his mind; and he might more properly be denominated a Deist than a Catholic. But in those revolutions of temper, when the love of raillery gave place to reflection, and his penetrating, but negligent understanding was clouded with fears and apprehension, he had starts of more sincere conviction; and a sect, which always possessed his inclination, was then master of his judgment and opinion. (*H* II, LXIII, 481)

"Sincere conviction," which sounds like a good thing, is paired with states of illness and fear which are hardly conducive to clear thinking. The reader is encouraged to wonder if sincerity of religious belief is a sickness of some sort.

There are ironic barbs even in passages which ostensibly make conciliatory gestures toward religion. In a passage discussing Charles I's cheerfulness in the face of death, Hume concedes that:

The great source whence the king derived consolation amidst all his calamities, was undoubtedly religion; a principle which in him seems to have contained nothing fierce or gloomy, nothing which enraged him against his adversaries, or terrified him with the dismal prospect of futurity. While everything around him bore a hostile aspect; while friends, family, relations, whom he passionately loved, were placed at a distance, and unable to serve him; he reposed himself with confidence in the arms of that Being who penetrates and sustains all nature, and whose severities, if received with piety and resignation, he regarded as the surest pledges of unexhausted favour. (*H* II, LIX, 378)

The final sentence startles the reader; why should a Being responsible for such an awful state of affairs be regarded as a Being in whom to repose oneself? What sort of "pledges of favour" are the experiences Charles has had to undergo? Is not Charles' cheerfulness somewhat irrational? Even though the religious principle in Charles is not manifested as violent zeal or severity and gloom, it betrays its misvaluation of values by allowing a man who has lost everything in life to remain undisturbed. Hume's irony disrupts the apparent self-evidence of religious platitudes.

Along with irony, Hume employs the rhetoric of sentimentalism most familiar to us from eighteenth-century sentimental novels.[50] At a few crucial points in his narrative, he describes in detail the emotional reactions of actors and spectators of a dramatic event. Within the context of eighteenth-century sentimentalism, such techniques are designed to evoke sympathetic responses in readers by making them feel they themselves are witnesses of the moving scene.[51] Sentimental scenes in history, unlike such scenes in poetry, are, Hume believes, in the service of moral education. Moral judgment requires an unjaundiced eye and impartial consideration of individuals and factions, but this should not be regarded as emotional detachment. On the contrary, moral judgment requires engagement and concern, not indifference. In the *Treatise*, Hume had discussed the relation between the "violent" and the "calm" passions. Both, he said, pursue good and avoid evil, but " 'tis certain, that when we would govern a man, and push him to any action, 'twill commonly be better policy to work upon the violent than the calm passions, and rather take him by his inclination, than what is vulgarly call'd his *reason*. We ought to place the object in such particular situations as are proper to encrease the violence of the passion. For we may observe, that all depends upon the situation of the object, and that a variation in this particular will be able to change the calm and the violent passions into each other" (*T* 419). The historian's task, therefore, is not only to work to detach readers from their prejudices and unexamined prepossessions, but also to foster readers' extensive sympathies, to stimulate their concern and motivate them to see even their enemies as fellow human beings, by placing objects in approximately moving situations. Hume therefore uses irony to weaken factional bonds, especially those based on what he considers to be imaginary distinctions,[52] and uses sentimentalism to evoke outrage at the enormities resulting from factionalism and to create more extensive bonds of connection. Hume does not try to substitute mere passive sympathy and feelings of compassion for the hard work of giving thick moral descriptions of actions and events, and is sparing in his recourse to the language of sentimentality. Nevertheless, sentimental scenes, embedded in discussions of belief, motivation, and cultural and historical context, are given a critical role to play in opening up readers' willingness to question their assumptions or to understand those different from themselves. Such scenes can therefore help to create the possibility of sympathetic understanding.

The revolt of Irish Catholics under Charles I is one occasion for the rhetoric of sentimentality. Having seized the property of the English people residing in Ireland:

A universal massacre commenced of the English, now defenceless, and passively resigned to their inhuman foes. No age, no sex, no condition was spared. The wife weeping for her husband, and embracing her helpless children, was pierced with them, and perished by the same stroke . . . In vain did flight save from the first assault: destruction was, everywhere, let loose, and met the hunted victims at every turn. In vain was recourse had to relations, to companions, to friends: all connexions were dissolved, and death was dealt by that hand, from which protection was implored and expected. Without provocation, without opposition, the astonished English, living in profound peace and full security, were massacred by their nearest neighbours, with whom they had long upheld a continual intercourse of kindness and good offices. (*H* II, LV, 295)

The account goes on at length, detailing the cruelties of the zealous Irish and the terrors of the suffering English; this is not the sort of account Hume gives of an ordinary war of conquest or border dispute. The reader, whose sympathies on behalf of the English are aroused, is now told that:

Amidst all these enormities, the sacred name of RELIGION resounded on every side; not to stop the hands of these murderers, but to enforce their blows, and to steel their hearts against every movement of human or social sympathy. The English, as heretics, abhorred of God, and detestable to all holy men, were marked out by the priests for slaughter; and, of all actions, to rid the world of these declared enemies to Catholic faith and piety, was represented as the most meritorious . . . While death finished the sufferings of each victim, the bigoted assassins, with joy and exultation, still echoed in his expiring ears, that these agonies were but the commencement of torments infinite and eternal. (*H* II, LV, 296)

Faith and piety are associated with cruelty, not sympathy or compassion. The reader who is affected by the suffering of these victims of religious zeal reaffirms the importance of the bonds of human fellowship and society and is thereby also aroused against the religious principles which are invoked to inspire and justify persecution.

Lest accounts of Catholic persecutions of Protestants should merely reinforce factionalism by inflaming Protestant hatred of Catholics,

Hume's *History* contains sentimental scenes dealing with Protestant atrocities as well, such as his account of the Earl of Stafford, who was accused of participating in the fabricated "Popish plot" against Charles II. Stafford admits that he has tried to secure toleration for Catholics, but denies participating in any treasonous plot. Nevertheless, he is condemned to death:

The populace, who had exulted at Stafford's trial and condemnation, were now melted into tears at the sight of that tender fortitude which shone forth in each feature, and motion, and accent of this aged noble. Their profound silence was only interrupted by sighs and groans. With difficulty they found speech to assent to those protestations of innocence, which he frequently repeated: "We believe you, my lord! God bless you, my lord!" These expressions with a faltering accent flowed from them. The executioner himself was touched with sympathy. Twice he lifted up the axe, with an intent to strike the fatal blow; and as often felt his resolution to fail him. A deep sigh was heard to accompany his last effort, which laid Stafford for ever at rest. All the spectators seemed to feel the blow. And when the head was held up to them with the usual cry, This is the head of a traitor, no clamor of assent was uttered. Pity, remorse, and astonishment, had taken possession of every heart, and displayed itself in every countenance. (*H* II, LXVIII, 582)

Here the zeal which is responsible for Stafford's death falters at the last moment and sympathy with the love of life reasserts itself, at least with the help of Hume's idealized sentimental rendering of events. Hume goes on to make the moral of the story plain: "This is the last blood which was shed on account of the popish plot: an incident which, for the credit of the nation, it were better to bury in oblivion; but which it is necessary to perpetuate, as well to maintain the truth of history, as to warn, if possible, their posterity and all mankind never again to fall into so shameful, so barbarous a delusion (*H* II, LXVIII, 582–583).[53]

The purpose of Hume's sentimental scenes is not to encourage readers to wallow in pity or to re-create emotions from the past, but to rouse them in ways that challenge their unreflective evaluations of character and action. It is a particularly important tool where religion is concerned, Hume believes, because cold and detached reasoning has little impact in this area dominated by various forms of irrational belief. Hume is convinced that there is no "instance that argument has ever been able to free the people from that enormous load of absurdity which superstition has everywhere overwhelmed them" (*H* I, XXIX, 555). Even "men of the greatest genius, where they relinquish by principle the use of their reason, are only enabled, by their vigor of mind, to work themselves the deeper into error and absurdity" (*H* II, LXIII, 479).

These statements appear to conflict with the opening sentences of "Of suicide," where Hume claims that "one considerable advantage that arises from philosophy consists in the sovereign antidote which it affords to superstition and false religion. All other remedies against that pestilent distemper are vain, or, at least uncertain . . . Superstition being founded on false opinion must immediately vanish when true philosophy has inspired juster sentiments of superior powers" (*D* 97). But superstition is excluded only "when sound philosophy has once gained possession of the mind," and this is more easily said than done. Moreover, Hume's analysis of superstition in the *Natural History of Religion* and throughout the *History of England* shows that superstition is not merely a matter of false opinion, but is rather much more like "love or anger, ambition or avarice," which Hume notes "have their root in the temper and affections, which the soundest reason is scarce ever able fully to correct" (*NHR* 97). The rhetoric of sentimentalism, by evoking compassion and outrage, refocuses readers' attention on the value of the goods of finite existence, like life, family, peace, and security, which are so often destroyed on behalf of abstract speculative allegiances. It is, for Hume, a sort of shock therapy which is capable of rousing the "natural principles of the mind" (*E* 343), those principles with which speculative reasoning and artificial manners interfere.[54]

It would be a mistake, however, to think that Hume is simply attempting to manipulate his readers psychologically, circumventing their own reasoning and judgment. It is true that Hume says that "eloquence, when at its highest pitch, leaves little room for reason or reflection; but addressing itself entirely to the fancy or the affections, captivates the willing hearers, and subdues their understanding (*E* 118). "Eloquence" refers to oration, however, not to written rhetoric, and this is the same complaint Hume makes about theater when praising, in contrast, history writing. Hume's rhetorical techniques, at their best, stimulate reflection and remove obstacles to clear, unprejudiced reasoning and judgment. If his rhetoric is capable of eliciting immediate extensive sympathy with suffering figures, he is not content with this immediate response, but seeks to encourage greater reflection and active sympathetic understanding. For example, Hume never allows his readers to become complacently detached from religious atrocities in the past, or to be inconsistent in their judgments, exonerating their own faction and indicting the enemy by denying his or her sincerity or humanity. He not only constantly draws parallels between zealots of different stripes, but also alludes to the present through his accounts of the past, forcing uncomfortable reassessments of present allegiances rather than allowing the past to recede into a distant unreality.[55]

Just as Hume in the *Treatise* tried to make the phenomenon of morality comprehensible apart from a God-given moral sense, and in the *Natural History of Religion* tried to make the phenomenon of religious belief comprehensible apart from revelation, in the *History of England* Hume attempts to show that history is comprehensible apart from divine Providence.[56] History is not to be read as proof that God is on the side of the Protestants or Catholics, the Whigs or the Tories, the Presbyterians or the Anglicans. There are things to be learned from history, but they are lessons about human mistakes and achievements, not revelations of divine action. Hume is spurred on in his attempt to account for the actions of religious believers by his desire to eliminate the temptation to have recourse to supernatural factors or providential action. He sees providential history as factional by nature. It cannot therefore fulfill the morally educative role of properly disinterested history, drawing readers into more enlarged and broadly sympathetic views.

ZEAL AND FACTION

The term "hypocrisy" and its counterpart, "sincerity," along with "zeal" and "faction," are crucial to understanding Hume's characterization of religious belief as irrational, rather than merely mistaken, and therefore as resistant to sympathetic understanding. By examining Hume's use of these terms in the *History*, I hope to identify distinctions among religious believers or beliefs which Hume treats as relevant to the possibility of sympathetic entrance into foreign points of view. I will also be examining the link Hume locates between religious belief and violence.

Lionel Trilling identified the preoccupation with sincerity, which has its origins in the mid-sixteenth century and remained prominent through the eighteenth, as a "response to the newly available sense of an audience, of that public which society created."[57] It is hardly surprising, then, that a thinker whose moral theory focuses on the moral judge as spectator, and hence on ethical relationships between actor and spectator, would also be concerned with sincerity and hypocrisy. The possibility of deceptive self-presentation implies a threat to sympathetic understanding and a concomitant falsification of moral judgment. For Hume the value of sincerity is public, and still involves "the reason that Polonius gives for being true to one's own self: that if one is, one cannot then be false to any man."[58] And yet Hume is also preoccupied with the possibility of a sort of sincere hypocrisy, particularly in religious belief, which involves the attempt to deceive oneself, rather than others. One's sincerity is thereby sustained, though at a high cost. Hume's exploration of this phenomenon casts doubt on the simplicity of the dichotomy between sincerity and hypocrisy; while sincerity sometimes only conceals absurdity and therefore makes way for zeal unopposed by considerations of interest, whether private or public, ordinary hypocrisy (redescribed as discretion) may have some redeeming features, at least in the realm of politics.[59] Furthermore, as it tends to be calculating rather than fanatical, it is less dangerous than sincere religious belief. In developing the category of sincere hypocrisy, Hume is questioning the notion, on the rise during the eighteenth century, that sincerity of belief is more important than objective rightness.[60] He does so by pointing out a case in which being wrong precludes true sincerity, where what appears to be sincerity involves self-deception.

Within the *History*, Hume treats all religious belief as a form of hypocrisy. Often, he suggests, those who claim to have religious reasons for their actions are self-consciously hypocritical – they seek to deceive others about the real reasons for their actions. Of Simon de Mountfort, Earl of Leicester, Hume writes that "by his hypocritical pretensions to devotion, he gained the favor of the zealots and clergy: by his seeming concern for public good, he acquired the affections of the public" (*H* I, XII, 255, also 261). When the duke of Bedford wishes to do away with Joan of Arc, whose inspiration of the French army had erased all his progress in France, he decides to accuse her of witchcraft, since "she was unstained by any civil crime: even the virtues, and the very decorums of her sex, had ever been rigidly observed by her: and ... had ... performed such signal service to her prince ... It was necessary, therefore, for the duke of Bedford to interest religion some way in the prosecution; and to cover, under that cloak, his violation of justice and humanity" (*H* I, xx, 432). Henry VIII was "impelled, both by his private passions, and by motives of public interest, to seek the dissolution of his inauspicious, and, as it was esteemed, unlawful marriage with Catharine," but he "afterwards affirmed that his scruples arose entirely from private reflection" about divine prohibitions against marrying one's brother's widow (*H* I, xxx, 569). This sort of hypocrisy or deception fosters vice, since it allows people to conceal evil actions which they would not dare to perform openly.[61] Yet the wrongdoing of hypocrites of this ilk is bounded by considerations of prudence. They will not carry cruelty or persecution to such a degree that it defeats their own concealed purposes.

Hume recognizes, however, that not all avowals of religious belief and motivation can fairly be attributed to such straightforward hypocrisy. Drawing on reflections in the *Natural History of Religion* about the precariousness and hidden falsehood of religious belief, he develops the notion of sincere hypocrisy. "The religious hypocrisy, it may be remarked, is of a peculiar nature; and being generally unknown to the person himself, though more dangerous, it implies less falsehood than any other species of insincerity" (*H* II, LXII, 460–461). Straightforward hypocrisy is, he suggests, relatively rare. More often, the desire to maintain sincerity and purity of conscience encourages what would now be called wishful thinking or self-deception. Elster defines wishful thinking as an unconscious "tendency to form beliefs when and because I prefer the state of the world in which they are true over the states in which they are false."[62] In wishful thinking, there is a causal relationship between my desires and my beliefs which disrupts the proper relationship between reasons and beliefs. When wishful thinking is at work in the realm of religion, people tend to come to believe things which happen, not accidentally, to coincide with their political interests or desire for power or glory. Braudy suggests that Hume's use of the word "sincerity" indicates "an effort to appreciate deeper levels of motivation, where what might on the surface seem more [sic] calculation and self-interest are shown to be the result of genuine beliefs, whether rationally or irrationally based."[63] But Hume's use of "sincerity" has an edge to it; it does not rule out an irrational relationship between interests, desires, and beliefs.

The story of the conversion of Henry IV of France is an example of wishful thinking at work. Henry, a Huguenot, desperately needed the support of his fellow Catholics, not only for the security of his reign, but for the stability of the kingdom. Hume claims that

the Hugonots also, taught by experience, clearly saw that his desertion of them was become absolutely necessary for the public settlement; and so general was this persuasion among them, that, as the duke of Sully pretends, even the divines of that party purposely allowed themselves to be worsted in the disputes and conferences; that the king might more readily be convinced of the weakness of their cause, and might more cordially and sincerely, at least more decently, embrace the religion which it was so much his interest to believe. If this self-denial in so tender a point should appear supernatural and incredible in theologians, it will at least be thought natural, that a prince so little instructed in these matters as Henry, and desirous to preserve his sincerity, should insensibly bend his opinion to the necessity of his affairs, and should believe that party to have the best arguments who could alone put him in possession of a kingdom. (*H* II, XLIII, 87–88)

Wishful thinking is particularly prevalent in the realm of religious belief because, Hume thinks, there is no good way to decide whom to side with on religious questions, which are either abstract and speculative or concrete and utterly frivolous. It is therefore understandable that belief would so often follow interest.

It is sometimes difficult to distinguish self-serving sincere belief from straightforward hypocrisy, since in both cases the non-religious desires or interests account for the appearance of religious devotion. Oliver Cromwell is a sort of borderline case. "Carried by his natural temper to magnanimity, to grandeur, and to an imperious and domineering policy, he yet knew, when necessary, to employ the most profound dissimulation, the most oblique and refined artifice, the semblance of the greatest moderation and simplicity. [He was] . . . devoted to religion, though he perpetually employed it as the instrument of his ambition" (*H* II, LVII, 346).[64] Although Cromwell was "transported to a degree of madness with religious ecstasies, he never forgot the political purposes to which they might serve" (*H* II, LX, 395). On the one hand, Hume is inclined to credit Cromwell with real religious devotion,[65] but Cromwell's ability to control his own zeal, to channel it to serve his own interests, calls the sincerity of his belief into question.

The truly sincere or self-deceived hypocrite, in contrast, is more apt to pursue his or her desires and interests, now honestly regarded as religious duties, without prudence or discretion. Only false zeal can be used instrumentally and strategically – true zeal takes control of the person it inhabits. This serves as a criterion by which Hume rejects, for instance, the notion that those who fought so violently against Charles I's extensions of royal authority consciously made use of religious pretenses in order to secure greater liberty:

The great courage and conduct displayed by many of the popular leaders, have commonly inclined men to do them, in one respect, more honor than they deserve, and to suppose, that, like able politicians, they employed pretences which they secretly despised, in order to serve their own selfish purposes. It is however probable, if not certain, that they were, generally speaking, the dupes of their own zeal. Hypocrisy, quite pure and free from fanaticism, is perhaps, except among men fixed in a determined philosophical skepticism, then unknown, as rare as fanaticism entirely purged from all mixture of hypocrisy. So congenial to the human mind are religious sentiments, that it is impossible to counterfeit long these holy fervors without feeling some share of the assumed warmth: and on the other hand, so precarious and temporary, from the frailty of human nature, is the operation of these spiritual views, that the religious ecstasies, if constantly employed, must often be counterfeit, and must be warped by those more familiar motives of interest and ambition, which insensibly gain upon the mind. This indeed seems the key to most of the celebrated characters of that age. Equally full of fraud and of ardor, these pious patriots talked perpetually of seeking the Lord, yet still pursued their own purposes; and have left a memorable lesson to posterity, how delusive, how destructive, that principle is by which they were animated. (*H* II, n. 3 G to ch. LV, 672–673)[66]

It is the fanaticism and lack of control which characterizes their pursuit of their purposes which is the best guarantee of their sincerity. The few who manage to be straightforward hypocrites without becoming sincere fanatics are those of a "determined philosophical skepticism," whom Hume discusses with a note of admiration, unlike the fanatical majority, whose lack of prudence receives Hume's contempt.

But religious beliefs and loyalties do not always obviously serve one's own secular interests, as when they call for a life of abstinence and self-denial, or when a person becomes a martyr for his or her beliefs.[67] Is this the mark of truly sincere belief? No, according to Hume; since theistic tenets cannot be comprehended or fully believed, even this must be an attempt at self-deception, rather than truly sincere belief. Here, zeal and factionalism become even more crucial to Hume's understanding of religious belief. Zeal is, according to Hume, a response to the faintness and instability of religious belief. Whereas Butler had simply seen religious zeal as a cloak for evil actions, Hume suggests that there is a genuine kind of religious zeal, which is engendered by the need to reassure oneself of the firmness and sincerity of one's religious convictions. Attempting to reconstruct an argument for religious toleration (an occasion which permits him to present his own arguments on its behalf), Hume suggests that

the theological animosity so fierce and violent, far from being an argument of men's conviction in their opposite sects, is a certain proof that they have never reached any serious persuasion with regard to these remote and sublime subjects. Even those who are the most impatient of contradiction in other controversies, are mild and moderate in comparison of polemical divines; and wherever a man's knowledge and experience give him a perfect assurance in his own opinion, he regards with contempt, rather than anger, the opposition and mistakes of others. But while men zealously maintain what they neither clearly comprehend nor entirely believe, they are shaken in their imagined faith by the opposite persuasion, or even doubts, of other men; and vent on their antagonists that impatience which is the natural result of so disagreeable a state of the understanding. (*H* I, XXXVII, 693)

Zeal is not just a rationalization for doing something one has a prior, distinct desire to do. A person caught up in zeal, far from calculatingly pursuing his or her own purposes, or even pursuing them while under the illusion of pursuing religious ends, may easily act in utterly destructive ways which serve no intelligible purpose, or insist on the vital importance of trifling details (*H* II, LIV, 277). The zealot may do things which are inspired only by religious devotion and serve no other desire or purpose, just in order to reaffirm and reinforce that devotion, and these things are not limited to religious ceremonies or self-denial, but extend to violent persecution of those who hold competing beliefs. In fact, if it were not for the emergence of zeal, Hume doubts that religious belief would make itself felt in the world at all, since it is so abstract and removed from concrete concerns.

Hume is persuaded that "no human depravity can equal revenge and cruelty covered with the mantle of religion" (*H* I, XXXVII, 695). Such zeal is, finally, a sort of madness which overcomes a person, and like madness it is a term invoked when understanding breaks down, and human beings cease to be intelligible as agents. The government of Charles II made a mistake in its dealings with Scottish non-conformists, Hume thinks, and "instead of treating them like madmen, who should be soothed, and flattered, and deceived into tranquility, thought themselves entitled to a rigid obedience, and were too apt, from a mistaken policy, to retaliate upon the dissenters, who had erred from the spirit of enthusiasm" (*H* II, LXVI, 546). Hume remarks that "the religious spirit contains in it something supernatural and unaccountable; and that, in its operations upon society, effects correspond less to their known causes than is found in any other circumstance of government" (*H* II, XLVII, 165).

Of course Hume is, precisely because of this apparent unaccountability, more forcefully impelled to discover the lesser-known causes, to which the "effects" of the operations of the religious spirit on society correspond. He finds these in the dynamics of zeal. The Catholics involved in the Gunpowder Conspiracy, an attempt to blow up Parliament during the reign of James I, were actuated by such zeal, which led them to throw caution to the wind:

So transported were they with rage against their adversaries, and so charmed with the prospect of revenge, that they forgot all care of their own safety; and trusting to the general confusion, which must result from so unexpected a blow, they foresaw not, that the fury of the people, now unrestrained by any authority, must have turned against them, and would probably have satiated itself, by a universal massacre of the Catholics . . . The holy fury had extinguished in their breast every other motive; and it was an indiscretion at last, proceeding chiefly from these very bigoted prejudices and partialities, which saved the nation. (*H* II, XLVI, 146; also 148)

Only "holy fury" can explain the indiscretion of their actions and their utter lack of prudence.

Religious zeal, as the examples just cited show, both reinforces and is fed by factionalism. Groups who profess different religious beliefs tend to become inflamed into irreconcilable factions. "Though theological principles," Hume writes, "when set in opposition to passions, have often small influence on mankind in general, still less on princes; yet when they become symbols of faction, and marks of party distinction, they concur with one of the strongest passions in the human frame, and are then capable of carrying men to the greatest extremities" (*H* II, LXVIII, 579). Human beings have a tendency to form factions based on interest and affection. These can lead to deplorable divisions in society, but there is at least a hope of keeping such divisions under control, or even of eventually resolving them, since they are based on real differences which might be amenable to adjustment.[68] For instance, Hume was convinced that "properly understood, the interests of government and society in relation to trade and manufactures are united. The greater the scope for individuals to pursue their natural interest in the production and exchange of luxuries, the greater the resources available for the public to draw on in emergencies." When it comes to religious factions, however, Hume finds no real differences of interest or sentiment to be settled between them, since "the controversy about an article of faith, which is utterly absurd and unintelligible, is not a difference in sentiment, but in a few phrases and expressions, which one party accepts of, without understanding them; and the other refuses in the same manner" (*MPL* 59).[69]

Confrontation with contradictory religious views, rather than destroying belief, as one might anticipate, tends instead to intensify the zeal which first emerged as a defense against the internal contradictions and instability which characterize religious belief. The introduction of zeal signals that religious belief has become ideology, in the service of a faction rather than of the search for truth. As Hume would say, zealous belief becomes "bigoted," deaf to challenges from the outside.[70]

Severity and self-denial, which are driven by the search to find something which can unambiguously be regarded as a sign of religious devotion, can also stimulate religious zeal. This is as true of monasticism as of Calvinism. The Benedictine monks,

carrying farther [than had previous monastic orders] the plausible principles of mortification, secluded themselves entirely from the world, renounced all claim to liberty, and made a merit of the most inviolable chastity . . . The Roman pontiff, who was making every day great advances towards an absolute sovereignty over the ecclesiastics, perceived that the celibacy of the clergy alone could break off entirely their connexion with the civil power, and, depriving them of every other object of ambition, engage them to promote, with unceasing industry, the grandeur of their order. (*H* I, II, 52)

When the usual social ties are absent and the social pleasures are denied, neither public good nor personal loyalties offer any competition to the wholesale commitment to faction.[71]

In the wake of the Reformation, reformers abolished what Hume considered inoffensive superstitious practices and sought to establish a pure and unadorned form of religion:

A mode of worship was established, the most naked and most simple imaginable; one that borrowed nothing from the senses; but reposed itself entirely on the contemplation of that divine essence, which discovers itself to the understanding only. This Species of devotion, so worthy of the Supreme Being, but so little suitable to human frailty, was observed to occasion great disturbances in the breast, and, in many respects, to confound all rational principles of conduct and behaviour. The mind, straining for these extraordinary raptures, reaching them by short glances, sinking again under its own weakness, rejecting all exterior aid of pomp and ceremony, was so occupied in this inward life, that it fled from every intercourse of society, and from every cheerful amusement, which could soften or humanise the temper. It was obvious to all discerning eyes, and had not escaped the king's [James I], that, by the prevalence of fanaticism, a gloomy and sullen disposition established itself among the people; a spirit, obstinate and dangerous, independent and disorderly; animated equally with a contempt of authority, and a hatred to every other mode of religion, particularly to the Catholic. (*H* II, XLVII, 166)

The reformers supplanted every sort of amusement with inflammatory sermons (*H* I, XXXIV, 655). Religious zeal became the only acceptable outlet for energies which might otherwise have been dissipated in mirth, feasting or dancing.

Religious zeal is further reinforced by passive sympathy, in the form of emotional infection, with those who share one's beliefs; "such is the nature of the human mind, that it always lays hold on every mind that approaches it; and as it is wonderfully fortified by an unanimity of sentiments, so is it shocked and disturbed by any contrariety ... This principle, however frivolous it may appear, seems to have been the origin of all religious wars and divisions" (*MPL* 61).[72] Contagious sympathy is a cause of, rather than a reason for, acquiring beliefs or zeal in defending them. Hume's attribution of the spread of religious zeal to passive sympathy echoes Shaftesbury who, in "A letter concerning enthusiasm," wrote that "one may with good reason call every passion panic which is raised in a multitude and conveyed by aspect or, as it were, by contact or sympathy."[73] Metaphors of disease are colorfully rampant as Shaftesbury proceeds to implicate sympathy in the spread and intensity of religious enthusiasm – "no wonder if the blaze rises so of a sudden; when innumerable eyes glow with the same passion, and heaving breasts are labouring with inspiration; when not the aspect only, but the very breath and exhalations of men are infectious, and the inspiring disease imparts itself by insensible transpiration."[74] Hume uses the same language of infection, though his rhetoric is somewhat tamer. The Scottish clergy who attempted to quell by persecution the spread of Reformation ideas, for example, "observed, that the enthusiastic zeal of the reformers, inflamed by punishment, was apt to prove contagious on the compassionate minds of the spectators. The new doctrine, amidst all the dangers to which it was exposed, secretly spread itself everywhere; and the minds of men were gradually disposed to a revolution in religion" (*H* I, XXXII, 621).[75] Contagious zeal is particularly apt to spread when subject to persecution, which makes a more indirect approach to quelling religious controversies necessary.

Zeal and faction work in concert to undermine morality. Members of religious factions perceive actions in defense of their party as selfless and principled, but this simply licenses them to do greater harm with a clean conscience. It is easier to do heinous things in the name of principle than flagrantly to commit a far lesser evil. Displaced self-interest, smothered by religion, is funneled into factional interests. During the reign of Charles I, for example, "the fanatical spirit, let loose, confounded all regard to ease, safety, and interest; and dissolved every moral and civil obligation . . . Never was there a people less corrupted by vice, and more actuated by principle, than the English during that period: never were there individuals who possessed more capacity, more courage, more public spirit, more disinterested zeal. The infusion of one ingredient, in too large a proportion, had corrupted all these noble principles, and converted them into the most virulent poison" (*H* II, LV, 312). The selfish pursuit of one's own private interests, although it is less principled, is far less dangerous than factional zeal, because it is restrained by one's desire for the good opinion of others. "It is no wonder," reflects Hume, "that faction is so productive of vices of all kinds: for, besides that it inflames all the passions, it tends much to remove those great restraints, honour and shame; when men find, that no iniquity can lose them the applause of their own party, and no innocence secure them against the calumnies of the opposite" (*H* II, LXIX, 603). Those who seek only to promote the strength of their faction do much more harm to the public good than do those who never move beyond private self-interest.

In a 1741 essay called "Of parties in general," Hume blamed factions for their tendency to "subvert government, render laws impotent, and beget the fiercest animosities among men of the same nation, who ought to give mutual assistance and protection to each other" (*MPL* 55). Parties of interest, however, unlike those of abstract speculative principle, can be directed toward the public good, and are therefore a far less serious threat to society.[76] Hume co-opts the civic republican preoccupation with faction while mitigating its censure of the private pursuit of material interests. The expression of private interests, unlike religious zeal, can contribute to economic prosperity at large and to the spread of polite culture and the arts and sciences, and need not be opposed to the interests of society as a whole. In the *History*, the phenomenon of irrational devotion to faction is seen most clearly during the reign of Charles I, when "the spirit of enthusiasm being universally diffused, disappointed all the views of human prudence, and disturbed the operation of every motive which usually influences society" (*H* II, LII, 238).

THE LIMITS OF SYMPATHETIC UNDERSTANDING

Factional zeal, and the passive, contagious sympathy by which it spreads, are directly opposed to the sympathetic understanding needed to appreciate different points of view. Narrow sympathies and factional prejudices, the phenomena on which Hume focuses much of his attention as he recounts the history of England, are also those which, as I argued above, his rhetoric aims at eliminating among his readers. Hume is never simply analyzing past events, but always also trying to shape contemporary attitudes and beliefs. He often deplores the narrow views of otherwise admirable leaders. Recounting the execution of Archbishop Laud by a revengeful parliament, for instance, Hume notes that "it is to be regretted, that a man of such spirit, who conducted his enterprises with so much warmth and industry, had not entertained more enlarged views, and embraced principles more favorable to the general happiness of society" (*H* II, LVII, 349). Charles I is criticized because he embraced episcopacy not for reasons of policy, for he "never attained such enlarged principles," but for religious reasons (*H* II, LVII, 347; see also 254, but also 674). Hence, he made no attempt to set in place forms of church government and liturgy which would encourage peace among rival religious factions. Henry IV of France, on the other hand, is praised for his enlarged views; "this excellent prince was far from being a bigot to his sect; and ... deemed these theological disputes entirely subordinate to the public good" (*H* II, XLIII, 87).

The moral assessment of self-deception takes one into murky waters. As Fingarette notes, "as deceiver one is insincere, guilty; whereas as genuinely deceived, one is the innocent victim. What, then, shall we make of the self-deceiver, the one who is both the doer and the sufferer?"[77] For Pascal and other thinkers in the Christian tradition of self-deception, self-deception is sin, and it is therefore crucial that individuals be responsible for their own self-deception. Hume, in contrast, has no religious reasons to hold individuals responsible for their doomed attempts at self-deception. For him, the question of responsibility and intentionality ultimately take a back seat to the issue of how to eliminate self-deceptive belief and zealous factions in the present among his readers. Hume's discussion of the conflict between Charles I and the Scots over the establishment of episcopal church government, a question still of passionate concern to eighteenth-century Scots, provides an opportunity for him to urge that "this narrowness of mind, if we would be impartial, we must either blame or excuse equally on both sides; and thereby anticipate, by a little reflection, that judgment, which time, by introducing new subjects of controversy, will undoubtedly render quite familiar to posterity" (*H* II, LIII, 258).[78] Trading denunciations of those in the past should not be made the occasion for present factional strife.

The murder of Thomas à Becket gives Hume another opportunity to reflect on the issue of responsibility for self-deceptive belief as he puzzles over the religious zeal and devotion of this "prelate of the most lofty, intrepid, and inflexible spirit," a man in whom Hume found much to admire. He would, Hume thinks, have been "an extraordinary personage, surely, had he been allowed to remain in his first station [as Chancellor to Henry II], and had directed the vehemence of his character to the support of law and justice; instead of being engaged, by the prejudices of the times, to sacrifice all private duties and public connexions to ties which he imagined or represented as superior to every civil and political consideration." Hume toys with the possibility that Becket was a simple hypocrite:

But no man who enters into the genius of that age can reasonably doubt of this prelate's sincerity. The spirit of superstition was so prevalent, that it infallibly caught every careless reasoner, much more ever one whose interest, and honor, and ambition, were engaged to support it. All the wretched literature of the times was enlisted on that side: some faint glimmerings of common sense might sometimes pierce through the thick cloud of ignorance, or, what was worse, the illusions of perverted science, which had blotted out the sun, and enveloped the face of nature: but those who preserved themselves untainted by the general contagion, proceeded on no principles which they could pretend to justify: they

indebted to their want of instruction, than to their knowledge, if they
d some share of understanding. (*H* I, VIII, 167–168)

ves from blaming superstitious belief on careless reasoning to
that one who did not accept the prevailing beliefs would not
be justified in his or her lack of belief. This implies that twelfth-century
religious believers were actually justified in holding what Hume regards
to be not only false but irrational beliefs. Hume makes a similar
comment elsewhere in the *History*, when remarking on the fact that
James I wrote a commentary on the Revelations and proved the pope to
be Antichrist: "From the grossness of its superstitions, we may infer the
ignorance of an age; but never should pronounce concerning the folly of
an individual, from his admitting popular errors, consecrated by the
appearance of religion" (*H* II, Appendix, 526). Religious belief was a
mass delusion, not merely isolated instances of self-deception, so the
culture as a whole inculcated and reinforced belief. It hardly seems just
to hold individuals responsible at this point in time. Yet Hume also insists
that such religious beliefs, no matter how prevalent and supported by the
intellectual authorities of the day, came into conflict with "common sense."

By "common sense," Hume seems to be pointing to knowledge of the
basic goods of human life – family bonds, social pleasures, public
security. These are goods which must in a practical way be recognized,
even if never attended to as consciously held beliefs, in order for human
life in community to be sustained. But this knowledge can be regarded in
various ways: as instinctive, as something learned by each individual in
the course of his or her own experience, or as a form of cultural wisdom,
learned within human community and passed on from generation to
generation.[79] If common sense were either instinctive or individual, it
would fail only on an individual basis, for sometimes there are
anomalous and defective individuals. If it were cultural, the wisdom
could be lost within a community as a whole, although with the result
that human community would begin to falter – as it doubtless would if all
"private duties and public connexions" were utterly disregarded.

Hume has a tendency to move between the latter two characterizations
of common sense, sometimes treating private experience as the locus of
this basic trustworthy knowledge, sometimes broadening this to include
social knowledge. When he considers religious belief he is particularly
tempted to privatize the source of common sense and to regard cultural
forms of knowledge as nests of superstition and contradiction. In doing
so, he suggests not only that individuals within such a misguided society
bear ultimate responsibility for their perverted beliefs, but also that they
possess the necessary resources for seeing through the darkness into light.

Thus he suggests in the passage about Becket that individuals would have been better off without any instruction at all than with the knowledge derived from membership in that superstitious community. On the other hand, if common sense is an individually obtainable possession of this sort, how could it come to be lacking in so many?

Perhaps the point is not that individuals should be able to determine that their artificial beliefs contradict a fund of common-sense beliefs which they have somehow figured out all on their own, but rather that beliefs can be identified as conflicting with common sense if they require self-deception in order to be lived out. Religious believers, despite the fact that they acquire their "poetical system" of religious reality in the usual way that beliefs are acquired in human communities, must end up engaging in voluntaristic efforts at self-deception in order to maintain this poetical system. An "artificial" way of life would be one in which basic goods constitutive of flourishing life in community were being systematically flouted, and in which social life was therefore beginning to disintegrate. This disintegration is, in fact, what Hume suspects religious belief to be guilty of bringing about. Hence, Hume's concern is not with contradictory beliefs in and of themselves, but with the artificial lives in which they result. If beliefs have no practical implications, we can afford to be quite indifferent about their absurdity or unintelligibility.

Twelfth-century Christians are not accused of irrational belief acquisition, but at most of being insufficiently sensitive to tensions among their beliefs, or, more significantly, to tensions between the commitments reflected in their actual lives and the propositions they consciously held. In such a situation, self-deception is the only way to maintain all of one's beliefs intact, although it need not have been involved in the initial acquisition of the beliefs. Individuals must continually disguise the instability of their beliefs and the available social reinforcement is not sufficient.

To recall individuals from superstition to "common sense" is precisely to heighten their awareness of their own attempts at self-deception. The perception of hypocrisy in others, of a mismatch between others' avowals and actions, plays an important role in this process. The English, for example, began to resist papal influence when they realized that papal actions were best understood not as promoting the glory of God, but as pursuing worldly power and wealth:

These causes, though they opened slowly the eyes of men, failed not to produce their effect: they set bounds to the usurpations of the papacy: the tide first stopped, and then turned against the sovereign pontiff: and it is otherwise inconceivable, how that age, so prone to superstition, and so sunk in ignorance, or rather so devoted to a spurious erudition, could have escaped falling into an absolute and total slavery under the court of Rome. (*H* I, XI, 218; XII, 251)

Luther's success at disaffecting people from Rome was also due to his ability to draw attention to hypocritical uses of church power for worldly gain (*H* I, XXIX, 554). People were utterly bewildered, in contrast, when forced to decide among sects on the basis of abstract differences of doctrine, such as the precise nature of the sacraments: "As soon, therefore, as a new opinion was advanced, supported by such an authority as to call up their attention, they felt their capacity totally unfitted for such disquisitions; and they perpetually fluctuated between the contending parties" (*H* I, XXXI, 588). Such fluctuation being understandably uncomfortable (we might say cognitively dissonant), zealous attachment to a particular sect, regardless of one's abilities to give reasons for its superiority, was the eventual result. But the perception of hypocrisy eventually disenchanted many with this enthusiastic zeal as well, so that by the reign of Charles II, "the spirit of enthusiasm had occasioned so much mischief, and had been so successfully exploded, that it was not possible, by any artifice, again to revive and support it. Cant had been ridiculed, hypocrisy detected; the pretensions to a more thorough reformation, and to greater purity, had become suspicious" (*H* II, LXVIII, 574).

Detection of hypocrisy is given as a primary reason for religious disaffection in the past. Once again, as with his critique of narrow sympathies, Hume's analysis of the past is turned toward present endeavors. Hume's strategy of extending the notion of hypocrisy to cover all religious belief, including sincere but self-deceptive belief, therefore seeks to create disenchantment with religion as a whole by replicating triggers of belief change which he believes to have been important in the past. He trains his readers to be on the lookout for hypocrisy and self-deception when they detect incongruities between avowals and actions, inconsistency in action, or actions which are unintelligible or self-defeating. Christian persecution of the Jews during the reign of Henry III, for example, was ostensibly carried out for religious reasons, but the plunder and rapine of Jews should make readers suspicious of such avowals. Greed and resentment of Jewish wealth were the true motives; "so far from desiring in that age to convert them, it was enacted by law in France, that if any Jew embraced Christianity, he forfeited all his goods, without exception, to the king or his superior lord. These plunderers were careful, lest the profits accruing from their dominion over that unhappy race should be diminished by their conversion" (*H* I, XII, 271). In this case, the actions cannot be accounted for by reference to the avowed religious motives, but can be easily understood with reference to greed.

Hypocrisy or self-deception can also, however, result in utter unintelligibility. When Cromwell is finally offered the crown, he cannot simply take it, because the army would never accept this abrupt unmasking of his ambition. His arguments before parliament, as he tries to juggle his hypocritical principles with the private ambition which they no longer serve to conceal, are unintelligible; "while the protector argued so much in contradiction both to his judgement and inclination, it is no wonder that his elocution, always confused, embarrassed, and unintelligible, should be involved in tenfold darkness, and discover no glimmering of common sense or reason" (*H* II, LXI, 437). Of course, it is easier to detect hypocrisy or self-deception in someone else than in oneself, but Hume's impartial treatment of different factions, which locates self-deception throughout, makes it more difficult for the reader to simply exempt him- or herself from critical examination. Once the reader recognizes that his or her factional loyalty rests on self-deception, and that zeal is not a reflection of true devotion and idealism, but of unsteadiness and inner tensions in a person's beliefs, he or she will be freed from self-deceptive belief and enabled to act in ways which are not self-defeating and destructive of others, but which foster social stability, prosperity, and happiness. The social fabric – and common sense – will be restored.

In the course of Hume's attempt to account for religious belief and action in the past, an attempt directed at locating and preventing its worst manifestations in the present and future, different kinds of religious belief are understood and accounted for in different ways. If he regarded theistic beliefs, like ancient polytheistic beliefs, as ordinary false beliefs, the actions of those who hold such beliefs could be understood simply by taking into account the intelligible ends they pursue; the means by which they pursue them will reflect these false beliefs. This is similar to the approach Hume takes in attempting to understand Greek infanticide or homosexual practices.

The possibility of a hypocritical profession of religious belief complicates matters somewhat, as there will be a mismatch between avowed (religious) ends and actual, hidden ends. Once the mismatch has been detected, however, which happens when actions do not correspond to expectations based on what is avowed, sympathetic understanding is once again possible; the hypocrite is pursuing wealth, or glory, or power, etc., understandable if not laudable ends.[80]

But Hume does not take theistic belief to be ordinary false belief, nor always a mere pretense of belief. Often, it is rather a faint and wavering sort of belief, due to the abstract speculative nature of its object. Moreover, the ends pursued by religious believers, in particular that of eternal life, are incoherent, and the pursuit of them undermines the possibility of the pursuit of real goods. This gives rise to the expectation that religious belief will not have a substantial impact on action, and that people will follow non-religious aims and interests regardless of their avowals of religious aims and motivation. Understanding these sincere believers is akin to understanding the straightforward hypocrite, except that in this case the mismatch is not between avowed ends and concealed ends, but between the person's ends, as he or she identifies them both publicly and privately, and his or her actions, which betray unrecognized or unconscious factors influencing action. In this case, it is not just the avowals, but the very self-understanding, of religious believers which are discounted by one who seeks to understand their actions. Sincerity does not guarantee that the impartial spectator will accept their own account of what they are doing and why. Their actions are not understood with reference to the religious reasons they themselves give, but by reference to reasons which they themselves would not give or are not aware of as relevant. Still, their actions can be explained by reasons rather than causes. Is this sympathetic understanding? I think not; it does involve taking into account the ends and goods an agent has in mind, but it discounts these as the true moral causes of his or her actions.

Sometimes, actions may be understood as being directed toward the preservation or dominance of a particular religious faction. As Hume regards most differences between religious factions to be imaginary or frivolous, however, a supplementary explanation must be given in this case as well. The differences which are given as reasons for the animosity among different religious factions are not proportional to the extremes of hatred they generate. Believers do not, therefore, have good reason to place factional interests above private interest and all other social bonds and responsibilities.

The dominance of factional loyalty is often linked to zeal. When religious belief becomes inflamed by zeal, people's actions are dispropor-tionate to any reasons they give and any interests they can be understood by a spectator to have. The contagious sympathy by which such zeal spreads and increases in intensity is regarded by Hume as something utterly irrational, a cause but not a reason for action. Here actions are (externally) explained, rather than understood. Sentimentalism can still evoke pity for a suffering martyr, but it does so by reminding the reader/spectator of the true goods of life which are being senselessly destroyed, not by achieving sympathetic understanding of the martyr's perception of the glory of sacrificing oneself for the holy cause. Factional zeal is, for Hume, the height of religious irrationality and incomprehensibility.

Hume assumes that the ends of theists are always either disguised worldly interests or incoherent otherworldly ones. In the former case, an internal explanation can be given, but it is one which disregards the avowed reasons of the actors; in the latter case, while a sort of sympathetic grasp of the emotional state of the actors is possible, they are regarded as possessing no coherent reasons of their own and an external explanation of their actions is given. Zeal and the contagious sympathy by which it spreads are invoked as non-moral causes of actions, rather than reasons for them, and sympathetic understanding is thus impossible.

Hume's analysis of religious belief provides a valuable exploration of how sympathetic understanding is complicated or blocked by various kinds of irrationality. Two things make sympathetic understanding impossible: when an agent's statements and actions reveal not simply disguised motives or mixed motives, but motives utterly pervaded with contradictions, and when the end being pursued by the agent is completely senseless, utterly lacking a positive connection to any intelligible end. This seems to be a nuanced and judicious account of the boundary line between internal and external explanation. Yet it is applied rather crudely by Hume to the case of theistic believers. Hume argues, in effect, that the only motives and ends of such believers which are intelligible are those which are non-religious, connected with the love of power, the pursuit of wealth, or lust – or simply the love of peace and general prosperity. For instance, he suggests that Luther was unwilling to return to the Catholic fold because leading the schism "brought him a glory superior to all others, the glory of dictating the religious faith and principles of multitudes" (*H* I, XXIX, 554). Firm conviction of the error of Catholic views is incomprehensible, but love of glory is easy to understand. *All* religious motives and ends are internally contradictory and display pragmatic contradictions when one attempts to follow them or put them into practice. The only exception to this is polytheism; here, Hume sees the beliefs simply as false, so internal understanding is nonetheless possible. Unless Hume is correct in his analysis of theistic belief, he is himself guilty of a failure of sympathetic understanding, a failure to work hard enough to discern the internal consistency of theistic belief and the connections between theistic ends and genuine human flourishing.

There are a few cases in which Hume encounters what for him is an anomaly – an individual who appears to be both sincere and steadfast in his or her religious belief, who does not betray a mismatch between avowal and action, and who does not have recourse to zeal in order to bolster his or her beliefs and way of life. Thomas More is one such; when Henry VIII moves toward a breach with Rome, More gives up his position as Chancellor, foreseeing "an alteration of religion, with which his principles would not permit him to concur." What impresses Hume is that "the austerity of this man's virtue, and the sanctity of his manners, had nowise encroached on the gentleness of his temper, or even diminished that frolic and gayety to which he was naturally inclined" (*H* I, xxx, 581). Here is a man who does not seem to display the telltale signs of an "artificial" life! Hume does not, however, allow that More's religious dedication might be the source of his sustained gentleness and joy, but suggests that these must be basic personality traits which not even his religion could obliterate. When More is eventually beheaded for treason, Hume suggests that "nothing was wanting to the glory of this end, except a better cause, more free from weakness and superstition. But as the man followed his principles and his sense of duty, however misguided, his constancy and integrity are not less the objects of our admiration" (*H* I, xxxi, 543). The virtues of constancy and integrity are hardly those which Hume should in theory discover in a theist, even the most sincere. So Hume in this instance seems to give the lie to his own assumptions about the nature of theistic belief and therefore to the limits of sympathetic understanding of a theist by a non-theist.

Another notable instance comes when Hume is comparing the principles of Cardinal Pole with those of Queen Mary's Chancellor Gardiner with respect to the persecution of heretics. Cardinal Pole, Hume writes, "was very sincere in his religious principles; and though his moderation had made him be suspected at Rome of a tendency towards Lutheranism, he was seriously persuaded of the Catholic doctrines, and thought that no consideration of human policy ought ever to come in competition with such important interests" (*H* I, xxxvii, 693). Gardiner, in contrast, was a religious hypocrite, making his beliefs and principles serve his interests. Yet Pole advised toleration of heretics, while Gardiner advised persecution. Hume does not consider the possibility that Pole is, for instance, inspired by a desire to follow Christ's peacefulness and forbearance. Rather, as with More, he puts Gardiner's anomalous tolerance, appearing where one would expect zeal, down to personality; "such is the prevalence of temper above system, that the benevolent disposition of Pole led him to advise a toleration of the heretical tenets, which he highly blamed; while the severe manners of Gardiner inclined him to support by persecution that religion which, at the bottom, he regarded with great indifference."

Although Hume is able to deal with these anomalous cases by appealing to personality, they nevertheless belie his general accusations against theism. While this is clearly not the place to mount a wholesale investigation into the issue of the intelligibility and coherence of theism, it is obvious that one's beliefs in this matter will determine one's assessment of the adequacy of Hume's capacity for sympathetic understanding. I will therefore briefly outline the aspects of Hume's argument on which a possible rebuttal in defense of theism would need to focus.

Hume claims, for instance, that theological propositions are incoherent and self-contradictory. But powerful defenses of the consistency and coherence of theological views have been mounted. What of Hume's charge that the pursuit of religious ends is self-defeating? This, for Hume, is of greater significance, since it is artificial lives, rather than absurd beliefs in and of themselves, which threaten human community. Of course, it would be self-defeating to pursue eternal happiness by destroying the conditions for the possibility of pursuing any goods, including eternal happiness. But this need not be the case. Much depends on how eternal happiness is conceived and how it is to be pursued. Moreover, Hume disregards the fact that the pursuit of religious ends may actually require fostering the flourishing of human communities in this world, searching for peace, and encouraging mutual understanding and forbearance. In fact, he considers such pursuits to be non-religious by definition, while religious pursuits, to deserve the name, must be utterly disconnected with all that is finite and this-worldly. But theological virtues may complement and perfect, not negate, moral virtues, and hence theistic lives need not be "artificial." It should in that case also be possible to find connections between the ends pursued by theists and non-theists, such that their actions become mutually intelligible despite their differences of belief.

If theistic ends are intelligible this, in turn, would cast doubt on Hume's claim that religious (at least, theistic) belief is always wavering and unsteady. There need not be huge contradictions among the beliefs which prevent full assent. Theological claims ned not run counter to the "common sense" understanding of the conditions for the pursuit of human goods. What of the charge that theological tenets are so abstract and speculative that full-blooded belief is impossible? If the measure of full-blooded belief is a tendency to act in light of it, then as long as religious belief makes a difference in the way believers understand their actions, it makes little sense to deny that they truly believe them. Is it really the case that the actions of all religious individuals belie their avowals of belief? Hume points out many instances of hypocrisy or self-deception, without showing decisively that there is something peculiar about religious belief that results necessarily in such perversions of rationality.

Finally, if religious belief is not always unsteady and wavering, then there is no reason to expect zeal and bigotry to emerge unfailingly as a form of internal reassurance. Hume's account of factional zeal is undeniably a powerful one; we learn to expect zeal where belief is tottering or under fire, to expect factions to emerge to supply reinforcement, to anticipate that insignificant details will be magnified and made the heart of violent and irreconcilable disputes, and that zealous belief will be deaf to reason, no longer just ordinarily conservative. Perhaps the reason that challenges to religious belief so often result in zeal, bigotry, and ideology is that the loss of religious belief would involve a wholesale transformation of one's sense of the shape and meaning of life as a whole, although Hume does not explore this end of things. But on the other hand, what appears to Hume as bigotry may reflect the fact that some individuals' religious beliefs are more certain for them than anything else, so that it is reasonable for them, when a conflict in belief becomes apparent, to reinterpret their other beliefs to bring them in line with their religious beliefs, rather than vice versa. A devoted defense of one's religious beliefs need not always signify uncontrolled, irrational zeal, which lashes out at those who disagree and refuses to hear a challenge, but may be reasonable, though firm. Where the "enthusiast" or "zealot" is recognized as honest, rather than as a self-deceiver who is trying to paper over blatantly contradictory beliefs, the possibility of sympathetic understanding exists. In contrast, despite first appearances, the "straightforward," self-interested hypocrite may actually end up being quite opaque, as the example of Cromwell's final lapse into unintelligibility suggests. The kinds of hypocrisy encouraged by an alliance between church and state may therefore present a more formidable challenge to sympathetic understanding than the energetic faith of a Dissenter.[81]

This sort of response which I have briefly sketched could be mounted against Hume's attack on theism in general. But Hume's attacks on "theism" are best understood as particular responses to theism as he knew it, and most particularly to Scottish Evangelical Calvinism. An abstract defense of the coherence of theistic belief, which does not show how these beliefs have actually been lived out in a coherent way in the life of a believer, may repel Hume's attack on theism in the abstract, but it does not deflect his concrete claims about religion in the *History*, which show in detailed ways how believers have engaged in self-deception, or wishful thinking, have held incoherent theologies, or have been bigoted and ideological. Not surprisingly, Hume's reflections on religion are most powerful and telling where he openly grapples with particular figures and events. A similarly detailed defense would need to be mounted (which is not to say, of course, that many of Hume's analyses and accusations could not be fully accepted by the defender). It would be of utmost importance that this defense go beyond a defense of the logical consistency of religious *beliefs* in the abstract and take up seriously the task of defending the coherence of religious *lives* and their capacity to sustain themselves within flourishing human communities.

What would it mean to accuse Hume of a failure of sympathetic understanding in the realm of theism? Would this lead inexorably to the conclusion that nonbelievers cannot understand believers and vice versa, meaning that the non-confessional study of religion and of history must provide solely external explanations of religious actors? Not at all; as Hume's exploration of polytheism indicates, beliefs may be regarded as false (or as unconfirmed) while still being sympathetically understood. Sympathetic understanding of another's point of view is not tantamount to accepting the other's beliefs or way of life. Had Hume regarded theistic beliefs as for the most part simply false, rather than as absurd and contradictory, he would have seen far greater scope for sympathetic understanding. He would also have found it easier to make sense of the existence of whole societies in the thrall of "superstition." But he would have had to relinquish the notion that common sense provides an inextinguishable light leading away from religious error, as well as the notion that theism can be immediately marked off from the "natural" and branded as "artificial."

Even if Hume was too quick to place theistic believers beyond the pale of sympathetic understanding, his reflections on the possibility of entering into foreign points of view do succeed in carving out a niche for a non-relativistic, non-confessional study of religion and of the human sciences more broadly. Just as importantly, however, in exploring the limits of sympathetic understanding and the ways in which it is blocked, he draws our attention to the pitfalls of ascriptions of irrationality. There are times when it is appropriate to resort to the category of insanity and, as Hume suggests would have been appropriate with those enthusiastic Scottish non-conformists mentioned above, to realize that certain individuals "should be soothed, and flattered, and deceived into tranquility," rather than reasoned with. But we should be wary of resorting too quickly to this label; all too often it is simply a confession of our own limitations of imagination and understanding, rather than a statement about the other. This is particularly true when we are tempted to consider practices and beliefs of entire communities as unintelligible. Accusations of this sort, even when made in measured tones, are reminiscent of the bigot's refusal to be open to the sound of disagreement. Far more fruitful is the effort to extend sympathetic understanding even to those with whom we sharply disagree.

Conclusion

The dramatic conclusion to Book I of the *Treatise*, where Hume compares himself to a solitary sea-voyager who, having just narrowly escaped shipwreck, dares to set sail again in the same leaky vessel, is undoubtedly the most famous conclusion written by Hume, and for that matter one of the most memorable conclusions ever written to a work of philosophy. Reflecting on the contradictions and total lack of certainty into which his "refin'd and metaphysical" reflections have led him, Hume observes that:

Most fortunately it happens, that since reason is incapable of dispelling these clouds, nature herself suffices to that purpose, and cures me of this philosophical melancholy and delirium, either by relaxing this bent of mind, or by some avocation, and lively impression of my senses, which obliterate all these chimeras. I dine, I play a game of back-gammon, I converse, and am merry with my friends; and when after three or four hour's amusement, I wou'd return to these speculations, they appear so cold, and strain'd, and ridiculous, that I cannot find in my heart to enter into them any farther. (*T* 269)

This is often read as a confession of the bankruptcy of Hume's skeptical approach and an embrace of the non-solution of distraction from one's doubts and the abandonment of serious reflection. But Annette Baier's brilliant reading of the conclusion suggests that "in its pages, Hume enacts for us the turn he wants us to imitate, a turn from a one-sided reliance on intellect and its methods of proceeding to an attempt to use, in our philosophy, all the capacities of the human mind: memory, passion and sentiment as well as a chastened intellect."[1] Having shown the contradictions and confusion which result from attempting to think in solitary Cartesian isolation, Hume continues on in Books II and III to a more social form of reflection, social in a dual sense in that it is reflection on matters of social concern, and that it is carried out in a way which acknowledges that our reflection must take place within the social world we always already inhabit.

One of the reasons Hume gives for dropping the mode of philosophizing typical of Book I is its failure to contribute to the service of mankind (*T* 270). If he is to engage in such strenuous intellectual effort, it must be with good reason. And there are questions, he suggests, concerning the principles of moral good and evil, of the nature and foundation of government, and of the passions, which remain to be addressed, thereby "contributing to the instruction of mankind" (*T* 271). These are questions to which "superstition," as well as philosophy, addresses itself, and Hume believes that the greatest contribution of philosophy in this sphere may perhaps be made, not by providing final solutions, but rather by presenting us with "mild and moderate sentiments," which are less likely than superstition to lead to "great extravagancies of conduct" (*T* 272). Philosophy's greatest service to mankind, therefore, is in creating a safe, nondogmatic form of speculation, one which will not disturb the peace of society. This concern for the public good must give pause even to those inclined to reject Hume's particular reflections on the passions and morals.

While I have said very little about this part of Hume's corpus, it is clear that even here, at the conclusion of his most abstract philosophical work, a work concerned primarily with epistemological problems, Hume is already embarked on his life-long voyage. Book I of the *Treatise*, along with each of Hume's other works, is part of his comprehensive endeavor to understand the conditions for the possibility of a flourishing society (where the ethical and economic aspects of such flourishing are inseparably entwined), to discern the greatest threats to such flourishing, and to develop strategies for diffusing these threats. I can say little more at this point which has not already been said in the preceding pages to make plausible my initial claim that only by appreciating Hume's central social and political concerns can we perceive the unity of his thought, and further, that this realization calls into question the tendency to study his "serious," philosophical works in isolation from his "popular" essays or his "obsolete" historical works. I shall, however, like Hume, pause "to ponder that voyage, which I have undertaken, and which undoubtedly requires the utmost art and industry to be brought to a happy conclusion" (*T* 263).

The initial context of Hume's reflection on social peace and flourishing had been framed by earlier discussions of self-interestedness. Self-interest had often been identified as the primary threat to human co-operation directed towards the public welfare. This threat was commonly seen not simply as an obstacle to human flourishing, but as an accusation against divine Providence. It was incumbent on Latitudinarian divines to battle Hobbesian assumptions concerning the egotism of human nature, for example, not simply because such assumptions undermined human co-operation, but, more importantly, because they cast aspersions on the goodness of the Creator. The Latitudinarians appealed to the notion of "sympathy" as evidence that God had indeed equipped human nature with instinctive ties which run counter to private interest. Hume, in contrast, borrowed the notion of "sympathy" not because it could give us information about the moral character of its Creator, but because it indicated that it was possible for individuals to escape the conflicts of judgment which arise out of viewing things only from the point of view of their own interests. It thereby made it possible for them to appreciate and approve of those things which benefit others. "Sympathy" was a way of coping with the fragmentation induced by thinking in terms of individual interests.

But private interest, while it does tend to isolate and alienate individuals from one another, was not for Hume the greatest threat to social co-operation; he was far more concerned with the sorts of conflict posed by groups of individuals united to form sects, parties, or factions. And the factions which he observed to have done the greatest damage to the social fabric, those which gave rise to the bitterest violence, that were least susceptible to compromise, were not parties arising out of shared interests, but parties of principle, especially of abstract speculative principle – first and foremost, religious factions.

Hume provided a theory of moral approbation not because he believed that ethical practice required the sustenance of a supporting theory, but in order to loosen the ties linking ethical convictions, beliefs about living and doing well, to intractable theological disputes. Like Hutcheson, Hume stands in the tradition of modern natural law, which seeks on the basis of observation of human nature to discern the shape of the good individual and the good society. In Hume's secularized account of moral approbation, sympathy filled the place Hutcheson reserved for Providence; it assured an intelligible connection between moral judgments and human flourishing in society. But it began to be clear that the form of sympathy capable of inhabiting such a role could not be the passive, instinctual notion of sympathy employed by the Latitudinarians. The sympathy appealed to by the Latitudinarians was limited and variable. It followed well-worn paths of pre-existing connections and resemblances, threatening to reinforce, rather than alleviate, family feuds, nationalist bloodbaths, and, uppermost in Hume's mind, religious zeal and sectarian conflict. If such sympathy is a tie which binds "similar" individuals together, it is at the same time a rope which cordons "them" off from "us."

In the course of Hume's reflections on sympathy, something new emerged – an active effort to move beyond prior affinities and to cross factional boundaries in entering into the situations and points of view of others. In "Of the standard of taste," Hume grappled openly with the problem of disagreement in taste and judgment and explored the possibility of sympathetic understanding of those regarded as "other." This capacity for entering into different points of view is akin to extensive sympathy, in that it regards actions within the alien way of life as a whole, rather than focusing on individual acts. Sympathetic understanding goes far beyond extensive sympathy, however, in that it actively strives to perceive how individual actions, as well as those traits considered by the community to be virtues, contribute to or are constitutive of goods pursued by individuals in that community. While generally confident of the possibility of understanding those of different ages and cultures, Hume suggested that sympathetic understanding comes to a dead stop when confronting those who live "artificial" religious lives, deducing practical consequences from speculative theories.

Hume devoted considerable effort to the task of understanding the barriers religious belief places in the way of sympathetic understanding – otherworldliness, self-deception, hypocrisy, and zeal. Hume's essay on the pleasures of tragedy, for instance, unmasked the pathologies of belief which lie behind Scottish Evangelicals' condemnation of theater. The Evangelical rejection of worldly existence exchanged this-worldly reality for what Hume took to be the fiction of spiritual reality and a Future State. This resulted in a distortion of sympathetic capacities which not only led to the rejection of tragic drama, but which induced a kind of aesthetic detachment from real life tragedy and the suffering caused by believers' own zeal. One's whole web of belief, it appears, affects one's capacity for sympathetic understanding. In the *Natural History of Religion*, Hume suggested that the pathologies of religious belief include not only the self-defeating pursuit of the other-worldly, but pervasive contradictions which render religious belief shadowy and wavering. Whenever religious belief lacks the stability derived from the intrinsic support of reasons (and Hume thinks this is always the case), it engenders the extrinsic reinforcements of zeal and faction. Zeal employs violence to display devotion to belief, while faction gathers bodies to lend the illusion of certainty in numbers. Where zeal and faction are rooted in irrationality and self-deception, a total impasse to sympathetic understanding threatens – the points of view of such zealots can no more be grasped by others than they themselves can sympathetically understand those outside of their own sect.

Since writing and reading history was, for Hume, the paradigm of sympathetic understanding, it is fitting that this study draws to a close by exploring the contribution made by the *History of England* to understanding the possibilities and limits of sympathetic understanding. It is here that Hume's delineation of the links among religious irrationality, zeal, and faction, along with the ways in which these links can be broken to allow sympathetic understanding among those of rival religious affiliations, attains its most concrete and persuasive form. Hume goes a long way towards exploring the conditions which make active sympathetic understanding possible, an understanding capable of detoxifying zealous factions of speculative principle. This in turn, he trusts, will help to calm overwrought fears about the threat posed to society by factions of interest and enable a more productive engagement with these practical conflicts of interest, conflicts which leave room for compromise, negotiation, and creative balance.

Yet Hume's assessment of theistic belief as irremediably incoherent and contradictory may be too quick, signaling an ironic failure on Hume's part to extend sympathetic understanding to religious believers. Hume can make sense of the possibility of sympathetically entering into the situation of someone without embracing his or her beliefs or way of life, but this possibility does not extend to theism since theism is not simply wrong but "absurd" and "artificial." Sympathetic understanding holds out the promise of healing factional divisions, but when so many are held to be beyond its reach, its promise fades. Where even a minimal internal understanding of the other is possible, so is conversation and the discovery of common ground and shared ends. Where it is not, the other is manipulated rather than spoken with. Peace achieved in the latter way would not be true concord, even if it were an absence of faction and conflict. The label of irrationality must therefore be applied with great hesitance and self-critical awareness, and the search for sympathetic understanding must never be permanently foreclosed.

That, then, is the shape of Hume's thought as I have drawn it. I hope, of course, that it will be helpful for scholars of Hume, to whom a new reading of Hume may be expected to be of intrinsic interest. But my aim has not been simply to contribute to the already vast body of Hume scholarship. From a broader perspective, a more "extensive" point of view, Hume's thought as here interpreted does not lie neatly within the usual boundary lines which delineate the stories of modern religious thought, the relationship between ethics and religion (and aesthetics), and of the history of the study of religion. This interpretation of Hume is at the same time, therefore, a call for a redrawing of these defining borders.

The starting-point of Hume's reflection on religion is not, as many interpretations imply, a desultory interest in arguments for the existence of God, but rather his experience of being caught in the crossfire of conflicts among Evangelical, Seceding, and Moderate religious factions within the Church of Scotland, and his observation of the impact these conflicts were having on Scotland's cultural and economic development. In the *History of England* these concerns are reflected in Hume's attention to zeal, hypocrisy, and faction in the various configurations of religious beliefs and institutions throughout English history. Only after reading Hume's *History* and his political essays is it possible fully to understand what Hume is up to in those works which are taken to be the only works "really" about religion.

To write the *Dialogues Concerning Natural Religion* was, on the one hand, to engage in the sort of open-ended discussion which Hume thought appropriate to such undecidable speculative issues. On the other hand, it was also to warn of the dangers of the seemingly laudable attempt to appeal to reason rather than revelation in order to secure final, certain answers to such speculative questions. The illusion of certainty, even if it arose out of free and open discussion, could only too easily encourage the re-emergence of dogmatism and religious zeal.[2] Thus there is a practical impetus behind Hume's skeptical arguments. Similarly, despite his employment of general terms such as "religion" and "theism," Hume is less interested in these abstractions than in how different sorts of religious beliefs and institutions shape different kinds of character, encourage hypocrisy or zeal, set up authorities which rival the state or do away with such authorities altogether. If the labels of "enthusiasm" and "superstition," or a story of the emergence of theism from polytheism, lump together different religions or sects, creating bedfellows who would find one another not only strange but repugnant, this can be seen as a sort of shock treatment which may only assist Hume's project of securing the peace and encouraging the flourishing of society by demanding greater self-awareness and critical reflection.

So Hume's place in modern religious thought cannot simply be that of the skeptic who forever closed off the avenue of "natural religion." Nor is his contribution best seen as summed up by his reflection on the causes of "religious belief" in general. But this implies that the history of modern religious thought must itself be understood in broader, more comprehensive terms. Rather than defining it solely as the development of reflection about the sources of religious knowledge and the justification of religious belief, or simply as the development of psychological and sociological explanations of the phenomenon of religion in general (although these are aspects of modern religious thought which have over the course of time become distinct, institutionally defined academic subfields), it is better to understand it in terms of the whole course of reflection about the relationship between religion and society, which emerges out of a concern about how to secure peace in a world of pervasive disagreement over theological matters. This is an area of intellectual endeavor that is comprehensive enough to embrace concerns about moral character, speculative knowledge, and social cohesion, yet that is concrete enough in its concerns to examine *particular* religious groups and *particular* societies. This alternate story-line of modern religious thought and the reading I have offered of Hume are mutually reinforcing, so that if my reading of Hume is accepted a shift in vision which makes this story-line plausible will seem natural, while the old boundary lines will seem increasingly artifactual and bound to contemporary academic self-definition.

This is not, admittedly, simply a broader definition of modern religious thought, but rather a redefinition of it, one which might seem to distract attention from the question of the truth of religious belief. But it is impossible to understand the course of modern religious thought without recognizing that one of the key defining features of modern reflection on religion is precisely that social and political concerns are not adventitious or secondary considerations to be sorted out after metaphysical or ontological or even epistemological puzzles are first solved, but that they are rather the starting points of reflection. So in telling the story of the secularization of ethics (of the emergence of accounts of morality which made no appeal to theological concepts), this approach to modern religious thought, which encourages sensitivity to the social and political context of modern religious thought, would draw attention to the centrality of practical concerns about the destructive effects of religious conflict, rather than focusing more narrowly on a crisis of belief which followed the challenge of the new science to traditional intellectual authorities. In the aftermath of the religious wars, questions about the consequences of holding certain religious beliefs, or of having certain sorts of religious institutions, had everything to do with the way in which questions about the truth of religious beliefs were posed. Thinkers began to ask, what does it mean to call "true" beliefs which have given rise to such passionate disagreement? While some thinkers strove to locate beliefs on which all could agree, or to redescribe or reconfigure beliefs in such a way that all could agree on them, others began to ask if it would not perhaps be wisest, in the absence of final guarantees of truth, to promote beliefs which would form good character and good communities.

This broader context of concern over the relation between religious beliefs and institutions and society gives greater intelligibility to the emergence of the study of the phenomenon of "religion" in general. The path toward inquiry into the causes and functions of religion was opened up by asking questions about the sorts of individuals and societies which particular religious communities help to constitute, for the latter sort of question, like the former, sets aside the question of the truth or falsity of particular religious beliefs, places all in the same plane, and assumes the appropriateness of asking the same questions of each. The categories of heretic, pagan, and heathen are thereby displaced.

This proposed redefinition of modern religious thought only seems to distract attention from truth questions because it draws attention to other sorts of questions which modern thinkers began to formulate. The course of modern religious thought becomes more intelligible when the driving force of social concerns is recognized. But this does not mean that truth questions disappear or become irrelevant, that false religious beliefs ought to be foisted on an unsuspecting populace if it will make them content and productive. What must be recongized and fully integrated into religious studies is that truth questions do not exist in a vacuum, waiting indifferently for evaluation by scholars, students, and seekers, but that they are formulated under particular conditions. When questions about the truth of the Christian doctrine of the Trinity are formulated in a classroom, for instance, they are, in effect, different questions than when formulated by a congregation of believers, and this fact must be raised to full awareness. It therefore makes little sense to attempt to isolate such questions from their particular contexts, from the concerns and questions to which they are linked. Truth questions *must* be formulated, but the scholar of religious studies is asking his or her own questions, even when these are questions about someone else's questions.

In providing a new reading of Hume's thought, then, I have also tried to hint at the ways in which it both calls for and contributes to a broader, more socially and politically sensitive understanding of the story-line of modern religious thought, the history of ethics and the history of the study of religion. But it might perhaps be suggested that what I have really done, in making sympathy the starting-point of my study, is a third thing. It might be thought that I have attempted to provide a Lovejoy-like history of the "idea-unit" of sympathy, or, at least, that I have told the "Hume episode" of the story of sympathy, with a quick glance back at the episode involving the Latitudinarian divines, and a few detours to consider the Adam Smith scene, the "sympathy and tragedy" scene, and so forth.

There is indeed a body of literature on the history of sympathy as a concept within modern thought to which I have been responding in discussing the emergence of interest in sympathy and the development of sympathy and related concepts in Hume's thought, and in suggesting subsequent lines of development of sympathy and the imagination. But my intention has certainly not been to suggest, as is the tendency in the history of ideas, that the act of separating out sympathy as an element of thought, looking at it apart from the changing complexes in which it combines with other ideas, will have the virtue of simplifying our understanding of eighteenth-century intellectual history or of its continuity with nineteenth- or twentieth-century thought. Nor have I wished to provide the idea of sympathy with a history of its own, implying that ambiguities internal to the idea (passive/active, emotional/intellectual) possess a motive force which generates change and development over time, within what must then be regarded as the relatively passive transmission fluid of the thought of Hume and others.

I did suggest that the notion of sympathy can be seen as uniting disparate aspects of Hume's thought. For it was in reflecting on the relationship of sympathy to moral approbation and disapprobation, and on sympathy's varieties, variability, scope, limits, and perversions, that Hume explored the conditions for the possibility of a flourishing society. Sympathy, together with the notion of entering sympathetically into foreign points of view, thus bind together Hume's moral philosophy, his literary and political essays, his history, and his analysis and critique of religion. I suggested, moreover, that the fact that the passive sympathy first introduced in the *Treatise* is replaced in the course of Hume's writings by an active capacity to enter into the situations of others opened up new ethical and political possibilities for sympathy which subsequent thinkers took up and continued to explore. Comments scattered throughout the preceding chapters give some indication of where one might look to find a continuation of this story about sympathy and the notions which it spawns in the subsequent Romantic period – sympathetic imagination, the moral imagination, sympathetic under-standing, and imaginative identification. Although Hume's primary concern with peace and stability made the notion of radical social change anathema to him, and he could not conceive of it ever bringing more good than harm, once sympathetic understanding is seen as capable of calling our factional loyalties into question, it may not simply contribute to the maintenance of social peace, but go on to contribute to social transformation.

This is a brief sketch of the contribution this study of Hume's thought makes to the literature on the history of sympathy. Part of my purpose has been to show, however, that we get things backwards if we think that the central questions to be asked are questions about the definition of the concept of sympathy, about whether it should be regarded as essentially active or passive, emotional or intellectual, instinctive or deliberate. Within the period I have been discussing, it is concerns with a cluster of *other* questions, questions of social and political import, which make people care about sympathy. Sympathy belongs with a cluster or web of interrelated concepts and concerns – not only sympathy, but situation, point of view, tragedy, hypocrisy, faction, zeal, and public good. Within Hume's thought, one can begin to explore any of these concepts and be led to each of the others. Starting with sympathy is one possibility, but it is only one; only from an inadequate and limited perspective does it seem to be the sole key to the unity of Hume's thought. Seeing sympathy as part of this cluster of concepts makes more intelligible the social and political stakes surrounding different interpretations of sympathy: active versus passive, reflective versus instinctive, requiring heightened self-awareness or loss of self, reinforcing existing bonds and factions or capable of challenging and reaching beyond them. Sympathy's primary significance lies not in itself but in its connections with these other concepts.

To try to tell just the history of the concept of sympathy, ignoring the questions which lent it import and looking only at changing definitions and understandings of the concept itself, not only robs us of any sense of why sympathy became a central preoccupation of Hume and other eighteenth-century thinkers; it also makes it impossible to distinguish semantic from substantial lines of inheritance. In light of the fact that conceptions of sympathy have, in fact, varied widely, and even that the term itself has been displaced by others, we can speak intelligently about whether there is in some sense an ongoing discussion taking place only if we look beyond sympathy to the questions and concerns which render it of interest. By tracing the interconnections within this cluster, therefore, I have been able to do something which I did not in fact set out to do when I began this project – to identify, at least tentatively, these substantial lines of inheritance. For it is shared concern with this cluster of concepts and issues, rather than any straightforward doctrinal or argumentative connection, which links Hume in significant ways with important thinkers in several subsequent generations. This cluster of concerns, because it extends across disciplinary boundaries, linking moral philosophy with aesthetics with politics with psychology with sociology, can easily be overlooked. This not only leads to a fragmentation of Hume's thought and a variety of "Humes" who are strangers to one another, but also encourages a blindness to very real connections with subsequent thinkers.

If we look only for a shared concern with the factional zeal of religious groups, for instance, we would miss the fact that Burke, like Hume, is concerned with the zeal of factions of "speculative principle," but believes that political, rather than religious, factions now pose the greatest danger to society. The persuasiveness of Burke's attack on the "literary cabal" or "political men of letters" rests in large part on the inherited power of the rhetoric of criticism of religious zeal. Burke also draws on the connection between sympathy and tragedy, although for his political purposes he does not acknowledge the ambiguities of sympathy and relies only on passive sympathy. He appeals to "natural" feeling, to the immediate sympathetic response to tragedy, in order to combat the French Revolution, claiming the importance to the health of the social organism of pre-existing affiliations and hierarchies. Burke's understanding of "natural" sympathy thus plays a key role in his conservatism and advocacy of gradual reform.

The same cluster of concepts also helped to frame the discussions of American statehood and republic formation. Jefferson puzzles over the connection between sympathy and the social bonds requisite to human society. But because he believes that mutual sympathy among citizens must be predicated on homogeneity, rather than conceiving of it as capable of extension across lines of difference, he concludes that apartheid will be necessary in former slave states. Madison draws on Hume's insights into the possibility of balancing factions of interest, as opposed to parties of speculative principle, in order to argue that a large republic need not be torn apart by factions.

Hazlitt, with his conviction of the basic identity between imaginative sympathy with someone else's future welfare and with one's own future welfare, emphasizes the possibilities for reform which lie within active sympathy. Stung by Burke's employment of "natural" sympathy to reinforce traditional hierarchies, Hazlitt employs his own considerable rhetorical powers to show that sympathy, properly understood, is rather the first step toward a recognition of human equality. Only habit, he insists, keeps us from extending sympathy beyond ourselves or our private societies. Sympathy with the "common" inspires forceful critique of the privileged classes, and claims that sympathy is "naturally" limited to those of one's own class and station in life must be unmasked as artificial limits used to justify the status quo.

Hazlitt thinks in terms of the powers of imagination versus the inertia of habit, rather than extensive versus limited or active versus passive, but sympathy remains intimately linked to concrete social and political issues. Because Hume is seen as politically conservative (although his "ideal commonwealth" was a form of indirect democracy) and Hazlitt is a radical, because Hume's focus is on the role of sympathetic understanding in controlling religious zeal and factions in order to secure social peace and public welfare, while Hazlitt's attention turns to the role of sympathetic imagination in the recognition of human equality and the fight against subjection to false authorities, it would be easy to overlook the continuities between Hume's and Hazlitt's thought. Hazlitt, however, continues to reflect on the connections within the same cluster of concepts which capture Hume's basic concerns.

Further evidence of this is found in Hazlitt's views on religion. Although Hume favors the state establishment of religion, while Hazlitt is a fierce critic of this establishment, the notion of "hypocrisy" is central to the discussion of religion in both thinkers. Both would agree that hypocrisy, because of its threat to sympathetic understanding, poisons society and jeopardizes public welfare, although they disagree about what particular form of religious institutions engenders the most problematic forms of hypocrisy.

If the thought of such figures as Burke, Jefferson and Hazlitt demonstrates how the web of concepts which gave unity and coherence to Hume's thought is carried on but transformed, as the child's game of cat's cradle forms a constantly transforming web, the Lake School Poets with whom Hazlitt was closely associated give some indication of the course of the breakdown of this web of concepts. At the outset, the connections between sympathy and social and political concerns are central to Wordsworth's aesthetic theory and practice. Poetry, by embracing the common, promises to create bonds of sympathy between the simple folk and the cultured gentry and usher in democracy. But an initial inebriation with the ideals of the French Revolution is quickly succeeded by political reaction and disaffection.

Among the poets of the Lake School, the sympathetic imagination, first hailed as an avenue toward realizing universal humanity, soon degenerates into the poet's projection of himself into other people or things; the link between sympathy and social and political concerns is dissolved and the ideal of aesthetic "autonomy" begins to develop. This encourages a relativistic interpretation of sympathetic activity; the "other" can be imaginatively identified with, sympathetically understood, but this requires a loss of self which makes it impossible ever to bring self and other into focus together. As self-absorption and self-reflection displace concern with others, the genre of tragedy is eclipsed by that of lyric poetry. To bring ethical concerns to bear within sympathetic activity easily comes to be seen as a failure to lay aside the self and therefore a failure to achieve sympathetic understanding.[3] Keats, deeply influenced by Hazlitt, attempts to escape this poetic egotism, but he nevertheless further cements the separation between politics and poetry and the aestheticization of sympathy.

It was not, as I say, my intention to trace the different configurations of this cluster of concepts in thinkers after Hume, nor to locate its breakdown. My observations in this regard must remain merely suggestive. But I hope that I have said enough to break a path for future reflection. We can now begin to discern how later social critics and nation-designers carry on a tradition of critical reflection which addresses itself to concrete social concerns with all available intellectual resources. It would not be inappropriate to call this a tradition of social criticism, or even of the "organic intellectual." For thinkers after Hume, the central problem was in most cases no longer the threat to social peace posed by factions made up of enthusiastic religious zealots. Still, several of Hume's central concerns remained alive for several subsequent generations: the issue of factional divisions and how to bridge them or redirect their harmful energies, that of the relationship between different sorts of religious beliefs or institutions and society, and the question of the resources provided by sympathy and related notions to enable mutual understanding and to create a sense of shared humanity. Discerning the breakdown of this cluster of concerns sheds light on the nature of the transition from the Enlightenment to Romanticism.

Skipping ahead nearly 200 years to the present, it is striking to find prominent contemporary authors once again interested, not in "sympathy" or "imagination" as isolated concepts, but in the links between these notions and social and political concerns about "factions," with the boundaries which separate various human communities, with the capacity to question dogmatic, zealous allegiance to one's communities, to foster understanding among them, and, more broadly, to promote the public good. Moreover, just as eighteenth-century thinkers saw tragedy as intimately linked with sympathy and faction, contemporary thinkers are beginning to regard literature (along with ethnography) as relevant to this cluster of concepts and social concerns, with a consequent shift in the understanding of the relationship between ethics and aesthetics.

Alasdair MacIntyre and Richard Rorty, different though they are, are quick to come to mind.[4] For MacIntyre, it is rationality (conceived in narrative terms) which requires us to take up the task of imaginative identification. Only through such imaginative identification can we evaluate our allegiance to a particular tradition:

What rationality then requires of . . . a person is that he or she confirm or disconfirm over time this initial view of his or her relationship to this particular tradition of enquiry by engaging, to whatever degree is appropriate, both in the ongoing arguments within that tradition and in the argumentative debates and conflicts of that tradition of enquiry with one or more of its rivals . . . The latter requires, so far as is possible, the acquisition of the language-in-use of whatever particular rival tradition is in question, as what I have called a second first language, and that in turn requires a work of the imagination whereby the individual is able to place him or herself imaginatively within the scheme of belief inhabited by those whose allegiance is to the rival tradition, so as to perceive and conceive the natural and social worlds as they perceive and conceive them.[5]

For Rorty, in contrast, even this modest sort of rationality is an illusion; imaginative identification, rather than being called for by rationality, itself substitutes for the "demands of reason." "For public purposes," Rorty insists, "it does not matter if everyone's final vocabulary is different, as long as there is enough overlap so that everybody has some words with which to express the desirability of entering into other people's fantasies as well as into one's own . . . For the liberal ironist, skill at imaginative identification does the work which the liberal metaphysician would like to have done by a specifically moral motivation – rationality, or the love of God, or the love of truth."[6] All we need for human solidarity is the recognition of our shared susceptibility to pain and humiliation, but we cannot provide any guarantee that this imaginative skill which we have developed will persist.

Both MacIntyre and Rorty, despite the gulf which separates them, draw on sympathy-derived notions in order to reflect on the borders and bridges among the various traditions, "languages," and "vocabularies" in which we human beings find ourselves. Both fear that the consequence of a failure in imaginative identification would be a dangerous form of complacency – for Rorty, a complacency which would place our shared public purposes in jeopardy and foster the growth of various forms of cruelty, while, for MacIntyre, a complacency which would result in corrupt allegiance to traditions which embody error and injustice.

Surely these fears and these remedies become more intelligible when placed in relationship to earlier reflections on sympathy and related notions. But this contemporary phenomenon poses a question whose answer lies beyond the scope of the present work. What sort of story would be required to fill the 200-year gap between the disintegration within Romantic thought of the cluster of concepts initially drawn together by Hume, and the contemporary reconnection of sympathy and imagination with political and social concerns? Is this a re-emergence of Hume's cluster, a reconnecting of sympathy with the body of concerns which made it interesting to eighteenth-century thinkers, or is there a continuous, though overlooked, tradition of reflection which holds these ethical, aesthetic, social, and political concepts and concerns together? Are contemporary thinkers reinventing a long-lost character, whom we might call the Humean social critic, or is Humean social criticism receiving renewed attention simply because it is being readmitted into the halls of the academy, where a different sort of criticism (one whose ideal of disciplinary purity required the isolation of aesthetic from ethical from political categories) long reigned supreme?

Notes

INTRODUCTION

1 See Donald W. Livingston, *Hume's Philosophy of Common Life* (University of Chicago Press, 1984), 222–223 and James Farr, "Hume, hermeneutics, and history: a sympathetic account," *History and Theory* 17 (1978): 285–310.

2 On the distinction between seeing things from "right and sound points of view" and seeing things from a detached, universal point of view, see Hans-Georg Gadamer, *Truth and Method*, eds. Garrett Barden and John Cumming (New York: Crossroad, 1975), 31. Gadamer's discussions of *sensus communis*, judgment and taste (19–39) offer an interpretation of eighteenth-century British thought which stresses the social and historical connotations of these concepts in ways which resonate with my interpretation of the development of Hume's accounts of sympathy and moral judgment.

3 Ironically, Norman Kemp Smith's 1935 introduction to the *Dialogues Concerning Natural Religion* (Indianapolis: Bobbs-Merrill, 1947; first edn 1935) provided a broader perspective on Hume's critique of religion, but initiated a discussion focused almost solely on Hume's arguments against natural religion in the *Dialogues*.

4 J. C. A. Gaskin, *Hume's Philosophy of Religion* (London: Macmillan, 1978), 5.

5 Gaskin, *Hume's Philosophy of Religion*, 2nd edn (London: Macmillan, 1988), 192.

6 Richard Wollheim, introduction to *Hume on Religion*, by David Hume (Cleveland: Meridian Books, 1963), 14–17.

7 Kenneth R. Merrill and Donald G. Wester, "Hume on the relation of religion to morality," *Journal of Religion* 60 (1980): 273, 276.

8 Keith E. Yandell, *Hume's Inexplicable Mystery: His Views on Religion* (Philadelphia: Temple University Press, 1990), 83.

9 Antony Flew, introduction to *Writings on Religion*, by David Hume (La Salle, IL: Open Court, 1992), vii–xi.

10 James Noxon, "Hume's concern with religion," in *David Hume: Many-Sided Genius*, eds. Kenneth R. Merrill and Robert W. Shahan (Norman, OK: University of Oklahoma Press, 1976), 59–60.

11 Richard H. Popkin, "Skepticism and the Study of History," in *David Hume: Philosophical Historian*, eds. David Fate Norton and Richard H. Popkin (Indianapolis: Bobbs-Merrill, 1965), xxx.

12 Donald Siebert, *The Moral Animus of David Hume* (Newark: University of Delaware Press, 1990). Siebert's project and conclusions are perhaps closest to my own. We differ in several significant respects, however. Siebert takes sympathy to be important primarily in terms of great feeling for those in distress. Although he stresses that Hume is not a typical sentimentalist, since sympathy is for Hume not enfeebling or a sign of weakness, he does not explore the relationship between Hume's early discussions of sympathy and similar notions in later works. Furthermore, Siebert believes that Hume accepts an innate moral sense and that he is a relativist, both of which I contest.

13 Nicholas Phillipson, *Hume* (New York: St. Martin's Press, 1989), especially 18, 34–35, 64, 73. Livingston's attention to history in Hume's thought also deserves mention.

14 See Phillipson's works, particularly his essays "Towards a definition of the Scottish Enlightenment," in *City and Society in the 18th Century*, eds. Paul S. Fritz and David Williams, (Toronto: Hakkert, 1973) 125–147 and "Culture and society in the 18th-century province: the case of Edinburgh and the Scottish Enlightenment," in *The University in Society*, vol. 2, *Europe, Scotland, and the United States from the 16th to the 20th Century*, ed. Lawrence Stone, (Princeton University Press, 1974), 407–448. The essays in *Wealth and Virtue: The Shaping of Political Economy in the Scottish Enlightenment*, eds. Istvan Hont and Michael Ignatieff (Cambridge University Press, 1983) are also relevant.

15 Alasdair MacIntyre's wholly negative characterization of Hume's relationship with Scotland strikes me as one-sided. MacIntyre writes that "David Hume's relationship to his Scottish upbringing and education was one in which throughout his life . . . he consistently discarded everything distinctively Scottish in matters of intellectual attitude and belief," (280) and claims that "two rival modes of social and cultural life had confronted each other in early eighteenth-century Scotland: one prizing the seventeenth-century Scottish past but recognizing the need to transform it so that the distinctively Scottish inheritance in religion, in law, and in education might be renewed as well as preserved; the other seeing no prosperous future for Scotland except as an increasingly anglicized part of the United Kingdom," *Whose Justice? Which Rationality?* (University of Notre Dame Press, 1988), 323. This fails to take into account past and contemporary social strife and economic problems in Scotland for which Hume sought a solution.

16 J. G. A. Pocock, "Cambridge paradigms and Scotch philosophers: a study of the relations between the civic humanist and the civil jurisprudential interpretation of eighteenth-century social thought," in *Wealth and Virtue*, 240.

17 Richard Sher and Alexander Murdoch, "Patronage and party in the Church of Scotland, 1750–1800," in *Church, Politics and Society: Scotland 1408–1929*, ed. Norman MacDougall (Edinburgh: John Donald Publishers Ltd., 1983), 213. See also Callum G. Brown, *The Social History of Religion in Scotland since 1730* (London: Methuen, 1987), 22–32, and Ian D. L. Clark, "From protest to reaction: the Moderate regime in the Church of Scotland, 1752–1805," in *Scotland in the Age of Improvement: Essays in Scottish History in the*

Eighteenth Century, eds. N. T. Phillipson and Rosalind Mitchison (Edinburgh University Press, 1970), 200–224.

18 Sher and Murdoch, "Partronage and party," 213.

19 J.Y.T. Greig, *David Hume* (London: Jonathan Cape Ltd., 1931).

20 James Boswell, *Private Papers of James Boswell*, vol. 12, eds. Geoffrey Scott and Frederick A. Pottle (Mount Vernon, New York: W. E. Rudge, 1931), 227–228.

21 [Richard Allestree,] *The Practice of Christian Graces or the Whole Duty of Man* (London: D. Maxwell for T. Garthwait, 1658), 598–603.

22 *Ibid.*, Part II, sections 1–3.

23 *LDH* I: 13, 34, Letter to Francis Hutcheson, September 17, 1739.

24 Alasdair MacIntyre, *Whose Justice?*, 245.

25 E. C. Mossner and John V. Price give an account of Hume's 1744 attempt to obtain a post in moral philosophy at the University of Edinburgh in their introduction to Hume's *A Letter from a Gentleman to his friend in Edinburgh* (Edinburgh University Press, 1967; first published in 1745), vii–xxv.

26 John Robertson, "The Scottish Enlightenment at the limits of the civic tradition," in *Wealth and Virtue*, 151.

27 See Phillipson, *Hume*, 73, 90, and Robertson, "Scottish Enlightenment," 152–153.

28 See *H* I, XXIX, 552ff. Hume worries, on the one hand, that ecclesiastics forced to provide for themselves will encourage zeal and hatred of other sects, and, on the other, that a rich independent clerical establishment like the Catholic one is a dangerous rival to civil authority. He concludes that the civil magistrate will find that "in reality the most decent and advantageous composition, which he can make with the spiritual guides, is to bribe their indolence, by assigning stated salaries to their profession, and rendering it superfluous for them to be farther active, than merely to prevent their flock from straying in quest of new pastures" (*H* I, XXIX, 552–553). It would be left to a later generation of critics, notably William Hazlitt, to turn the social critic's eye toward the evils and corruption associated with church establishment. Hazlitt argues that the establishment of religion in England has transformed clergy into sycophants of power and encouraged the doctrine of divine right.

Priests are naturally favourers of power, inasmuch as they are dependent on it. – Their power over the mind is hardly sufficient of itself to insure absolute obedience to their authority, without a reinforcement of power over the body. The secular arm must come in aid of the spiritual. . . . Kings and conquerors make laws, parcel out lands, and erect churches and palaces for the priests and dignitaries of religion: "they will have them to shew their mitred fronts in Courts and Parliaments"; and in return, Priests anoint Kings with holy oil, hedge them round with inviolability, spread over them the mysterious sanctity of religion, and, with very little ceremony, make over the whole species as slaves to these Gods upon earth by virtue of divine right!

"On the clerical character," in *The Complete Works of William Hazlitt*, ed. P. P.

Howe, vol. 7 (London and Toronto: J. M. Dent and Sons, 1930), 256. It is important to see that Hazlitt's central concern is no longer, as with Hume, the threat of violent social upheaval deriving from religious zeal and faction, but rather the threat to liberty of thought and action posed by, among other phenomena, that of the alliance between church and state.

29 Siebert, *Moral Animus of Hume*, 118–119.

30 For further discussion of the role of the *Dialogues* in Hume's campaign against faction, see Jennifer A. Herdt, "Opposite sentiments: Hume's fear of faction and the philosophy of religion," *American Journal of Theology and Philosophy* 16 (1995): 245–259.

1 SETTING SYMPATHY'S STAGE

1 Hobbes is not always classed with the modern natural lawyers, although historically sensitive readers are arriving at this consensus. For a brief account, see Richard Tuck, *Hobbes* (Oxford University Press, 1989), 92–100.

2 Duncan Forbes, *Hume's Philosophical Politics* (Cambridge University Press, 1975), 3–90.

3 *Ibid.*, 17.

4 Hugo Grotius, *On the Law of War and Peace*, trans. Francis W. Kelsey (Oxford University Press, 1925), Prolegomena.

5 A helpful introduction to sixteenth-century Thomism is found in Quentin Skinner, *The Foundations of Modern Political Thought*, vol. 2, *The Age of Reformation* (Cambridge University Press, 1978), 135–173.

6 I should note that Aquinas' understanding of "the" common good was as a plurality of goods common to individuals and the community. He did not, moreover, believe that action-guiding principles could be deduced from the first principles of natural law; we can understand ethics in light of our social nature and its perfection, but we cannot derive concrete precepts from human nature. My understanding of Aquinas is indebted to conversations with Victor Preller. For an interpretation which supports this reading of Aquinas, see John R. Bowlin, "Contingency, chance, and virtue in Aquinas," (Ph.D. dissertation, Princeton University, 1993), 11–20; 191–192. For my present purposes, however, I am not trying to give the best interpretation of Aquinas' thought, but am more interested in how he was interpreted by subsequent thinkers, who, influenced by neo-Stoicism, emphasized the natural law elements in his thought.

7 Thomas Aquinas, *Summa Theologica*, trans. Fathers of the English Dominican Province, 5 vols. (New York: Benziger Brothers, 1947–8), *S.T.* IA IIAE Q. 1, *S.T.* IA IIAE Q. 1 A. 5.

8 *S.T.* IA IIAE Q. 109 A. 3. Aquinas elsewhere writes that "every part is ordained to the whole, as imperfect to perfect; and . . . one man is a part of the perfect community," *S.T.* IA IIAE Q. 90 A. 2.

9 *S.T.* IA IIAE Q. 2 A. 8, Q. 4 A. 8, Q. 90 A. 2.

10 J. B. Schneewind, "The Divine Corporation and the history of ethics," *Philosophy in history: Essays on the historiography of philosophy*, eds. Richard Rorty, J. B. Schneewind, and Quentin Skinner (Cambridge University Press, 1984), 176.

11 Thomas Hobbes, *Leviathan*, ed. Richard Tuck (Cambridge University Press, 1991), 117 (Part II, ch. 17). *Leviathan* was originally published in 1651.

12 *Ibid.*, 119 (Part II, ch. 17).

13 Skinner, *Age of Reformation*, 160.

14 Calvin's views on human fallenness, though often conflated with those of Luther, leave more room for the continued perception of natural law. Calvin believed that fallen human reason is utterly blind to spiritual truth, but that natural, fallen human reason continues to be able to perceive truth in matters social and political. David Little comments that "Apparently, Calvin believed that men naturally affirm the duties of humanity, which were but the second table of the Decalogue," "Calvin and the prospects for a Christian theory of natural law," in *Norm and Context in Christian Ethics*, eds. Gene H. Outka and Paul Ramsey (New York: Charles Scribner's Sons, 1968), 183. Calvin's followers, however, adopted more skeptical views about fallen human reason, even in the earthly political realm.

15 Martin Luther, *Luther's Works*, vol. 45. *The Christian in Society* II, ed. Walther I. Brandt (Philadelphia: Muhlenberg Press, 1962), 90–91.

16 For a view which stresses the influence of sixteenth-century skeptics like Montaigne and Charron, see Richard Tuck, "The 'modern' theory of natural law," in *The Languages of Political Theory in Early-Modern Europe*, ed. Anthony Pagden (Cambridge University Press, 1987), 99 – 119. My suspicion is that conflict arising among those who held strong beliefs and attacked those who did not was more crucial to the development of natural law thought than was the thought of those who avoided conflict by embracing skepticism.

17 Pufendorf, who was influenced by both Hobbes and Grotius, is closer to Hobbes in his denial of the social instinct. He suggests instead that sociability can be derived from our self-interestedness in light of our weakness; we are dependent on human society for our own survival. For Pufendorf, therefore, the natural laws which teach us how to be good members of society come much closer to being simply laws of expediency, although Pufendorf avoids this conclusion by insisting that what renders them morally obligatory is the command of a superior. Samuel Pufendorf, *The Duty of Man and Citizen*, trans. Frank Gardner Moore (Oxford University Press, 1927), Bk. 1, ch. 2, paras. 3–5; ch. 3, para. 3.

18 Hugo Grotius, *On the Law of War and Peace*, Prolegomena, section 11.

19 Forbes, *Hume's Philosophical Politics*, 41.

20 Charles Taylor, *Sources of the Self: The Making of the Modern Identity* (Cambridge, MA: Harvard University Press, 1989), 275.

21 Samuel Y. Edgerton, Jr. *The Renaissance Rediscovery of Linear Perspective* (New York: Basic Books, 1975). My colleague Mark Larrimore suggested this connection to me in conversation.

22 So ethics now often seems to be fundamentally about altruism, despite the fact that altruism is seen as problematic. As we saw with Hutcheson, if we derive pleasure from serving the interests of others, this seems to threaten the purity and moral praiseworthiness of our service to others. See Alasdair MacIntyre, *After Virtue*, 2nd edn (University of Notre Dame Press, 1984), 228–229. An example of the continuing tendency to see ethics in this way is Thomas Nagel's *The Possibility of Altruism* (Princeton University Press, 1970).

23 See R. S. Crane, "Suggestions toward a genealogy of the 'man of feeling,'" in *The Idea of the Humanities* (University of Chicago Press, 1967), 188–213.

24 Shaftesbury borrowed from the optimism of the Latitudinarian divines about human nature under grace in developing his notion of "moral sense." See Ernest Tuveson, "The importance of Shaftesbury," *Journal of English Literary History* 20 (1953): 267–299 and "The origins of the moral sense," *Huntington Library Quarterly* 11 (1947–48): 241–259, which discusses the ideas of Thomas Burnet and their possible influence on Shaftesbury's doctrine of moral sense.

25 Of course, they argued that *sinners* acted only selfishly, and might very well be induced to obey God only through fear of punishment. The *Elect* were not, however, understood as obeying God's law in an interested fashion.

26 [Richard Allestree,] *The Practice of Christian Graces or the Whole Duty of Man* (London: D. Maxwell for T. Garthwait, 1658), Preface, section 1.

27 *Whole Duty*, Preface, section 8.

28 A reductivist account would, of course, violate Hume's famous but ill-understood is – ought distinction. When read in its context, which is Hume's attack on the rationalists, the import of the is–ought passage is that morals have to do with things insofar as they matter to human beings, that is, insofar as they are possible ends of human action, something neiether voluntarists nor rationalists had grasped (*T* 469–470). For a similar interpretation, see W. D. Hudson, "Hume on *is* and *ought*," in *The Is–Ought Question*, ed. Hudson (London: Macmillan, 1969), 73–80.

29 In the very beginning of Book III of the *Treatise*, the book "Of Morals," Hume writes that "Morality is a subject that interests us above all others: We fancy the peace of society to be at stake in every decision concerning it" (*T* 455). It should be noted that Hume was much less preoccupied with law as a model for morality than were the modern natural lawyers, due to influence on them from neo-Stoicism. One result of this is Hume's relative lack of concern about the question of obligation. In this sense he is actually closer to the classical natural lawyers.

30 Forbes, *Hume's Philosophical Politics*, 8.

31 James Moore and Michael Silverthorne, "Gershom Carmichael and the natural jurisprudence tradition in eighteenth-century Scotland," in *Wealth and Virtue: The Shaping of Political Economy in the Scottish Enlightenment*, eds. Istvan Hont and Michael Ignatieff (Cambridge University Press, 1983), 77–78.

32 Francis Hutcheson, *A System of Moral Philosophy* (London, 1755; New York: August M. Kelley, 1968), 1.

33 The sense that our ability to bridge this gap between persons requires special explanation is still with us today. See, for example, H. B. Acton, who insists that "a certain amount of sympathy is required if anyone is even to notice that someone else is in need of help, for, it might be said, it is under the stimulus of fellow-feeling that an objective or contemplative attitude towards others is transformed into a sensitive awareness of ways in which they may be helped or harmed and have a moral claim upon our services," "The ethical importance of sympathy," *Philosophy* 30 (1955): 62. See also David Ernest Cartwright, "The ethical significance of sympathy, compassion, and pity" (Ph. D. dissertation, University of Wisconsin at Madison, 1981), 4, and Robert J. Lipkin, "Altruism and sympathy in Hume's ethics," *Australasian Journal of Philosophy* 65 (March 1987): 21, 25–26.

34 Taylor continues: "One of the fruits of this is the new political atomism which arises in the seventeenth century, most notably with the theories of social contract of Grotius, Pufendorf, Locke, and others," *Sources*, 193.

35 Crane, "Man of Feeling," 188–213. Among the "Latitudinarian divines" Crane includes Isaac Barrow, John Tillotson, Richard Cumberland, Samuel Parker, Gilbert Burnet, Benjamin Whichcote, and Samuel Clarke.

36 Current reinterpretations suggest that Hobbes believed that human actions were necessarily self-centered, not that they were necessarily self-interested. For recent work on Hobbes, see Tuck's *Hobbes* and *Perspectives on Thomas Hobbes*, eds. G. A. J. Rogers and Alan Ryan (New York: Oxford University Press, 1989). For my purposes, however, how Hobbes was read is more important than what he meant, and I therefore give a more traditional account of his views.

37 Hobbes, *Leviathan*, 88 (part 1, ch. 13).

38 Tuveson, "Importance of Shaftesbury," 267–299.

39 Hobbes, *Leviathan*, 43 (Part 1, ch. 6). On Hobbes' behalf it can be said that it is hard to see how a being unable to suffer could be said to feel pity, but this is of course different than saying that each instance of pity is necessarily self-referential.

40 William Clagett, *Of the Humanity and Charity of Christians*, (1686, 1687 edn), 4; quoted in Crane, "Man of feeling," 194–195.

41 Isaac Barrow, *Theological Works* (1830; sermons published during 1660s and 70s), II, 140–141; quoted in Crane, "Man of feeling," 206.

42 Samuel Parker, *Demonstration of the Divine Authority of the Law of Nature*, (1681), 55; quoted in Crane, "Man of feeling," 207. Sympathy is not so clearly distinguished from compassion and pity as it is from benevolence. Compassion and pity, unlike sympathy, however, are limited to responses to something negative, and involve a positive attitude toward the sufferer, while sympathy refers only to the fact of being *affected* by someone else's joy or sorrow.

43 For references to explicit anti-Stoicism, see Crane, "Man of feeling," 200–201.

44 John B. Radner, "The art of sympathy in eighteenth-century British

thought," in *Studies in Eighteenth-Century Culture*, ed. Roseann Runte, vol. 9 (Madison: University of Wisconsin Press, 1979), 191.

45 Henry Grove, *Spectator* 588 (1714).

46 Anthony Ashley Cooper, Third Earl of Shaftesbury. *Characteristics of Men, Manners, Opinions, Times*, ed. John M. Robertson (Indianapolis: Bobbs-Merrill, 1964), 298.

47 *Ibid.*, Shaftesbury, 77.

48 On civic republicanism in relationship to eighteenth-century Scotland, see Peter Jones, "The Scottish professoriate and the polite academy, 1720–46," in *Wealth and Virtue*, 89–117. In the same volume see also John Robertson, "The Scottish Enlightenment at the limits of the civic tradition," 137–178 and J. G. A. Pocock, "Cambridge paradigms and Scotch philosophers: a study of the relations between the civic humanist and the civil jurisprudential interpretation of eighteenth-century social thought," 235–252. It was Pocock's *The Machiavellian Moment* which drew the attention of contemporary scholars to civic humanism (Princeton University Press, 1975), and the significance of this tradition of reflection is still just beginning to be explored.

49 Shaftesbury, *Characteristics*, 299.

50 See Tuveson, "Importance of Shaftesbury.'

51 Bernard Mandeville, *The Fable of the Bees*, ed. F. B. Kaye (Oxford: Clarendon, 1924), 254.

52 *Ibid.*, 257.

53 *Ibid.*, 56.

54 Joseph Butler, *Fifteen Sermons*, ed. W. R. Matthews (London: G. Bell & Sons, 1914), "Upon compassion," Sermon v, 83–6; also "Upon the love of our neighbor," Sermon xi, 188.

55 *Ibid.*, v, 86.

56 *Ibid.*, v, 86.

57 At the end of the following chapter, I return to consider ambiguities surrounding the goal of locating the "source" of moral distinctions. It is not quite clear what sort of explanation is being proffered here.

58 Philip Mercer is quite right to insist on the distinction between sympathy's role in determining conduct and its role in evaluating conduct, but wrong, I think, to claim that Hume's reflections on the role of sympathy in moral judgment can be understood wholly apart from the preceding and contemporaneous "altruism versus egoism" debate. As a result, he fails to see that Hume begins with an adopted understanding of sympathy which proves inadequate to its new role and which must be revised throughout the *Treatise* and beyond. *Sympathy and Ethics: A Study of the Relationship between Sympathy and Morality with Special Reference to Hume's Treatise* (Oxford: Clarendon Press, 1972), 1.

59 P. H. Nidditch, *An Apparatus of Variant Readings for Hume's "Treatise of Human Nature"* (University of Sheffield Press, 1976), 14.

60 All three additions are to Part II of Book III. The only reference to sympathy found in the published version of this Part of the *Treatise* is in Hume's discussion of the moral approbation which attends justice. He inserts a

further reference to sympathy in this section, and adds references to sympathy to his discussions of the moral obligation to allegiance and to chastity.

61 Subtitle to *A Treatise of Human Nature.*

62 J. B. Schneewind, Introduction to "David Hume," in *Moral Philosophy from Montaigne to Kant: An Anthology*, vol. 2, (Cambridge University Press, 1990), 545. See also Forbes, *Hume's Philosophical Politics*, 59–65.

63 The principle of association is much less evident in Hume's later work.

64 See also Walter Saul Brand, *Hume's Theory of Moral Judgement: A Study in the Unity of "A Treatise of Human Nature"* (Dordrecht: Kluwer Academic Publishers, 1992), 71.

2 DISPLACING PROVIDENCE

1 For fine-tuned reflections on Hume's account of pride, see Annette Baier, "Hume's analysis of pride," *Journal of Philosophy* 75 (1978): 27–40 and "Master passions," in *Explaining Emotions*, ed. Amélie Oksenberg Rorty (Berkeley: University of California Press, 1980), 403–423.

2 Annette Baier's response to the problem of the missing impression of self is close to my own. She argues that "Hume never retracts his Book One denial of a 'simple' persisting self, the sort of thing of which we might have a simple impression. The self is complex, changing, dependent on others for its coming to be, for its emotional life, for its self-consciousness, for its self-evaluations" *A Progress of Sentiments: Reflections on Hume's Treatise* (Cambridge, MA.: Harvard University Press, 1991), 130. But she adds that, since the idea of the self is produced by pride, and pride is "that agreeable passion in which he thinks our minds tend to rest and invigorate themselves whenever possible" (143), it is vivid enough to raise communicated ideas of passions into their corresponding impressions. For an opposing view, which sees Hume as contradicting himself, see Norman Kemp Smith, *The Philosophy of David Hume: A Critical Study of its Origins and Central Doctrines* (London: Macmillan, 1964), 171.

3 See Baier, "Master passions," 422 n. 7. Baier argues that the most stable sort of pride is pride in virtue, 415ff.

4 Páll S. Árdal, *Passion and Value in Hume's Treatise* (Edinburgh University Press, 1966), 45.

5 Philip Mercer, *Sympathy and Ethics: A Study of the Relationship between Sympathy and Morality with Special Reference to Hume's Treatise* (Oxford: Clarendon Press, 1972), 36. Mercer acknowledges that extensive sympathy may broaden sympathy into something of greater practical moral relevance, but he denies that a consistent interpretation of extensive sympathy is possible (21).

6 Max Scheler points out this aspect of emotional infection in order to distinguish it from fellow-feeling, in which we are aware of an emotion as belonging to someone else. *The Nature of Sympathy*, trans. Peter Heath (Hamden, CN: Archon Books, 1970), 11–12, 14–17. While Hume does not make this distinction clearly in the *Treatise*, I will argue that he does see the need for a corrective to passive emotional infection, and that this comes in the form of an intentional form of sympathetic understanding of the situations of

others. As we have already seen, Hume insists that our own self is *not* the object of any passion in sympathy; this can be read as a normative insistence that our attention *ought* to be focused on the other person. Sympathy as emotional infection will therefore be problematic for Hume.

7 Mandeville had held the love of praise to be original, but Hume shows it to be no more original than our approval of virtue, managing to side neither with Mandeville nor Hutcheson on the question of original sentiments. Moreover, while Hume, like Mandeville, relates the love of praise to the motivation to virtue, he manages to do so without reducing virtue to a mere means to the pleasure which attends flattery and pride.

8 See R. J. Butler, "T and sympathy," *Proceedings of the Aristotelian Society Supplement* 49 (1975), 16–19, and James Farr, "Hume, hermeneutics, and history: a 'sympathetic' account," *History and Theory* 17 (1978): 291. Lest this seem an overly irrationalistic account of belief formation, consider whether the process by which most beliefs are acquired in childhood is "rational" in any strict sense. Beliefs acquired in this manner are certainly as open to critical appraisal as beliefs acquired in any other way. In chapter 3, I discuss ways in which Hume confronts inadequacies in his theory of belief and introduces modifications. For a critical account of Hume's account of sympathetic belief acquisition, see John J. Jenkins, "Hume's account of sympathy – some difficulties," in *Philosophers of the Scottish Enlightenment*, ed. V. Hope (Edinburgh University Press, 1984), 94–98.

9 In this passage the roots of Hume's notion of sympathy in the *sensus communis* of the ancients are particularly evident. See Hans-Georg Gadamer, *Truth and Method* (New York: Crossroad, 1975), 24. This view of sympathy as multiplying pleasure and ameliorating pain is technically inconsistent with Hume's more fully developed understanding of sympathy, in which the communication of a painful emotion is painful. He becomes more aware of this inconsistency as time wears on, as is evident in his response to Adam Smith's *Theory of Moral Sentiments*.

10 See Mercer, *Sympathy and Ethics*, 16.

11 For criticisms of Hume's attempt to account for how the transition between being affected by another's condition to being concerned for someone's welfare is made, see Mercer, *Sympathy and Ethics*, 39, and Douglas Chismar, "Hume's confusion about sympathy," *Philosophy Research Archives* 14 (1988–89), 242–246. When it comes to extensive sympathy, Chismar argues that "at best, Hume makes a well-supported empirical observation: increased participation 'over all the related ideas' of R's present situation, as well as his past history and future prospects, makes it harder to deny him personhood . . . As we get to know a person better, we become more likely to care about what happens to him" (244). I hope to show that Hume has a more adequate response, although perhaps not one that is fully developed within the *Treatise*.

12 For more details on the contrast between the double relation of ideas and impressions and the constant tendency of a passion, see *T* 381ff.

13 "For what reason," he asks, "shou'd the same passion of pity produce love to the person, who suffers the misfortune, and hatred to the person, who causes

it; unless it be because in the latter case the author bears a relation only to the misfortune; whereas in considering the sufferer we carry our view on every side, and wish for his prosperity, as well as are sensible of his affliction" (*T* 389). See also *T* 385 on sympathy's extension in time, where he writes that "'tis certain, that sympathy is not always limited to the present moment, but that we often feel by communication the pains and pleasures of others, which are not in being, and which we only anticipate by the force of imagination." What Hazlitt termed his "discovery" concerning "the Natural Disinterestedness of the Human Mind" is a development of this observation and of Hume's reflections on the idea of the self, which was published in 1805 as *An Essay on the Principles of Human Action*. Hazlitt argues that we are selfish only out of habit, and that our capacity to take an interest in the welfare of others differs in no way from our capacity to take an interest in our own welfare. In both cases we are forced to rely on our imagination and its ability to conceive of the future and to aim at something in it. "As an affair of sensation, or memory," Hazlitt writes:

I can feel no interest in any thing but what relates to myself in the strictest sense. But . . . I have not the same sort of exclusive, or mechanical self-interest in my future being or welfare, because I have no distinct faculty giving me a direct present interest in my future sensations, and none at all in those of others. The imagination, by means of which alone I can anticipate future objects, or be interested in them, must carry me out of myself into the feelings of others by one and the same process by which I am thrown forward as it were into my future being, and interested in it,

An Essay on the Principles of Action, in *The Complete Works of William Hazlitt*, ed. P. P. Howe, vol. 1 (London: J. M. Dent and Sons, 1930), 1.
For Hazlitt, the imagination takes center stage as the power of the mind which may be cultivated to extend the scope of sympathy; hence, countering Godwin, he writes that general benevolence is an abstraction which "can only arise from an habitual cultivation of the natural disposition of the mind to sympathize with the feelings of others by constantly taking an interest in those which we know, and imagining others that we do not know," 14.

14 Ernest C. Mossner, *The Life of David Hume* (Austin: University of Texas Press, 1954), 133.

15 Mandeville, too, had characterized his approach as that of an anatomist. See "A search into the nature of society," in *Fable of the Bees*, ed. F. B. Kaye (Oxford, 1924) 1:324. One would have thought that Hume's defense of his approach would have been undermined by the fact that it involved overtly aligning himself with one of Hutcheson's main enemies.

16 *LDH* no. 13, pp. 32–35, Letter to Hutcheson, September 17, 1739.

17 In his discussion of the natural virtues, Hume highlights the simpler situations in which virtuous characters contribute to present sense of well-being and vicious characters to present misery, but attention to the complexities of extensive sympathy as discussed in Book II allows us to make sense of the more complex situations as well.

18 Mossner, *Life of Hume*, 135. For what remains a helpful introduction to

Hutcheson, see William Robert Scott, *Francis Hutcheson: His Life, Teaching and Position in the History of Philosophy* (Cambridge University Press, 1900).

19 Francis Hutcheson, *An Inquiry into the Original of our Ideas of Beauty and Virtue* (Hildesheim: Georg Olms Verlagsbuchhandlung, 1971; facsimile of the 1725 edn), 217, also 141.

20 *Ibid.*, section 143–144 .

21 Hutcheson, *An Essay on the Nature and Conduct of the Passions and Affections* (Hildesheim: Georg Olms Verlagsbuchhandlung, 1971; facsimile of 1728 edn), 5. Hutcheson tends to put his own definitions into quotation marks.

22 Indeed, a few pages later he refers to it as such. See Hutcheson, *Passions*, 14. Hutcheson also equates the public sense with the *sensus communis* of the ancients. Shaftesbury characterized *sensus communis* very differently: as a "sense of public weal, and of the common interest; love of the community or society, natural affection, humanity, obligingness, or that sort of civility which rises from a just sense of the common rights of mankind, and the natural equality there is among those of the same species." Anthony Ashley Cooper, Third Earl of Shaftesbury, *Characteristics of Men, Manners, Opinions, Times*, ed. John M. Robertson (Indianapolis: Bobbs-Merrill, 1964), 70.

23 Hutcheson, *Passions*, 13–21.

24 *Ibid.*, 14–15.

25 Hutcheson, *Virtue*, 150–151.

26 Hutcheson, *Passions*, 21.

27 In fact, Hutcheson makes just this criticism of the attempt to make sympathy central to moral theory in his 1755 work, *A System of Moral Philosophy*, (New York: August M. Kelley, 1968), 47–48. Hume would have protested that Hutcheson had misunderstood his theory, which places sympathy at the heart of moral approbation and disapprobation, not directly of motivation to do good, except perhaps in the specific case of compassion. Hutcheson's other criticisms, of the variability of sympathy, Hume strives to address within the *Treatise*. In the process of doing so, sympathy is transformed in ways which Hutcheson overlooks.

28 *LDH* no. 15, pp. 36–38, Letter to Hutcheson, March 4, 1740.

29 Hutcheson, *Passions*, 234.

30 *Ibid.*, 223.

31 Hutcheson, *Virtue*, 175

32 Ironically, Hutcheson does provide formulas for calculating the moment of moral excellence in various actions, and these do involve degrees of natural advantage. These are not intended to be used in moral evaluation, however, and Hutcheson later withdrew them. The moral sense takes care of these operations behind the scenes. So Hutcheson comments that "in comparing the moral qualitys of actions, in order to regulate our election among various actions propos'd, or to find which of them has the greatest moral excellency, we are led by our moral sense of virtue thus to judge, that in equal degrees of happiness, expected to proceed from the action, the virtue is in proportion to the number of persons to whom the happiness shall extend" (*Virtue*, 163).

Moreover, advantage which is not intended does not increase moral excellence, since the crucial thing is always benevolent *intention*.

33 The "autonomy" of morality can mean many things. Here, I use it to refer to an independence from prudential considerations in general, including, but not limited to, self-interested considerations.

34 John Balguy, *The Foundation of Moral Goodness* (New York: Garland Publishing, 1976; facsimile of 1728–29 edn), Bk. 1, 21.

35 *Ibid.*, 1, 8–9.

36 Apparently, when it comes to approving of God, we can conclude directly from the tendency of God's creation to enhance natural good to the presence of true benevolence, and we need not worry that God's apparent benevolence might perhaps be disguised self-interest, motivated by his desire for sympathetic pleasure with the beneficial results of the way he has constructed us.

37 Knud Haakonssen, "Moral philosophy and natural law: From the Cambridge Platonists to the Scottish Enlightenment," *Political Science* 40 (1988): 107.

38 For evidence of Hutcheson's concerns about voluntarism, refer to the way he sets up his task in the Introduction to "An Inquiry concerning the original of our ideas of virtue or moral good," *Virtue*, especially 104–106, and the concluding section of the same work, in particular his discussion of obligation. See also *Passions*, 316–320. These passages reflect Hutcheson's commitment to the Moderate Party in the Church of Scotland, which stressed God's benevolence and human goodness, not God as judge of human wickedness.

39 Hutcheson, *Virtue*, 275.

40 Hutcheson, *System*, 77.

41 *LDH* no. 13, p. 33, Letter to Hutcheson, September 17, 1739.

42 Hutcheson, *System*, 78.

43 Hume gives a parallel analysis of indirect sources of our desire for riches. Although the power which riches bring are their original source of satisfaction, the sympathy-derived esteem of others, which is a secondary source of satisfaction, becomes the "chief reason" why we desire them for ourselves and further enhances our esteem of them in others (*T* 365). Similarly, although the opinions of others are a secondary cause of pride and humility, Hume says that they have an equal influence on our affections (*T* 316).

44 See Bernard Wand, "A note on sympathy in Hume's moral theory," *The Philosophical Review* 64 (1955): 276–277.

45 See the following section.

46 In his *Inquiry Concerning Virtue or Merit*, for instance, Shaftesbury discusses the importance of possessing a mind which is able to bear its own inspection and review. *Characteristics*, 302–305. Joseph Butler equated reflection with conscience, and insisted that it bore its own mark of authoritative moral judgment. Hume is interested in the process of reflection as a source of authoritative judgment, not in a separate principle with marks of authority. Still, he would probably have gone along with Butler in saying "Thus a parent has the affection of love to his children; this leads him to take care of,

to educate, to make due provision for them; the natural affection leads to this, but the reflection that it is his own proper business, what belongs to him, that it is right and commendable so to do – this added to the affection becomes a much more settled principle." Joseph Butler, *Fifteen Sermons*, ed. W. R. Matthews (London: G. Bell & Sons, 1914), "Upon human nature," Sermon 1, 39. The subject of reflexivity is a central theme in Baier's interpretation of Hume. See, for instance, *Progress of Sentiments*, 97–100, 134, 215–218, and "Master passions."

47 Hutcheson, *Virtue*, 106.

48 *Ibid.*, v. Pleasure is built into Hutcheson's definition both of internal sense and moral sense – "These determinations to be pleas'd with any Forms or Ideas which occur to our Observation, the Author chuses to call senses; distinguishing them from the powers which commonly go by that name, by calling our power of perceiving the beauty of regularity, order, harmony, an internal sense; and that determination to be pleased with the contemplation of those affections, actions, or characters of rational agents, which we call virtuous, he marks by the name of a moral sense" (*Virtue*, vi). Hume insists that "no object is presented to the senses, nor image form'd in the fancy, but what is accompany'd with some emotion or movement of the spirits proportion'd to it" (*T* 373). He specifically includes virtue and vice, along with wit and folly, riches and poverty, happiness and misery, among those objects "which are always attended by an evident emotion" (*T* 374). Unlike Hutcheson, however, Hume refers to unspecified emotion, rather than pleasure. This creates the possibility of asking why the emotion varies from case to case, and makes more urgent the need to explain why and how certain things cause pleasure.

49 The point of such observations is to show that

human nature was not left quite indifferent in the affair of virtue, to form to it self observations concerning the advantage or disadvantage of actions, and accordingly to regulate its conduct . . .very few of mankind could have form'd those long deductions of reason, which may show some actions to be in the whole advantageous to the agent, and their contrarys pernicious. The author of nature has much better furnish'd us for a virtuous conduct, than our moralists seem to imagine, by almost as quick and powerful instructions, as we have for the preservation of our bodys: he has made virtue a lovely form, to excite our pursuit of it; and has given us strong affections to be the springs of each virtuous action, *Virtue*, vii.

50 This may raise the specter of infinite regress. Why stop asking this sort of question when Hume does? Does not he, too, stop, if not with a moral sense, then with sympathy? What prevents the appeal to divine Providence at this point? Hume probes just to sympathy and no further because this establishes a connection between approval and human flourishing, not reducible to self-interest, without making an appeal to Providence. There would be no need to appeal to Providence at any further stage of questioning, he believes, since the problem of intelligibility has already been solved.

51 In a later letter responding to Adam Smith's *Theory of Moral Sentiments*, Hume comes out firmly against the notion that sympathy is always agreeable. He is still willing to grant that "when we converse with a man with whom we can

entirely sympathize, that is, where there is a warm & intimate friendship, the cordial openness of such a commerce overpowers the pain of a disagreeable sympathy, and renders the whole movement agreeable." In most cases, this is not the case, however. Therefore we cannot, as Smith suggests, simply desire the increase of sympathy in general. *LDH* no. 169, pp. 311–314, Letter to Adam Smith, July 28, 1759.

52 The question of who "resembles" us is not an objective matter, but rather depends on what features are regarded by us as salient. Lucinda Cole makes the perceptive remark that sympathy in eighteenth-century letters has no stable referent, but is "best read as a kind of literary topos of potential community, where particular versions of the 'communal' were in fact being created," "Sympathy, gender, and the writing of value in late eighteenth-century English letters" (Ph.D. dissertation, Louisiana State University, 1990), 15.

53 The use of the term "naturalistic" is highly problematic. For helpful clarification, see Jeffrey Stout, "Naturalism," in the *Encyclopedia of Religion*, ed. Mircea Eliade (New York: MacMillan, 1987). I use it here to indicate Hume's dedication to an account which makes no reference to supernatural powers or to divine Providence, neither in order to affirm nor to deny their existence.

54 This insistence should be seen specifically as a disavowal of Mandeville's views. Read as such, it is clear that the appropriate contrast with "natural" is "excited by politicians," not "artificial" in the Humean sense in which justice is artificial although never designed by anyone.

55 Nicholas Capaldi argues that in Hume "the moral sense is a set of feelings, not the faculty that perceives the feelings," *Hume's Place in Moral Philosophy* (New York: Peter Lang, 1989), 50.

56 R. J. Butler points out that "the content of some simple ideas can only be specified relationally and identified by reference to past experience," "T and sympathy," 8. Donald Livingston says that "the moral world, for Hume, is simply the natural world viewed in the light of our passions or impressions of reflection ordered from a certain point of view. Objectivity in the moral world is constituted by these points of view and is manifest in the conventions of common life and the language that informs them ... tenseless standards grow historically, as it were, out of existing practices and are reflections of them," *Hume's Philosophy of Common Life* (University of Chicago Press, 1984), 137–138; also 82–84. Peter Jones is right to insist, however, that it would be a misrepresentation of Hume's theory to suggest that reference to internal sentiments can be dropped altogether, despite the fact that "sentiments can be picked out only by means of publicly learned, rule-governed concepts," *Hume's Sentiments: Their Ciceronian and French Contexts*, (Edinburgh University Press, 1982), 114. Although we learn to use color concepts only within a social and linguistic context, a blind person can never use them in the same way as a sighted person.

57 David Fate Norton, in contrast, holds that Hume assumes a *natural*

uniformity of sentiments and that only this gives him the assurance that there can be a right and a wrong sentiment in morals, *David Hume: Common-sense Moralist, Sceptical Metaphysician* (Princeton University Press, 1982), 135. To some extent, the disagreement can be resolved by recognizing that Hume uses the word "sentiment" to refer to different levels of reaction. The most immediate are, he believed, naturally uniform, whereas the more reflexive levels take shape only in society and are therefore subject to greater variation.

58 Hume does not distinguish between the development of moral judgment in a particular individual with the emergence of moral distinctions among human beings in general; some implications of this will be discussed in the final section of this chapter. This is accompanied by insufficient recognition of how moral distinctions are passed down directly from generation to generation; i.e. the role of tradition is overlooked.

59 For an example of the latter interpretation, see Mercer, 60.

60 Walter Brand emphasizes this aspect, claiming that we always judge of values and there is only a contrast between partial and impartial moral judgements, never of pre-moral judgments, *Hume's Theory of Moral Judgement: A Study in the Unity of "A Treatise of Human Nature"* (Dordrecht: Kluwer Academic Publishers, 1992), 95. I believe this overlooks Hume's recognition of the inadequacy of our partial judgments, whatever we choose to call them.

61 Moreover, if Hume claims that we feel moral sentiments even when we are not considering things from a general or disinterested point of view, he has turned the notion of a distinct moral sense into a fifth wheel, since we do not need to postulate it in order to account for interested or preferential sorts of responses to character – these are continuous with gratitude and other sorts of love.

62 See Barry Stroud, *Hume* (London: Routledge and Kegan Paul, 1977), 191. See also Capaldi, *Hume's Place*, 225.

63 W. D. Falk makes the helpful suggestion that we think in these terms: reason attempts to discover truth and falsehood, while taste is concerned with the importance or relevance of things for us. "Hume on is and ought," in *Ought, Reasons, and Morality* (Ithaca: Cornell University Press, 1986), 126. See also Livingston, *Philosophy of Common Life*, 58, and Baier, *Progress of Sentiments*, 167–173.

64 At one point Hume seems to suggest that acting solely from a sense of duty or a regard to virtue happens *only* when one lacks the normal virtuous motive of gratitude or natural affection or whatever it may be, and that only the original motive is worthy of approbation (*T* 478–479). What Hume is really saying, I think, is that some motive other than regard for virtue is required in order to get the practice of a virtue as such off the ground. This does not mean that the regard for virtue cannot later come to receive our approbation as a virtuous motive. In the case of the natural virtues, regard for virtue supplements, but does not supplant, the original motives. In the case of the artificial virtues, however, the sole motive may well be, as Hume himself suggests, regard to duty, once the practice is fully established (*T* 479,

483). This is true despite the fact that the *original* motive was self-interest and the original reason for approbation had to do with sympathetic appreciation of the general benefits of the practice.

65 Therefore, although the practice is thus in some sense artificial, it is predicated on certain natural features of human beings. For an account of the natural emergence of morality which traces its lineage back to Hume, see Baier's "Theory and reflective practices," in *Postures of the Mind: Essays on Mind and Morals* (Minneapolis: University of Minnesota Press, 1985), 220–223. Baier suggests that "if we see morality essentially as control of our natural responses to the mixed risk of evil and chance of good inherent in our interdependent situation, we can see moral response, in the form of training, criticism, and so on, as a response to a natural response, and we can see the evils and goods which come from morally disapproved and approved action as themselves the offspring of those evils and goods responses [to] which morality controls" (220). In focusing on moral development, Baier is led to suggest that moral goods arise out of natural goods in the course of an experience of conflict among goods and an adjustment or equilibration process resulting in reflective equilibrium. This is reminiscent of Hume's account of the correction of sympathy, in which the experience of conflict among transient and particular points of view results in the emergence of a stable and general point of view. I will argue, however, that this account, from which moral judgment seems to emerge automatically, as it were, is insufficient to Hume's subsequent attempts to characterize the nature of moral judgment, and I will strive to elucidate from these later works a more adequate model of moral judgment, one which is less interested in tracing moral judgment back to a pre-social, preconventional nature.

66 In chapter 5, the threats posed to moral character by self-deception will be more fully discussed, particularly in relation to the nature of religious belief.

67 Baier's work highlights the importance of reflexive survey in Hume's work as a whole. See, for example, *Progress of Sentiments*, 14, 99–100, 134; *Postures of the Mind*, 225, 260.

68 On goods internal and external to a practice, see Alasdair MacIntyre, *After Virtue* (University of Notre Dame Press, 1981), ch. 14, especially 187–191.

69 MacIntyre comments that "although the virtues are just those qualities which tend to lead to the achievement of a certain class of goods, nonetheless unless we practice them irrespective of whether in any particular set of contingent circumstances they will produce these goods or not, we cannot possess them at all," *After Virtue*, 198. This seems right, but it does not tell against Hume's position, as MacIntyre seems to think.

70 MacIntyre, *After Virtue*, 197. Aristotle, too, thought that the virtuous person takes pleasure in being virtuous. *Nichomachean Ethics* 1099a 7–21, 1166a 23–29.

71 [Richard Allestree,] *The Practice of Christian Graces or the Whole Duty of Man* (London: D. Maxwell for T. Garthwait, 1658), Part 6, section 3.

72 *Ibid.*, Part 2, section 4.

73 Baier notes that Hume's moral viewpoint "is not a 'view from nowhere'; it is a view from a common *human* viewpoint . . . It aims not at detachment from

human concerns but at impartiality, and interpersonal agreement," *Progress of Sentiments*, 182.

74 Árdal, *Passion and Value*, 118. He adds that "we form the habit of looking upon a person's situation in such a way as to take into consideration only those characteristics that are independent of the special situation in which any one spectator may find himself," 119. See also Geoffrey Sayre–McCord's discussion of how Hume's general point of view differs from an ideal point of view, "On why Hume's 'general point of view' isn't ideal – and shouldn't be," *Social Philosophy and Policy* II (1994): 202–228, and his list of those who have "idealized" Hume's general point of view, 202 fn. 1.

75 Capaldi suggests that Hume tries to overcome these problems by introducing general rules, but goes on to reveal the insufficiency of this solution, *Hume's Place*, 192, 215–235. While not claiming that Hume ever satisfactorily overcomes these problems, I am interested in how sympathy changes in response to them.

76 Mark Burch comments that, for Hume, sympathy is "an emotional process operating too swiftly and unconsciously to be reduced to interest. Less a moral faculty than the ground which guarantees the humanity of and our obedience to moral categories, this capability causes us to identify society's interests as our own," "Eighteenth-century sentimentality: a study of literature and its contexts" (Ph.D. dissertation, University of Texas at Austin, 1984), 52.

77 See Jeffrey Stout, *The Flight from Authority* (Notre Dame, University of Notre Dame Press, 1981) 234–235. See also J. B. Schneewind, "Natural law, skepticism, and methods of ethics," *Journal of the History of Ideas*, 1991: 300–302. Schneewind suggests that Hume's theory provides a "skeptical method of ethics" which accepts the premises of contemporary skepticism about moral knowledge but nonetheless preserves morality intact.

78 Even within the *Treatise*, Hume's disavowals of practical intent are somewhat disingenuous, in that he did think that proper theoretical understanding would have an *indirect* effect on moral beliefs, reinforcing certain beliefs and undermining others (like those which endorse the monkish virtues).

79 See W. D. Falk, who suggests that "the active force of the merit judgement is not, for Hume, in its conclusion, but in the judgemental process that leads to it," "Hume on practical reason," in *Ought, Reasons, and Morality*, 52.

80 We might even expect comparison rather than sympathy to be the expected response in these circumstances. Baier notes, however, that Hume treats sympathy as natural and comparison as the result of blurred vision or a cognitive defect, *Progress of Sentiments*, 149–150.

81 This is not, however, a problem with sympathy's range of operation. Árdal mistakenly insists that "one can sympathize only with experiences that one has had oneself. One cannot, on Hume's account, form the idea of another person's emotion unless one has had the corresponding impression," *Passion and Value*, 45. The latter sentence is unexceptionable, but the former does not follow from it, as Árdal tries to suggest. Sympathy requires that we have experienced the full range of *emotions*, not that we have already had the particular *experiences* with which we sympathize.

82 At several points Hume refers to the efforts of the imagination. See, for example, *T* 385, 386, and 398. For another interpretation which also stresses the activity of the imagination, see R. W. Altmann, "Hume on sympathy," *Southern Journal of Philosophy* 18 (March 1980): 129. Peter Jones makes similar observations about Hume's remarks on criticism in his *Essays*. Jones suggests that "the peculiar interest of Hume's albeit fragmentary comments [on criticism, art, beauty and language] is that he amplifies his account in the *Treatise* of the causes of human reactions, by assigning certain constructive tasks to the mind; by so doing, he prepares the ground for a notion of appropriate response, and for a notion of criticism as a rational endeavour," *Hume's Sentiments*, 3. See also 44, 122. Jones does not, however, seem to fully appreciate Hume's reasons for resisting the transformation of judgment into a capacity which is actively developed and exercised.

83 R. J. Butler suggests that "Hume's initial statement of the doctrine of sympathy contains a mixture of causal language and the language of signs," "T and sympathy," 10. Unlike causal language, the language of signs opens up room for conscious, active processes of inference and interpretation. Moreover, once the language of signs becomes dominant, not solely the external evidence of emotion, but also the context as a whole, is opened up for interpretation. Farr insists emphatically that "We must first decode the signs or effects which embody another's ideas. Secondly, we then come to share not only those ideas, but their related impressions as well, because of the mechanism of the association of ideas . . . Sympathy or communication presupposes the interpretation of signs and /or the analysis of effects" "Hume, hermeneutics, and history," 292. Although he decries Hume's lack of clarity about the nature of the decoding operations, he observes that often Hume speaks in such a way as to invoke "not a species of verification and causal analysis, but of interpretation and the hermeneutic circle" (293). Farr goes overboard in his attempt to clear Hume from charges of engaging in subjectivist, intuitivist psychology and promotion of empathetic projection. Hume's account of sympathy is multifaceted and some varieties of sympathy suit Farr's thesis more than others.

84 Imagination is for Hume always a *mental* activity, but he did not speak of imagining as something an *agent* could do. Amélie O. Rorty suggests that "when reason is assigned only the functions of discovering regularities among matters of fact and analysing the relations among ideas, it is the imagination that becomes the active faculty" and passions go from being something suffered to being activities of the mind. "From passions to emotions and sentiments" *Philosophy* 57 (1982): 160. She locates this transformation between Descartes and Rousseau.

85 John B. Radner provides a similar analysis which places Hume at the beginning of a shift in eighteenth-century thought from sympathy as passive and instinctual to sympathy (or, more often, compassion) as deliberate and active. He suggests that Hume occupies a straddling position, since "focus on the degree of the misery suggests the passivity of compassion . . . Focus on how strongly a person sympathizes . . . hints that compassion may largely

depend on deliberate mental activity. The key to whether or not a person sympathizes strongly is the imagination," "The art of sympathy in eighteenth-century British thought," *Studies in Eighteenth-Century Culture*, ed. Roseann Runte, vol. 9 (Madison: University of Wisconsin Press, 1979), 198–199.

86 David Fate Norton suggests that, since Hume's later works were popular and not directed towards a sophisticated philosophical audience, particulars about sympathy were unimportant. "Hume's common sense morality," *Canadian Journal of Philosophy*, 5. 4 (1975), 542. While it is true that Hume did strive to be less abstruse in his later works, he did not simplify his ideas, but rather worked on the assumption that any philosophical thoughts of any merit could be clear and comprehensible to the general reader. On the issue of philosophical rhetoric and style, see M. A. Box's *The Suasive Art of David Hume* (Princeton University Press, 1990). Norman Kemp Smith argues that Hume dropped sympathy from his moral theory when he realized that it depended illegitimately on an impression of the self, *Philosophy of David Hume*, 151. I have already discussed the issue of the impression of self in the first section of this chapter, and do not find Kemp Smith's argument persuasive.

87 Perhaps the most influential contemporary discussion of the moral point of view is that of John Rawls' *A Theory of Justice* (Cambridge, MA: Belknap Press, 1971. Rawl's position has been modified over the years, however, and the claims he makes on behalf of "the original position" are no longer so large.

88 I am indebted to Victor Preller for helping me to think through this issue.

89 Baier, "Natural virtues, natural vices," *Social Philosophy & Policy* 8 (1990): 25.

90 *Ibid.*, 27.

91 *Ibid.*, 31.

92 I do not mean by this to undercut Hume's account of the "artificial" virtues. Such accounts presuppose moral distinctions and so take up the account of origins at a very different point.

93 This is true even if, as scholars would argue, Hume was not even attempting to give an account of the origin of moral distinctions, but only an account of how the sentiments of moral approbation and disapprobation are caused in each individual.

94 Passages such as these reveal Hume's affinity for the modern natural law problematic of conflict. In *De Cive*, Hobbes wrote that "the desires of men are different, as men differ among themselves in temperament, custom and opinion; we see this in sense-perceptions such as taste, touch or smell, but even more in the common business of life, where what one person praises – that is, calls good – another will condemn and call evil. Indeed, often the same man at different times will praise and blame the same thing. As long as this is the case there will necessarily arise discord and conflict." *Philosophical Rudiments Concerning Government and Society*, vol. 2, *The English Works of Thomas Hobbes of Malmesbury*, ed. William Molesworth (London: John Bohn, 1839–45; 2nd reprint Aalen: Scientia Verlag, 1966), III.31, pp. 47–48 (this is a 1651 translation of *De Cive*, approved and perhaps written by Hobbes himself.) Richard Tuck comments that "it was conflict over what to praise, or morally to approve, which Hobbes thus isolated as the cause of discord,

rather than simple conflict over wants. What he was frightened of, it is reasonable to assume, were such things as the Wars of Religion, or other ideological wars; not (say) class wars, in which the clash of wants could more clearly be seen" *Hobbes* (Oxford University Press, 1989), 56. Whereas Hobbes thought that only an absolute sovereign could overcome such conflict, however, Hume thought that it could be overcome in the course of human social interaction.

95 In the process, the issue of the criteria for determining what really counts as extensive sympathy are addressed. This raises problems, of course, for Hume's *Treatise* depiction of the automatic development of good moral judgment, an issue which will be discussed in the following chapters.

3 "POETICAL SYSTEMS" AND THE PLEASURES OF TRAGEDY

1 See Jean Baptiste Dubos, *Réflexions critiques sur la poesie et sur la peinture* (1719; Genève: Slatine Reprints, 1967), translated as *Critical Reflections on Poetry, Painting, and Music*, trans. Thomas Nugent (London: J. Nourse, 1748; from the 5th edn), vol. 2, ch. xxii, on the chief end of poetry.

2 See Jerome Stolnitz, "'Beauty': Some Stages in the History of an Idea," *Journal of the History of Ideas* 22 (1961): 185–204; René Wellek, *A History of Modern Criticism 1750–1950*, vol. 1, *The Later Eighteenth Century* (New Haven: Yale University Press, 1955), 12–30; Walter Jackson Bate, *From Classic to Romantic: Premises of Taste in Eighteenth-Century England* (New York: Harper & Row, 1946). Ernst Cassirer sees this in terms of an empiricist revolt against the a priori approach of classical aesthetic theory. "The method of explanation and deduction," he writes, "gradually approaches that of pure description. But description does not begin directly with the work of art; it attempts first to characterize and ascertain the mode of aesthetic contemplation." *The Philosophy of the Enlightenment*, trans. Fritz C. A. Koelln and James P. Pettegrove (Princeton University Press, 1951), 298. The empiricism of the focus on effects does not, of course, explain why other empirical aspects were not pursued.

3 Diderot's 1769 *Paradox Sur le Comedien*, however, broke with this consensus to claim that the actor must be cold in order to carefully portray the external *signs* of feeling. Cibber, Garrick, and Riccoboni embraced similar ideas. See Jonas Barish, *The Antitheatrical Prejudice* (Berkeley, Los Angeles, and London: University of California Press, 1981), 277–279. This disagreement is tied up with ongoing discussions about how the audience was affected, whether by some sort of mystical identification with the actor, or by inference from external signs to the emotions they signify. A parallel discussion concerned the mechanism of sympathy outside of the poetic context.

4 See Northrop Frye, "Towards defining an age of sensibility," in *Eighteenth Century English Literature: Modern Essays in Criticism*, ed. James L. Clifford (New York: Oxford University Press, 1959), 316.

5 Literary scholars continue to do battle over the proper application of the

terms sentimentality and sensibility to literature. R. F. Brissenden uses the term "novels of sentiment" to refer to literature in which sympathetic feelings are seen as valuable in themselves and wholly take the place of active response. *Virtue in Distress: Studies in the Novel of Sentiment from Richardson to Sade* (London: Macmillan, 1974). Mark Burch, in contrast, claims that sentimentality is concerned with feeling precisely as the source of moral knowledge and action. He links sensibility with the rising mechanistic science, saying that it obliterates the will and negates the possibility of action by focusing instead on private feeling. "Eighteenth-century sentimentality: a study of literature and its contexts" (Ph.D. dissertation, University of Texas at Austin, 1984), v–vi, 6–8. Regardless of the labels, it does seem that there was a trend in eighteenth-century literature toward focusing on feeling detached from action, a trend which resulted in the taint associated with the contemporary word "sentimental."

6 David Marshall, *The Surprising Effects of Sympathy* (The University of Chicago Press, 1988), 26–27.

7 Despite the fact that Aristotle's views were developed in direct response to Plato's notorious opposition to theater, Plato's views about mimesis had little influence on the eighteenth-century tragedy debate, so I will not discuss them here. See Barish, 29–30.

8 Aristotle, *Politics* 1341b35–1342a15, *Poetics* 1450a 15–20. Citations to Aristotle in this chapter will be from *Poetics*, with the *Tractatus Coislinianus*, reconstruction of *Poetics* II, and the fragments of the *On Poets*, trans. by Richard Janko (Indianapolis and Chicago: Hackett Publishing Company, 1987).

9 There is continuing controversy over what Aristotle means by catharsis, which is hardly surprising, since the part of the *Poetics* in which Aristotle most fully discusses catharsis has been lost. My own understanding of catharsis has been influenced by Janko, whose interpretation hearkens back to Lessing's understanding of catharsis and resonates in interesting ways with Hume's understanding of the relationship between the passions and moral judgment.

10 On the growing positive attitude toward the passions, see Albert O. Hirschman, *The Passions and the Interests: Political Arguments for Capitalism before Its Triumph* (Princeton University Press, 1977), 47.

11 Aristotle, *Politics* 1340a 15–24.

12 M. A. Box's *The Suasive Art of David Hume* reveals Hume's conviction of the importance of reaching a broader audience with his philosophical ideas, and discusses his understanding of philosophy and history as *belles-lettres* and his developing strategies for making philosophy more palatable to the non-scholarly reader (Princeton University Press, 1990).

13 *LDH* III, p. 223, Letter to Andrew Millar, June 12, 1755.

14 E. C. Mossner, *The Life of David Hume* (Austin: University of Texas Press, 1954), 321.

15 Hence, it is surprising that Jonas Barish does not so much as mention this event in *The Antitheatrical Prejudice*, which in other respects is quite a complete

account of debates concerning theater. It is true that the debate over *Douglas* broke no new theoretical ground, but it did serve to spur the debate about theater far beyond the borders of Scotland.

16 Mossner, *Life of Hume*, 359.

17 *Scots Magazine* 19 (1757), 18. Quoted in E. C. Mossner, *The Forgotten Hume: "Le bon David"* (New York: Columbia University Press, 1943), 44. My account of the controversy surrounding *Douglas* is indebted to this work and to Mossner's *Life of Hume*.

18 Quoted in Mossner, *Life of Hume*, 368.

19 Quoted in *ibid.*, 363.

20 In *The Works of John Witherspoon*, vol. 6 (Edinburgh: Ogle & Aikman, Pillans & Sons, J. Ritchie, and J. Turnbull, 1805).

21 Saint Augustine, *Confessions*, trans. Henry Chadwick (Oxford University Press, 1991), *III*.ii.

22 See Charles Taylor, *Sources of the Self* (Cambridge, MA: Harvard University Press, 1989), ch. 7. Ironically, this sense of the moral importance of the inner disposition of the will, which stems from Augustine, influenced the development of eighteenth-century "sentimentality," although advocates of sentiment and Augustine held diametrically opposed evaluations of tragedy. Novels of sensibility were Augustinian in their focus on inner states rather than external action, but they valorized passive emotional responses and held up as exemplary those who savored sympathetic suffering and wallowed in helpless grief at the sight of distress.

23 Witherspoon, *Works VI*, 50.

24 *Ibid.*, 54.

25 *Ibid.*, 59.

26 *Ibid.*, 59.

27 *Ibid.*, 59.

28 *Ibid.*, 100.

29 *Ibid.*, 93.

30 The extent to which Jean-Jacques Rousseau's well-known *Lettre à d'Alembert* (1758) echoes the sentiments of Witherspoon is striking. One of Rousseau's first observations is "qu'un spectacle est un amusement; et s'il est vrai qu'il faille des moins qu'ils ne sont permis qu'autant au'ils sont nécessaires, et que tout amusement inutile est un mal, pout un être dont la vie est si courte et le temps si précieux" (Paris: Garnier-Flammarion, 1967), 65. Rousseau also argues that plays must simply reflect the manners of the audience, and worries that we will become accustomed to the sight of horrors. Rousseau shares with Witherspoon, moreover, a distrust of the passions: "L'émotion, le trouble, et l'attendrissement qu'on sent en soi-même et qui se prolonge après la pièce, annoncent-ils une disposition bien prochaine à surmonter et régler nos passions? ... Ne sait-on pas que toutes les passions sont sœurs, qu'une seule suffit pour en exciter mille, et que les combattre l'une par l'autre n'est qu'un moyen de rendre le cœur plus sensible à toutes?," 73. Rousseau presents us with a secularized version of Calvinism, with similar

pessimism about human nature, but stripped of the idiom of "sin" and "grace."

31 John Home, *Douglas*, ed. Gerald D. Parker (Edinburgh: Oliver & Boyd, 1972).

32 *Ibid.*, Act I, ln. 212–216.

33 *Ibid.*, Act V, ln. 172–174.

34 Mossner, *Life of Hume*, 321–324. For further discussion of this incident, see chapter 4.

35 This quotation captures Hume's somewhat incongruous pairing of classical asthetic sensibilities (viz. his view of Shakespeare as barbaric) with the newer sentimentalist focus on emotional impact.

36 René Descartes, *The Philosophical Works of Descartes*, trans. E. S. Haldane and G. R. T. Ross (Dover Publications, 1911; 1931), "The passions of the soul," vol. 1, p. 373, art. 94. See also p. 398, art. 147.

37 *Ibid.*, p. 398, art. 158.

38 Dubos, *Critical Reflections*, 1, 5, 8.

39 *Ibid.*, 11, 237, also 11, 1. At other times he does discuss a possible morally instructive role for theater, but it is always regarded as parasitic on theater's role as amusement.

40 *Ibid.*, 1, 10.

41 *Ibid.*, 18.

42 *Ibid.*, 21.

43 Barish echoes these concerns when he writes that "pity, it would seem, intrinsically involves spectatordom, and passive spectatordom at that. We look upon the vexations of another and identify with him as we would if witnessing his sufferings in the theater. The more helpless we feel to come to his aid, the sharper our pity. The moment we reach out to grapple actively and energetically with his problems, we lose the theatrical distancing, the ingredient of imagination, that pity requires," *Antitheatrical Prejudice*, 270. This, however, comes close to identifying pity with emotional infection.

44 Dubos, *Critical Reflections*, 1, 32.

45 *Ibid.*, 11, 268.

46 Norman Fiering suggests that just such a shriveling of response occurred in the eighteenth century as compassion came to be seen more and more as an element in literature and less a matter of practical morals, "Irresistible compassion: an aspect of eighteenth-century sympathy and humanitarianism." *Journal of the History of Ideas* 37 (1976): 195–218.

17 Edmund Burke, *A Philosophical Enquiry into the Origin of our Ideas of the Sublime and Beautiful*, ed. James T. Boulton (Oxford: Basil Blackwell, 1958; reprinted from the 2nd edn, 1759), 46.

48 *Ibid.*, 136.

49 *Ibid.*, 46.

50 Samuel Johnson had earlier espoused a similar view, that the differences between our responses to reality and to fiction have to do primarily with differences in the immediacy and nearness of the need with which we are confronted, rather than with a difference between reality and representation

as such. *The Rambler* (London: Jones & Company, 1826; originally published 1750–52), nos. 60 and 81. According to John B. Radner, Johnson held that "sympathizing with distresses described in literature is somewhat pleasing, while sympathizing with real and present unhappiness is not; and sympathizing with troubles that are real and near sometimes prompts people to help, while sympathy with what is fictional or historical does not." In "Samuel Johnson, the deceptive imagination, and sympathy," *Studies in Burke and His Time* 16 (1974–75): 33.

51 Joseph Addison experimented with this line of argument in *Spectator* 418 (1712).

52 Hume seems not to see that Smith is often talking of something quite different than Hume when he speaks of sympathy. When Smith claims that sympathy is always pleasurable, he is not making the Burkean claim about our attraction to scenes of distress, but rather claiming that we find it pleasurable when others agree with us in our reactions to various objects and situations. Sympathy *is* this agreement, according to Smith, and the pleasure is due to this convergence of reaction, not to its content. Smith clarifies this in a footnote in a later edition of the *Theory of Moral Sentiments*, although this may be the only place at which he is fully clear about it. See *The Theory of Moral Sentiments*, intr. E. G. West (Indianapolis: Liberty Classics, 1969), 106.

53 ". . . le mouvement du plaisir, poussé un peu trop loin, devient douleur, et que le mouvement de douleur, un peu modérée, devient plaisir. De-là vient encore au'il y a une tristesse douce et agréable; c'est une douleur affoible et diminuée." Bernard Le Bovier de Fontenelle, *Reflexions sur la poetique*, in *Oeuvres de Fontenelle*, vol. 3 (Paris: Jean-François Bastien, 1790), para. 36. Quoted (in English) by Hume, *MPL* 218.

54 ". . . suffit pour diminuer la douleur de voir souffrir quelqu'un que l'on aime, et pour réduire cette douleur au degré où elle commence à se changer en plaisir."

55 ". . . comme cette affliction, qui est causé par l'impression des objects sensible et extérieurs, est plus forte que la consolation qui ne part que d'une réflexion intérieure, ce sont les effets et les marques de la douleur qui doivent dominer dans ce composé."

56 See Earl R. Wasserman, "The pleasures of tragedy," *English Literary History* 14 (1947): 286.

57 *Ibid.*, 286–287.

58 Plutarch, *Table-Talk*, I–VI, trans. Paul A. Clement and Herbert B. Hoffleit, *Moralia*, VIII, Loeb Classics (London, 1969), 376–383. Quoted by Barish, *Antitheatrical Prejudice*, 32. This classical theory was often alluded to by thinkers who held widely differing views. Thus, for example, it is partially endorsed by both Witherspoon, *Works* VI, 53 and Burke *Sublime and Beautiful*, 49.

59 See the critical comments of Eric Hill, "Hume and the delightful tragedy problem." *Philosophy* 57 (1982): 319–326.

60 Hume has been accused of developing Lockean empiricism "in the direction of an extreme fictionalism which threatened to subvert the very basis of Englightenment reason." Richard Kearney, *The Wake of Imagination:*

Ideas of Creativity in Western Culture (London: Hutchinson, 1988), 164. On my interpretation, Hume problematizes common understandings both of reality and of fiction, not, finally, in order to reject the distinction, but to render it more complex.

61 See also *Enquiry*, 47ff., and the discussion in Antony Flew, *Hume's Philosophy of Belief: A Study of His First Inquiry* (London: Routledge and Kegan Paul, 1961), 100–101.

62 Flew offers a similar interpretation of Hume on belief; he is critical of Hume's official theory while finding in it hints towards a more fruitful understanding of belief which is in accord with Hume's "informal working assumptions," *Hume's Philosophy of Belief*, 31. To my mind, the essay "Of tragedy" is an extremely valuable place in which to see these "informal working assumptions" in full swing.

63 Flew, *Hume's Philosophy of Belief*, 39.

64 *Ibid.*, 212.

65 As Annette Baier comments, "Hume's project all along has been not so much to dethrone reason as to enlarge our conception of it, to make it social and passionate," *A Progress of Sentiments* (Cambridge, MA: Harvard University Press, 1991), 278.

66 'What stands fast does so, not because it is intrinsically obvious or convincing; it is rather held fast by what lies around it." Ludwig Wittgenstein, *On Certainty*, eds. G. E. M. Anscombe and G. H. von Wright (Oxford: Basil Blackwell, 1969), section 144. See also Donald W. Livingston's discussion of narrative association in Hume in *Hume's Philosophy of Common Life* (University of Chicago Press, 1984), 130–136, and Annette Baier's discussions of association and repetition in *A Progress of Sentiments* (Cambridge, Mass.: Harvard University Press, 1991), esp. 32, 38, 70ff.

67 Normally, we do not even *try* to interact with fictional characters, although it is true that a former Vice President of the United States did attempt to send a baby gift to a television personality. It is conceivable that the stuffed elephant could have shown up on the TV show (although in fact the link between reality and fiction was abruptly broken by its being sent to an organization which collects toys for homeless children), but it is harder to imagine the gift reaching the fictional baby at her fictional address through the U.S. Postal service. We do, however, provide a post office address for Santa Claus so that children can write to him; we even try to make sure that they get the right gift in response. We thereby set up a "poetical system," that is, we set up the connections that help sustain belief.

68 Baier, *Progress of Sentiments*, 46–47.

69 R. F. Brissenden traces Hume's increasing reliance on the term "sentiment" in attempting to characterize belief, " 'Sentiment': Some Uses of the Word in the Writings of David Hume," *Studies in the Eighteenth Century*, ed. R. F. Brissenden (Canberra: Australian National University Press, 1968). Brissenden suggests that, for Hume, "our impressions of reality are not simply feelings, but feelings which are inevitably accompanied by a process of judgement"

(101). The term sentiment, which could be used to refer either to a 'mental feeling' or to an 'emotional thought' (95), lent itself well to the notion of belief as a sort of feeling mingled with judgment.

70 When we watch television, our deliberations tend to be about when to take a bathroom break and whether to go get a Coke from the fridge, and this is so whether what we are watching is "The Simpsons" or footage from Bosnia. If the war were actually brought into our living rooms, our deliberations would presumably be quite different! When we ourselves feel the effects of something, we tend to react to it without bothering to "decide" whether it is relevant or not.

71 *Politics and the Arts: Letter to M. D'Alembert on the Theatre.* Trans. and with notes by Allan Bloom (Ithaca: Cornell University Press, 1960), 24–26.

J'entends dire que la tragédie mène à la pitié par la terreur; soit, mais quelle est cette pitié? Une émotion passagère et vaine, qui ne dure pas plus que l'illusion qui l'a produite; un reste de sentiment naturel étouffé bientôt par le passions; une pitié stérile qui se repaît de quelques larmes, et n'a jamais produit le moindre acte d'humanité . . . En donnant des pleurs à ces fiction, nous avons satisfait à tous les droits de l'humanité, sans avoir plus rien à mettre du nôtre; au lieu que les infortunés en personne exigeraient de nous des soins, des solagements, des consolations, des travaux qui pourraient nous associer à leurs peines, qui coùteraient du moins à notre indolence . . . Plus j'y réfléchis, et plus je trouve que tout ce qu'on met en représentation au théâtre, on ne l'approche pas de nous, on l'en éloigne.
Lettre à d'Alembert, 79–80.

72 Chapter 5 contains a fuller discussion of the irrationality of religious belief.

73 See Hume's "Of the immortality of the soul," *MPL* 590–598, which was first printed along with "Of tragedy" and withdrawn before publication, but not before a few copies had found their way into Evangelical hands. "What cruelty, what iniquity, what injustice in nature," writes Hume, "to confine thus all our concern, as well as all our knowledge, to the present life, if there be another scene still awaiting us, of infinitely greater consequence? Ought this barbarous deceit to be ascribed to a beneficent and wise being?" (*MPL* 593).

4 SYMPATHETIC UNDERSTANDING AND THE THREAT OF DIFFERENCE

1 Walter Jackson Bate, *From Classic to Romantic* (New York: Harper & Row, 1946), 35, 84.

2 *Ibid.,* 43.

3 *Ibid.,* 58; see also 84.

4 And yet the separation between aesthetics and ethics is being disputed once again, if not openly. Usually the attack on the separation takes the form of a claim that something is not art after all, and is therefore subject to ethical evaluation. If something is pornography, or contains senseless violence, or advocates racial or sexual subordination, it is not art. The assumption remains that once something is admitted into the realm of art, ethical criticism is wholly out of place. But artists do admit to having moral intentions in their work – they hope, for example, to increase our capacity to

recognize those who are very different from ourselves as fellow human beings, or to communicate true insights about what makes life worth living, and it is hard to fathom what "pure" aesthetic criticism could make of such intentions.

5 Jerome Stolnitz, "On the significance of Lord Shaftesbury in modern aesthetic theory," *Philosophical Quarterly* 11 (1961), 99.

6 René Wellek, *A History of Modern Criticism:, 1750–1950*, vol. 1, *The Later Eighteenth Century* (New Haven: Yale University Press, 1965), 107.

7 Edmund Burke, *A Philosophical Enquiry into the Origin of Our Ideas of the Sublime and the Beautiful*, ed. James T. Boulton (Oxford: Basil Blackwell, 1958), 13. After trying to make a clear distinction between taste and morals, however, Burke admits that, since many works of the imagination depict human character and action, moral judgment and therefore reason cannot be wholly excluded from aesthetic judgments of these works (22). On the moral ambiguity of taste in Burke, see David Bromwich, "How moral is taste?" *Yale Review* 82 (1994): 1–23. If reason cannot be excluded from aesthetic judgment, neither is Burke consistent about requiring reason alone to make moral judgments, at least if by reason we understand a reflective capacity. This I already discussed in chapter 3 in relation to Burke's understanding of the moral role of pity and our delight in it. One example of how Burke exploited what he regarded as the instinctive, unreflective nature of sympathetic responses to tragedy is his *Reflections on the Revolution in France* (1790), ed. J. G. A. Pocock (Indianapolis: Hackett Publishing Company, 1987), 70–71. Burke asks himself:

Why do I feel so differently from the Reverend Dr. Price and those of his lay flock who will choose to adopt the sentiments of his discourse?–For this plain reason: because it is natural I should; because we are so made as to be affected at such spectacles with melancholy sentiments upon the unstable condition of mortal prosperity and the tremendous uncertainty of human greatness; because in those natural feelings we learn great lessons; because in events like these our passions instruct our reason; because when kings are hurled from their thrones by the Supreme Director of this great drama and become the objects of insult to the base and of pity to the good, we behold such disasters in the moral as we should behold a miracle in the physical order of things.

Burke's gut reaction to the revolution is, he claims, the true *natural* response to a tragedy of such sublime dimensions; it is thus unnecessary for him to give any argument in defense of his position, since it is obvious to all but the "perverted" that his response is the right one. After having first characterized actual events in theatrical terms, Burke goes on to suggest that what causes pity and delight among (not already "perverted") audiences in the theater is a trustworthy guide to what is true tragedy and worthy of pity in actuality:

Indeed, the theatre is a better school of moral sentiments than churches, where the feelings of humanity are thus outraged. Poets who have to deal with an audience not yet graduated in the school of the rights of men and who must apply themselves to the moral constitution of the heart would not dare to produce such a triumph as a matter of exultation. There, where men follow their natural impulses, they would not bear the odious maxims of a Machiavellian policy.

If the proper sympathetic response is instinctive and unreflective, this of course favors the status quo, rather than opening space for challenges to our current attitudes and views.

8 Bate, "The sympathetic imagination in eighteenth-century English criticism" *ELH* 12 (1945): 156–158.

9 Leo Braudy, *Narrative Form in History and Fiction: Hume, Fielding and Gibbon* (Princeton University Press, 1970), 74.

10 Annette Baier, *Postures of the Mind* (Minneapolis: University of Minnesota Press, 1985), 228–245, contrasts normative moral theory with reflective practice and mental geography, where the latter are exemplified by Hume. She does not, however, take note of the difference between what Hume is doing in the *Treatise* and what he does in "Of the standard of taste."

11 This phrase from Gilbert Ryle has been made famous by Clifford Geertz in "Thick description: toward an interpretive theory of culture," in *The Interpretation of Cultures* (New York: Basic Books, 1973), 3–32.

12 On the importance of "serenity of mind," cf. Jean Baptiste Dubos: "To be a good spectator, one must have that peace of soul, which rises not from the exhausting, but from the serenity of the imagination." *Réflexions critiques sur la poesie et sur la peinture* (1719); English translation *Critical Reflections on Poetry, Painting, and Music*, trans. Thomas Nugent from the 5th edn (London: J. Nourse, 1748), ii, 294.

13 *Ibid.*, 256.

14 *Ibid.*, 238

15 Bate, *Classic to Romantic*, 116.

16 *Ibid.*, 117, 131.

17 As Wittgenstein remarks, "a wheel that can be turned though nothing else moves with it, is not part of the mechanism," Ludwig Wittgenstein, *Phiosophical Investigatioins*, trans. G. E. M. Anscombe (New York: Macmillan, 1953, 1958), section 271.

18 Dubos, *Critical Reflections*, ii, 294.

19 *Ibid.*, i, 334.

20 *Ibid.*, ii, 39.

21 This resonates with Jerome Stolnitz's notion of "aesthetic disinterestedness," with its emphasis on selflessness and forgetting the "proprietary self" in order to enable attention to become truly object-centered. "On the origins of 'aesthetic disinterestedness'," *Journal of Aesthetics and Art Criticism* 20 (1961): 131–142. If only the object to be evaluated is allowed into consideration, this suggests that the object must be carefully isolated from context. This would imply that Hume's understanding of aesthetic evaluation differs radically from his understanding of moral evaluation, in which, as I argued in chapter 2, the context of the actions which cause our immediate moral responses are absolutely crucial. Hume's next sentence, however, makes clear that freedom from prejudice amounts to something closely akin to the context-sensitive moral point of view.

22 Hume does not, however, invoke a Hutchesonian "sense of beauty," even in the radically transformed guise in which he invoked a "moral sense" in the *Treatise*.

23 Of course, Hume's actual judgments seem to us to be rather parochial, despite his claims of "naturalness" and "universality, but Hume deserves credit nonetheless for leaving these judgments open to reflective criticism. On Hume's parochiality, see Wellek, *A History of Modern Criticism*, 108.

24 Just as, according to Aristotle, we can recognize the *phronimos* without ourselves being fully virtuous.

25 This debate between the partisans of the ancients and the partisans of the moderns began as a literary controversy in the 1680s and developed in the eighteenth century into a discussion of the idea of progress in all realms of culture. See Allan Megill, "Aesthetic theory and historical consciousness in the eighteenth century," *History and Theory* 17 (1978): 35. Also A. Owen Aldridge, "Ancients and Moderns in the eighteenth century," *Dictionary of the History of Ideas*, vol. 1 (New York, 1973), 76–87. Mossner has examined Hume's various contributions to the debate in "Hume and the Ancient-Modern Controversy, 1725–1752: A study in creative scepticism," *Texas Studies in English* 28 (1949): 139–153.

26 Interestingly, when he does not have the ancients specifically in mind, he claims that "the misfortunes of the wicked are not a proper subject to move us" and that "a poet would be blamed for dressing his villainous personages with qualities capable of engaging the benevolence of the spectator," Dubos, *Critical Reflections* 1. 93, 97.

27 The second edition appeared in 1759.

28 It is interesting that he includes both imagination and judgment under the heading of taste, rather than opposing taste to judgment as earlier neoclassicists would have tended to do.

29 Burke, *Sublime and Beautiful*, 12.

30 *Ibid.*, 21.

31 *Ibid.*, 23.

32 *Ibid.*, 26.

33 Of course, it might not always be the case that we judge the poet to have been justified, even given his context, in holding the moral beliefs he held. For an illuminating discussion of the relationship between justified and true moral beliefs which resonates with Hume's suggestions, see Jeffrey Stout, *Ethics after Babel* (Boston: Beacon Press, 1988), 24–26, 93–94. For a different conclusion about Hume's comments on morals in "Of the standard of taste," see Donald Livingston, *Hume's Philosophy of Common Life* (University of Chicago Press, 1984), 241–243. Livingston, who suggests that Hume *is* erecting barriers to sympathetic understanding of alien moral sentiments, implies that there is no distinction between sympathetically entering into an alien point of view, identifying the goods which others pursue, and accepting their moral judgments.

34 See Livingston, *Philosophy of Common Life*, chs. 10 and 12.

35 On the barriers to understanding "barbarians," see *ibid.*, 235–246.

36 Thomas McCarthy, "On misunderstanding 'understanding,'" *Theory and Decision* 3 (1972–73): 351–70. This awareness of the importance of description raises questions about the link between rhetoric and sympathetic understanding which will be taken up in chapter 5.

37 The criticism of Hume's belief in the uniformity of human nature stems from influential philosophers of history, such as J. B. Black, R. G. Collingwood, and Friedrich Meinecke. See Duncan Forbes' account in *Hume's Philosophical Politics* (Cambridge University Press, 1975), ch. 4. Those who regard Hume as more of a historicist and relativist include Wellek, *History of Modern Criticism*, 107–108, *The Rise of English Literary History* (Chapel Hill: University of North Carolina Press, 1941), 51–52 and Peter Gay, *The Enlightenment: An Interpretation* (New York: Alfred A. Knopf, 1969), 2:381. Donald T. Siebert finds what he takes to be Hume's tendency toward relativism disturbing; *The Moral Animus of David Hume* (Newark: University of Delaware Press, 1990), 184–185. See also John J. Burke, Jr., "Hume's *History of England*: Waking the English from a dogmatic slumber," *Studies in Eighteenth-Century Culture*, vol. 7, ed. Roseann Runte (Madison: University of Wisconsin Press, 1978), 245–247, and Mossner, "Hume and the Ancient – Modern controversy," 146.

38 My position is close to that of S. K. Wertz, who suggests that "human nature" is for Hume a formal, not a substantial, uniformity, needed to understand history "Hume, history, and human nature," *Journal of the History of Ideas* 36 (1975): 481–496. See also Forbes' account, which makes clear that "the *Enquiry*, which appears to be putting forward a uniformitarian view of human behaviour, is not really doing so. Not of course that Hume's position is any kind of ethical relativism," *Hume's Philosophical Politics*, 110. Livingston's view is also very close to my own, although I disagree with Livingston' contention that, for Hume, to understand is to excuse, if this implies that moral truth, not simply justification, is relative, *Philosophy of Common Life*, 218–225, 243. These three thinkers also take sympathy to be crucial to understanding those historically or culturally distant from ourselves, although their understandings of sympathy differ. Livingston, for example, speaks of a "process of *verstehen*" made possible by "the original principle of sympathy" without clarifying what the original principle of sympathy itself is for Hume (222). Forbes addresses sympathy as the social glue which makes for national character as well as sympathy as a sense of common humanity, but does not discern the tension between the two or recognize that they might work at cross purposes when it comes to understanding those who belong to communities other than one's own (106–110).

39 The term "hermeneutic of charity" is indebted to Donald Davidson's notion of the necessity of employing a principle of charity in translation and interpretation. See "On the very idea of a conceptual scheme," *Proceedings of the American Philosophical Association* 47 (1973–74): 5–20; reprinted in *Relativism: Cognitive and Moral*, ed. Michael Krausz and Jack W. Meiland (University of Notre Dame Press, 1982), 66–79, especially 78–79.

40 Livingston, *Philosophy of Common Life*, 222, also 225. My interpretation of

Hume's sympathetic understanding is indebted to Livingston's notion of internal understanding, according to which "to understand the moral cause of an action is to see how it is directed to some good the agent had in mind" (242). See also James Farr, who writes that "when the moral scientist wants to explain, say, a human action, as distinct from a physical movement, he must have recourse to sympathy in order to decode the 'external signs' and thereby recover the motives, maxims, and principles which give the action meaning," "Hume, hermeneutics, and history: a 'sympathetic' account," *History and Theory* 17 (1978): 298.

41 See also Baier, *A Progress of Sentiments: Reflections on Hume's Treatise* (Cambridge, MA: Harvard University Press, 1991), 210–212.

42 This is quite a radical implication of Hume's discussion. Even Diderot, a strong advocate of the theater, worried that the capacity to assume an imaginary self indicated a lack of a self of one's own. See Jonas Barish, *The Antitheatrical Prejudice* (Berkeley: University of California Press, 1981), 281.

43 Clifford Geertz, *Local Knowledge* (New York: Basic Books, 1983), 44.

44 *Ibid.*, 56, 58.

45 Ernest Tuveson, "The importance of Shaftesbury," *Journal of English Literary History* 20 (1953): 291.

46 Jean-Jacques Rousseau, *Politics and the Arts: Letter to M. D'Alembert on the Theatre*, trans. Allan Bloom (Ithaca: Cornell University Press, 1960), 19 ("on ne saurait se mettre à la place de gens qui ne nous ressemblent point," *Lettre a M. D'Alembert sur son Article Genève*, ed. Michel Launay, (Paris: Garnier-Flammarion, 1967), 70).

47 *Ibid.*, 19 ("qu'on n'attribue donc pas au théâtre le pouvoir de changer des sentiments ni des mœurs qu'il ne peu que suivre et embellir," 69).

48 *Ibid.*, 46 ("Qui ne devient pas un moment filou soi-même en s'intéressant pour lui? Car s'intéresser pour quelqu'un qu'est-ce autre chose que se mettre à sa place?," 112).

49 *Ibid.*, 58 ("il n'est pas possible que la commoditè d'aller tous les jours régulièrement au même lieu s'oublier soui-même et s'occuper d'objets étrangers ne donne au citoyen d'autres habitudes et ne lui forme de nouvelle mœurs" (129).

50 Hazlitt will suggest that the important division is between past and present, on the one hand, and future, on the other, rather than between self and other. See n. 13, chapter 2. While it is true that my present sensations, that which "interests" me, are related to me in a peculiarly intimate way, it is only the imagination which can make me care about anyone's welfare, since welfare has to do with *future* benefits either to ourselves or to others; "the mind can take, it can have no interest in any thing, that is an object of practical pursuit, but what is strictly imaginary: it is absurd to suppose that it can have a real interest in any such object directly whether relating to ourselves, or others . . . neither can the reality of my future interest in any object give me a real interest in that object at present," *An Essay on the Principles of Human Action*, in *The Complete Works of William Hazlitt*, ed. P. P.

Howe, vol. 1 (London: J. M. Dent and Sons, 1930), 10. Hazlitt is not, of course, disagreeing with Hume; the imagination does not make us think that we *are* the other person, but Hazlitt does want to suggest, by invoking the Romantic faculty of "imagination" (grown much more powerful and active than imagination in the late seventeenth-century), that sympathy with others is properly understood in the same terms as our concern for our own imagined future welfare.

51 James Farr's reading of sympathy even in the *Treatise* is as an interpretive principle. Farr notes that "we must first decode the signs or effects which embody another's ideas. Secondly, we then come to share not only those ideas, but their related impressions as well, because of the mechanism of the association of ideas . . . Sympathy or communication presupposes the interpretation of signs and/or the analysis of effects," "Hume, hermeneutics, and history," 292. The emphasis of Hume's account of sympathy "is on communication, not empathy or individual psychology. In this respect Hume's version of sympathy or *verstehen* is more akin to Gadamer's than to the early Dilthey's," 289. I am in basic agreement with Farr, although I think it is important to recognize the significance of Hume's shift from speaking of sympathy in primarily passive terms to speaking of actively entering into alien points of view.

52 This is true of German as well as French and English Romanticism, although in the brief remarks that follow I will, as I have throughout, limit myself to the latter. It would be a fascinating project to explore the increasing cross-fertilization of ideas which begins to occur as German thinkers not only read, but are read by, English and French authors. Hume was well known in Germany by the 1770s. Lessing's insistence on the moral importance of *Mitleid* (pity, compassion, sympathy; literally suffer-with) in his aesthetic writings was certainly influenced by his reading of Adam Smith; whether or not he read Hume is less clear. Herder, searching, much like his contemporaries elsewhere, for a more active concept, used the word *Einfühlen* (feel-into) to characterize the sympathetic imagination. Herder believed that "only a combination of historical scholarship with a responsive, imaginative sensibility can find a path into the inner life, the vision of the world, the aspirations, values, ways of life of individuals or groups or entire civilizations," and insisted that these different visions of the world possessed a distinct integrity which requires that they be evaluated only in their own terms. Isaiah Berlin, *Vico and Herder* (London: The Hogarth Press, 1976), xxii; see also 154–155, 171–174, 186–188. For Herder (and the same is true, much later, of Dilthey), *Einfühlen* results in evaluative incommensurability, a view which contrasts, I have argued, with a Humean notion of sympathetic understanding. This word was the seed for the late nineteenth-century aesthetic doctrine of *Einfühlung*, which was then translated back into English by the invented word "empathy." See James Engell's *The Creative Imagination: Enlightenment to Romanticism* (Cambridge, MA: Harvard University Press, 1981), which traces the development of both British and German understandings of the imagination and includes a helpful chapter on sympathy and the imagination, 143–160.

53 R. F. Brissenden writes that "the sentimental tribute of a tear exacted by the spectacle of virtue in distress was an acknowledgment at once of man's inherent goodness and of the impossibility of his ever being able to demonstrate his goodness effectively," *Virtue in Distress: Studies in the Novel of Sentiment from Richardson to Sade* (London: MacMillan, 1974), 29. According to Norman S. Fiering, "the cultivation of humane literature, ironically, may be a refuge from and a substitute for feelingful responses to painful human situations in the real world," "Irresistible compassion: an aspect of eighteenth-century sympathy and humanitarianism," *Journal of the History of Ideas* 37 (1976): 213.

54 Bate, *From Classic to Romantic*, 132.

55 John B. Radner, "The art of sympathy in eighteenth-century British thought," in *Studies in Eighteenth-Century Culture*, vol. 9, ed. Roseann Runte (Madison: University of Wisconsin Press, 1979), 196.

56 This was not such a radical notion, but rather a natural development of the principles of the literary movement of which Hume was a part, which sought to rescue *belles-lettres* and philosophy from "scholastic" pedantry, abstruse reasoning, and unintelligible prose. Typified by the short essays of Addison's *Spectator*, this movement reached out to the growing reading public, rather than remaining within the walls of the university. See M. A. Box, *The Suasive Art of David Hume* (Princeton University Press, 1990), ch. 1. Hume's shift from treatise-writing to essay-writing should not be despised as a mere desire for fame, but recognized as a commitment to making criticism and philosophical reflection accessible and socially and politically relevant. Hazlitt inherited Hume's mantle as essayist; Coleridge, in contrast, though initially joining in Wordsworth's embrace of the common, ended up expressing his distrust and disdain for the 'reading public'; "From a popular philosophy and a philosophic populace," he exclaimed, "Good Sense deliver us!" See "A lay sermon addressed to the higher classes of society," in *The Collected Works of Samuel Taylor Coleridge: Lay Sermons*, ed. R. J. White (Cambridge: Routledge and Kegan Paul, 1972), 38. Coleridge adopted a more learned, convoluted style, which has left a lasting influence on the style of academic prose. I am indebted to Jeffrey Stout for increasing my awareness of this tradition of essayists and social critics which includes not only Hume and Hazlitt, but also Cobbett and eventually Orwell, and which reaches back (self-consciously, in Hazlitt's case) to Montaigne.

57 William Wordsworth, *Preface* to the second edn. of *Lyrical Ballads*, (1800) in *Selected Poems and Prefaces by William Wordsworth*, ed. Jack Stillinger (Boston: Houghton Mifflin Company, 1965), 447.

58 *Ibid.*, 453.

59 William Hazlitt, "On the living poets" in *Lectures on the English Poets* (1818), *Works*, vol. 5, 163.

60 Brissenden, *Virtue in Distress*, 77. Hazlitt saw the poetic failure of the Lake Poets as intrinsically linked to their political failure – not just their disillusionment with the French Revolution, which was understandable, but their consequent abandonment of democratic ideals and endorsement

of the legitimacy of the English monarchy, which was unforgivable. Hazlitt worried that their failure was somehow inevitable; the imagination is entranced, he reasoned, with things exalted and grand; poetry is ill-suited to democratic purposes. He applied the same explanation to account for the persuasiveness of Edmund Burke's *Reflections on the Revolution in France*. Burke was able to engage the sympathies of his readers because his subject – the glory of the monarchy, the nobility of the aristocracy, the venerability of tradition – was able to capture their imaginations. Although the imagination is an active faculty, nevertheless it is better-suited to certain subjects than others. To be successful, the democratic impulse in poetry, while it introduces equality and thus sameness in the political realm, must compensate by finding forms of excellence and greatness of other sorts. See "Coriolanus," in *Characters of Shakespear's Plays* (1817), *Works*, vol. 4, "Character of Mr. Burke" (1807), *Works*, vol. 7. The novel is perhaps a form of poetry more suited to a liberal democratic age; certainly lyric poetry has gone into eclipse. This sentiment is voiced by Milan Kundera in *The Art of the Novel*, trans. Linda Asher (New York: Grove Press, 1986), 42, 159,165, and Richard Rorty in *Contingency, Irony, and Solidarity* (Cambridge University Press, 1989), 93–94, both of whom link imaginative identification in the novel with awareness of difference and the liberal virtue of tolerance. I leave to others the task of reflecting on the relationship between tragic drama, so important to eighteenth-century aesthetic and ethical reflection, and the novel.

61 Letter to Richard Woodhouse, October 27, 1818, *The Selected Letters of John Keats*, ed. Lionel Trilling (New York: Farrar, Straus and Young, Inc., 1951), 151–153.

62 Hazlitt, "On effeminacy of character," *Works*, vol. 8, 255.

63 David Bromwich, *Hazlitt: The Mind of a Critic* (Oxford University Press, 1983), 386.

64 *Ibid.*, 375.

65 Samuel Johnson, *The Rambler* (London: Jones & Company, 1826), no. 60, 105.

66 *Ibid.*, 81, 140.

67 *Ibid.*, 60, 105.

68 Johnson, *Rasselas* (1759), ch. 10. *The Rambler* (London: Jones & Company, 1826), no. 60, 105.

69 Johnson, *Rambler* 60, 105.

70 *Ibid.*

71 Bate, *Classic to Romantic*, 134.

72 To do justice to Adam Smith's theory of sympathy would require at least a chapter, if not more. Nonetheless, it is worth providing a brief account of Smith's theory in order to highlight the differences between the two thinkers, thereby indicating why I find in Hume more of an indication of how it is possible to come to terms with difference through sympathy.

73 Adam Smith, *The Theory of Moral Sentiments*, intr. E. C. West (Indianapolis: LibertyClassics, 1969), 47; hereafter abbreviated *TMS*.

74 Occasionally, Smith's language suggests that the power of the imagination is such that it allows us first to conceive and then to feel what the sufferer actually feels; "we enter as it were into his body, and become in some measure the same person with him, and thence form some idea of his sensations, and even feel something which, though weaker in degree, is not altogether unlike them," *TMS*, 48. Just as Smith focused on certain strands of Hume's discussion of sympathy and developed them into a substantially different account of sympathy than that developed by Hume, the poetic and dramatic rhetoric Smith uses in the passage just quoted fed in turn into the romantic notion of the sympathetic imagination. According to Bate, "the development of the sympathetic imagination came largely from a group of Scottish critics who almost agreed with Archibald Alison's estimate of the *Moral Sentiments* as 'the most eloquent work on the subject of morals that modern Europe has produced,'" *Classic to Romantic*, 135.

75 Smith, *TMS*, 58.

76 *Ibid.*

77 *Ibid.*, 514.

78 *Ibid.*, 502.

79 Philip Mercer, *Sympathy and Ethics: A Study of the Relationship between Sympathy and Morality with Special Reference to Hume's "Treatise"* (Oxford: Clarendon Press, 1972), 86.

80 See also Smith, *TMS*, 331–332.

81 This is the conclusion encouraged by Romantic understandings of sympathy.

82 Marshall writes that "although the person suffering is really present, we can experience what our senses deny us only through what Kames in his *Elements of Criticism* calls 'ideal presence . . . even an eyewitness must depend upon an imagined representation, at least in order to feel sympathy." *The Figure of the Theater* (New York: Columbia University Press, 1986), 171. For both Kames and Smith, the spectator's attention is focused on the imagined representation rather than the other person in actuality.

83 Smith, *TMS*, 90–91.

84 *Ibid.*, 50–51.

85 *Ibid.*, 110–111.

86 Because of Smith's tendency to focus on the intensity of passions, it is difficult to distinguish between a failure of the first and a failure of the second sort of sympathy. The result of both sorts of failure seems to be passions of lesser intensity than those of the person observed, rather than inappropriate kinds of passions.

87 Smith, *TMS*, 108.

88 *Ibid.*, 86. Ironically, as David Marshall points out in *The Figure of the Theater*, Smith has a knack for sympathetic understanding especially in those situations in which he denies that sympathy will take place (182, 192). This is particularly striking in the chapter "Of the influence of custom and fashion upon moral sentiments," where Smith displays his own capacity for sympathetic understanding of a Humean sort, rather than the imaginative

sympathy which he advocates but thinks impossible under such circumstances.

89 Smith, *TMS*, 233. Apparently our capacity to view things as the impartial spectator does, unlike our capacity to sympathize with others, is something we can and should develop. See also 248.

90 *Ibid.*, 247.

91 Lucinda Cole highlights this aspect of Smith's thought in her "Sympathy, gender, and the writing of value in late eighteenth-century English letters," (Ph.D. dissertation, Louisiana State University, 1990), 73, 81, 208. Cole provides an insightful analysis and criticism of Smith, but unfortunately conflates his views with those of Hume, rather than recognizing the significant distinctions between them.

92 Smith, *TMS*, 369.

93 Mercer, *Sympathy and Ethics*, 91.

94 As we have already seen, sympathy on Smith's account is not limited just to one's own society, but within it to one's social and economic class, and restricted further to those who share the same intensity of sentiment. This conviction that homogeneity is requisite to sympathy could be used, as by Smith, to harden the boundaries between existing social classes; in the American colonies, where identity was shaped around the category of race, it was applied to the slavery question. Garry Wills argues persuasively that Thomas Jefferson drew on this notion in developing his argument that blacks ought to be freed (since equal with whites in the crucial capacity of moral sentiment, if not in mind or body), but could never be integrated into Virginia society. Instead, they would have to be deported to form their own, homogenous colonies elsewhere. Only then could bonds of sympathy flourish within both white societies and black societies. *Inventing America: Jefferson's Declaration of Independence* (New York: Vintage Books, 1978), 301–306; 289–292. A Humean understanding of sympathetic understanding, in contrast, does not predicate sympathy on homogeneity, and would not have lent support to systems of apartheid. I cannot here give a full treatment of Hume's beliefs concerning the issues of race and slavery, but I will venture a few remarks, as the subject is clearly related to the question of sympathy and its limits. It is true that Hume suspects "the negroes to be naturally inferior to the whites," basing this conclusion on his limited knowledge about the state of the arts and sciences in African nations, and this does run against his rejection of physical causes for national differences in general ("Of national characters," *MPL* 208). But he does not employ these racist assumptions in order to deny freedom to blacks. In "Of the populousness of ancient nations," Hume takes a detour from his discussion of the relative population of the ancient and modern worlds to denounce the evils of slavery. "A chained slave for a porter," he remarks, "was usual in Rome, as appears from Ovid, and other authors. Had not these people shaken off all sense of compassion towards that unhappy part of their species, would they have presented their friends, at the first entrance, with such an image of the severity of the master, and the misery of the slave?" (*MPL* 385). Unlike Jefferson, Hume does not deny that

sympathy extends from master to slave. Indeed, this bond which links them with one another is the basis for arguing against slavery, and could not therefore be used to argue that former masters and former slaves be kept separate.

Nevertheless, the link between sympathy and homogeneity persisted, and a half century after Jefferson argued for racial separation, Alexis de Tocqueville wrote that "once one admits that whites and emancipated Negroes face each other like two foreign peoples on the same soil, it can easily be understood that there are only two possibilities for the future: the Negroes and whites must either mingle completely or they must part" *Democracy In America*, ed. J. P. Mayer (New York: Harper & Row, 1969), 355. He then goes on to express his deep pessimism about the first possibility, citing Jefferson, and worries that the second option may involve the extermination of blacks or whites. Underlying his pessimism about American race-relations is his sense that "what keeps a great number of citizens under the same government is less a reasoned desire to remain united than the instinctive and, in a sense, involuntary accord which springs from like feelings and similar opinions," 373. Tocqueville's prediction of the inveteracy of the problem of race in America has been fulfilled, but it is perhaps also true that the belief that sympathy and social concord could only emerge out of uniformity is a self-fulfilling prophecy, undermining active efforts to extend sympathy to those different from oneself and one's own.

95 Smith, *TMS*, 328.
96 *Ibid.*, 334.
97 Glenn R. Morrow, "The significance of the doctrine of sympathy in Hume and Adam Smith," 71, 73.
98 Smith, *TMS*, 341.
99 *Ibid.*, 228.
100 This seems at first glance to be a striking reversal of Aristotle's opinion on the comparative value of poetry and history. According to Aristotle, poetry possesses a more general truth than does history, which is always preoccupied with the contingent and particular, rather than the probable or necessary and the general. *Poetics* 1451b 5–15. Scott Davis has persuaded me, however, that it is less of a reversal of Aristotle than a conviction on Hume's part that historians always aspire to poetry, or at least that they too are preoccupied with the probable and the general, even if they reach it through different means.
101 Meineke, of course, regarded Hume as utterly unhistorical and considered historism a German phenomenon, while Megill extends it to Vico and the "English pre-romantics," 31–33. Certainly Herder, often considered the originator of historism, was deeply influenced by eighteenth-century Scottish and English critics. Wellek, *History of Modern Criticism*, 181. David Fate Norton regards Hume solely as a philosophical historian. See *David Hume: Philosophical Historian*, ed. David Fate Norton and Richard H. Popkin (Indianapolis: Bobbs-Merrill, 1965), xxxii-l.
102 Megill, "Aesthetic theory and historical consciousness," 30.

103 *Ibid.*, 34.
104 Ernst Cassirer, *The Philosophy of the Enlightenment*, trans. Fritz C. A. Koelln and James P. Pettegrove (Princeton University Press, 1951), 226.
105 John Burke , "Hume's *History of England*," 243.
106 Wellek, *Rise of English Literary History*, 25.
107 Peter Gay fails to distinguish between attaining sympathetic understanding of historical actors and situations and lapsing into a relativism which can do no more than "apply the internal standards that a nation would apply to itself." He writes that "the philosophes' capacity to appreciate historical individuality, mirrored and produced a relativist conception of the past, a certain willingness to suspend judgment and to see other epoches from the inside. In 1751, David Hume put the still fairly rudimentary relativism of the little flock into an amusing dialogue," *The Enlightenment* II:381. Because Gay thinks Hume espoused a relativism which applied only internal standards, he fails to see that Hume's critique of Christianity might be something other than a "polemical passion" which contravened Hume's own relativist historicism, II. 383.
108 John Witherspoon, "A serious inquiry into the nature and effects of the stage," in *The Works of John Witherspoon*, vol. 6 (Edinburgh: Ogle & Aikman, Pillans & Sons, J. Ritchie & J. Turnbull, 1805), 97.
109 *Ibid.*, 92–93.
110 Barish, *Antitheatrical Prejudice*, 298.
111 Witherspoon, "Serious inquiry," 120.
112 Mossner, *Life of Hume*, 321–324.
113 *Ibid.*, 343.
114 Hume seems almost to have resigned himself to excommunication at this time, for he remarks: "Meanwhile I am preparing for the Day of Wrath, and have already bespoken a number of discreet families, who have promised to admit me after I shall be excommunicated." Letter to Allan Ramsay, quoted in Mossner, *Life of Hume*, 343.
115 *Ibid.*, 325.
116 Dubos, *Critical Reflections* II, 353–354.
117 Hume's strategy of separating speculative, artificial systems from ordinary life and its natural principles stands in striking contrast to a common strategy of separation employed in the defense, not of religious skepticism, but of religious belief. Enlightenment thinkers did not, in general, endorse Hume's skepticism about speculative knowledge in general, but rather regarded scientific and mathematical statements as the paradigm of knowledge, while casting suspicion on religious statements, which seemed plagued by endless controversy and void of definitive procedures of rigorous justification. Some defenders of religion (Schleiermacher is a prime example) responded to the aspersions cast on religion by claiming that religious claims were not a poor attempt at scientific statements, but belonged rather in a different realm altogether – a realm of feeling rather than of reason. Whereas Hume invoked a strategy of separation in order to

justify religious toleration, once religion is on the defensive rather than the offensive, it invokes a similar strategy of separation in order to justify its continued existence.

118 See H. B. Acton, "The ethical importance of sympathy," *Philosophy* 30 (1955): 62, and Robert J. Lipkin, "Altruism and sympathy in Hume's ethics," *Australasian Journal of Philosophy* 65 (1987): 21, 25–26.

5 RELIGION AND IRRATIONALITY IN HISTORY

1 Hume's *Dialogues Concerning Natural Religion* provides a rather different perspective on religion than do the *Natural History of Religion* and the *History of England,* since it is directed primarily at philosophers who attempt to prove, empirically or logically, speculative religious hypotheses, rather than at the man-on-the-street believer, who accepts revelation and traditional authorities. Philosophical error, unlike self-deception and factional zeal, is subject to correction by philosophical argument. I do think that Parts X and XII of the *Dialogues* use some of the same rhetorical techniques and provide the same sort of analysis of religion as the other works I will be discussing, and I will therefore have occasion to refer to these sections below.

2 R. G. Collingwood, *The Idea of History* (Oxford: Clarendon Press, 1946), 78, 80. Collingwood's conviction of Hume's lack of sympathetic understanding for religious, pre-modern ages leads him to conclude that Hume's attitude, and the Enlightenment more generally, was not truly historical, but rather polemical and anti-historical, 77.

3 This may seem to be a somewhat precipitous conclusion, since we can at least see that Pascal's manners make some sense in light of his pursuit of the goods of eternal life. Hume's account suggests, however, in ways which I hope to clarify in what follows, that the goods of eternal life cannot *really* be grasped and understood as goods.

4 Since reasons can be causes, not all causal accounts set aside sympathetic understanding. The "external" isolates only those which do not attend to the purported reasons of the agents, or which analyze them as positively deceptive or misleading.

5 Peter Brown, the eminent scholar of late antiquity, believes Hume's *Natural History of Religion* has had a lasting deleterious impact on the study of religion:

it seems to me that our curiosity has been blunted by a particular model of the nature of religious sentiment and a consequent definition of the nature of "popular religion." We have inherited from our own learned tradition attitudes that are not sensitive enough to help us enter into the thought processes and the needs that led to the rise and expansion of the cult of the saints in late antiquity . . . It was precisely the "armchair" quality of Hume's essay that accounts for the continued subliminal presence of its leading ideas in all later scholarship . . . [it] seems to carry the irresistible weight of a clear and judicious statement of the obvious.

The Cult of the Saints (University of Chicago Press, 1981), 12–13.

6 Donald W. Livingston, *Hume's Philosophy of Common Life* (University of Chicago Press, 1984), 163. Chapters 6 and 7 of Livingston's book contain an insightful discussion of Hume's accounts of causal explanation in various domains – science, metaphysics, and morals.

7 *Ibid.*, 192.

8 Jon Elster discusses the importance, but also the difficulty, of being able to characterize belief as rational while false in *Sour Grapes: Studies in the Subversion of Rationality* (Cambridge University Press, 1983), 2–16.

9 A related interpretation of Hume's analysis of religion is developed by Keith E. Yandell in *Hume's "Inexplicable Mystery": His Views on Religion* (Philadelphia: Temple University Press, 1990). Yandell suggests that the tensions between the propensity to polytheism and the propensity to theism "serve to weaken or disorder the efficacious operations of propensities to belief that (in part) comprise human nature. Too many conflicting propensities, or too much conflict among propensities, within a single system of human nature may reduce, or even abolish, its capacity for belief altogether" (31). Hume seems to me to be more interested in tensions internal to theistic belief than in tensions between polytheistic and theistic tendencies. Moreover, while Yandell argues that Hume's primary concern is epistemic stability (82–84), I believe Hume thought that the real threat lay in the moral, rather than the epistemic, realm. Religious beliefs are shadowy competitors to common-sense beliefs, but their very shadowiness motivates zealous religious practices and persecutions, which are very real indeed.

10 Although the term "self-deception" is not Hume's own, I believe it captures the irrational feature of religious belief which Hume is attending to here. The *OED* gives 1677 as the date of the first use of the word "self-deception," but it here means complying with someone else who is seeking to deceive you. The word is used in its modern sense in 1745 by J. Mason, who considers it a particularly dangerous form of deceit because usually unsuspected. I do not mean to claim that "self-deception" is itself a clear concept. There is a sizeable and by no means univocal contemporary philosophical literature which explores self-deception, wishful thinking, and other related kinds of irrationality. Some of the sources I have found most helpful are: Herbert Fingarette, *Self-deception* (London: Routledge and Kegan Paul, 1969); Elster, *Sour Grapes*; David Pears, *Motivated Irrationality* (Oxford: Clarendon Press, 1984); Donald Davidson, "Deception and division," and Amélie O. Rorty, "Self-deception, *akrasia* and irrationality," in *The Multiple Self: Studies in Rationality and Social Change*, ed. Jon Elster (Cambridge University Press, 1985); Mike W. Martin, *Self-Deception and Morality* (Lawrence, KS: University Press of Kansas, 1986); Robert Audi, "Self-deception, rationalization, and reasons for acting," and "Bas C. van Fraassen, "The peculiar effects of love and desire," in *Perspectives on Self-Deception*, eds. Brian P. McLaughlin and Amélie O. Rorty (Berkeley: University of California Press, 1988). At times I will attempt to place Hume in dialogue with these thinkers, but I do not want to import too many foreign distinctions or get side-tracked into a theoretical discussion of self-deception, as my primary interest is in understanding the role of

self-deception and other forms of irrationality in Hume's account of religion.

11 Fingarette, *Self-deception*, 1–33.

12 Davidson, "Deception and division," 91–92; see also Pears, *Motivated Irrationality*, 103.

13 Both Martin, *Self-deceptin and Morality*, 6 and Fingarette, *Self-deception*, 28–29 insist on the importance of intentionality. See also Pears, *Motivated Irrationality*, 103.

14 Amèlie O. Rorty suggests that self-deception is a corruption of a strong conservatism of beliefs and motives which itself is justified because it helps make rational agency possible by allowing the compartmentalization of beliefs. "Self-deception, *akrasia*, and. irrationality," 126.

15 Elster, *Sour Grapes*, 149.

16 *Ibid.*, 150.

17 Elster points out that wishful thinking gives only temporary relief; "when reality reasserts itself, frustration and dissonance will also reappear," *ibid.*, 142. See also Davidson, "Deception and division," 90.

18 Hume's use of the colorless term "deity" here does not, of course, obscure the fact that he is speaking of the Calvinist God of wrath.

19 Elster, *Sour Grapes*, 46.

20 Although most of the contemporary literature on irrationality in general and self-deception in particular is ahistorical, Bas van Fraassen draws attention to the rootedness of western thought about self-deception in Christian reflection in "The peculiar effects of love and desire," which discusses both Augustine and Pascal. See also Martin's *Self-Deception and Morality*.

21 See Martin, *Self-deception and Morality*, 31–33, which places both Butler and Pascal in the "Inner Hypocrisy" tradition of reflection on self-deception.

22 Joseph Butler, *Fifteen Sermons*, ed. W. R. Matthews (London: G. Bell & Sons, 1914), Sermon VII, 129, 114.

23 Butler, "On hypocrisy," in *The Works of Joseph Butler*, ed. J. H. Bernard (London: 1900), 318.

24 See *D* 84 and *NHR* 75 as well as discussions of Thomas à Becket, Simon de Mountfort, Joan of Arc, Cardinal Wolsey, Henry VIII, and Thomas More in the *History of England*. He also continues to make use of its more conventional meaning as well (for example, NHR 64), which results in a lack of clarity about just what his claims about the nature of theistic belief are. I will discuss this more fully later in this chapter. Donald Siebert has a helpful discussion of Hume on the hypocrisy of religious belief in *The Moral Animus of David Hume* (Newark: University of Delaware Press, 1990), 101–103, 125–126.

25 E. C. Mossner, *The Life of David Hume* (Austin: University of Texas Press, 1954), 102.

26 Blaise Pascal, *Pensées*, trans. A. J. Krailsheimer (London: Penguin Books, 1966), 377 (655). I give Krailsheimer's numbering of the *Pensées* in parentheses.

27 Pascal, *Pensées*, 139 (136).

28 *Ibid.*, 100 (978).

29 *Ibid.*, 428 (148).

30 *Ibid.*

31 *Ibid.*, 434 (131).

32 *Ibid.*, 468 (220).

33 *Ibid.*, 195 (428).

34 [Richard Allestree], *The Practice of Christian Graces or the Whole Duty of Man* (London: D. Maxwell for T. Garthwait, 1658), Part 17, section 22.

35 This is reminiscent of remarks in the *Treatise* on the power of eduction to instill belief even where "the constant and inseparable union of causes and effects" is lacking (*T* 116), although Hume seems in the *Treatise* to have attributed more power (or vivifying capacity) to education than in later reflections.

36 Hume discusses our tendency to weight the present more than the past and future in *T* 427–438. Like Pascal, Hume thinks that the fact that things which are closer to us in space and time have a proportionally stronger effect on our will and passions often works to our detriment; "this is the reason why men so often act in contradiction to their known interest; and in particular why they prefer any trivial advantage, that is present, to the maintenance of order in society, which so much depends on the observance of justice" (*T* 535). The remedy is to take up a more detached, less prejudiced point of view. Hume confines this analysis and remedy to this-wordly concerns, however.

37 Elster, *Sour Grapes*, 11.

38 Pascal, *Pensées*, 233 (418).

39 For a valuable group of essays on rationality, including a debate about the rationality of religious belief, see Bryan Wilson, ed. *Rationality* (Oxford: Basil Blackwell, 1970).

40 The six volumes of Hume's *History of England* appeared between 1754 and 1762.

41 Religion is not the only important subject of the *History of England,* although I think it is an absolutely central one. Hume is also very interested in the story of the development of the English constitution, of the mixed form of government, and the rise of liberty and its limitation of the power of the monarchy, for example.

42 Several writers have traced changes in Hume's treatment of religion, or his approach to the writing of history more generally, from the Stuart volumes, which Hume wrote first, backwards through time. See Mossner, *Life of Hume*, 307; Leo Braudy, *Narrative Form in History and Fiction: Hume, Fielding, Gibbon* (Princeton University Press, 1970), 33ff. I believe that Hume's treatment of religion varies with the historical material he is writing about, however, and is otherwise consistent over time. I will therefore be drawing on all volumes of the history without paying special attention to when particular passages were written.

43 See, for example, *NHR* 49; "Of parties in general," in *MPL* 59–60.

44 Butler, "On hypocrisy," 326.

45 See Mossner's account, *Life of Hume*, 305ff.

46 Braudy attacks what he calls "Hume's false ideal of detachment" (13), and claims that Hume's own "faith in the possibilities of impartiality grows weaker as his claims of impartiality grow more shrill" (90), but Braudy seems to think there is a tension between "the demands of sympathetic character analysis and those of detached narrative" (35). See also J. C. Hilson, "Hume:

The historian as man of feeling." In *Augustan Worlds*, eds. J. C. Hilson, M. M. B. Jones, and J. R. Watson (Leicester University Press, 1978), 219. Hume's claim, I think, is that sympathetic understanding, far from being in tension with impartiality, requires it. Impartiality is not a refusal to make judgments, but a determination to stay out of factionalism and party politics.

47 In what follows, I refer frequently to "the reader." This is difficult to avoid in a discussion of rhetoric. Of course, I do not want to imply that everyone reacted or was expected to react in the same way to every feature of the *History*, and I will attempt to make relevant distinctions among various sorts of theoretical "readers."

48 On Hume's use of irony in the *History*, see John Vladimir Price, *The Ironic Hume* (Austin: University of Texas Press, 1965), chap. 3.

49 wayne c. booth, "The pleasures and pitfalls of irony: or, why don't you say what you mean?" In *Rhetoric, Philosophy and Literature: An Exploration*, ed. Don M. Burks (West Lafayette, IN: Purdue University Press, 1978), 13.

50 Hilson provides a useful corrective to what he complains of as "a tendency to read Hume through Gibbonian spectacles; to focus on his detachment, irony, or even satire." Hilson wants to place Hume's history in the context of "the sentimental tradition in mid-century ethics and aesthetics," 205–206. See also Siebert, *Moral Animus of Hume*, especially ch. 1.

51 See chapter 2 above.

52 In fact, James I comes under fire for failing to discover that irony and humor are the secret to cooling factional fury. He made the mistake of getting involved in speculative disputes in order to try to restore agreement about religious matters; "by entering zealously into frivolous disputes, James gave them an air of importance and dignity which they could not otherwise have acquired; and being himself enlisted in the quarrel, he could no longer have recourse to contempt and ridicule, the only proper method of apeasing it" (*H* II, XLV, 138).

53 Other notable sentimental scenes in Hume's *History* are the executions of the Catholics Mary Queen of Scots and Charles I, both of which Siebert discusses, *Moral Animus of Hume*, 45–57.

54 See also Part X of the *Dialogues Concerning Natural Religion*, where Hume uses sentimental rhetoric in his discussion of evil. The tone of this section is strikingly different from the detached and playful tone of the rest of the work.

55 See, for instance, *H* I, XXXVIII, 719.

56 Richard H. Popkin, "Skepticism and the study of history," in *David Hume: Philosophical Historian*, eds. David Fate Norton and Richard H. Popkin (Indianapolis: Bobbs-Merrill, 1965), xxx.

57 Lionel Trilling, *Sincerity and Authenticity* (Cambridge, MA: Harvard University Press, 1972), 25.

58 *Ibid.*, 9. Hume's conviction of the importance of being able to withstand one's own gaze suggests a movement towards the more private ideal of authenticity, but even this self-reflexiveness is in the service of social, rather than private, ends, and social existence is not regarded as alienating.

59 Hume's approval of the strategic employment of hypocrisy for the public good may be indebted to the civic republican tradition, in particular to Machiavelli's advocacy of strategic behavior in the political realm. See J. G. A. Pocock, *The Machiavellian Moment* (Princeton University Press, 1975), 165–180, and Vittorio Hösle, "Morality and politics: reflections on Machiavelli's *Prince*," *International Journal of Politics, Culture and Society* 3 (1989): 51–69.

60 John Kilcullen suggests that Pierre Bayle was the first to "put a higher value upon sincerity than on actually being right." *Sincerity and Truth: Essays on Arnauld, Bayle, and Toleration* (Oxford: Clarendon Press, 1988), 15. Bayle's comment to this effect comes in the context of an argument on behalf of religious toleration. By claiming that theistic belief is incurably hypocritical, Hume is cutting the ground out from under the appeal to conscience which is crucial to this argument for toleration.

61 See also Hume's attack on the hypocrisy of the clergy in the essay "Of national characters," *MPL* 199–201. Hazlitt's main concern is with this sort of hypocrisy, and he is quick to point out that nothing fosters it more than church establishment: "Those who make a regular traffic of their belief in religion, will not be backward to compromise their sentiments in what relates to the concerns between man and man. He who is in the habit of affronting his Maker with solemn mockeries of faith, as the means of a creditable livelihood, will not bear the testimony of a good conscience before men, if he finds it a losing concern," "On the clerical character," in *The Complete Works of William Hazlitt*, ed. P. P. Howe, vol. 7 (London and Toronto: J. M Dent and Sons, 1930), 253. Hume might not be swayed by this observation from his endorsement of church establishment, however, as he regards this as the most harmless form of hypocrisy, because less likely to result in violent outbursts of zeal. Hazlitt's concern, on the other hand, is not with violence, but with the way in which the established clergy have an invested interest in giving religious sanction to unlimited royal power and thus in increasing the subjection of subjects. See fn. 28, Introduction.

62 Elster, *Sour Grapes*, 148.

63 Braudy, *Narrative Form*, 59.

64 Hume's characterization of Philip II of Spain is similar: "Philip, though a profound hypocrite, and extremely governed by self-interest, seems also to have been himself actuated by an imperious bigotry; and, as he employed great reflection in all his conduct, he could easily palliate the gratification of his natural temper under the color of wisdom, and find, in this system, no less advantage to his foreign than his domestic politics. By placing himself at the head of the Catholic party, he converted the zealots of the ancient faith into partisans of Spanish greatness" (*H* I, xxxix, 734).

65 See also *H* II, LXI, 430.

66 Elsewhere in the *History*, Hume writes that "the habits of hypocrisy often turn into reality" (*H* I, xxxvii, 694). See also Hume's discussion of the Scholastics, *H* I, viii, 168.

67 Of course, even in these cases, personal glory can provide a rather worldly compensation for suffering.

68 John Robertson, "The Scottish Enlightenment at the limits of the civic tradition," in *Wealth and Virtue*, eds. Istvan Hont and Michael Ignatieff (Cambridge University Press, 1983), 154. Hume's reflection on parties of interest was not without political significance; Douglass Adair has demonstrated the direct influence of Hume's thinking about faction on James Madison. In *Federalist* 10, Madison drew on Hume's "Of parties in general" and "Of the idea of a perfect commonwealth" in developing his argument in favor of a large republic. Following Hume, Madison argued that a large republic, if painstakingly organized as an indirect democracy, would actually be more stable and less prone to faction than a smaller republic. Although it would encompass a greater variety of interests, it would be more difficult for a minority to inflame the whole with passion to act against the public interest. Variety of interests need not inevitably lead to irreconcilable factional conflict. See Douglass Adair, "That politics may be reduced to a science': David Hume, James Madison, and the Tenth Federalist," in *Fame and the Founding Fathers: Essays by Douglass Adair*, ed. Trevor Colbourn (New York: W. W. Norton, 1974), 96–105.

69 Religious factions were, for Hume, an instance of parties of abstract speculative principle. Edmund Burke, carrying on while transforming Hume's suspicion of abstract speculation, places in this class, not religious factions, but rather the party of the "political men of letters," whom Burke holds responsible for the French Revolution. "The literary cabal," as he also calls them,

> had some years ago formed something like a regular plan for the destruction of the Christian religion. This object they pursued with a degree of zeal which hitherto had been discoverd only in the propagators of some system of piety. They were possessed with a spirit of proselytism in the most fanatical degree; and from thence, by an easy progress, with the spirit of persecution according to their means . . . A spirit of cabal, intrigue, and proselytism pervaded all their thoughts, words, and actions. And as controversial zeal soon turns its thoughts on force, they began to insinuate themselves into a correspondence with foreign princes, in hopes through their authority, which at first they flattered, they might bring about the changes they had in view. *Reflections on the Revolution in France*, ed. J. G. A. Pocock (Indianapolis: Hackett Publishing Company, 1987), 97–98.

> For an interpretation which stresses the continuities, rather than the notable differences between Burke and Hume's critiques of parties of abstract principle, see Livingston, *Philosophy of Common Life*, 313–329.

70 On bigotry, see *H*I, xxxiv, 661; xxxv, 676; II, LIII, 258; II, LXX, 609, 619. Zeal takes to extremes the tendency Amèlie O. Rorty sees in self-deception in general, to "block the movement to correction, block the logical rational processes oriented towards truth." "Self-deception, *akrasia*, and irrationality," 128. See also Clifford Geertz, "Ideology as a cultural system," in *The Interpretation of Cultures: Selected Essays* (New York: Basic Books, 1973), 232–233,

and *Islam Observed*, (University of Chicago Press, 1968), 103–107. I am indebted to G. Scott Davis for many interesting conversations on the subject of the ideologization of religious belief.

71 See also "Of national characters," *MPL* 200–201.

72 Hume's theory of religious violence is reminiscent of cognitive dissonance theories. See L. Festinger, *A Theory of Cognitive Dissonance* (Stanford University Press, 1957). Hume's analysis suggests that religious persecution, like proselytization, can be understod as an expression of cognitive dissonance.

73 Anthony Ashley Cooper, Third Earl of Shaftesbury, *Characteristics of Men, Manners, Opinions, Times*, ed. John M. Robertson (Indianapolis: Bobbs-Merrill, 1964), 13.

74 *Ibid.*, 32.

75 On contagion, see also *H* II, XLV, 138; LIV, 273; LV, 295.

76 John Robertson discusses factions of interest in "The Scottish Enlightenment and the civic tradition," suggesting that "Hume's response . . . to the problem of faction reveals a clear commitment to identifying the institutional framework which would ensure a harmony of interest between government and society. It was, he believed, the test of a 'wise and happy' government that by a skilful division of power among the separate courts and orders of men within it, the separate interest of each 'must necessarily, in its operation, concur with the public,'" 160–161; also 153–154.

77 Fingarette, *Self-Deception*, 1.

78 For a similar exoneration, see *H* II, LVII, 350.

79 On changing understandings of common sense, see Hans-Georg Gadamer, *Truth and Method*, (New York: Crossroad, 1975), 19–28. David Fate Norton details Hume's references to "common sense," "common life," "common experience," and related terms in his "Hume's common sense morality," *Canadian Journal of Philosophy* 5 (1975): 534–538. He argues that common sense, for Hume, arises out of sympathy, so that "through the agency of sympathy we create a *common* point of view and perceive *common* interests, and, further, create a shared or *common* moral standard by which we can determine the rightness and wrongness of acts," 539. But he fails to see that the morally relevant form of sympathy is not natural in the sense of pre-social or instinctive, and so ends up with a version of common sense naturalized via instinctive sympathy. Not surprisingly, he regards Hume's view of human nature as substantial, universal, and unchangeable. See *David Hume: Common-sense Moralist, Sceptical Metaphysician* (Princeton University Press, 1982), 136 n.50.

80 The hypocrite might also be a politician (one of civic republican persuasion, perhaps?) who is seeking the public good and realizes that only the appearance of religious belief of some particular sort will bring peace to the nation.

81 Hazlitt argues that the Dissenters are the most incorruptible and honest members of English society; "nothing else can sufficiently inure and steel

a man against the prevailing prejudices of the world, but that habit of mind which arises from non-conformity to its decisions in matters of religion," "On court influence," *Works*, vol. 7, 240. See also Hazlitt, "On the clerical character," *Works*, vol. 7, and note 61 above. I owe this insight to Jeffrey Stout. Hazlitt, ironically, praises just what Hume would abhor, that Dissenters are a party based not on interest but on abstract speculative principle: they "are the safest partizans, and the steadiest friends. Indeed they are almost the only people who have an idea of an abstract attachment to a cause or to individuals, from a sense of fidelity, independently of prosperous or adverse circumstances, and in spite of opposition," "On court influence," 240. The crucial differences here are, first, Hume's conviction that religious belief is self-contradictory and therefore inherently hypocritical, and, second, the context – for Hume, but not for Hazlitt, religious enthusiasm is seen as posing a real threat to the viability of society.

CONCLUSION

1 Annette Baier, *A Progress of Sentiments* (Cambridge, MA: Harvard University Press, 1991), 1.
2 For a more developed version of these reflections on Hume's *Dialogues*, see Jennifer A. Herdt, "Opposing sentiments: Hume's fear of faction and the philosophy of religion," *American Journal of Theology and Philosophy* 16 (1995): 245–259.
3 Many contemporary understandings of the sympathetic imagination continue to betray this leaning towards relativism or evaluative incommensurability. According to Milan Kundera, for instance, the art of the novel "created the fascinating imaginative realm where no one owns the truth and everyone has the right to be understood." *The Art of the Novel*, trans. Linda Asher (New York: Grove Press, 1986), 165. The novelist does not simply preach his or her own personal moral convictions – one who does this is what Kundera calls an *agélaste*, one who does not laugh. The *agélastes* are "convinced that the truth is obvious, that all men necessarily think the same thing, and that they themselves are exactly what they think they are. But it is precisely in losing the certainty of truth and the unanimous agreement of others that man becomes an individual. The novel is the imaginary paradise of individuals," 159. Kundera seems to think that active living requires a certain degree of dogmatism, while within the novel reflection is hypothetical and tentative. The world of the novel is a world in which moral judgments are left behind. At times, Kundera betrays a longing to escape forever into the world of the novel, to refrain from the affirmation required by living and acting in the world. But the options here are too starkly drawn. When a Humean sort of sympathetic understanding becomes central to the moral life, affirmation without dogmatism is possible.

4 Another contemporary thinker who could be mentioned is Martha Nussbaum, whose essays on literature and philosophy suggest that novels train their readers in a characteristic mode of seeing which attends to particularity and complexity. This mode of seeing, she argues, engenders a compassionate imaginative response to situations which better equips people to attend to problems of social justice than does an abstract impersonal approach. See *Love's Knowledge: Essays on Philosophy and Literature* (Oxford University Press, 1990).

5 Alasdair MacIntyre, *Whose Justice? Which Rationality?* (University of Notre Dame Press, 1988), 395.

6 Richard Rorty, *Contingency, Irony, and Solidarity* (Cambridge University Press, 1992), 92–93.

Select bibliography

WORKS BY DAVID HUME

Dialogues Concerning Natural Religion. Edited by Richard H. Popkin. Indianapolis: Hackett Publishing Company, 1980.

Enquiries Concerning Human Understanding and Concerning the Principles of Morals. Edited by L. A. Selby-Bigge. Text revised by P. H. Nidditch. From the 1777 edn. Oxford: Clarendon Press, 1975.

Essays Moral, Political, and Literary, revised edn. Edited by Eugene F. Miller. Indianapolis: Liberty Classics, 1987.

Four Dissertations. London: A. Millar, 1757.

The History of England, 2 vols. Philadelphia: M'Carty & Davis, 1836.

The Letters of David Hume. Edited by J. Y. T. Grieg. Oxford: Clarendon Press, 1976.

The Natural History of Religion. Edited by H. E.. Root, Stanford University Press, 1957.

A Treatise of Human Nature. Edited by L. A. Selby-Bigge. Text revised by P. H. Nidditch. Oxford: Clarendon Press, 1978.

OTHER WORKS

Acton, H. B. "The ethical importance of sympathy." *Philosophy* 30 (1955): 62–66.

Adair, Douglass. "'That politics may be reduced to a science': David Hume, James Madison, and the Tenth Federalist." In *Fame and the Founding Fathers: Essays by Douglass Adair.* Edited by Trevor Colbourn. New York: W. W. Norton, 1974.

Addison, Joseph. *Spectator* 418 (1712).

Aldridge, A. Owen. "Ancients and Moderns in the eighteenth century." *Dictionary of the History of Ideas.* New York, 1973.

[Allestree, Richard.] *The Practice of Christian Graces or The Whole Duty of Man.* London: D. Maxwell for T. Garthwait, 1658.

Altmann, R. W. "Hume on sympathy." *Southern Journal of Philosophy* 18 (March 1980): 123–136.

Aquinas, St Thomas. *Summa Theologica.* Translated by Fathers of the English Dominican Province. New York: Benziger Brothers, 1908.

Árdal, Páll. *Passion and Value in Hume's Treatise*. Edinburgh University Press, 1966.

Aristotle. *Poetics*, with the *Tractatus Coislinianus*, reconstruction of *Poetics* II, and the fragments of the *On Poets*. Translated by Richard Janko. Indianapolis and Cambridge: Hackett Publishing Company, 1987.

Audi, Robert. "Self-deception, rationalization, and reasons for acting." In *Perspectives on Self-Deception*. Edited by Brian P. McLaughlin and Amélie O. Rorty, 92–122. Berkeley: University of California Press, 1988.

Augustine. *Confessions*. Translated by Henry Chadwick. Oxford University Press, 1991.

Baier, Annette. "Hume's analysis of pride." *Journal of Philosophy* 75 (1978): 27–40.

"Master passions." In *Explaining Emotions*. Edited by Amélie O. Rorty, 403–423. Berkeley: University of California Press, 1980.

"Natural virtues, natural vices." *Social Philosophy and Policy* 8 (1990): 24–34.

Postures of the Mind: Essays on Mind and Morals. Minneapolis: University of Minnesota Press, 1985.

A Progress of Sentiments: Reflections on Hume's Treatise. Cambridge, MA: Harvard University Press, 1991.

Balguy, John. *The Foundation of Moral Goodness*. New York: Garland Publishing, 1976; facsimile of 1728–29 edn.

Barish, Jonas. *The Antitheatrical Prejudice*. Berkeley: University of California Press, 1981.

Barrow, Isaac. *Theological Works II*. 1830, 140–141. Quoted in Ronald S. Crane. "Suggestions toward a genealogy of the 'man of feeling,'" 206. In *The Idea of the Humanities*. University of Chicago Press, 1967.

Bate, Walter Jackson. *From Classic to Romantic: Premises of Taste in Eighteenth-Century England*. New York: Harper & Row, 1946.

"The sympathetic imagination in eighteenth-century English criticism." *English Literary History* 12 (1945): 144–164.

Berlin, Isaiah. *Vico and Herder*. London: The Hogarth Press, 1976.

Booth, Wayne C. "The pleasures and pitfalls of irony: or, why don't you say what you mean?" In *Rhetoric, Philosophy and Literature: An Exploration*. Edited by Don M. Burks, 1–14. West Lafayette, IN: Purdue University Press, 1978.

Boswell, James. *Private Papers of James Boswell*. Edited by Geoffrey Scott and Frederick A. Pottle, vol. 12. Mt. Vernon, NY: W. E. Rudge, 1931.

Bowlin, John. "Contingency, chance and virtue in Aquinas." Ph.D. dissertation, Princeton University, 1993.

Box, M. A. *The Suasive Art of David Hume*. Princeton University Press, 1990.

Brand, Walter Saul. *Hume's Theory of Moral Judgment: A Study in the Unity of "A Treatise of Human Nature."* Dordrecht: Kluwer Academic Publishers, 1992.

Braudy, Leo. *Narrative Form in History and Fiction: Hume, Fielding, and Gibbon*. Princeton University Press, 1970.

Brissenden, R. F. "Sentiment: some uses of the word in the writings of David Hume." In *Studies in the Eighteenth Century*. Edited by R. F. Brissenden, 89–107. Canberra: 1968.

Virtue In Distress: Studies in the Novel of Sentiment from Richardson to Sade. London:

Macmillan, 1974.

Bromwich, David. *Hazlitt: The Mind of a Critic.* New York and Oxford: Oxford University Press, 1983.

"How moral is taste?" *Yale Review* 82 (1994): 1–23.

Brown, Callum G. *The Social History of Religion in Scotland since 1730.* London and New York: Methuen, 1987.

Brown, Peter. *The Cult of the Saints.* University of Chicago Press, 1981.

Burch, Mark Hetzel. "Eighteenth-century sentimentality: a study of literature and its contexts." Ph.D. dissertation, University of Texas at Austin, 1984.

Burke, Edmund. *A Philosophical Enquiry into the Origin of Our Ideas of the Sublime and the Beautiful.* Edited by James T. Boulton. Oxford: Basil Blackwell, 1958; reprint of 2nd edn, 1759.

Reflections on the Revolution in France. Edited by J. G. A. Pocock. Indianapolis: Hackett Publishing Company, 1987.

Burke, John J. Jr. "Hume's *History of England*: waking the English from a dogmatic slumber." In *Studies in Eighteenth-Century Culture.* Edited by Roseann Runte, 235–250, vol. 7. Madison: University of Wisconsin Press, 1978.

Butler, Joseph. *Fifteen Sermons.* Edited by W. R. Matthews. London: G. Bell & Sons, 1914.

The Works of Joseph Butler. Edited by J. H. Bernard. London: 1900.

Butler, R. J. "'I' and sympathy." *Proceedings of the Aristotelian Society Supplement* 49 (1975): 15–16.

Capaldi, Nicholas. *Hume's Place in Moral Philosophy.* New York: Peter Lang, 1989.

Cartwright, David Ernest. "The ethical significance of sympathy, compassion, and pity." Ph.D. dissertation, University of Wisconsin at Madison, 1981.

Cassirer, Ernst. *The Philosophy of the Enlightenment.* Translated by Fritz C. A. Koelln and James P. Pettegrove. Princeton University Press, 1951.

Chismar, Douglas. "Hume's confusion about sympathy." *Philosophy Research Archives* 14 (1988-89): 237–246.

Claggett, William. *Of the Humanity and Charity of Christians.* 1686, 1687 edn, 4. Quoted in Ronald S. Crane. "Suggestions toward a genealogy of the 'man of feeling,'" 194–195. *The Idea of the Humanities.* University of Chicago Press, 1967.

Clark, Ian D. L. "From protest to reaction: The Moderate regime in the Church of Scotland: 1752–1805." In *Scotland in the Age of Improvement: Essays in Scottish History in the Eighteenth Century.* Edited by N. T. Phillipson and Rosalind Mitchison, 200–224. Edinburgh University Press, 1970.

Cole, Lucinda. "Sympathy, gender, and the writing of value in late eighteenth-century English Letters." Ph.D. dissertation, Louisiana State University, 1990.

Coleridge, Samuel Taylor. *The Collected Works of Samuel Taylor Coleridge.* Edited by R. J. White, vol. 2, *Lay Sermons.* Cambridge: Routledge and Kegan Paul, 1972.

Collingwood, R. G. *The Idea of History.* Oxford: Clarendon Press, 1946.

Crane, Ronald S. "Suggestions toward a genealogy of the 'man of feeling.'" In *The Idea of the Humanities,* 188–213. University of Chicago Press, 1967.

Davidson, Donald. "Deception and division." In *The Multiple Self: Studies in Rationality and Social Change*, ed. Jon Elster. Cambridge University Press, 1985.

"On the very idea of a conceptual scheme." *Proceedings of the American Philosophical Association* 47 (1973–74): 5–20. Reprinted in *Relativism: Cognitive and Moral*, Edited by Michael Krausz and Jack W. Meiland, 66–79. University of Notre Dame Press, 1982.

Descartes, René. *The Philosophical Works of Descartes*. Edited by E. S. Haldane and G. R. T. Ross, vol. 1. Dover Publications, 1911.

Dubos, Jean Baptiste. *Critical Reflections on Poetry, Painting and Music*. Translated by Thomas Nugent. London: J. Nourse, 1748; from the 5th French edn. *Réflexions critiques sur la poesie et sur la peinture*. Geneva: Slatine Reprints, 1967; reprint of 7th edn, 1770.

Edgerton, Samuel Y. Jr. *The Renaissance Rediscovery of Linear Perspective*. New York: Basic Books, 1975.

Elster, Jon. *Sour Grapes: Studies in the Subversion of Rationality*. Cambridge University Press, 1983.

Elster, Jon, ed. *The Multiple Self: Studies in Rationality and Social Change*. Cambridge University Press, 1985.

Engell, James. *The Creative Imagination: Enlightenment to Romanticism*. Cambridge, MA: Harvard University Press, 1981.

Falk, W. D. *Ought, Reasons, and Morality*. Ithaca: Cornell University Press, 1986.

Farr, James. "Hume, hermeneutics, and history: a 'sympathetic' account." *History and Theory* 17 (1978): 285–310.

Festinger, L. *A Theory of Cognitive Dissonance*. Stanford, CA: Stanford University Press, 1957.

Fiering, Norman S. "Irresistible compassion: an aspect of eighteenth-century sympathy and humanitarianism." *Journal of the History of Ideas* 37 (1976): 195–218.

Fingarette, Herbert. *Self-Deception*. London: Routledge and Kegan Paul, 1969.

Flew, Anthony. *Hume's Philosophy of Belief: A Study of His First 'Inquiry'*. London: Routledge and Kegan Paul, 1961.

Introduction to *Writings on Religion*, by David Hume. La Salle, IL: Open Court, 1992.

Fontenelle, Bernard Le Bovier de. "Reflexions sur la poetique." *Oeuvres de Fontenelle*. Paris: Jean-François Bastien, 1790.

Forbes, Duncan. *Hume's Philosophical Politics*. Cambridge University Press, 1975.

Fraassen, Bas C. van. "The peculiar effects of love and desire." In *Perspectives on Self-Deception*. Edited by Brian P. McLaughlin and Amélie O. Rorty, 123–156. Berkeley: University of California Press, 1988.

Frye, Northrop. "Towards defining an age of sensibility." In *Eighteenth-Century English Literature*. Edited by James L. Clifford, 311–318. Oxford University Press, 1959.

Gadamer, Hans-Georg. *Truth and Method*. Edited by Garrett Barden and John Cumming. New York: Crossroad, 1975.

Gaskin, J. C. A. *Hume's Philosophy of Religion*. London: Macmillan Press, 1978; 2nd edn, 1988.

Gay, Peter. *The Enlightenment: An Interpretation*, vol. 2, *The Science of Freedom*. New York: Alfred A. Knopf, 1969.

Geertz, Clifford. "Ideology as a cultural system." In *The Interpretation of Cultures*, 193–233. New York: Basic Books, 1973.

Islam Observed. University of Chicago Press, 1968.

Local Knowledge. New York: Basic Books, 1983.

"Thick description: toward an interpretive theory of culture." In *The Interpretation of Cultures*, 3–32. New York: Basic Books, 1973.

Greig, J. Y. T. *David Hume*. London: Jonathan Cape Ltd., 1931.

Grotius, Hugo. *On the Law of War and Peace*. Translated by Francis W. Kelsey. Oxford University Press, 1925.

Grove, Henry. *Spectator* 588 (1714).

Haakonssen, Knud. "Moral philosophy and natural law: from the Cambridge Platonists to the Scottish Enlightenment." *Political Science* 40 (1988): 97–110.

Hazlitt, William. *The Complete Works of William Hazlitt*. 21 vols. Edited by P. P. Howe. London: J. M. Dent and Sons, 1930.

Herdt, Jennifer A. "Opposite sentiments: Hume's fear of faction and the philosophy of religion." *American Journal of Theology and Philosophy* 16 (1995): 245–259.

Hill, Eric. "Hume and the delightful tragedy problem." *Philosophy* 57 (1982): 319–326.

Hilson, J. C. "Hume: The historian as man of feeling." In *Augustan Worlds*. Edited by J. C. Hilson, M. M. B. Jones, and J. R. Watson, 205–222. Leicester University Press, 1978.

Hirschman, Albert O. *The Passions and the Interests: Political Arguments for Capitalism before Its Triumph*. Princeton University Press, 1977.

Hobbes, Thomas. *Leviathan*. Edited by Richard Tuck. Cambridge University Press, 1991.

"Philosophical rudiments concerning government and society." In *The English Works of Thomas Hobbes of Malmesbury*. Edited by William Molesworth. London: John Bohn, May 1966.

Hollis, Martin. "The limits of irrationality." In *Rationality*. Edited by Bryan Wilson, 214–220. Oxford: Basil Blackwell, 1970.

Home, John. *Douglas*. Edited by Gerald D. Parker. Edinburgh: Oliver & Boyd, 1972.

Hont, Istvan, and Michael Ignatieff, eds. *Wealth and Virtue: The Shaping of Political Economy in the Scottish Enlightenment*. Cambridge University Press, 1983.

Hösle, Vittorio. "Morality and politics: reflections on Machiavelli's *Prince*." *International Journal of Politics, Culture and Society* 3 (1989): 51–69.

Hudson, W. D. "Hume on *is* and *ought*." In *The Is-Ought Question*. Edited by W. D. Hudson, 73–80. London: Macmillan, 1969.

Hutcheson, Francis. *An Essay on the Nature and Conduct of the Passions and Affections*. Hildesheim: Georg Olms Verlagsbuchhandlung, 1971; facsimile of the 1728 edn.

An Inquiry into the Original of our Ideas of Beauty and Virtue. Hildesheim: Georg Olms Verlagsbuchhandlung, 1971; facsimile of the first edn, 1725.

A System of Moral Philosophy. London: 1755; reprint, New York: August M. Kelley, 1968.

Jenkins, John J. "Hume's account of sympathy – some difficulties." In *Philosophers of the Scottish Enlightenment.* Edited by V. Hope, 91–104. Edinburgh University Press, 1982.

Johnson, Samuel. *The Rambler.* London: Jones & Company, 1826.

Rasselas. London: 1759.

Jones, Peter. *Hume's Sentiments: Their Ciceronian and French Contexts.* Edinburgh University Press, 1982.

"The Scottish Professoriate and the polite academy, 1720–46." In *Wealth and Virtue: The Shaping of Political Economy in the Scottish Enlightenment.* Edited by Istvan Hont and Michael Ignatieff, 89–117. Cambridge University Press, 1983.

Kearney, Richard. *The Wake of the Imagination: Ideas of Creativity in Western Culture.* London: Hutchinson, 1988.

Keats, John. *The Selected Letters of John Keats.* Edited by Lionel Trilling. New York: Farrar, Straus and Young, Inc., 1951.

Kilcullen, John. *Sincerity and Truth: Essays on Arnauld, Bayle, and Toleration.* Oxford: Clarendon Press, 1988.

Kundera, Milan. *The Art of the Novel.* Translated by Linda Asher. New York: Grove Press, 1986.

Lipkin, Robert J. "Altruism and sympathy in Hume's ethics." *Australasian Journal of Philosophy* 65 (1987): 18–32.

Livingston, Donald W. *Hume's Philosophy of Common Life.* University of Chicago Press, 1984.

Luther, Martin. *Luther's Works.* Edited by Walther I. Brandt. *The Christian in Society* ii, vol. 45. Philadelphia: Muhlenberg Press, 1962.

MacIntyre, Alasdair. *After Virtue,* 2nd edn. University of Notre Dame Press, 1984.

Whose Justice? Which Rationality? University of Notre Dame Press, 1988.

Mandeville, Bernard. *The Fable of the Bees.* Edited by F. B. Kaye. Oxford: 1924.

Marshall, David. *The Figure of the Theater.* New York: Columbia University Press, 1986.

The Surprising Effects of Sympathy: Marivaux, Diderot, Rousseau, and Mary Shelley. University of Chicago Press, 1988.

Martin, Mike W. *Self-Deception and Morality.* Lawrence, KS: University Press of Kansas, 1986.

McCarthy, Thomas. "On misunderstanding 'understanding.'" *Theory and Decision* 3 (1973): 351–370.

McLaughlin, Brian P. and Amèlie O. Rorty, eds. *Perspectives on Self-Deception.* Berkeley: University of California Press, 1988.

Megill, Allan. "Aesthetic theory and historical consciousness in the Eighteenth century." *History and Theory* 17 (1978): 29–62.

Mercer, Philip. *Sympathy and Ethics: A Study of the Relationship between Sympathy and Morality with Special Reference to Hume's "Treatise."* Oxford: Clarendon Press, 1972.

Merrill, Kenneth R., and Robert W. Shahan, eds. *David Hume: Many-Sided Genius*, Norman, OK: University of Oklahoma Press, 1976.

Merrill, Kenneth R., and Donald G. Wester. "Hume on the relation of religion to morality." *The Journal of Religion* 60 (1980): 272–284.

Moore, James, and Michael Silverthorne. "Gershom Carmichael and the natural jurisprudence tradition in eighteenth-century Scotland." In *Wealth and Virtue: The Shaping of Political Economy in the Scottish Enlightenment*. Edited by Istvan Hont and Michael Ignatieff, 73–87. Cambridge University Press, 1983.

Morrow, Glenn R. "The significance of the doctrine of sympathy in Hume and Adam Smith." *Philosophical Review* 32 (1923): 60–78.

Mossner, Ernest C. "Hume and the Ancient–Modern controversy, 1725–1752: A study in creative scepticism." *Texas Studies in English* 28 (1949): 139–153.

The Forgotten Hume: "Le Bon David" New York: Columbia University Press, 1943.

The Life of David Hume. Austin: University of Texas Press, 1954.

Mossner, Ernest C., and John V. Price. Introduction to *A Letter from a Gentleman to his friend in Edinburgh*, by David Hume. Edinburgh: Edinburgh University Press, 1967; from 1745 edn.

Nagel, Thomas. *The Possibility of Altruism*. Princeton University Press, 1970.

Nidditch, P. H. *An Apparatus of Variant Readings for Hume's "Treatise of Human Nature."* University of Sheffield Press, 1976.

Norton, David Fate. "Hume's common sense morality." *Canadian Journal of Philosophy* 5 (1975): 523–543.

"History and philosophy in Hume's thought." In *David Hume: Philosophical Historian*. Edited by David Fate Norton and Richard Popkin, xxxii-l. Indianapolis: Bobbs-Merrill, 1965.

David Hume: Common-sense Moralist, Sceptical Metaphysician. Princeton University Press, 1982.

Noxon, James. "Hume's concern with religion." In *David Hume: Many-Sided Genius*. Edited by Kenneth R. Merrill and Robert W. Shahan, 59-82. Norman, OK: University of Oklahoma Press, 1976.

Nussbaum, Martha. *Love's Knowledge: Essays in Philosophy and Literature*. Oxford University Press, 1990.

Parker, Samuel. *Demonstration of the Divine Authority of the Law of Nature*, 1681, 55. Quoted in Ronald S. Crane. "Suggestions toward a genealogy of the 'man of Feeling,'" 207. In *The Idea of the Humanities*. University of Chicago Press, 1967.

Pascal, Blaise. *Pensées*. Translated by A. J. Krailsheimer. London: Penguin Books, 1966.

Pears, David. *Motivated Irrationality*. Oxford: Clarendon Press, 1984.

Phillipson, Nicholas T. "Towards a definition of the Scottish enlightenment." In *City and Society in the 18th Century*. Edited by Paul S. Fritz and David Williams, 125–147. Hakkert: Toronto, 1973.

"Culture and society in the 18th-century province: the case of Edinburgh and the Scottish Enlightenment." In *The University in Society: Europe, Scotland, and the United States from the 16th to the 20th Century*. Edited by Lawrence Stone, 407–448. Princeton University Press, 1974.

Hume. New York: St. Martin's Press, 1989.

Phillipson, Nicholas T., and Rosalind Mitchison, eds. *Scotland in the Age of Improvement*. Edinburgh University Press, 1970.

Plutarch. *Table-Talk, I-VI*. Translated by Paul A. Clement and Herbert B. Hoffleit. *Moralia*, VIII. London: Loeb Classics, 1969. Quoted in Jonas Barish, *The Antitheatrical Prejudice*, 32. Berkeley: University of California Press, 1981.

Pocock, J. G. A. "Cambridge paradigms and Scotch philosophers." In *Wealth and Virtue: The Shaping of Political Economy in the Scottish Enlightenment*, ed. Istvan Hont and Michael Ignatieff, 240–251. Cambridge: Cambridge University Press, 1983.

The Machiavellian Moment. Princeton: Princeton University Press, 1975.

Popkin, Richard. "Skepticism and the study of history." In *David Hume: Philosphical Historian*. Edited by David Fate Norton and Richard Popkin, ix-xxxi. Indianapolis: Bobbs-Merrill, 1965.

Price, John V. *The Ironic Hume*. Austin: University of Texas Press, 1965.

Pufendorf, Samuel. *The Duty of Man and Citizen*. Translated by Frank Gardner Moore. Oxford University Press, 1927.

Radner, John B. "The art of sympathy in eighteenth-century British thought." In *Studies in Eighteenth-Century Culture*. Edited by Roseann Runte, 192–201, vol. 9. Madison: University of Wisconsin Press, 1979.

"Samuel Johnson, the deceptive imagination, and sympathy." *Studies in Burke and His Times* 16 (1905): 23–46.

Rawls, John. *A Theory of Justice*. Cambridge, MA: Belknap Press, 1971.

Robertson, John. "The Scottish Enlightenment at the limits of the civic tradition." In *Wealth and Virtue: The Shaping of Political Economy in the Scottish Enlightenment*. Edited by Istvan Hont and Michael Ignatieff, 137–178. Cambridge University Press, 1983.

Rogers, G. A. J., and Alan Ryan, eds. *Perspectives on Thomas Hobbes*. New York: Oxford University Press, 1989.

Rorty, Amélie O. "From passions to emotions and sentiments." *Philosophy* 57 (1982): 159–172.

"Self-deception, *akrasia* and irrationality." In *The Multiple Self*. Edited by Jon Elster, 115–129. Cambridge University Press, 1985.

Rorty, Richard. *Contingency, Irony, and Solidarity*. Cambridge University Press, 1989.

Rorty, Richard, Quentin Skinner, and J. B. Schneewind, eds. *Philosophy in History: Essays on the Historiography of Philosophy*. Cambridge University Press, 1984.

Rousseau, Jean-Jaques. *Politics and the Arts: Letter to M. D'Alembert on the Theatre*. Translated and with notes by Allan Bloom. Ithaca: Cornell University Press, 1960.

Lettre à M. d'Alembert sur son Article Genève. Edited by Michael Launay. Paris: Garnier-Flammerion, 1967.

Sayre-McCord, Geoffrey. "On why Hume's 'general point of view' isn't ideal – and shouldn't be," *Social Philosophy and Policy* 11 (1994): 202–228.

Scheler, Max. *The Nature of Sympathy*. Translated by Peter Heath. Hamden, CN: Archon Books, 1970.

Schneewind, J. B. "The Divine Corporation and the history of ethics." In *Philosophy in History: Essays on the Historiography of Philosophy*. Edited by Richard Rorty, J. B. Schneewind, and Quentin Skinner, 173–191. Cambridge University Press, 1984.

"Natural Law, skepticism, and methods of ethics." *Journal of the History of Ideas* 52 (1991): 289–308.

Schneewind, J. B., ed. *Moral Philosophy from Montaigne to Kant: An Anthology*, 2 vols. Cambridge University Press, 1990.

Scott, William Robert. *Francis Hutcheson: His Life, Teaching and Position in the History of Philosophy*. Cambridge University Press, 1900.

Shaftesbury, Anthony Ashley Cooper, Third Earl of. *Characteristics of Men, Manners, Opinions, Times*. Edited by John M. Robertson. From the 1710 edn. Indianapolis: Bobbs-Merril, 1964.

Sher, Richard, and Alexander Murdoch. "Patronage and party in the Church of Scotland, 1750–1800." In *Church, Politics and Society: Scotland 1408–1929*. Edited by Norman MacDougall, 197–220. Edinburgh: John Donald Publishers Ltd., 1983.

Siebert, Donald T. *The Moral Animus of David Hume*. Newark: University of Delaware Press, 1990.

Skinner, Quentin. *The Foundations of Modern Political Thought*, vol. 2, *The Age of Reformation*. Cambridge University Press, 1978.

Smith, Adam. *The Theory of Moral Sentiments*. Introduction by E. C. West. Indianapolis: LibertyClassics, 1969.

Smith, Norman Kemp. Introduction to *Dialogues Concerning Natural Religion*, by David Hume, 1–75. Indianapolis: Bobbs-Merrill, 1935.

The Philosophy of David Hume: A Critical Study of its Origins and Central Doctrines. London: Macmillan, 1964.

Stolnitz, Jerome. " 'Beauty': some stages in the history of an idea." *Journal of the History of Ideas* 22 (1961): 185–204.

"On the origins of 'aesthetic disinterestedness'." *Journal of Aesthetics and Art Criticism* 20 (1961): 131–142.

"On the Significance of Lord Shaftesbury in Modern Aesthetic Theory." *Philosophical Quarterly* 11 (1961): 97–113.

Stout, Jeffrey. *The Flight from Authority: Religion, Morality and the Quest for Autonomy*. University of Notre Dame Press, 1981.

Ethics After Babel. Boston: Beacon Press, 1988.

"Naturalism." *Encyclopedia of Religion*. Edited by Mircea Eliade. New York: Macmillan, 1987.

Stroud, Barry. *Hume*. London: Routledge and Kegan Paul, 1977.

Taylor, Charles. *Sources of the Self: The Making of the Modern Identity*. Cambridge, MA: Harvard University Press, 1989.

Tocqueville, Alexis de. *Democracy in America*. Translated by George Lawrence. Edited by J. P. Mayer. New York: Harper & Row, 1969.

Trilling, Lionel. *Sincerity and Authenticity*. Cambridge, MA: Harvard University Press, 1972.

Tuck, Richard. *Hobbes*. Oxford University Press, 1989.

Tuveson, Ernest. "The origins of the moral sense." *Huntington Library Quarterly* 11 (1947-48): 241–259.

"The importance of Shaftesbury." *Journal of English Literary History* 20 (1953): 267–279.

Wand, Bernard. "A note on sympathy in Hume's moral theory." *Philosophical Review* 64 (1955): 275–279.

Wasserman, Earl R. "The pleasures of tragedy." *Journal of English Literary History* 14 (1947): 283–307.

Wellek, René. *The Rise of English Literary History*. Chapel Hill: University of North Carolina Press, 1941.

A History of Modern Criticism: 1750–1950, vol. 1, *The Later Eighteenth Century*. New Haven: Yale University Press, 1965.

Wertz, S. K. "Hume, history, and human nature." *Journal of the History of Ideas* 36 (1975): 481–496.

Wills, Garry. *Inventing America: Jefferson's Declaration of Independence*. New York: Vintage Books, 1978.

Wilson, Bryan, ed. *Rationality*. Oxford: Basil Blackwell, 1970.

Witherspoon, John. "A serious inquiry into the nature and effects of the stage." In *The Works of John Witherspoon*, vol. 6. Edinburgh: Ogle & Aikman, Pillans & Sons, J. Ritchie, & J. Turnbull, 1805.

Wittgenstein, Ludwig. *Philosophical Investigations*. Translated by G. E. M. Anscombe. New York: Macmillan, 1953, 1958.

On Certainty. Edited and translated by G. E. M. Anscombe and G. H. von Wright. Oxford: Basil Blackwell, 1969.

Wollheim, Richard. Introduction to *Hume on Religion*, by David Hume, 7–30. Cleveland: Meridian Books, 1963.

Wordsworth, William. *Selected Poems and Prefaces by William Wordsworth*. Edited by Jack Stillinger. Boston: Houghton Mifflin Company, 1965.

Yandell, Keith E. *Hume's "Inexplicable Mystery": His Views on Religion*. Philadelphia: Temple University Press, 1990.

Index